New England
TRIPS

53 THEMED ITINERARIES **1012** LOCAL PLACES TO SEE

Ray Bartlett, Gregor Clark,
Dan Eldridge, Brandon Presser

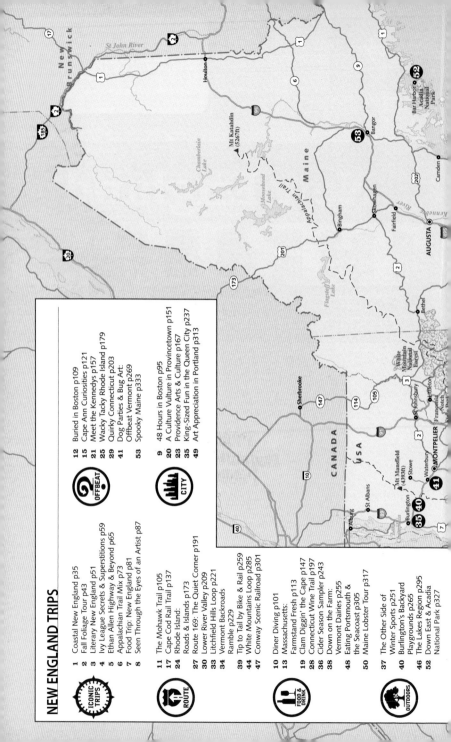

NEW ENGLAND TRIPS

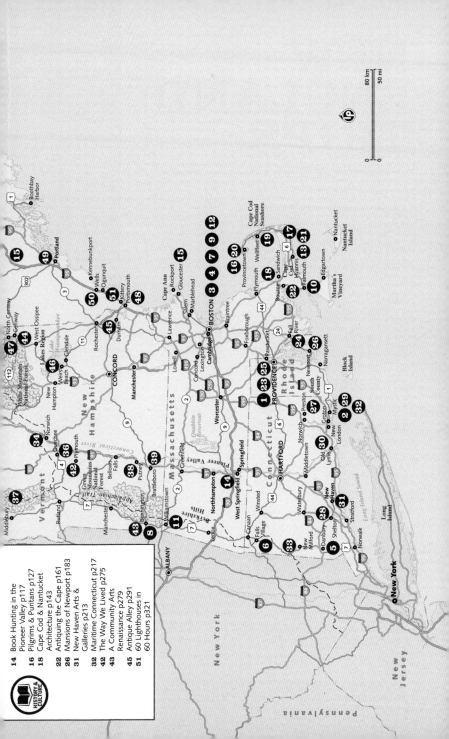

HISTORY &
CULTURE

80 km
50 mi

0
0

NEW ENGLAND TRIPS

You know the drill: it's 3pm on a Friday, and your mind is drifting off to a place with coast-hugging roads, clam shacks, historic towns, mountain vistas and boutique breweries. Does such a place really exist, or is it all just a post-traumatic work-week-induced fantasy? Luckily, this dreamy destination is quite real: it's New England. So that's where you want to be, but where to go? When? How? As trip-takers and travelers ourselves, we know that condensing information down into simple, inspirational journeys can be tough. There are just so many sources and opinions. We just want to pick a trip and go.

Our local authors have scoured New England to bring you 53 of the best trips for food lovers, history buffs, outdoor enthusiasts, culture-vultures and families, as well as unique and off-the-beaten track options. Our most inspirational trips range from an insider's look at Ivy League schools to Vermont's best dairy farms; from a bicycle ride through kitschy Rhode Island to a clam digger's tour of Cape Cod. Trips are themed to suit your interests, perhaps even your mood. For day trippers we have picked our favorite short trips from Boston, covering music, history and museums.

Now that you've got the inspiration, all you need is to pack your bags and go. Oh, and tell your boss you won't be in on Monday.

ETHAN ALLEN HIGHWAY & BEYOND p65
Pretty Moss Glen Falls provides respite from Route 100

"Does such a place really exist, or is it all just a post-traumatic work-week-induced fantasy?"

ON THE BIG SCREEN

The many facets of New England culture make ideal film settings and plots, from the Ivy League (*Good Will Hunting*; 1997) to perfect suburbia (*The Stepford Wives*; 1975) and transcendentalism (*Little Women*; 1949).

MAINE LOBSTER TOUR p317
Fresh Maine lobster by the sea

FALL FOLIAGE TOUR p43
The fall colors of Maine

COASTAL NEW ENGLAND p35
Explore Massachusetts' coast from the water

"This dreamy destination is quite real: it's New England."

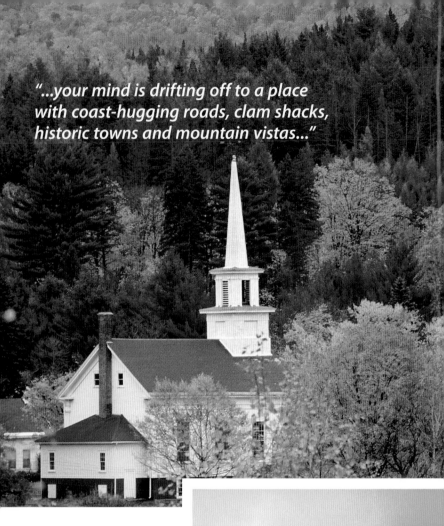

"...your mind is drifting off to a place with coast-hugging roads, clam shacks, historic towns and mountain vistas..."

Iconic Trips

Nowhere is American iconography more present than in the birthplace of the New World: New England. Glimpse the inspiring **paintings** (p87) and **books** (p51) of New England's sons and daughters. Follow the scenic roads and **classic routes** (p65) that zigzag along the rugged **coastline** (p35) and through the fiery **fall foliage** (p43), sample what was really on the menu at that first Thanksgiving – **seafood** (p81) – and hike the storied **Appalachian Trail** (p73). However you decide to sample New England, stop and appreciate the beauty, quirkiness and history that abound in this most American of regions.

IN HONOR
OF THE
SECOND MASSACHUSETTS VOLUNTEER INFANTRY
AND IN REMEMBRANCE OF THE
OFFICERS AND MEN WHO FELL IN ITS RANKS
THE MONUMENT HAS BEEN GIVEN TO THE CITY OF BOSTON

WINCHESTER · 1862 · CEDAR MOUNTAIN ·
ANTIETAM · CHANCELLORSVILLE ·
GETTYSBURG · RESACA · ATLANTA ·
THE MARCH TO THE SEA · SAVANNAH ·
SHERMAN'S CAROLINA CAMPAIGN ·

"Follow the scenic roads and classic routes that zigzag along the rugged coastline."

IN A LEAGUE OF YOUR OWN

Make an educational trip to one of New England's Ivy League universities: Brown (RI), Dartmouth (NH), Harvard (MA), and Yale (CT) – check out www.go4ivy .com for more information.

IVY LEAGUE SECRETS & SUPERSTITIONS p59
"The big H, the H-bomb": Harvard epitomises the Ivy League

COASTAL NEW ENGLAND p35
The rugged coast of Maine

ETHAN ALLEN HIGHWAY & BEYOND p65
Route 100 provides the quintessential Vermont image: a big red barn

⊕ **Routes**
ROUTE

If taking a road trip through New England makes you feel like you've mistakenly climbed into a time machine instead of your car, don't adjust your odometer. That's just New England. Start in the 18th century as you thread your way through the tree-lined tunnels of **Vermont** (p229), passing churches and graveyards dating back to 1749. Continue on to the early 19th century, edging along the same granite cliffs that smugglers of the War of 1812 used (p259). Ramble the back-roads dotted with early 20th-century farmhouses, or travel all 63 miles of the **Mohawk Trail** (p105), New England's first scenic road which first opened in 1914. Finally, park your DeLorean in the present day and do the green thing – board a **train** (p259, p301) and enjoy the quiet countryside from the comfort of a railcar, or travel by your own **steam** (p137, p259).

IT'S ALL IN THE NUMBERS

With 72,000 square miles of land within New England – 4,965 of them coastline – there are thousands of routes to explore in this beautiful region. Grab your keys and get lost.

"...park your DeLorean in the present day and do the green thing..."

Food & Drink

Oh sure. You *think* you know **New England food** (p81). **Maine lobster** (p317). Clams from the **Cape** (p147). Maple syrup in **Vermont** (p243), and of course, the *chowdah*. But dig deep enough, and beneath its crustacean-catching, tree-tapping, traditional surface, you'll find that there's more to eating in New England than meets the eye. Discover an up-and-coming wine region in **Connecticut** (p197), the rebirth of the farmers market in **Massachusetts** (p113) and the best spots for that famous **New England seafood** (p147, p317) And if you're smart, you'll save room for some fresh-from-the-dairy **ice cream** (p255). The cutting edge dining scene is giving the home of the first Thanksgiving a run for its money, and we've compiled eight trips that let these different culinary styles duke it out for the blue ribbon in eating. We guarantee you won't be going home hungry.

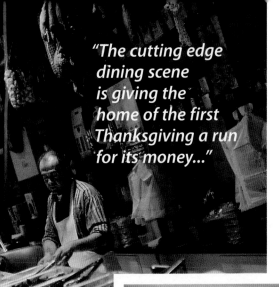

"The cutting edge dining scene is giving the home of the first Thanksgiving a run for its money..."

GO ON, BE PICKY

For a comprehensive list of orchards that allow you to hand-pick your own apples, visit www.apples-ne.com/pickyourownapples.html. Grab a ladder and a basket, and get to pickin'.

⊕ **FOOD TRIP: NEW ENGLAND** p81
Boston's North End has more than 300 restaurants and Italian shops

⊗ **CLAM DIGGIN' THE CAPE** p147
Cape Cod provides an abundance of seafood

⊕ **DOWN ON THE FARM: VERMONT DAIRIES** p255
The next Miss Ver-mooont outside a Vermont barn

> *"...take refuge in the verdant valleys, rolling hills and rocky peaks that perforate this landscape."*

HOME ON THE RANGE

Check out www.aroundthecampfire .homestead.com for reviews of New England campsites, plus songs, recipes and ghost stories – all good for sharing around the campfire.

# Outdoors

A weather-beaten coastline and hundreds of glacial lakes, rushing rivers and placid ponds make New England a water-lover's dream. But fear not, aquaphobes; while New England is intrinsically tied to H_2O, you can take refuge in the verdant valleys, rolling hills and rocky peaks that perforate this landscape. Hike through quarries and mountains on the **Appalachian Trail** (p73), camp amidst old growth trees in **Acadia National Park** (p327), or discover the **Green Mountains** on skis (p251). With snow-covered slopes, windswept beaches and the multi-colored tapestries of fall foliage, New England draws millions of outdoor adventurers every year.

DOWN EAST & ACADIA NATIONAL PARK p327
Hiking trails abound in this coastal national park in Maine

BURLINGTON'S BACKYARD PLAYGROUNDS p265
From Stowe, 4393ft Mt Mansfield looks like a nice little hike

THE OTHER SIDE OF WINTER SPORTS p251
Middlebury: a great hiking area in summer, full of mad-cap graduates in winter

History & Culture

New England's personality is a two-sided coin. On one side, it's traditional – landmarks remembering New England's humble **Pilgrim beginnings** (p127), **maritime museums** (p217) proudly reflecting on their port town pasts, historical homes lining some of the country's **oldest streets** (p183), and **antiques** (p161, p291) and **literature** (p117). But get to know New England, and you'll see her wild side – cutting-edge galleries filled with modernist paintings and sculptures, trendy boutiques hawking local wares and current fashions, performance spaces and theaters showcasing **avant-garde arts** (p213, p279). In this book you'll find a collection of trips that are steeped in history and culture, demonstrating the diversity that makes New England what she is: colorful, controversial, free-thinking, and forward-looking, yet always remembering her heritage.

WHO WAS FIRST?

It's a hotly debated topic, but Rhode Island – not New Hampshire – was technically the first colony to declare independence from Great Britain.

"Colorful, controversial, free-thinking, and forward-looking, yet always remembering her heritage."

"...there's something offbeat and eerie to counterbalance the region's charming perfection."

Offbeat

For each classic image that New England conjures up – white clapboard churches on well-manicured greens; granite mountains majestically ablaze with fall colors; paint-peeling fishing boats bobbing at their moors – there's something offbeat and eerie to counterbalance the region's charming perfection. At the **Bread & Puppet Theater** (p269) in Vermont, carnivalesque pageants are performed by life-size marionettes, while the owners serve up warm homemade bread and blackberry jelly. In the tiniest state in the nation you can pay a visit to the **biggest bug in the world** (p269) and in **Bridgeport** (p203) you can stop and meet a Merman, or admire artfully recycled debris at the **Trash Museum** (p203) in Hartford. In between the lobsters and lighthouses, it's OK to let your inner freak run wild. Go on, New England doesn't mind.

NEW ENGLAND'S ATLANTIS

In 1942, the town of Billingsgate was swallowed by enormous waves. It is now only visible at very low tide as a shoal off northern Wellfleet, making it Cape Cod's very own Atlantis.

DOG PARTIES & BUG ART: OFFBEAT VERMONT p269
Bread, puppets and outdoor theater

BURIED IN BOSTON p109
The Granary Burial Ground is an American Revolution–afficionado's mecca

SPOOKY MAINE p333
Maine's spooky past still lingers

SAMUEL PECK
Son of MOSES
& ELIZABETH PECK
died 7th Augst 1775
Aged 6 Y...

CARRIAGE XING

CITY TRIPPING

For everything from local news to reviews of cheap eateries to weekend happenings, see www.bostonist.com, a blog for all things Boston.

48 HOURS IN BOSTON p95
Beantown: wicked good

PROVIDENCE ARTS & CULTURE p167
Providence's WaterFire installation fires up several times a year

KING-SIZED FUN IN THE QUEEN CITY p237
The Church St Marketplace in Burlington

⟨🏙️⟩ Cities
CITY

You might not believe us when we tell you, but New England is all about urban grit. Industrial and port cities were built on the backs of factory workers, mill girls and sailors. As well as the obvious metropolis of **Boston** (p95), towns such as **Provincetown** (p151), **Providence** (p167), **Burlington** (p237) and **Portland** (p313) are remaking themselves as trendsetters and cosmopolitan destinations. Former factories are now modern museums and galleries, old warehouses are transforming into hip restaurants, and even canals, harbors and former railroads are now a part of the metropolitan make-up. No matter what new identity these cities take on, they retain their resilient undersides, fuelling innovative art, nonstop nightlife, and cutting-edge culture.

MARITIME CONNECTICUT p217
New England's lobster obsession is evident along the coast

CAPE COD RAIL TRAIL p137
The Rail Trail provides equal measures of exercise and entertainment

Contents

Trips by Theme

🚗 ROUTES
TRIP

🍴 FOOD & DRINK
TRIP

🌳 OUTDOORS
TRIP

HISTORY & CULTURE

OFFBEAT

CITIES

Trips by Season

SPRING (MAR–MAY)

SUMMER (JUN–AUG)

Expert-Recommended Trips

The Authors

RAY BARTLETT

Ray Bartlett began travel writing at 18 by jumping a freight train for 500 miles and selling the story to a local newspaper. Two decades later he is still wandering the world with pen and camera in hand. He has been published in *USA Today,* the *Denver Post, Miami Herald,* and other newspapers and magazines, and recently appeared on PRI's *The World*. His Lonely Planet titles include *Japan, Mexico, Yucatán,* and *Korea*. More about him can be found at his website, www.kaisora.com. When not travelling, he surfs, writes fiction, drinks way too much coffee, and burns way too much midnight oil.

GREGOR CLARK

Gregor Clark lives in Vermont. After six previous Lonely Planet assignments in Europe, South America and California, exploring his beloved home state with family has been a dream come true. Favorite new discoveries include Derby's Haskell Opera House and West Rutland's Carving Studio.

DAN ELDRIDGE

Born in the San Francisco Bay Area and currently based in Philadelphia with his wife and their five cats, Dan Eldridge is the author of a travel guide to Pittsburgh, and the founding editor of *Young Pioneers* magazine. Dan has written about Turkey and Thailand for Lonely Planet, and his journalism has appeared in the *Daily Telegraph, Houston Chronicle* and *Paste,* among other publications.

BRANDON PRESSER

After spending his childhood summers collecting starfish along the Maine coast, Brandon perfected his *'pahk the cah'* Bostonian drawl while attending Harvard University. When he's not writing his way across the globe, Brandon still calls New England home.

LONELY PLANET AUTHORS

Why is our travel information the best in the world? It's simple: our authors are independent, dedicated travelers. They don't research using just the internet or phone, and they don't take freebies, so you can rely on their advice being well researched and impartial. They travel widely, to all the popular spots and off the beaten track. They personally visit thousands of hotels, restaurants, cafés, bars, galleries, palaces, museums and more – and they take pride in getting all the details right, and telling it how it is. Think you can do it? Find out how at lonelyplanet.com.

CONTRIBUTING EXPERTS

Taylor Brown A Cape Cod native living in Chatham, Taylor Brown is a professional clam digger who also works as an accessory designer, and as a vintage clothing online retailer. Visit www.sweetwatervintage.etsy.com and www.myspace.com/sweetwatervinatge to learn more. She takes us clam diggin' on p147.

Chef Harry Chef Harry is the creator and host of PBS' *Chef Harry and Friends.* He is a regular contributor on NBC's *Today Show,* and the KTLA-CBS *Food Guru* in Los Angeles and the Fox *Food Guru* in Nashville. He has authored five books, and is currently the Culinary and Creative Director for Heritage Trail Vineyards and Winery. His expertise

on the Connecticut wine industry is shared on p197. To learn more, visit www.chefharry.com.

Stephanie Elsener As a lover of the lakes, mountains and fresh air, the Lakes Region was the ideal spot for Stephanie to be raised. Currently traveling the world and spending more time in her husband's native Switzerland, she still keeps a warm place in her heart for NH and the Lakes Region, which she shares on p295.

Silas Finch Originally from Massachusetts, Silas Finch is a found-object sculptor based in New Haven, CT. Finch uses cast-off and discarded metals and leathers to build a diverse cast of characters – from dancing elephants and drummer boys to biomechanical monsters. Photographs of his work can be seen at www.myspace.com/silasfinch. Silas takes us through the ins and outs of New Haven's art galleries on p213.

Lissy Heminway Lissy, founder of Vermont Dog Sledding (www.vermontdogsledding.org), grew up on a small farm in New England, where her dreams of becoming a musher began. She settled in Vermont in 1992 and has been running sled dogs ever since. Her expertise on the other side of winter sports is shared on p251.

Melissa Jenks Melissa was raised in Thailand and has travelled solo since she was eleven. Lately, she's hiked the Appalachian Trail (see p73 for the best sections to hike), bicycled from Key West to Maine, and sailed to the Bahamas, while blogging at www.casting-off.blogspot.com.

Daniel Kany An art historian, author, foodie and co-founder of the Gallery Association of Portland Maine, Daniel grew up in central Maine and attended nearby Bowdoin College. His contemporary art gallery specializes in international glass art (http://kany.net), but for this book Daniel has returned to the familiar art scene of Portland on p313.

Kimberly Keefe A Newportite through and through, Kimmie's been hobnobbing with the best of 'em for as long as she can remember. She is currently in medical school with plans to become a doctor, but took time out to show us the mansions of Newport on p183.

Charlotte Clews Lawther Charlotte is an Acadia National Park ranger and naturalist. She's worked for the park for three years and grew up in nearby Blue Hill. She's been coming to the park all her life to hike, swim and eat popovers (learn more at www.wildravenarts.com), and has shared her favorite Acadia spots with us on p327.

Matthew Perry Visual artist Matthew Perry is cofounder and Artistic Director of the Vermont Arts Exchange (www.vtartxchange.org). His paintings and sculptures are inspired by his surroundings, whether in Vermont or through his travels abroad, where he has also taught and exhibited. On p279 he uncovers the arts renaissance in Vermont.

David Webber David is the Farmers Market Coordinator for the Massachusetts Department of Agricultural Resources, working with local communities to set up and promote farmers markets. David is a Massachusetts native and enjoys traversing the Massachusetts countryside, enjoying the local bounty area farmers provide. He helps us out with the best farmers markets to visit on p113.

NEW ENGLAND ICONIC TRIPS

New England. Those two words immediately bring to mind a cacophony of images. Craggy coastline, dotted with lighthouses. Lobsters, fresh from the sea, served up on rustic tables with boiled corn and potatoes. The spectacular display of autumnal color along a quiet Vermont country road. History-rich Ivy League campuses, buzzing with creativity and a thirst for knowledge. New England is indeed all these things, but it's also greater than the sum of its parts. It's these tangible sights, sounds and tastes, but it's also a feeling – the emotion of this special place brought to life by artists and writers so inspired by this legendary landscape.

The following chapter is a collection of trips that encompass the best of New England's best. Grouped together, they create unique vignettes that will twist and turn you through the scenic roads, making stops for the best food and drinks along the way, and possibly inspiring you to pick up a paintbrush, dust off your typewriter, or even reenroll in college. Somehow, the northeastern corner of the country has that effect on folks.

Six states. Eight iconic trips. One New England.

 PLAYLIST

New England may be famous for churning out some of the world's best writers, but it's also made a significant contribution to the music scene. Here are some of our favorites for a long coastal or mountain drive:

- "More Than a Feelin," Boston
- "Sweet Rhode Island Red," Ike & Tina
- "Moonlight in Vermont," Willie Nelson
- "U-Mass," The Pixies
- "The Beautiful Song," Willard Grant Conspiracy
- "The State of Massachusetts," Dropkick Murphys
- "Old Cape Cod," John Prine & Mac Wiseman
- "Dream On," Aerosmith

 BEST ICONIC TRIPS

ICONIC TRIPS

Coastal New England

WHY GO For many of us, the northeast's craggy, wind-swept coasts and its salty-aired islands are synonymous with the very spirit of New England. This mammoth expedition, which spans four states and thousands of miles, is for any inquisitive traveler with an unyielding desire to discover the true spirit of this pioneering region.

Pull out the worn and folded American map that hides in your car's glove box. Then take a good look at the curving outline of the northeastern United States, all the way from Connecticut to the Canadian border. Even on paper, it is quite obviously a massive and mighty place, especially in the northernmost reaches of the country, where Frenchman Bay and the Gulf of Maine finally give way to the wilds of Canada.

With that in mind, it's probably worth mentioning that a grand tour along the coast of New England – one of the best possible ways to explore the area, as far as we're concerned – could hypothetically begin almost anywhere. A good number of New England–based tour companies, for example, offer coastal journeys that begin in the charming Connecticut seaside city of Mystic. If you'd like to do the same, simply refer to the "Maritime Connecticut" trip in this book's Connecticut chapter, where the city of Mystic is covered in depth.

Boston is another popular starting point, in part because it has the busiest airport north of New York. For reasons of convenience and common sense, however, we've decided to kick things off in the city of ❶ **Providence**, Rhode Island, which, contrary to popular belief, is by no means the most destitute locale in the northeast. In fact, as the city's boosters are fond of saying, "If you haven't seen Providence lately, you

TIME
7 days

DISTANCE
750 miles

BEST TIME TO GO
Sep – Nov

START
Providence, RI

END
Bar Harbor, ME

ALSO GOOD FOR

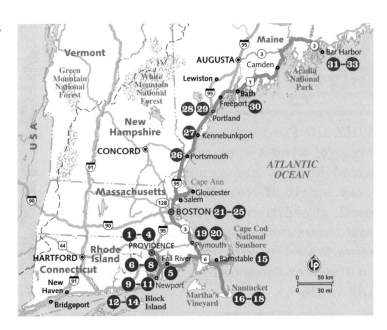

haven't seen Providence." And it's true: in recent years, the downtown area has experienced a successful redevelopment project, with the newly beautified Providence River as its shining centerpiece.

During the day, explore the city's Federal Hill neighborhood, a still-authentic Little Italy with Atwells Ave as its main thoroughfare. Try the popular **2 Al Forno Restaurant** for dinner, a contemporary Italian bistro that has been absolutely showered with well-deserved praise from locals, tourists and journalists alike since its opening in 1980. Get the grilled pizza. And if you're in town sometime between May and October, don't miss the opportunity to experience **3 WaterFire**, an astonishing installation and performance art project featuring 100 small bonfires at the confluence of the city's three rivers.

Literary-minded folks usually find the **4 Providence Athenaeum** to be another of the city's must-see sights. Founded in 1753 and housed in a 19th-century Greek Revival building, it's the country's fourth-oldest membership library. Edgar Allen Poe was once a member, and today even out-of-towners can borrow books. Aside from its rare collection, the library features exhibits of particularly exceptional texts.

Make your way to the state's East Bay region next. Still rich in Colonial heritage, this particular stretch of Rhode Island has only recently become a popular destination with visitors. To quickly and affordably get a feel for the area, take a bicycle ride along the 14.5-mile ❺ **East Bay Bike Path**. Aside from a few minor interruptions, the Narragansett Bay will keep you company along the entire route.

The town of ❻ **Bristol** sits along the bike path; it's also the host of the country's oldest Fourth of July parade, which first took place in 1785. No matter what time of year you're in town, however, consider making plans to dine at Bristol's ❼ **DeWolf Tavern**, where contemporary American entrees are served in a restored 1818 warehouse. The restaurant is also known for its superb Indian dishes and for its impressively wide selection of rum.

To get a taste of Bristol's remarkably wealthy yesteryears, spend an hour or so at the ❽ **Blithewold Mansion, Gardens & Arboretum**, an English-style garden estate with 45 rooms and a fantastic collection of antiques. Perhaps even more impressive is the

WANT TO BE A LIGHTHOUSE KEEPER?

Although it's highly unlikely that anyone is keeping track, visiting lighthouses has got to be one of the most popular tourist activities in all of New England. And yet on the tiny Rose Island, which is just off the coast of Newport in Rhode Island's Narragansett Bay, it's possible to actually live and work in a lighthouse for one week. This is a popular program, and as such it's necessary to reserve your week well in advance. For full details, visit www.roseisland lighthouse.org.

foliage of the arboretum. The estate's outer appearance was so important to its original inhabitants, in fact, that at one point sand was trucked in from Martha's Vineyard and used to create a beach.

Next stop: ❾ **Newport**, Rhode Island, home to the legendary Newport Folk Festival, where Bob Dylan infamously "went electric" way back in the summer of 1965. The 50-acre ❿ **Newport Vineyards** is also becoming legendary, and today it's known for growing more wine grapes than any other farm in New England. Public tours take place daily at 1pm and 3pm. To knock back a drink or two in an entirely different environment that nevertheless still offers a quintessentially Newport experience, pull up a seat inside one of the many dining rooms of ⓫ **Clarke Cooke House**. This is a much-loved local restaurant, and one that has long been a favorite haunt of Newport's sailing elite. In fact, you're unlikely to find a more impressive collection of America's Cup memorabilia anywhere else in town. The menu is heavy on seafood and other regionally influenced cuisine.

"Bob Dylan infamously 'went electric' way back in the summer of 1965"

To reach this trip's next destination, ⓬ **Block Island**, which is often called the "Bermuda of the North," you'll need to alight at Point Judith, where the Block Island ferry departs multiple times throughout the day. It arrives at the island's solitary village, Old Harbor, which is conveniently located right down the street from the **⓭ 1661 Inn & Hotel Manisses**. Guests can choose from a half-dozen different properties, including the 1661 Inn itself, which comes complete with a remarkable ocean view, and the slightly stuffier hotel, where a fine collection of Victorian antiques are on display.

Traveling on foot is without a doubt the best way to experience the natural beauty of Block Island. So if you're game for a good hike, set out in search of the **⓮ Southeast Lighthouse**. The 52ft brick tower, a combination of the Italianate and Gothic Revival styles, is perched atop the dramatic Mohegan Bluffs, which are often compared to Ireland's Cliffs of Mohr. In years past, seafarers who worked along the New England coast knew the bluffs as the region's "stumbling block," and indeed a good number of ships sunk after sailing too near. As a result, the North Light was erected on Sandy Point in 1829. Southeast Light, however, didn't come along for 46 more years, in 1875.

After sailing back to Point Judith, hop on I-195 east and make your way to the village of Barnstable on Cape Cod; the drive takes a little over two hours. Departing two or three times a day from the Barnstable Harbor are a number of unique **⓯ Hyannis Whale Watcher Cruises**, each one led by a highly trained and well-informed naturalist guide, all seasoned environmentalists and ecologists. In fact, you'll learn not only about whales during your four-hour journey but also about the Cape's unique ecology. Humpback whales and the absolutely enormous fin whales are just two of the species you may encounter.

After touring the Great Atlantic and returning to Barnstable, you'll want to cut directly across the mid-Cape and head for Hyannisport, where you'll board yet another sea-worthy vessel, this one bound for the island of **⓰ Nantucket**. Hy-Line Cruises (www.hylinecruises.com) and Steamship Authority (www.islandferry.com) both operate Nantucket-bound boats out of Hyannisport, with Steamship coming in as the slightly more affordable option. (A round-trip adult ticket on the two-hour slow boat is about $35.)

While many visitors to Cape Cod make day-trips to Martha's Vineyard, those going to Nantucket tend to stay for at least one night. We happen to be partial to the **⓱ Veranda House**, an endlessly stylish boutique hotel with priceless Nantucket Harbor views that literally must be seen to be believed. And if you happen to still be reeling from your recent date with the whales and would like to learn more, you're certainly in the right place: Nantucket was once known as the whaling capital of the world, and it's an absolute pleasure to learn about the island's seafaring past at the **⓲ Whaling Museum**. The museum recently experienced an extensive restoration, and visitors can now view the enormous skeleton of a sperm whale before retiring to the rooftop observation deck.

True American patriots will find more than enough to keep them busy at our next stop: America's Hometown, **20** **Plymouth**, Massachusetts, which is just 45 minutes by car from the Hyannis harbor. Joining an organized tour is one of the easiest ways to take in all of Plymouth's most important attractions in one fell swoop; one of the town's more professional tour outfits is **21** **Colonial Lantern Tours of Plymouth.** The tours always take place at night – that explains the lanterns – so it makes perfect sense that the frightful Ghost & Legends Lantern Tour would be one of the company's best on offer. Also available is the Historic Colonial Lantern Tour.

22 **Boston** is only 40 miles away, and even if you're just passing through town on your way to Cape Ann, it's tough to go wrong with a stroll down the city's 2.5-mile **23** **Freedom Trail**, which winds past 16 important historic sights. The trail begins at the visitor information center in Boston Common, and passes Faneuil Hall, the Paul Revere House, and the Old North Church before crossing the Charles River and ending at the Bunker Hill Monument.

DRINK YOUR WAY UP THE COAST

Many visitors to this part of the country aren't aware that the southeastern region of New England has its very own **Coastal Wine Trail**. But it's true! Officially known as the Southeastern New England Wine Growing Appellation, the region stretches all the way from the coast of Connecticut to Cape Cod, although only three Massachusetts and four Rhode Island wineries are currently represented. For more information about the trail and its Passport Contest, visit www.coastalwinetrail.com.

If you are planning on making a day or two of it in Boston, you've certainly got enough time to head to the **24** **John F Kennedy Presidential Library & Museum**. The size of the JFK archives at the library is absolutely stunning, although most visitors come for the museum, which documents the life and many achievements of JFK. Don't forget to get a good look at the building itself before leaving; it was designed by the world-renowned architect IM Pei.

Boston is awash with good hotels, although one of the most unusual is the **25** **Hotel @ MIT**, which sits near the MIT campus in Cambridge. It's something of a boutique hotel for the technologically obsessed traveler.

As you travel up the coast toward the massive expanse of Maine, you'll pass a good number of interesting destinations worth an extended stop. In the Cape Ann area, the rugged port town of Gloucester is certainly worth your time, as is Portsmouth, New Hampshire – supposedly the country's third-oldest city. The **26** **Strawbery Banke Museum** there uses a combination of exhibits and restored houses to recreate what life was like in the area as far back as the late 1600s.

Only 30 miles away from Portsmouth is the summer retreat town of Kennebunkport, Maine, popular with artists, writers, and the former US President

George HW Bush. Head inland to the **㉗ Brick Store Museum** in Kennebunk to learn about a side of the city most visitors fail to explore: its history. The range of the museum's collection is vast, with exhibits documenting everything from the area's Native American legacy to its obscure professional sports heroes.

㉘ Portland is the next sizable town along the coast, and like Kennebunkport, it too has a substantial artistic community. It's also home to the Maine College of Art, while the highly regarded Bowdoin College sits on the opposite end of Casco Bay, in the town of Brunswick. There's no doubt that much of this local talent finds inspiration on the walls of the **㉙ Portland Museum of Art**, which has a strong collection of both American and European masters.

Those of you who plan to follow this trip to its very end may want to first consider stopping at the **㉚ LL Bean Flagship Store** in Freeport, which is nothing if not the pure epitome of destination retail. The shop offers clinics for hunters, fishers, bicyclists, boaters and skiers, and it even has a free summer concert series. More importantly for your purposes, however, it's got a heck of a lot of fleece. That's a fabric that's almost certain to come in handy in **㉛ Bar Harbor**, one of the last vestiges of civilization before the United States becomes Canada.

"An unusual city, of course, calls for unusual activities"

An unusual city, of course, calls for unusual activities, and perhaps no other experience in town fits the bill better than a two-hour-long **㉜ Lulu Lobster Boat Ride**. Lulu's Captain John is particularly renowned for his wide knowledge of area lore and the inner workings of the lobster industry.

And finally, the **㉝ Harborside Hotel & Marina**, which sits right on the unspoiled Frenchman Bay, is by leaps and bounds the finest resort in town. Everything about the place, from its exterior to the very mattresses on its beds, simply screams pure luxury. And if you've managed to come this far, friend, you've earned it, pure and simple.

Dan Eldridge

TRIP INFORMATION

GETTING THERE
I-95 runs directly between Boston and Providence.

DO

Blithewold Mansion, Gardens & Arboretum
Take a peak into the unusual lives of Rhode Island's mansion millionaires. ☎ 401-253-2707; www.blithewold.org; 101 Ferry Rd, Bristol, RI; adult/child $10/free; ☽ 10am-4pm Wed-Sat, 10am-3pm Sun

Brick Store Museum
If it's notable and it came from Kennebunk, you'll likely find it here. ☎ 207-985-4802; www.brickstoremuseum.org; 117 Main St, Kennebunk, ME; donation $5; ☽ 10am-4:30pm Tue-Fri, 10am-1pm Sat; ☝

Colonial Lantern Tours of Plymouth
Learn about the often frightful legends of Colonial Plymouth by night and with lantern in hand. Call for the tour schedule. ☎ 774-454-8126; www.lanterntours.com; Plymouth, MA; adult/child $15/12

Hyannis Whale Watcher Cruises
The mid-Cape's only whale-watching company employs whale-friendly boats without propellers. Call for the cruise schedule. ☎ 508-362-6088; www.whales.net; 269 Millway Rd, Barnstable, MA; adult/child $45/26; ☝

John F Kennedy Presidential Library & Museum
Easily the greatest memorial to America's most charismatic and beloved leader. ☎ 617-514-1600; www.jfklibrary.org; Columbia Point, Boston, MA; adult/child $10/7; ☽ 9am-5pm

LL Bean Flagship Store
A full schedule of free events, and there's enough fleece to clothe a small African village. ☎ 800-441-5713; www.llbean.com; 95 Main St, Freeport, ME; ☽ 24hr daily

Lulu Lobster Boat Ride
Learn about the wily ways of the lobster with Captain John. ☎ 207-963-2341; www.lulu-lobsterboat.com; 56 West St, Bar Harbor, ME; adult/child $27/15; ☽ tours daily May-Oct

Portland Museum of Art
Maine's largest and oldest art gallery, with a 17,000-piece collection. ☎ 207-775-6148; www.portlandmuseum.org; 7 Congress Sq, Portland, ME; adult/child $10/4; ☽ 10am-5pm Tue-Thu, Sat & Sun, 10am-9pm Fri

Providence Athenaeum
This subscription library is a bibliophile's fantasy come to life. ☎ 401-421-6970; www.providenceathenaeum.org; 251 Benefit St, Providence, RI; admission free; ☽ 9am-7pm Mon-Thu, 9am-5pm Fri, 9am-1pm Sat

Southeast Lighthouse
Come here for dramatic, show-stopping views of the craggy Mohegan Bluffs. ☎ 401-466-5009; www.lighthouse.cc; 122 Mohegan Trail, Block Island, RI; admission free; ☽ 10am-4pm Jul & Aug

Strawbery Banke Museum
Exhibits and restored houses take visitors back in time to New Hampshire's very earliest days. ☎ 603-433-1100; www.strawberybanke.org; 14 Hancock St, Portsmouth, NH; adult/child $15/10; ☽ 10am-5pm May-Oct

Whaling Museum
Nantucket's legacy as the world's whaling capital is proudly on display here. ☎ 508-228-1894; www.nha.org; 15 Broad St, Nantucket, MA; adult/child $15/8; ☽ 10am-5pm daily Jun-Oct

EAT & DRINK

Al Forno Restaurant
This world-renowned Italian eatery is heavy on both creativity and regional ingredients. ☎ 401-273-9760; www.alforno.com; 577 S Main St, Providence, RI; mains $12-28; ☽ 5-10pm Tue-Fri, 4-10pm Sat

Clarke Cooke House
From the Boom Boom Room to the Candy Store, this is the pure epitome of Newport. ☎ 401-846-4500; www.clarkecooke.com; 1 Bannister's Wharf, Newport, RI; mains $20-40; ☽ 11:30am-4pm & 5pm-late

DeWolf Tavern
The building is age-old, and the food is contemporary and cutting-edge. Try the rum. ☎ 401-254-2005; www.dewolftavern.com; 259 Thames St, Bristol, RI; prix fixe $20; 🕑 5-10pm Mon-Sat, 5-9pm Sun

Newport Vineyards
Take a tour of New England's biggest grower of wine grapes, then sample its vintages. ☎ 401-848-5161; www.newportvineyards .com; 909 E Main Rd, Rte 138, Middletown, RI; 🕑 10am-5pm Mon-Sat, noon-5pm Sun

SLEEP

1661 Inn & Hotel Manisses
A mini-village of inns and hotels for all tastes, conveniently located near the ferry terminal. ☎ 401-466-2421; www.block islandresorts.com; 1 Spring St, Block Island, RI; r $90-445

Harborside Hotel & Marina
This downtown resort and spa is so pretty and endlessly luxurious, you'll think you're dreaming. ☎ 207-288-5033; www.theharbor sidehotel.com; 55 West St, Bar Harbor, ME; r from $300

Hotel @ MIT
A wired hotel from the folks who brought you the search engine and the webpage. ☎ 617-577-0200; www.hotelatmit.com; 20 Sidney St, Cambridge, MA; r from $223; ⑤

Veranda House
Convenient to town, this flawlessly decorated and classically cool boutique hotel has unbelievable views of Nantucket Harbor. ☎ 508-228-0695; www.theverandahouse.com; 3 Step Lane, Nantucket, MA; r $189-589

USEFUL WEBSITES
www.massport.com/tourism
www.visitmaine.com

LINK YOUR TRIP
www.lonelyplanet.com/trip-planner

Fall Foliage Tour

WHY GO Touring through small-town New England in search of autumn's changing colors has become such a popular activity, it has sprouted its own enthusiastic subculture of "leaf-peepers." But this trip is about much more than just flora and fauna: become immersed in the bountiful harvest spirit that envelops the entire region each fall.

TIME
5 – 7 days

DISTANCE
785 miles

BEST TIME TO GO
Sep – Nov

START
Mystic, CT

END
Kennebunkport, ME

ALSO GOOD FOR

OUTDOORS

Let us be the first to admit it: if the region of the country in which you happen to live is lucky enough to experience all four seasons, there's no reason at all for you not to enjoy the bounty of autumn in your own hometown. But the thing about New England and the fall season, as anyone who has ever experienced the two together can no doubt confirm, is that they have always gone together with such seamless, picture-perfect grace. Aesthetically speaking, it doesn't get much better than seeing the fiery reds of a sturdy oak tree juxtaposed with an old wooden clapboard church in a small Massachusetts town. Or maybe for you it's the burnt orange leaves of a yellow sugar maple tree, perched atop a modest hill and overlooking a storybook Vermont village below.

But enough already with the talking – autumn doesn't last forever, after all. (Peak fall foliage season in New England, by the way, starts at the beginning of September and runs through the end of October.) To get yourself in an appropriately autumnal frame of mind then, plan a trip to ❶ **BF Clyde's Cider Mill** in Old Mystic. It's a National Historic Landmark where six generations of the same family have been producing cider since the late 1800s. Visitors can watch the cider mill in action – this is the only such mill in the country still powered by steam – and then purchase alcoholic or nonalcoholic cider in plastic jugs.

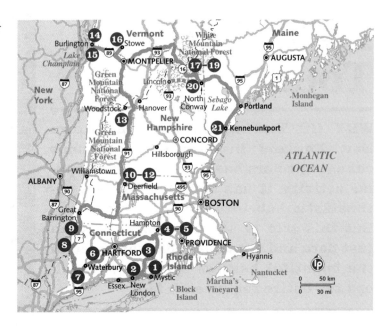

As soon as you're properly hydrated and fortified at the mill (don't forget to pick up a bottle of maple syrup and a bit of Indian corn), head west to the town of Essex, where the Connecticut River Expeditions company launches its ❷ **Fall Foliage Cruise** aboard the *RiverQuest*, a twin-hulled catamaran with wide windows for sightseeing and a large outdoor deck. The *RiverQuest* embarks on its 90-minute leaf-peeping expedition of the lower stretch of the Connecticut River at 1pm and 3pm on weekends, and at 1pm on weekdays.

About 30 miles north of Mystic, the ❸ **Blue Slope Country Museum** in Franklin is essentially a celebration of all things bucolic: wagon and sleigh rides for the kids; basket weaving and blacksmithing demonstrations; donkey and mule shows – you name it, really. And during the fall season, life at the museum gets even more interesting: how about pie-eating contests and Amish outdoor furniture for sale?

And if you plan on staying put in this relaxed region of Connecticut, often referred to as the Last Green Valley, there are two appropriately countrified choices in the villages of Hampton and Chaplin; both are about 15 miles north of Franklin. In Hampton, the ❹ **Safe Haven B&B** sits on 90 acres of farmland dotted not only with trees and winding rivers but also with alpacas – those are the unusual and peaceful creatures that look a bit like llamas, and whose hair is used to make blankets, sweaters, and other knitted items. Guests can also take advantage of the nearby hiking trails and, at day's end, the on-site hot tub. The ⑤ **Old Gurley Tavern Country Inn** is another smart choice nearby. It's located in the village of Chaplin, and unlike the Safe Haven B&B, this two-story house is located in a residential neighborhood. There's an old tavern room where guests can socialize, and a few of the bedrooms come complete with working fireplaces.

On the opposite end of Connecticut, the Litchfield Hills region is the state's other major destination for serious leaf-peeping. Incidentally, it's also a popular region in which to visit one of Connecticut's famous sugar houses, especially during the spring months of February and March, which is when the houses produce Connecticut's famous maple syrup. Some of the houses choose to stay open year-round, however, and among them is ⑥ **Lamothe's Sugar House** in Burlington (not to be confused with the Vermont town of the same name!). Tours are given daily at Lamothe's, and the gift shop, where luscious maple candies are sold, is open year-round as well. To find other area houses that may be open during your visit, pick up a copy of the annual *Guide to Connecticut Sugarhouses,* available in some tourism information centers. It's also available online, at www .ctmaple.org, as a downloadable PDF.

DIY FARM TOUR

Connecticut may be one of the nation's smallest states, but after touring its country roads for a day or two, you'll be amazed at the sheer mass of farmland. And what's more, many of Connecticut's farms have value-added entertainment benefits for visitors: you've got wineries, pick-your-own farms, farmers markets, farm stands – they're everywhere!

To maximize your agrarian experience, pick up a free copy of the absolutely indispensable *Connecticut Farm Map: A Guide to Connecticut's Agricultural Destinations.* It's available at most state tourism info centers.

About a half-hour drive to the west is the fifth-generation ⑦ **Bunnell Farm,** where an unusual twist on the popular pick-your-own-fruit-and-vegetable trend is offered – namely, pick-your-own flowers. There are also horse-drawn hay rides and tractor rides at the farm, both of which lead guests to a PYO pumpkin farm, which is naturally at its peak during fall foliage. And like many PYO farms, Bunnell is solidly in on the corn-maze craze as well – if you happen to arrive after sunset, they'll even loan you a flashlight and let you stumble around in the dark.

Before venturing north into Massachusetts, stop by one more of Litchfield County's PYO farms, the ⑧ **Ellsworth Hill Orchard & Berry Farm.** Just a bit southwest of Falls Village and close to the New York state line, this farm is home to a particularly challenging six-acre corn maze. And naturally, berries, plums, peaches, and apples can be snapped right off the vine by your very own hands. Just 15 miles north of here, the ⑨ **Rustling Wind Creamery & Stables** can be found. Originally a simple daily farm, the creamery now produces six

different natural cow's-milk cheeses and a number of goat's-milk cheeses. Jams, jellies, and three different flavors of goat's-milk fudge are available at the creamery as well.

Continue heading north, and cross the state border to reach this trip's next stop, which is in the northern Massachusetts town of Deerfield. Hopping on I-91 north in Connecticut is the most convenient way to reach Deerfield from the Litchfield Hills, although if you haven't yet sampled this chapter's "Ethan Allen Hwy & Vermont Rte 100" trip, this is the perfect stretch in which to do so. Simply take Rte 7 (aka the Ethan Allen Hwy) north into Massachusetts instead of I-91; you'll find plenty to keep you busy on the stretch between Kent, CT, and Stockbridge, MA, where you can transfer to I-90 east, and then to I-91 north, which leads directly to Deerfield.

After such a long drive, there's a decent chance you'll be in need of quality food and lodging by the time you reach town. And in that case, the laid-back country atmosphere of the **10** **Deerfield Inn** will almost certainly cure what ails you. Conveniently located right within the Historic Deerfield village, the Deerfield Inn has all the comfort and hominess of an age-old country B&B and all the conveniences and modern amenities of a boutique hotel: wi-fi, flat-screen TVs with cable and DVD players in every room, premium toiletries, and so on. For a romantic candlelit dinner, try the consistently award-winning **11** **Chandler's Restaurant** in South Deerfield's Yankee Candle Village. The menu at Chandler's is known for changing on a regular basis, but exemplary service and an impressive wine selection are unswerving standards.

"Electra Havemeyer Webb – a woman with a truly unique artistic vision and a serious shopping compulsion"

The **12** **Historic Deerfield** village itself is a collection of 14 houses, all decorated in the popular styles of the 18th and 19th centuries. Visitors are led from house to house by a well-informed guide, and for those without a strong grounding in American history, a larger building known as the Flynt Center for the Study of Early American Life does a decent job of explaining it all in smaller and more easily digestible chunks.

Travel north for about 90 miles along I-91 to reach the town of Woodstock, VT, and the **13** **Billings Farm and Museum**. Billings is indeed a working dairy farm, and visitors who tour the grounds here are taken to a horse barn and a calf nursery before going on a self-guided tour through a series of 19th-century barns. Show up at just the right time, and you may get to see the daily milking of the herd, which happens at 3:30pm.

From Woodstock, hop right on I-89 north and take it all the way to Burlington, which sits directly on the shores of Lake Champlain; the Adirondacks of

New York are located on the opposite side of the lake. With a 15-minute rest stop included, the drive should take about two hours.

Burlington, of course, is home to a wealth of indoor and outdoor activities, so if you'd like to briefly get off the cycle of country farm- and fall foliage-specific activities, the Lake Champlain Valley, as this area is known, is a great place to do that.

One of the area's snazziest B&B operations is an ivy-covered, red-brick Victorian mansion known as the ⑭ **Willard Street Inn**. A chef prepares breakfast each morning in a wide solarium overlooking the lawn and, best of all, the inn is located in the city and within easy walking distance of the University of Vermont and Champlain College. Some of the fourteen individually designed rooms have striking views of Lake Champlain and the Adirondacks.

One of Vermont's most unusual and most visited attractions, the ⑮ **Shelburne Museum**, is seven miles south of Burlington and right in the heart of Lake Champlain valley. Founded in 1947 by Electra Havemeyer Webb, a woman with a truly unique artistic vision and a serious shopping compulsion, the museum is home to nearly 200,000 pieces of distinctive American folk art and crafts. But Webb was also collected buildings and historic structures, and her art is now housed in literally dozens of them, including a jail and a 220ft-long steamship.

A 45-minute drive east – I-89 south, then Rte 100 – leads to Stowe, where anyone in search of a truly unforgettable culinary experience should run – that's *run,* not walk – directly to the ⑯ **Trapp Family Lodge**. Believe it or not, this Austrian-style alpine mountain resort is still operated by the same von Trapp family that inspired the musical and movie *The Sound of Music.* Not surprisingly, European-style dining is what's on offer, although visitors can choose from three completely different restaurants: a formal dining room for the stiff-upper-lip experience; an Austrian Tea Room where blond-haired blue-eyed beauties serve bratwurst and sauerkraut; and the Lounge, which bears a significant resemblance to cafés in more standard-issue mountain lodges.

 DETOUR If you're in the mood to try a new trip but don't have an extra weekend to spare, consider going for a drive along Rte 112, known as the **Kancamagus Scenic Byway**, which passes through the White Mountains from Lincoln to Conway in New Hampshire. You'll see the craggy Lost River Gorge and the wide open spaces of Franconia Notch State Park, where the foliage in September and October is simply spectacular. The 26.5-mile drive takes roughly an hour to complete, or much longer if you choose to stop and admire the view.

You're now about 120 miles away from this trip's next stop, which happens to sit atop New Hampshire's Wildcat Mountain, but trust us on this one: the zip cable ride known as the

Wildcat Express Gondola is well worth it, and the views of Mt Washington will absolutely blow your mind. And no, you won't be hanging on with your fingers: the Wildcat is essentially a cross between a hammock and a chair. It does soar at speeds of up to 45 mph, though, and the trip is a half-mile long.

Hiking or driving to **Mount Washington State Park** is also a popular activity, and an unusual one too, especially considering you'll need to ascend a 6288ft mountain to get there. Reaching the peak via the 7.6-mile **Mt Washington Auto Road** makes for one of the most remarkable drives in New Hampshire. But be sure to check the mountaintop weather situation online before leaving your inn, as conditions can change with little warning. The rather steep toll fee comes complete with an audio tour on CD or cassette, and it's meant to be played during your drive, which should take between 30 and 45 minutes each way.

Many visitors to the White Mountains choose to stay somewhere in or around the town of North Conway, which is where you'll find the **Cranmore Inn**, a relaxed, country-style bed and breakfast that is nonetheless conveniently located for restaurants and retail districts in North Conway Village. And not only does the Cranmore have both a hot tub and a swimming pool, it also has the distinction of being the oldest continuously operating lodge in the entire Mt Washington Valley. In other words, they're clearly doing something right.

"The only serious downside is that you won't ever want to pack up and leave. "

This trip comes to its decidedly laid-back conclusion in the resort town of Kennebunkport, Maine, where generations of writers, artists, and even world leaders have come for a mix of inspiration and down-time. Kennebunkport is about two hours by car from North Conway. When you arrive, check into one of the 16 designer **Cottages at Cabot Cove**, which, yes, actually are lined up inside a breathtakingly gorgeous tidal cove. And while the prices are admittedly high, they graciously include beach passes, a fully equipped kitchen, and the use of kayaks and rowboats. In fact, the only serious downside to staying at the cottages is that you probably won't ever want to pack up and leave.

Of course, hordes of travelers before you have said the very same thing about New England itself. And yet there's really only one way to find out if you'll end up feeling the same.

We'll see you there.
Dan Eldridge

TRIP INFORMATION

GETTING THERE

To reach Mystic from Hartford, take Rte 2 E to Rte 11 S, to Rte 85 S. From there, take I-95 N straight into town.

DO

BF Clyde's Cider Mill

See an historic steam-powered mill pressing apples into crisp cider here. ☎ 860-536-3354; www.bfclydescidermill.com; 129 North Stonington Rd, Old Mystic, CT; tours free; ⊙ 9am-5pm daily Sep-Dec; ♿

Billings Farm & Museum

Vermont farming culture is serious business at this slick museum. ☎ 802-457-2355; www.billingsfarm.org; Rte 12 & River Rd, Woodstock, VT; adult/child $11/6; ⊙ 10am-5pm daily; ♿

Blue Slope Country Museum

Immerse yourself in rural living with the many farm activities here. ☎ 860-642-6413; www .blueslope.com; 138 Blue Hill Rd, Franklin, CT; call for event schedule and prices; ♿

Bunnell Farm

Hayrides, pick-your-own pumpkins, turkeys, and a great corn maze: what's not to like? ☎ 860-567-9576; www.bunnellfarm.org; 498 Maple St, Litchfield, CT; ⊙ farm 10am-5:30pm Thu-Mon; maze 11am-6pm Fri-Sun; ♿

Ellsworth Hill Orchard & Berry Farm

Enjoy apple orchard tours and a six-acre corn maze at this pick-your-own farm. ☎ 860-364-0025; www.ellsworthfarm.com; 461 Cornwall Bridge Rd, Sharon, CT; ⊙ 9am-5:30pm; ♿

Fall Foliage Cruise

Go leaf-peeping in style on a 90-minute cruise of the lower Connecticut River. Call ahead for schedules. ☎ 860-662-0577; www.ctriver expeditions.org; Steamboat Dock, Main St, Essex, CT; adult/child $20/15

Historic Deerfield

Learn about 18th-century American life by touring 14 homes in this historic village.

☎ 413-775-7214; www.historic-deerfield .org; 80 Old Main St, Deerfield, MA; adult/ child $14/5; ⊙ 9:30am-4:30pm daily Apr-Dec

Lamothe's Sugar House

This maple syrup producer gives tours and sells all manner of sweet stuff. ☎ 860-675-5043; www.lamothesugarhouse.com; 89 Stone Rd, Burlington, CT; admission free; ⊙ 10am-6pm Mon-Thu, 10am-5pm Fri & Sat, noon-5pm Sun

Mount Washington State Park

A state park located on the summit of a mountain? Good stories are (almost) guaranteed. ☎ 603-466-3347; www.nhstateparks .org; Rte 302, Sargent's Purchase, NH; adult/ child $4/2; ⊙ 8am-6pm

Mt Washington Auto Road

Survive the 30-minute drive up New England's highest peak, then display the bumper sticker. ☎ 603-466-3988; www.mountwashington autoroad.com; Rte 16, Pinkham Notch, NH; car & driver/additional adult/additional child $20/7/5

Rustling Wind Creamery & Stables

A small dairy farm with sheep, goats, and a hodgepodge of crafts and foodstuffs for sale. ☎ 860-824-7084; www.rustlingwind.com; 164 Canaan Mountain Rd, Falls Village, CT; admission free; ⊙ 9am-5pm; ♿

Shelburne Museum

All manner of folksy Americana is displayed inside historic buildings here. ☎ 802-985-3346; www.shelburnemuseum.org; 6000 Shelburne Rd (Rte 7), Shelburne, VT; adult/child $18/9; ⊙ 10am-5pm daily May-Oct; ♿

Wildcat Express Gondola

Mountainside zipline and gondola rides. ☎ 603-466-3326; www.skiwildcat.com; Wildcat Mountain, Rte 16, Pinkham Notch, Jackson, NH; zipride $20, gondola adult/ child $15/7; ⊙ 9am-5pm daily mid-Jun–mid-Oct); ♿

EAT

Chandler's Restaurant

A romantic and award-winning restaurant with traditional New England fare. ☎ 413-

665-1277; www.chandlers.yankeecandle
.com; 25 Greenfield Rd, South Deerfield, MA;
mains $22-29; 🕙 10:30am-4pm Mon & Tue,
10:30am-8pm Wed-Sun

Deerfield Inn
This pristine country inn with hotel-type
amenities is right inside the historic Deerfield
Village. ☎ 413-774-5587; www.deerfieldinn
.com; 81 Main St, Deerfield, MA; mains $18-
32; 🕙 7:30-10am & 5-9pm Thu-Mon

Trapp Family Lodge
An Austrian-themed lodge with three dining
options (call ahead for opening hours), dramatically overlooking the village of Stowe.
☎ 802-253-8511; www.trappfamily
.com; 700 Trapp Hill Rd, Stowe, VT; mains
$9.50-33; 🚹

SLEEP
Cottages at Cabot Cove
These romantic and unusual cottage accommodations are delightfully tucked into a cove
on the Kennebunk. ☎ 207-967-5424; www
.cabotcovecottages.com; 7 S Maine St, Kennebunkport, ME; r $345-695; 🐾

Cranmore Inn
This 150-year-old inn is convenient to the
White Mountains and close to town. ☎ 603-
356-5502; www.cranmoreinn.com; 80 Kear-
sarge St, North Conway, NH; r $99-210; 🐾

Old Gurley Tavern Country Inn
A lovingly restored 1822 Federal-style house
in Connecticut's Last Green Valley. ☎ 860-
455-1457; www.oldgurleytavern.com; 42
Chaplin St, Chaplin, CT; r $80

Safe Haven B&B
This country inn sits on a working alpaca
farm. Hiking trails and a stocked river keep
visitors busy. ☎ 860-455-1101; www.stay
withsafehaven.com; 39 Drain St, Hampton,
CT; r $150-250

Willard Street Inn
A luxurious Victorian mansion in Burlington's
Hills District; some rooms have splendid Adi-
rondack and Lake Champlain views. ☎ 802-
651-8710; www.willardstreetinn.com; 349 S
Willard St, Burlington, VT; r $135-230

USEFUL WEBSITES
gonewengland.about.com
www.visit-vermont.com

LINK YOUR TRIP
TRIP

www.lonelyplanet.com/trip-planner

28 Connecticut Wine Trail p197
34 Vermont Backroads Ramble p229
51 60 Lighthouses in 60 Hours p321

Literary New England

WHY GO From Edith Wharton to Edward Gorey, Herman Melville to Harriet Beecher Stowe, the writers of New England have inspired generations with their poignant prose. Make this trip a mea culpa to your English teacher for not having read the great American classics you were assigned in school.

TIME
3 – 4 days

DISTANCE
610 miles

BEST TIME TO GO
Sep – Nov

START
Boston, MA

END
Middlebury, VT

ALSO GOOD FOR

HISTORY & CULTURE

The ❶ **Boston Public Library** is a fitting place to begin the ultimate literary tour. Constructed in 1852, the eye-catching structure lends credence to Boston's reputation as the "Athens of America." After thumbing through fragile tomes containing some of the region's greatest published works (including John Adams' personal library), pick up a free brochure and take a self-guided tour through the sumptuous neoclassical space. Note the hard-to-miss murals by John Singer Sargent. Before hitting the road, grab a book by your favorite local author and stop by the BPL's adorably named café, ❷ **Novel**. Swig a smooth cappuccino while memorizing bits of Robert Frost (it'll come in handy later), and enjoy the calm atmosphere overlooking an enchanting Italianate courtyard.

If you don't have the courage to confront Boston's post–Big Dig concrete jungle, retreat to the opulent ❸ **Omni Parker House**. The nation's longest continuously operating hotel (it opened in 1855) is a veritable sea of velvet drapes, overstuffed pillows and lavish swatches of floral wallpaper. Charles Dickens frequented the hotel, and it was here that he gave his first reading of *A Christmas Carol*.

When you're ready to hit the road, drive along I-93 (heading north) and take Hwy 1, then Rte 107 until you arrive in the quiet seaside town of Salem. Known for its bevy of spell-spewing witches, this little colonial haven also features the ❹ **House of the Seven Gables**. The

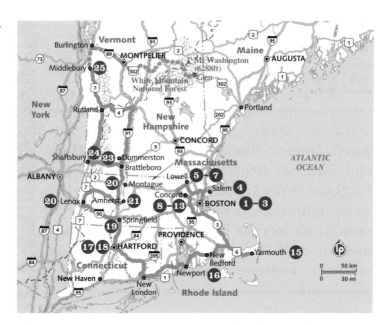

house was made famous by Nathaniel Hawthorne's novel of the same name, which used the manse as a metaphor to explore the gloomy Puritanical way of life in early New England. There are four historic buildings to be explored and a luscious, waterfront garden to remind ourselves that New England is much less dour than Hawthorne's depictions.

For something a bit more modern, hop back on the highway and take I-95 to I-93 until the turnoff for I-495. Here you will find the grumbling industrial town of Lowell, home to the Beat Generation's beloved Jack Kerouac. A small landscaped path on Bridge St, known as the **5** **Jack Kerouac Commemorative**, makes for a lovely place to stretch your legs and read several passages from his best-known works. His grave at **6** **Edson Cemetery**, on the corner of Gorham and Saratoga Sts, has become an unofficial pilgrimage site for free spirits. Try a **7** **Jack Kerouac Walking Tour**, compiled by the Jack Kerouac Subterranean Information Society. The fantastically detailed route stops at various sites throughout Lowell featured in five of his novels.

Woodsy Concord, just a short jaunt down Rte 3, is another step back in time. Nestled within the quaint collection of pitches and gables are the former residences of two of New England's most beloved authors. Check out the **8** **Ralph Waldo Emerson Homes**, which boasts most of the original furnishings purchased by the writer, and a luscious organic garden planted by Henry David Thoreau for Nathaniel Hawthorne (he also inhabited the estate).

Louisa May Alcott wrote her famous semiautobiographical *Little Women* in her home Orchard House, which is now part of a small estate of historical buildings called **9** **Louisa May Alcott Homes**. Complete Concord's literary hat-trick with a stay at **10** **Wayside Inn**, made famous by Longfellow's poems *Tales from a Wayside Inn*.

After a day in the life of some of Concord's finest, check out their final resting place at **11** **Sleepy Hollow Cemetery** (no relation to Ichabod Crane). Sleepy Hollow's wooded grounds challenge the stereotype of a spooky graveyard with towering evergreens, rolling hills, and plenty of space to gleefully spread a checkered tablecloth for a shady afternoon picnic. Head to the oft-visited Author's Ridge to visit the graves of Thoreau, Hawthorne, Emerson and two Alcotts, all quietly buried in the stunning setting that inspired each of their oeuvres.

"I went to the woods because I wished to live deliberately, to front only the essential facts of life, and see if I could not learn what it had to teach, and not, when I came to die, discover that I had not lived." Follow Henry David Thoreau's inspirational words from the non-fiction success *Walden; or, Life in the Woods* and enjoy an early-morning trip to nearby **12** **Walden Pond**. It was here that Thoreau put Transcendentalism's naturalist beliefs into practice and built himself a rustic cabin on the shores of the pond. Beat the crowds and delight in crunching freshly fallen leaves underfoot while taking in the serene setting orbiting the quiet glacial shore. Today, tombstone-like boulders mark the site of Thoreau's cabin, and its original furnishings are now preserved at the **13** **Concord Museum**, which also features other important pieces of 'New Englandiana' such as Emerson's desk and chair, and Paul Revere's 'one if by land' lantern.

OH! THE PLACES YOU CAN'T GO!

If Dr Seuss' inspirational words have you jonesing for your own literary adventure, beware of New England's literary decoys! Although they sound like honest-to-goodness New England towns, the following spots are figments of the authors' imaginations:

- Starkfield, Massachusetts – in *Ethan Frome* by Edith Wharton, supposedly located in the Berkshires.

- Arkham, Massachusetts – in several works by HP Lovecraft, home of the faux Ivy-League Miskatonic University.

- Castle Rock, Maine – in *The Dead Zone* by Stephen King, one of many made-up towns in King's scary state.

For a double dose of divinity, stop for lunch at the **14** **Fruitlands Tearoom**, in the nearby town of Harvard. The restaurant sits on a former vegetarian commune founded by Louisa May Alcott's father, Bronson Alcott, who aspired to set up a place for Transcendentalists to thrive.

After some contemplative kumbaya-ing, it's time to blaze a trail down I-95 for something a little more light-hearted. Follow the turnoff on Rte 3 for

Cape Cod and switch to Rte 6 as you approach Yarmouth, home to weirdo wordsmith Edward Gorey (yes, that is actually his real last name.) His former home has since been transformed into the **⑮ Edward Gorey House**, a museum featuring exhibits about his life and work. Don't forget to stop by the gift shop to grab some wickedly twisted bits of Gorey-ana.

If Gorey's gory stories of impaled children give you nightmares, calm your nerves at the plush, Victorian **⑯ Melville House** in New Bedford. Herman Melville often visited his sister here, and his memory has been preserved in the aptly named Herman Melville room, which features a handsome portrait of the writer.

Start the day with a drive along I-195, I-395, and Rte 2 until you reach Connecticut's capital, Hartford. For 17 years, Samuel Langhorne Clemens (better known as Mark Twain) and his family called Hartford home and lived in a stunning orange-and-black brick Victorian home on Farmington Ave. His years here were known to be the most productive of his life and the most tragic (two of his children died here), and the **⑰ Mark Twain House & Museum** carefully illustrates his history through photos, films, artifacts and manuscripts. He penned some of his most famous works here, including *The Adventures of Tom Sawyer, The Adventures of Huckleberry Finn* and *A Connecticut Yankee in King Arthur's Court.*

> *"The squat figure of the Lorax looks beseechingly up at passersby"*

Next door to the Twain residence is the former home of the esteemed author Harriet Beecher Stowe. Now a museum in the **⑱ Harriet Beecher Stowe Center**, the sun-drenched manse pays tribute to the author of *Uncle Tom's Cabin,* which bolstered the antislavery movement. Built in 1871, the Stowe house reflects the author's strong ideas about decorating and domestic efficiency, as expressed in her bestseller *American Woman's Home,* which sold almost as many copies as her ubiquitous novel.

As you head towards the rolling Berkshires, make a quick stop in Springfield to see the **⑲ Dr Seuss National Memorial Sculpture Garden** before turning off of I-91. Born in Springfield in 1904, Theodor Seuss Geisel passed through the gates of Dartmouth College and worked as a political cartoonist before earning his doctorate in gibberish and settling down to write his first children's book. The sculpture garden, created by his stepdaughter Lark Grey Dimond-Cates, features large-scale incarnations of his literary oeuvre. There's a 10ft-tall 'book' displaying the entire text of *Oh! The Places You'll Go!* and an impish-looking Geisel sitting at his drawing board, the Cat standing by his shoulder. In the opposite corner of the quad, the squat figure of the Lorax looks beseechingly up at passersby, his famous environmental warning engraved at his feet: "*Unless.*"

Follow I-90 west of Springfield and head to Lenox just before the highway crosses the state border into New York. Almost 50 years after Nathaniel Hawthorne left his home in this quaint hamlet (now part of Tanglewood), another writer found inspiration in the pine-scented Berkshires. Pulitzer-prize–winner Edith Wharton came to Lenox in 1899 and proceeded to build her palatial estate, the **20 Mount**. When not immersed in her craft, she would entertain a colorful array of guests including Henry James. Wharton summered at the Mount for a decade before moving permanently to France.

DETOUR If you're tired of the backseat peanut gallery screaming "Are we there yet?!", then make a beeline to the tiny town of Glen for a visit to **Story Land** (www.storylandnh.com). This refreshingly non-Disneyfied theme park caters to the three- to nine-year-old crowd with miniature rides and activities.

From patricians to poets – move along Rte 7 to Rte 8a and finally Rte 9 until you reach the birch-clad college town of Amherst, once home to the reclusive Emily Dickinson. During her lifetime, Emily Dickinson published only seven poems, but after her death, more than 1000 were discovered and published, and her verses on love, death, nature, and immortality have made her one of the most important poets of her time. It is not known why she was so hermitic as she aged, although some say she fell in love (unrequitedly) with a married clergyman and withdrew from the world into a private realm of pain, passion and poignancy. Her home is now the **21 Emily Dickinson Museum**, which features a tour of her house and the one next door, which belonged to her brother Austin. Continue north along Rte 63 and slip through the sleepy town of Montague to the find the **22 Montague Bookmill**, a converted cedar gristmill from 1842 whose multiple rooms contain stacks of used books ripe for the picking.

Travel north into Vermont to find the ultimate place for a lit lover to hang their hat. **23 Naulakha**, in Dummerston, offers guests the chance to spend the night in Rudyard Kipling's home – a truly unique experience closely guarded and maintained by the Landmark Trust USA. Kipling penned the ubiquitous *Jungle Book* here in little Naulakha, tucked in a valley that dimples the state's mountainous spine. He dreamed up Mowgli and his mates as a child in colonial India, but used the quiet hideaway in the thick Vermont forests to bring his critters to life on the page. Kipling also wrote *Captains Courageous* here.

NOT HALF BAKED

The **Bread Loaf Writers' Conference**, usually held in August, is the oldest writers' conference in America, having started long before 'creative writing' became a college course. Robert Frost inaugurated the idea in the 1920s, and today a mix of famous and aspiring writers still gather in the hill above Middlebury. Many events are open to the public; check out www.middlebury .edu/~blwc for more information.

In Shaftsbury, Vermont, west along Rte 9, Frost fanatics will get their fill at the ㉔ **Robert Frost Stone House Museum**. It was here, in this modest country home, that Frost composed some of his most memorable works. In fact the guides will tell you that the beloved *Stopping by Woods on a Snowy Evening* was actually composed at the dining room table on a sweltering summer night. The poem was featured in his fourth volume of poetry, *New Hampshire*, which earned him his first coveted Pulitzer Prize.

"At the end you'll find Frost's ubiquitous fork in the road... decide which way you want to go."

Let a stroll along the ㉕ **Robert Frost Interpretive Trail**, further north along Rte 7 (near Middlebury), be your final stop on your journey. As you wend your way through a picturesque thicket, pause to read the plaques featuring memorable quotes from his poetry. At the very end you'll find Frost's ubiquitous fork in the road. Now it's up to you to decide which way you want to go. The rest of the journey is yours.

Brandon Presser

TRIP INFORMATION

GETTING THERE
Start your trip in the heart of downtown Boston.

DO

Boston Public Library
A beautiful neoclassical structure affirming Boston's reputation as the "Athens of America." ☎ 617-536-5400; www.bpl.org; 700 Boylston St, Boston, MA; admission free; 🕙 9am-9pm Mon-Thu, 9am-5pm Fri & Sat year-round, 1-5pm Sun Oct-May; 🐧

Edward Gorey House
This museum in Gorey's former home has exhibits about his life and work and a gift shop. ☎ 508-362-3909; 8 Strawberry Lane, Yarmouth, MA; adult/child $5/2; 🕙 11am-4pm Wed-Sat, noon-4pm Sun; 🐧

Emily Dickinson Museum
This museum details the reclusive and introspective life of poet Emily Dickinson. ☎ 413-542-8161; www.emilydickinsonsmuseum.org; 280 Main St, Amherst, MA; adult/child $8/5; 🕙 9am-5pm May-Oct

Harriet Beecher Stowe Center
The manse here pays tribute to the author of *Uncle Tom's Cabin,* which bolstered the antislavery movement. ☎ 860-525-9317; www.harrietbeecherstowe.org; 77 Forest St, Hartford, CT; 🕙 9:30am-4:30pm Mon-Sat, noon-4:30pm Sun

House of the Seven Gables
The house made famous by Nathaniel Hawthorne's novel of the same name. ☎ 978-744-0991; www.7gables.org; 54 Turner St, Salem, MA; adult/child $12/11; 🕙 10am-5pm Nov-Jun, 10am-7pm Jul-Oct

Jack Kerouac Walking Tour
This fantastically detailed route stops at various sites throughout Lowell featured in five of his novels. Tour times fluctuate with demand. ☎ http://ecommunity.uml.edu/jklowell; Lowell, MA

Louisa May Alcott Homes
The setting of best-selling *Little Women,* Alcott's home is now a museum detailing her life surrounded by Transcendentalism. ☎ 978-369-4118; www.louisamayalcott.org; 399 Lexington Rd, Concord, MA; adult/child $8/5; 🕙 10am-4:30pm Mon-Sat, 1-4:30pm Sun Apr-Oct, reduced winter hours; 🐧

Mark Twain House & Museum
This museum carefully illustrates Mark Twain's life in Hartford through photos, films, artifacts and manuscripts. ☎ 860-247-0998; www.marktwainhouse.org; 351 Farmington Ave, Hartford, CT; adult/child $13/8; 🕙 9:30am-5:30pm Mon-Sat, noon-5:30pm Sun, closed Tue Jan-Mar

Montague Bookmill
This bookstore is a converted cedar gristmill from 1842 with many rooms of used books on offer. ☎ 413-367-9206; www.montaguebookmill.com; 440 Greenfield Rd, Montague, MA; 🕙 10am-6pm Sun-Wed, 10am-8pm Thu-Sat

The Mount
Award-winning writer Edith Wharton came to Lenox in 1899 and built this palatial estate where she entertained a colorful array of guests. ☎ 413-637-1899; www.edithwharton.org; 2 Plunkett St, Lenox, MA; adult/child $18/free; 🕙 9am-5pm May-Oct

Ralph Waldo Emerson Homes
Emerson's home boasts original furnishings and a luscious organic garden planted by Henry David Thoreau for Nathaniel Hawthorne. ☎ 978-369-2236; www.thetrustees.org; 28 Cambridge Turnpike, Concord, MA; adult/child $7/free; 🕙 10am-4:30pm Thu-Sat, 1-4:30pm Sun mid-Apr–Oct

Walden Pond
This stunning, silent glacial pond made famous by Henry David Thoreau and surrounded by multicolored trees was the epicenter of Transcendental thought. ☎ 978-369-3254; www.mass.gov/dcr/parks/northeast/wldn.htm; 915 Walden St, Concord, MA; admission free, parking $5; 🕙 dawn-dusk; 🐧

EAT & DRINK

Fruitlands Tearoom
This restaurant sits on a former Transcendentalist commune founded by Louisa May Alcott's father. ☎ 978-456-3924; 102 Prospect Hill Rd, Harvard, MA; lunch $11-14; ⏱ 11am-3pm Wed-Sat, 10am-1pm Sun

Novel
A quaint coffee shop in the heart of the Boston Public Library. Grab a coffee and curl up with a borrowed book. ☎ 617-536-5400; www.bpl.org; 700 Boylston St, Boston, MA; coffee $2; ⏱ 9am-9pm Mon-Thu, 9am-5pm Fri & Sat year-round, 1-5pm Sun Oct-May; ⏱

SLEEP

Melville House
Herman Melville often visited his sister at this 1855 Victorian manse. Check out his portrait in the aptly named Herman Melville bedroom. ☎ 508-990-1566; www.melvillehouse.net; 100 Madison St, New Bedford, MA; d $100-150

Naulakha
Catch your Zs in the former cottage of Rudyard Kipling. ☎ 802-257-7785; www.landmarktrustusa.org/naulakha/about.html; 707 Kipling Rd, Dummerston, VT; r $275-425

Omni Parker House
The nation's longest continuously operating hotel is a veritable sea of velvet drapes, overstuffed pillows and lavish swatches of floral wallpaper. Dickens loved to stay here. ☎ 617-227-8600; www.omnihotels.com; 60 School St, Boston, MA; r from $199

Wayside Inn
This lovely 10-room inn, made famous by Longfellow's poems *Tales from a Wayside Inn*, has an extensive archive of the history of the inn, which has been operating since 1700. ☎ 978-443-1776; www.wayside.org; 76 Wayside Inn Rd, Sudbury, MA; s/d $125/160

USEFUL WEBSITES
www.bpl.org

LINK YOUR TRIP
www.lonelyplanet.com/trip-planner

Ivy League Secrets & Superstitions

WHY GO Traditionally known for their "old boys club" attitude and ridiculously large endowments (we're talkin' money here), these redbrick bastions of higher learning are steeped in centuries of mystery and intrigue. Get the skinny on what these institutions are really about: parties, public nudity and pizza.

There's no better place to begin than America's first institution of higher learning: Harvard – the "big H", the "H-bomb," *Hahhhhvahh-hhd.* No matter how you spell it or say it, this saucy institution finds its way into the spotlight more than Paris Hilton. Some of the world's most interesting characters have passed through Harvard's gates: over a dozen American presidents, scores of Nobel prize winners, and a bevy of notable screen actors. Fictional characters too: there was that girl from *Legally Blonde,* the nerd in *With Honors,* the protagonist of the *Da Vinci Code* taught at Harvard, and who could forget *Love Story's* ill-fated Jennifer Cavalleri.

Give the admissions tour a miss if you aren't into watching prospective students sweat bullets as they sheepishly ask about the SATs. Instead, head to the Holyoke Center for the ❶ **Harvard University Campus Tours**, which are geared to tourists. The one-hour tour ambles between ivy-clad buildings while animated guides chat about the college's humble beginnings. Apparently the sordid history of higher learning in America reads like a twisted Dickens novel (although maybe a little less wordy). You'll learn about Harvard's "house system," which is similar to the dormitories in the Harry Potter series. Students are separated into different houses (*sans* sorting hat, of course) each named for an early president of the university (except Harvard's fourth president – Leonard Hoar – apparently no one wanted a Hoar House on campus…). The tour ends at the infamous ❷ **John Harvard Statue.**

TIME
2 – 3 days

DISTANCE
150 miles

BEST TIME TO GO
Sep – Nov

START
Cambridge, MA

END
New Haven, CT

ALSO GOOD FOR

HISTORY & CULTURE

BEST TRIP

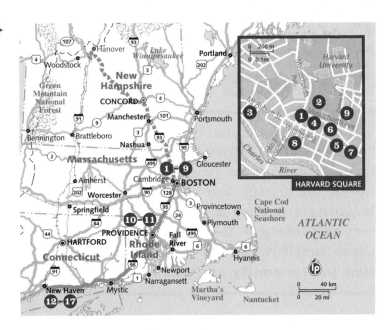

This sculpture, by Daniel Chester French, is inscribed with "John Harvard, Founder Of Harvard College, 1638" and is commonly known as the statue of three lies: John Harvard was *not* the college's founder, Harvard was actually founded in 1636, and the man depicted isn't even in Mr Harvard himself! This ubiquitous symbol hardly lives up to the university's motto, *Veritas* (truth). Most tourists rub John Harvard's shiny foot for good luck; little do they know that campus pranksters regularly use the foot like dogs use a fire hydrant.

"The sordid history of higher learning in America reads like a twisted Dickens novel (although maybe a little less wordy. "

After an hour of touring it's time to get off the beaten track and check out the college from a student's perspective. If you've worked up an appetite, try **3** **Darwin's Ltd** on Mt Auburn Street, just west of Harvard Square. This relaxed deli-cum-café is the choice spot for intellectual types and confirms the theory of "Survival of the Fittest." Grab a leather chair (if you can find a free one), snuggle up with your iMac and enjoy highly evolved sandwiches fusing regional produce and savory meats.

After lunch, head back to Massachusetts Ave to find **4** **Leavitt & Peirce**. This awesome remnant of old-school Harvard sells an endless selection of hand-made pipes, sending Cantabrigians to an early grave for centuries. Give your lungs a break and sneak upstairs to play parlor games in the dark salon under the watchful eyes of taxidermic elk. Let your new pipe purchase dangle languidly from your puckered lips as you meander among the colonial gridiron between the Harvard's Old Yard and Charles River. Here you will find Harvard's collection of not-so-secret societies, known on campus as Final Clubs. These single-sex clubs are sprinkled all over the place. Have a stroll past the impressive colonial exteriors of the Fox (44 JFK St), Spee (76 Mt Auburn St), Phoenix (72 Mt Auburn St), and the Porcellian (1324 Massachusetts Ave), to name just a few. The most spectacular facade belongs to the ❺ **Lampoon Castle** on Mt Auburn St. Although not technically a Final Club, the *Lampoon* is Harvard's humor magazine, and their hangout just so happens to be a Flemish-style castle chock full of oddities like czarist silverware, props from obscure B-list movies, and even a secret bookcase that opens to reveal a hidden study.

If you aren't sick of pop collars and crimson brick then head up to Hanover, New Hampshire, to check out **Dartmouth College**. Surprise! Free guided walking tours are also available on campus departing from the second floor of McNutt Hall. Be sure to swing past the **Sphinx Tomb** on East Wheelock St, which belongs to the secretive Sphinx Senior Society.

When it's time to refuel, pack an artery at ❻ **Bartley's Burger Cottage** on Massachusetts Ave. Wonderfully kitsch paraphernalia smothers the walls at this carnivore paradise. Tacky debris aside, the juicy burgers are unbeatable and are even named after contemporary celebs. Drool over 'Brad Pitt' or one of the other hunks of meat, or try 'Dick Cheney', lavished with heart-attack-inducing greasy fixings. Salads are available for the faint of heart, but coming to Bartley's for a hummus platter is like going to the Louvre and not seeing the Mona Lisa. After dinner, walk off the meat sweats and check out ❼ **Daedalus**, the choice nightspot for undergrads with a valid ID (or a really good phony). This sleek bar with a tantalizing roof deck bounces virtually every night of the week with gaggles of Final Club folks. When the bars start to close their doors (lest we forget that Massachusetts was founded under Puritanical jurisdiction) head west along Mt Auburn St and make a left on JFK Street to find ❽ **Pinocchio's**. Soak up that Long Island iced tea with an oh-so-tasty slice of square Sicilian pizza (tomato basil is the student fave) served by surly bakers. During the day this tiny pizza parlor flies under the radar, but in the late evenings it transforms into a stronghold for procrastinating Harvardites.

As the students retreat in the wee hours of the night to tackle their books, hang your hat at the gorgeous ❾ **Harvard Faculty Club** on Quincy St, just east of the Old Yard. Despite the name, this stunning colonial mansion is open to all members and friends of the Harvard community (so you better bust out the Rolodex to track down an invitation!). The upstairs bedrooms are swathed in floral prints and covered in a blizzard of doilies. Each room also comes with Cambridge's most precious commodity: a parking space.

In the morning get an early start and take I-95 south out of the Boston city limits to quieter Providence. Here you will find beautiful Brown, the rambunctious younger child of an uptight New England household. Big brothers Harvard and Yale carefully manicure their public image, while the little black sheep of the family prides itself on staunch liberalism and occasional bouts of indecent exposure. A campus tour is a good way to get your bearings and to learn about the artsy-fartsy student body, so stop by the Brown admissions office for a ❿ **Brown University Campus Tour**, led by ubermanic students who have clearly taken lessons in walking backwards without getting plowed by oncoming traffic. If you're in need of more luck after touching John Harvard's foot, head to the ⓫ **John Hay Library** and rub the nose of the John Hay statue (although who knows what those cheeky Brown students do to that man's poor honker). Make sure you don't visit all four of the other libraries on campus, as it is commonly believed that those who venture into each structure will be cursed forever and will never marry. If you happen to be bopping around the libraries at the beginning of exam period you might find yourself amid scores of students passing out doughnuts in the buff to their fellow classmates who are busy burning the midnight oil.

Nothing's more "quintessential college" than the doo-wop of unaccompanied voices. Download mp3 samples from the websites of these groups and shoo-bee-doo your way across New England.

• "McDonalds Girl," Harvard Din & Tonics
• "We Didn't go to Harvard," Cayuga Waiters
• "Whiffenpoof Song," Yale Whiffenpoofs
• "Who Are You," Brown Derbies
• "Change in My Life," Harvard Opportunes
• "Sally in Our Alley," Yale Alley Cats
• "Danny Boy," Harvard Krokodiloes
• "Build Me Up Buttercup," Yale Spizzwinks(?)

Hop back in your car and continue in a southeasterly direction along I-95. Turn off the highway when you see signs for downtown New Haven and follow the arrows for about a half-mile until you reach the gorgeous gothic realm that is Yale University, America's third-oldest university. Head to the corner of Elm and Temple Sts to catch a free ⓬ **Yale University Campus Tour** led by a current undergraduate. The tour does a good job of fusing historical and academic facts and passes by several standout architectural flourishes, including Yale's tallest building ⓭ **Harkness Tower**, a stunning bell tower and the preferred spot of some for a bit of late-night hanky-panky.

Although the walking tours overflow with tidbits about life at Yale, the guides refrain from mentioning the handful of tombs scattered around the campus. No, these aren't filled with corpses; in fact, it's quite the opposite – these tombs are the secret hangouts for a select group of senior students. The most notorious ⓮ **Tomb**, located at 64 High St, is the HQ for the notorious Skull & Bones Club, founded in 1832. Its list of members reads like a *Who's Who* of high-powered politicos and financiers over the last two centuries. Members keep mum, letting rumors fly about the artifacts hidden deep within the crypt like Geronimo's skull and Hitler's fine china.

With all those 'Type A' personalities milling about, one might think that the competition is fierce; however, the biggest rivalry on campus actually takes place beyond the classroom. It all revolves around pizza, and two greasy joints have been battling it out for the crown ever since Roosevelt was president (the second one). ⓳ **Frank Pepe Pizzeria Napoletana**, known simply as Pepe's, is the original don of the dough. Then there's ⓰ **Sally's Apizza**, which sprang up down the street a couple years later. Yale's heated two-(pizza)-party politics will undoubtedly rage on for centuries to come. Take a break between slices and head to 306 York St and try smooth-talking your way into ⓱ **Mory's Temple Bar**, a private dining club and Yale institution, which seats around 100. If you're lucky, you might catch a homemade melody sung by the Whiffenpoofs, the oldest collegiate a cappella troupe in the country.

Brandon Presser

TRIP INFORMATION

GETTING THERE
From Boston, cross over the Charles River to Cambridge and make your way down I-95.

DO

Brown University Campus Tours
Offers free tours of the campus and heaps of academic information. ☎ 401-863-2378; www.brown.edu; 45 Prospect St, Providence, RI; ⊙ 8:30am-5pm Mon-Fri, 9am-noon Sat

Harvard University Campus Tours
Guided by members of the Crimson Key Society, focusing on history and humorous anecdotes. ☎ 617-495-1573; www.harvard .edu; Holyoke Center Arcade, 1350 Massachusetts Ave, Cambridge, MA; ⊙ tours 10am & 2pm Mon-Fri, 2pm Sat

Leavitt & Peirce
A remnant of old-school Harvard, L&P sells an endless selection of handmade pipes. ☎ 617-547-0576; 1316 Massachusetts Ave, Cambridge, MA; ⊙ 9am-5:30pm Mon-Wed & Fri & Sat, 9am-8pm Thu

Yale University Campus Tours
Free campus maps and a self-guided walking-tour pamphlet ($1). ☎ 203-432-2300; www.yale.com.visitor; cnr Elm & Temple Sts, New Haven, CT; ⊙ 9am-4:30pm Mon-Fri, 11am-4pm Sat & Sun

EAT & DRINK

Bartley's Burger Cottage
Kitschy paraphernalia smothers the walls while patrons devour juicy burgers. ☎ 617-354-6559; www.mrbartley.com; 1246 Massachusetts Ave, Cambridge, MA; burgers from $8.50; ⊙ 11am-9pm Mon-Sat

Daedalus
Slap on a beret and join the fray of anonymous jetsetters brazenly swigging their designer cocktails, and enjoy the roof deck in summer. ☎ 617-349-0071; www.daedalus harvardsquare.com; 45 Mt Auburn St, Cambridge, MA; cocktails from $8; ⊙ 11am-2am

Darwin's Ltd
Highly evolved sandwiches fuse regional produce with savory meats. ☎ 617-354-5233; www.darwinsltd.com; 148 Mt Auburn St, Cambridge, MA; sandwiches from $7.50; ⊙ 6:30am-9pm Mon-Sat, 7am-9pm Sun

Frank Pepe Pizzeria Napoletana
Immaculate pizza fired in a coal oven, just as it has been since 1925, in frenetic white-walled surroundings. ☎ 203-865-5762; www.pepes pizzeria.com; 157 Wooster St, New Haven, CT; pizza pie $12; ⊙ 4-10pm Mon, Wed & Thu, 11:30am-11pm Fri & Sat, 2:30pm-10pm Sun

Pinocchio's
Famous for square Sicilian slices, Pinocchio's is popular late at night with procrastinating Harvardites. ☎ 617-876-4897; www.pinoc chiospizza.com; 74 Winthrop St, Cambridge, MA; pizza slice $2.25; ⊙ 11am-midnight Sun, 11am-1am Mon-Thu, to 2:30am Fri & Sat

Sally's Apizza
Giving Pepe's a run for its money since 1938. The white clam pie is legendary. ☎ 203-624-5271; www.sallysapizza.net; 237 Wooster St, New Haven, CT; white clam pie $10; ⊙ 5-10pm Tue-Sun, closed in Sep

SLEEP

Harvard Faculty Club
Bedrooms swathed in floral prints and covered in a blizzard of doilies. Open to members and friends of the Harvard community. ☎ 617-495-5758; www.hfc.harvard.edu; 20 Quincy St, Cambridge, MA; s/d from $199/$224

USEFUL WEBSITES
www.harvard.edu
www.brown.edu
www.yale.edu

www.lonelyplanet.com/trip-planner

LINK YOUR TRIP

Ethan Allen Highway & Beyond

WHY GO The Ethan Allen Hwy cuts a convenient path through some of the most perfectly picturesque scenery in Connecticut's Litchfield Hills before entering the Berkshires. Vermont's Rte 100, meanwhile, is the classic VT highway, threading its way through beautiful valleys and ski towns as it follows the Green Mountains' eastern edge.

TIME
3 days

DISTANCE
320 miles

BEST TIME TO GO
Sep – Nov

START
Danbury, CT

END
Burlington, VT

ALSO GOOD FOR

Officially, the 308-mile-long Ethan Allen Hwy begins in the southwestern Connecticut town of Norwalk – I-95 Exit 15, if you want to get technical. While central Norwalk is a pleasant enough place to visit, it certainly isn't the quiet and countrified town Rte 7 explorers are probably looking for, so unless you have plans to visit Norwalk's excellent maritime aquarium, continue north to Danbury, home of this trip's first stop, the ❶ **Danbury Museum and Historical Society**. The purpose of this museum is to preserve, exhibit and interpret the town's heritage, although most visitors find the museum's tours of its six historic area buildings to be of greater interest. The Marian Anderson Studio, which was owned by the legendary contralto opera singer, is one such building. Also of interest is the museum's John Dodd Hat Shop, which chronicles the history of hats and hat-making in Danbury. Tours are also given of the birthplace of composer Charles Ives. The museum changes its tour schedule annually, so be sure to call or check online before stopping by.

Next, travel to the historic town of ❷ **New Milford** where, thanks to an influx of wealthy New Yorkers, some of whom commute to Manhattan, you'll find eclectic boutique shopping along Bank St. To get a feel for the New Milford of the 18th century, stop by the town's historical society, where some of the exhibits on display include an antique toy collection and cooking hearth.

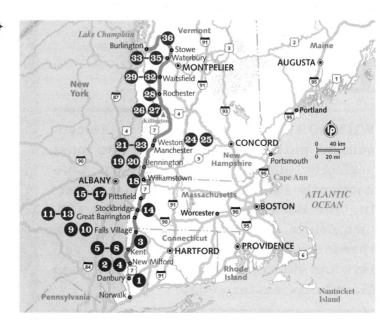

The drive from New Milford to the small village of ❸ **Kent**, which is also popular with New Yorkers, is simply stunning. Aside from the occasional cluster of antique shops and the covered ❹ **Bull's Bridge**, however, roadside attractions along this stretch are far and few between. It's the overwhelming beauty of nature that draws visitors, and with this portion of the highway running parallel to the Housatonic River, you'll be spoiled for photo opportunities.

The equally lovely drive from Kent to the Massachusetts border has the added benefit of a good number of state parks. The ❺ **Housatonic State Forest** and ❻ **Housatonic Meadows State Park**, both popular with hikers and campers, are just north of Kent, in between Cornwall Bridge and Falls Village. And in fact the Appalachian Trail runs directly through Kent, which is also where you'll find the ❼ **Starbuck Inn B&B**, an ideal choice for anyone planning to explore the area's great outdoors. The owners of the Starbuck Inn, formerly known as the Chaucer House, put a great deal of emphasis on the art of hospitality. High tea is served daily at 4pm, and a generously large breakfast spread is included.

Just north of the Housatonic State Forest on Rte 112 is ❽ **Lime Rock Park**, an autoracing facility and NASCAR track proudly known as the "Road Racing Center of the East." For those of you visiting from abroad, taking in a race at Lime Rock will afford you the rare opportunity of experiencing the often elusive local creature known as the blue-collar American in his or her native habitat. Bring beer, and try not to stare.

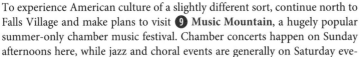

To experience American culture of a slightly different sort, continue north to Falls Village and make plans to visit ⑨ **Music Mountain**, a hugely popular summer-only chamber music festival. Chamber concerts happen on Sunday afternoons here, while jazz and choral events are generally on Saturday evenings. More eclectic offerings such as klezmer music or West African drum ensembles are scheduled at least a couple of times throughout the season. Built by Sears Roebuck back in 1930, the 335-seat Gordon Hall is where the magic happens; the hall's acoustics are simply second to none.

Also worth a visit is the nearby ⑩ **Falls Village-Canaan Historical Society**, which operates not only a museum where regional artifacts and antiques are displayed but also the South Canaan Meeting House and the Beebe Hill School. The meeting house is an incredibly iconic, New England–style church – you half expect to find Hester Prynne herself kneeling at the altar inside.

GET BIFFED IN THE BERKSHIRES

Cinema hounds traveling through the west Massachusetts in mid-May are in luck: that's when the **Berkshire International Film Festival** presents its annual celebration of documentary, short and independent films. Known as BIFFMA, the week-long event has become known over time as one of the industry's leading festivals, and many of the programs sell out fast. Visit www.biffma.com to check out the schedule and to order festival passes.

Cross into Massachusetts and head straight to Great Barrington, one of the Berkshires' most popular ski and snow sporting destinations. Regardless of whether the snow happens to be falling during your visit, this is a wonderfully slow-paced part of the region in which to be based. ⑪ **Thornewood Inn** is a bright and beautifully restored Dutch Colonial house located in Great Barrington with a pool, private gardens, and a deck that overlooks the Berkshire Hills. A ten-minute drive south along Rte 7 will take you to the appropriately named ⑫ **Route 7 Grill**, a barbeque house where all the meat is naturally and locally raised, and where literally everything else on the menu – from soups and salads to veggie quesadillas and grilled meatloaf – is made from scratch. Do a bit of exploring around Great Barrington's downtown area before dark, and don't miss a stroll along the ⑬ **Housatonic Riverwalk**, a paved path that was constructed by a team of volunteers. The public greenway is at its prettiest during the fall foliage season.

Travel north to Stockbridge next and visit the ever-popular ⑭ **Norman Rockwell Museum**. The museum lays claim to the largest collection of works by the illustrious painter of mid-century Americana, including a huge archive of personal effects. Probably the museum's most important exhibit – and certainly its most popular – is Rockwell's actual studio, easel and all.

Not far away in Pittsfield is the unusual ⑮ **Hancock Shaker Village**, which was established in the late 1800s, and existed as a successful Shaker community for almost 200 years. Today, the area is a "living history museum" where visitors can learn about the lifestyle and culture of the Shakers by exploring a total of 20 historic buildings, including a rare example of a round stone barn. The ⓰ **Berkshire Museum** is also in Pittsfield, and no matter who you're traveling with, there's a decent chance they'll find something there to get excited about: there's a natural science gallery, an aquarium, an art gallery, and a permanent Alexander Calder exhibit. (Calder got his first big break at the Berkshire Museum some 80 years ago.) Even better is the Feigenbaum Hall of Innovation, which introduces museum-goers to area entrepreneurs and bright scientific minds. Before leaving Pittsfield, you might want to consider investigating a local innovation of another sort at ⓱ **Asters**, an elegant restaurant considered to be among the best in the Berkshires. This is a steak and chop sort of place, although there's also a popular raw bar and a wine room.

THE LITERARY LIFESTYLE

Anyone with literary ambitions should expand their itinerary to include two historic home visits: Herman Melville's **Arrowhead** (www.mobydick.org) in Pittsfield and the **Mount** (www.edithwharton.org), Edith Wharton's former residence in Lenox and a stunning revivalist estate. The architecturally composed gardens were designed by Wharton herself. Arrowhead, where Melville composed *Moby Dick,* is a more modest domicile operated as a museum by the Berkshire County Historic Society.

And before continuing north into Vermont, experience one of the most popular contemporary art institutions in the country, ⓲ **MASS MoCA**, or the Massachusetts Museum of Contemporary Art, in North Adams. Because of the large industrial spaces here, complex installation art projects have become almost expected at MASS MoCA. Music, dance and film events of the decidedly unusual and unconventional sort are also scheduled on a regular basis.

Enter the lovely Valley of Vermont, a narrow gap sandwiched between the Taconic Mountains to the west and the Greens to the east. Just north of the border lies one of Vermont's oldest towns, chartered in 1749. ⓳ **Old Bennington**'s cluster of colonial buildings, a mile west of Rte 7, feels literally frozen in time, with Vermont's longest continuously functioning church and its oldest graveyard sitting side by side. The church's floor plan consists of old-fashioned "box pews," each like a small corral for a family of parishioners. Every post in the church's interior is made from a single old-growth tree, its base extending down to the basement. The cemetery, set on a rise with mountain vistas to the east and old maples rustling overhead, contains numerous American Revolution–era gravestones, together with the tomb of Vermont's one-time poet laureate Robert Frost, simply marked, "I had a lover's quarrel with the world."

Before continuing north, treat your taste buds to a historic relic of a different sort. North of downtown on Rte 7, ⓴ **Sonny's Blue Benn Diner,** prefabricated in New Jersey in the 1940s, serves breakfast all day. The menu's account of the diner's history is interesting, but even better are the great little tabletop jukeboxes where you can play Willie Nelson's "Moonlight in Vermont" or Cher's "Gypsies, Tramps and Thieves" till your neighbors scream for mercy.

Continuing north, veer off of Rte 7 and opt for historic two-lane Rte 7A through the towns of Shaftsbury, Arlington and Manchester Center. Outdoor enthusiasts should stop at Arlington's **㉑ Batten Kill Canoe**, which offers boat rentals and trips along the Batten Kill River. For a different perspective, history buffs shouldn't miss **㉒ Hildene**, south of Manchester, the former mansion of Abraham Lincoln's son Robert. The 24 rooms filled with family memorabilia are as extravagant as the formal gardens and the eyrie-like setting

"...even better are the little tabletop jukeboxes where you can play Willie Nelson's 'Moonlight in Vermont' "

high above the Batten Kill. Manchester itself is a bizarre blend of ostentatious historic homes and modern outlet stores. Java fiends and bookworms seeking shelter from this storm of filthy lucre and crass commercialism should head to **㉓ Northshire Bookstore and Spiral Café**, a wonderful independent bookstore with cozy nooks and a jam-packed schedule of author events. It's a great place to read up on Vermont and discover the works of local authors.

Cut across the Green Mountains on Rte 11 to join Rte 100, widely considered Vermont's most beautiful highway. Five miles north of Londonderry, the picturesque village of **㉔ Weston** is home to Vrest Orton's **㉕ Vermont Country Store**, founded in 1946 and still a fun place to browse. Crowds flock to the town's playhouse, just off the gazeboed circular town green (a former frog pond), for summer theater, and the views upstream to Weston's waterfall and 19th-century mill (now a museum) are the stuff of tourist legend.

Schuss on north through the heart of Vermont ski country – Ludlow, home of Okemo resort, and Killington, known as the "Beast of the East" thanks to its 3050ft vertical drop. In Killington, you'll find **㉖ Hemingway's**, a venerable Vermont restaurant; nosh in the cozy wine cellar or dine in the chandelier-bedecked "vault room". West of town on US-4, sip a pint of Guinness or Harp and catch some live Irish music at the **㉗ Inn at Long Trail**, a wonderfully rustic log-beamed lodging and pub sitting astride Vermont's century-old Long Trail, a 272-mile hiking route from the Massachusetts border to Quebec.

North of Killington, Rte 100 threads through the gorgeous White River valley, filled with classic red barns and long vistas of Green Mountain–fringed farmland. In Rochester, an eye-catching ensemble of historic buildings surrounds the town green. Across the street, duck into the **㉘ Rochester Café** to soak up the old-timey atmosphere over a milkshake at the vintage soda fountain. Ten miles further north, Rte 100 enters a narrow and wild corridor of protected land. A little pullout on the left provides viewing access to pretty **㉙ Moss Glen Falls**. A mile or so later, the small ponds of **㉚ Granville Gulf** comprise one of the state's most accessible moose-watching spots. Come through at dawn or dusk for the best chance of seeing these big critters.

SECESSION OBSESSION

At town meetings in recent years, Killington endorsed a proposal to secede from Vermont and join New Hampshire. The cause? Taxes. Vocal secessionists objected to Vermont laws requiring higher school funding contributions from well-heeled ski towns. Feeling abused as a cash cow, Killington kicked and balked. Perhaps secessionists would like to take their town but give Vermont back its forests? After all, in the 1950s the ski area was launched with the leasing of state forest land to developers!

Descending into the Mad River Valley, detour via the well-marked side road into the pretty village of Warren. Stop in at the **㉛ Warren Store**, popular for its great gourmet deli, picturesque creekside setting and creaky-floored upstairs store – a hodge-podge of jewelry, crafts, Vermont casual clothing, and toys selected as much for grown-ups as for kids.

Next stop, Waitsfield – a haven for outdoors enthusiasts and creative spirits. **㉜ Mad River Valley Artisans' Gallery**, just above the covered bridge in the center of town, is an artists' cooperative showcasing the work of dozens of Vermonters. Other studios and galleries are sprinkled throughout town. Rte 100 leaves the Mad River and jogs left in the pretty village of Waterbury. Here the **㉝ Alchemist Pub & Brewery**, a relatively young but intensely popular brew pub, will do its best to lure you off the road. If you make it past that hurdle without incident, you'll still have to contend with the temptation of **㉞ Ben & Jerry's** famous ice-cream factory. Yeah, the ice cream's hard to argue with, but a visit to the factory also offers a glimpse of the fun in-your-face corporate culture that made these two ice-cream pioneers so successful.

The crown jewel of Vermont ski resorts glimmers ten miles further up Rte 100. For many people, the picturesque pointy church steeple in **㉟ Stowe** juxtaposed with the massive flanks of Mt Mansfield is *the* classic Vermont picture-postcard scene. Aside from skiing, there's plenty else to keep visitors busy year round, including galleries, tennis and golf, a ski museum, a beautiful recreation path along the river, and dozens of restaurants.

There's no better way to bid farewell to Rte 100 than by climbing Rte 108 northwest through the twisty heights of **㊱ Smugglers Notch**, an almost impossibly narrow cleft between granite cliffs that was used to smuggle goods both during the War of 1812 and again during Prohibition. At the summit are some fine (uphill!) hiking trails, including the scenic 1.2-mile scramble through the boulders to Sterling Pond. From here it's all downhill to Burlington, where you can pick up the interstate again and and – sigh – return to normal life.

Dan Eldridge & Gregor Clark

TRIP INFORMATION

GETTING THERE
The Ethan Allen Hwy begins in Norwalk, CT, which is on I-95 just east of Stamford.

DO

Batten Kill Canoe
This long-established outfitter can guide you through the Batten Kill's turbulent waters or simply rent you a boat. ☎ 802-362-2800; www.battenkill.com; 6328 Rte 7A, Arlington, VT; canoe/kayak rental per day $65/40

Ben & Jerry's
No iconic trip to Vermont would be complete without a visit to America's most famous ice-cream factory. ☎ 802-882-1240; www.benjerry.com; 1281 Waterbury-Stowe Rd, Waterbury, VT; ⊙ 9am-9pm Jul & Aug, 10am-6pm Sep-Jun; ⑤

Berkshire Museum
This museum offers American art, natural history exhibits, an aquarium and more. ☎ 413-443-7171; www.berkshiremuseum.org; 39 South St (Rte 7), Pittsfield, MA; adult/child $10/5; ⊙ 10am-5pm Mon-Sat, noon-5pm Sun

Danbury Museum and Historical Society
Investigate Danbury's notable history and visit its most historically important homes. ☎ 203-743-5200; www.danburyhistorical.org; 43 Main St, Danbury, CT; general/child under 5/student/senior $6/free/2/5; ⊙ 1-4pm Tue-Thu & Sat

Falls Village-Canaan Historical Society
Explore an historic church building and school house after a visit to this village museum. ☎ 860-824-8226; 44 Railroad St, Falls Village, CT

Hancock Shaker Village
A "living museum," complete with rare artifacts. ☎ 413-443-0188; www.hancockshakervillage.org; 1843 W Housatonic St, Pittsfield,

MA; adult/child $15/7.50; ⊙ 10am-4pm Apr 12-May 23, 10am-5pm May 24-Oct 19

Hildene
The Lincoln family's legacy lives on in Vermont, in this imposing hilltop mansion overlooking the Batten Kill. ☎ 802-362-1788; www.hildene.org; 1005 Hildene Rd, Manchester, VT; adult/child $5/2, tour $12.50/5; ⊙ 9:30am-4:30pm

Lime Rock Park
Experience a NASCAR event, an amateur road race, or a vintage car show at this road course. Phone for tickets. ☎ 800-435-5000; www.limerock.com; 60 White Hollow Rd, Lakeville, CT

Mad River Valley Artisans' Gallery
The work of dozens of Vermont artisans is nicely displayed in a historic Waitsfield house. ☎ 802-496-6256; www.vermontartisansgallery.com; Bridge St, Waitsfield, VT; ⊙ 10am-5pm

MASS MoCA
Possibly the country's best contemporary art museum, with extraordinary installation art and cutting-edge performances. ☎ 413-662-2111; www.massmoca.org; 1040 Mass Moca Way, North Adams, MA; adult/child $12.50/5; ⊙ 10am-6pm

Music Mountain
A long-running and well-regarded chamber- and folk-music festival featuring string quartets and touring acts. Call or check the website for the schedule. ☎ 860-824-7126; www.musicmountain.org; 225 Music Mountain Rd, Falls Village, CT

Norman Rockwell Museum
Located in the legendary artist's hometown, this museum has the world's largest Rockwell collection. ☎ 413-298-4100; www.nrm.org; 9 Glendale Rd, Stockbridge, MA; adult/child $15/free; ⊙ 10am-5pm; ⑤

Northshire Bookstore and Spiral Café
This corner bookstore-café is one of Vermont's best, with an author events program second to none. ☎ 802-362-2200; www.northshire.com; 4869 Main St, Manchester,

VT; 10am-7pm Sun-Wed, 10am-9pm Thu-Sat

Vermont Country Store
Touristy but fun, this place brims with shelves full of Vermont products and a colorful history. ☎ 802-824-3184; www.vermont countrystore.com; 657 Main St, Weston, VT; 9am-5:30pm

Warren Store
This historic general store still functions as the social hub of its small village, albeit with some nods to 21st-century tastes. ☎ 802-496-3864; www.warrenstore.com; Main St, Warren, VT; 8am-7pm

EAT & DRINK

Alchemist Pub & Brewery
Come for the food, stay for the homebrew at this convivial downtown pub brightened with local artwork. ☎ 802-244-4120; www .alchemistbeer.com; 23 S Main St, Water-bury, VT; 4pm-late

Asters
This exquisite steak restaurant offers one of the very finest dining experiences in the Berkshires. ☎ 413-499-2075; www.berkshire dining.net; 1015 South St, Pittsfield, MA; mains $12-30; 4-10pm Sun-Thu, 4-11pm Fri & Sat

Hemingway's
Fine dining in Killington for over a quarter century. Choose from the wine cellar, garden room, or vaulted room. ☎ 802-422-3886; www.hemingwaysrestaurant.com; 4988 Hwy 4, Killington, VT; mains $13-36; 6pm-closing Wed-Sun

Rochester Café
Sidle up to the soda fountain for their trade-mark maple milkshake, or enjoy a Vermont-themed breakfast in one of the cozy booths. ☎ 802-767-4302; Rte 100, Rochester, VT; mains $4-9; 7am-4pm;

Route 7 Grill
These purveyors of Slow Food dish up Berkshire-raised meats, barbeque by the pound, and the occasional outdoor pig roast. ☎ 413-528-3235; www.route7grill.com; 999 Main St (Rte 7), Great Barrington, MA; mains $12-32; hours vary seasonally

Sonny's Blue Benn Diner
An American classic, both for its décor and its food. ☎ 802-442-5140; 314 Rte, Bennington, VT; mains from $4; 6am-5pm Mon & Tue, 6am-8pm Wed-Fri, 7am-4pm Sat & Sun;

SLEEP

Inn at Long Trail
This rustic lodge on Vermont's historic Long Trail has its own Irish pub playing live music every weekend. ☎ 802-775-7181, 800-325-2540; www.innatlongtrail.com; 709 Hwy 4, Killington, VT; r $75-130

Starbuck Inn B&B
Enjoy English-style hospitality with all mod-cons and a full breakfast in a Colonial Kent home. ☎ 860-927-1788; www.starbuckinn .com; 88 North Main St, Kent, CT; r $189-250

Thornewood Inn
Period antiques and French doors inside, with a view of the Berkshires and the Housatonic River from a second-floor balcony. ☎ 413-528-3828; www.thornewood.com; 453 Stock-bridge Rd, Great Barrington, MA; r $145-295

USEFUL WEBSITES
www.visit-massachusetts.com
www.vermontvacation.com

LINK YOUR TRIP
www.lonelyplanet.com/trip-planner

Appalachian Trail Mix

WHY GO Few hikes in history are as filled with romance and mystery as the Appalachian Trail. Stretching 2175 miles from Georgia into Maine, the trail's 700 New England miles are the most majestic and challenging. Appalachian Trail thru-hiker and travel blogger Melissa Jenks takes us through the highlights, both on and off the trail.

The first part of the Appalachian Trail (AT) to tackle in New England is the 8.3 miles from Falls Village to Salisbury, where the trail winds through old iron smelts and armament factories. Prepare by getting a room or just a drink at the historic ❶ **Falls Village Inn & Tavern**, where, on martini night, flavored martinis are just $5. Name your flavor and a bartender will whip up a concoction to your liking. The tavern boasts a German restaurant, restored to its 1834 grandeur, with hardwood floors, period lighting and the original bar.

Those who would rather sleep amid the peace of nature can climb the 4.7 miles to the ❷ **Limestone Spring Lean-to**, one of the quintessential three-sided shelters that dot the AT. Curl up in your sleeping bag, listen to the silence and drink a nightcap of fresh spring water – drinking water bubbling out of bedrock is one of hiking's simple joys.

Wake up before dawn and take a brief hike to watch the sunrise from exquisite Rand's View, with a panorama stretching all the way to Massachusetts. A half-mile later you'll pass Giant's Thumb, a rock monolith said to be an ancient Viking monument. Make the steep descent of Wetauwanchu Mountain, where Native Americans once built caves. Take a left through on Lower Cobble Rd to ❸ **White Hart Inn & Restaurant**, a charming 19th-century dining establishment and taproom in Salisbury. The chef makes especially delicious grilled chicken and

TIME
3 – 4 weeks

DISTANCE
250 miles

BEST TIME TO GO
May – Oct

START
Falls Village, CT

END
Mt Katahdin, ME

ALSO GOOD FOR

OUTDOORS

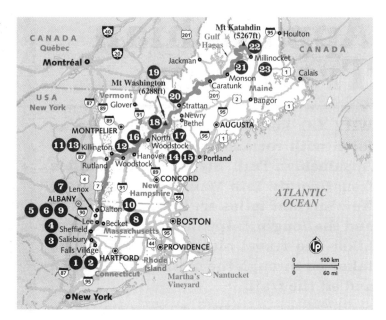

smoked onion quesadillas, with ingredients locally grown at nearby Twin Lakes Farm.

The next section of the trail (19.6 miles) to check out is 17 miles north, in Great Barrington, MA. Breakfast in Sheffield at ④ **Sunrise Diner**, where the Appalachian Mountain Club (AMC) ridgerunners dine, then hike north through stands of pine. You'll begin to cross hand-hewn bog bridges, built by volunteers to protect fragile wetlands. Push on toward ⑤ **Upper Goose Pond Cabin**, where you can use the rustic facilities or camp on a nearby tent platform. Borrow the cabin's ⑥ **canoe** and paddle through the glacial pond's blue periphery, then end the day by listening to music under the stars at the ⑦ **Tanglewood Music Festival**, near Lenox. Music and dance aficionados come from all over for the Tanglewood summer concert series and the famous ⑧ **Jacob's Pillow Dance Festival**, east of the trail in Becket, where the innovative troop founded by dance pioneer Ted Shawn has been an institution since 1930. Breakfast in Lee at ⑨ **Joe's Diner**, the inspiration for Norman Rockwell's painting *The Runaway*. With its low prices and small-town feel, eating here is like stepping back in time to Rockwell's idyllic world.

"Canoe the glacial pond's blue periphery, then end the day listening to music under the stars"

Press north for a taste (and smell!) of authentic hiker experience at the ⑩ **Birdcage**. Your host operates the underground hostel by donation, so you'll have to be a section hiker to stay. If you're not a section hiker, you can still drop by with a case of beer or soda and trade refreshment for a story. Stinky hikers are adept at singing for their supper and are always grateful for trail magic.

Head into Vermont, 125 miles north, for the next section (Killington to Pomfret; 19.9 miles), where you can break at the ⑪ **Inn at Long Trail**, an Irish pub situated where the 270-mile Long Trail divides from the AT, at Killington. Rest on the boulder couch and enjoy Guinness beef stew and a toasty Long Trail Ale or, better yet, visit the ⑫ **Long Trail Brewing Company** to try a brew fresh from the barrel.

Cross overgrown meadows to Kent Pond, where you can camp and cast for your dinner. This trail section is little used, so you could have the glassy, quiet pond to yourself. In the morning, ascend to three vistas in 6 miles, then hike 7.2 miles to the ⑬ **Lookout**. Cozy up before a blazing fire, avoid the leaks in the roof and wake up to watch the fog clear and the mountains stretch.

Ascend through gently graded fields of wildflowers, pass lowing bovines, then descend through vast tracts of maple trees, hooked to taps that harvest syrup in autumn. In Hanover you'll find college-style nightlife, the ⑭ **Hood Museum of Art** and the ⑮ **Four Aces Diner**. Some say the Four Aces is the best institution in the Dartmouth College area. The diner's magnum opus "the Joker" – a steaming pile of flapjacks, eggs, hash browns and meat – will provide ample fuel for the next day's hiking.

BASIC TRAIL LINGO

Thru-hiker A backpacker hiking the entire trail at once

Section hiker A person hiking the trail in sections, intending to complete its entirety

White blaze 2"x6" painted markers that lead the way

Blue blaze Blue markers that lead to AT shortcuts

Purist Someone who hikes by every white blaze

Blue-blazer A thru-hiker who doesn't mind taking shortcuts

Yellow-blazer A hitchhiker who uses his thumb to catch rides by the "yellow blaze" of the highway's middle line

Continue through to New Hampshire, where you can begin the Mt Moosilauke section (Glencliff to Kinsman Notch; 9.5 miles) at homey ⑯ **Hiker's Welcome Hostel**, where the hosts run an ultralight gear company out the back. If you need a backpack or tarp-tent, stop here. Pick up your winter gear before heading into the White Mountains: hats, extra wool socks, polypropolene long underwear. Don't take chances – no matter what the weather on the ground, hypothermia is public enemy number one on New Hampshire trails.

Mt Moosilauke is the first of the White Mountains you'll encounter as you head north, and the alpine views from its peak are extraordinary. You gain

3400ft in 5 miles and the descent is notoriously slippery. Although the trail is steep, it isn't as rocky as much of the rest of the Whites, so it's a good introduction to what's to come. Brutal winter storms, damaging winds and heavy snowfall daunt the ability of vegetation to grow above 3000ft here, meaning that you'll experience spectacular ridge-top views stretching all the way to Maine. The last mile to Moosilauke's apex is bald; the trail, marked only by mysterious cairns to mark the way, wanders to the top of the mountain ridge.

DETOUR If you have extra time, visit the **Bread & Puppet Theater** (www.breadandpuppet.org) near Glover, a politically active commune where you'll get exactly what it sounds like: bread and puppets. Lounge on grass during the show, then feast on hearth-baked bread and spring water. To get there, take I-91 to Exit 24, then take a right onto Rte 122 and continue 13 miles.

The best time to summit is at dusk in autumn, when the crowds have disappeared for the day and the surrounding forests are touched with golden light. Then hike 2.2 miles in the gloaming and spend the night at Beaver Brook Shelter before attempting the descent into Kinsman Notch in the morning.

Continuing northward to the Mt Washington section of the trail (Franconia Notch to Pinkham Notch; 53.7 miles), you will eventually come to the cozy **Woodstock Inn, Station & Brewery**. Enjoy a Brew Sampler before bed, then order the lobster scrambled eggs for breakfast.

Ascend steeply from Franconia Notch, hiking toward the AMC-run **Zealand Falls Hut**. The expensive hut system in the Whites is controversial among thru-hikers, who are accustomed to free shelters. Still, the area's alpine ecosystem needs protection from heavy use, meaning fee-based campsites and huts. The hut here, built in the rugged style of a Swiss *auberge*, is staffed by an eager young "croo" who carry kitchen provisions up the mountain, bake fresh bread and provide musical entertainment as you dine.

ASK A LOCAL "There is a plaque at the trail's southern terminus that reads: 'The Appalachian Trail: a footpath for those who seek fellowship with the wilderness.' But the AT experience is more than that. There are four things a hiker learns on the AT: how to carry all your worldly goods on your back, how to live with other people, how to make peace with yourself, and how to avoid mice!"
Lawdon aka "Happy Camper"

On good days, perfect skies allow for thousand-mile vistas from the Presidential Range, the highlight of this section. Even then, the wind whips mercilessly, so bring good gear and don't wear the souvenir clothing sold at the huts (any thru-hiker can tell you: cotton kills). Approaching **Mt Washington**, stop at the Lakes of the Clouds Hut to visit the eerie Dungeon, haunted by a drowned girl's ghost. As you near the summit, watch the cog engine chug to the cluster of towers at the top, a futuristic city above the clouds.

"You'll be alone, except for the occasional skinny, battered thru-hiker showing up at your campfire"

Mt Washington is home of the self-proclaimed "world's worst weather." A museum and observatory at the top are staffed year-round by researchers. Winds here have been measured at up to 231mph, the strongest recorded on land.

Push on to Maine and tackle the Mahoosuc Range (Gorham, NH, to Grafton Notch, ME; 31.1 miles). Far fewer services are offered along the trail here than in other states, the advantage being that you have the trail to yourself. Wind between lakes where red-eyed loons croon, startling stolid bull moose. Fragrance from endangered alpine flowers, carpets of pine and pure arctic air coalesce into a spicy-sweet pungency. Crossing the border, you'll encounter a sign: Welcome to Maine – The Way Life Should Be. Indeed.

Payment for these pleasures is the pain of aching muscles. You'll encounter boulders in your path as if there by a giant's whim and struggle over 5ft rock faces, and in the center of the range is the most difficult half-mile of the 2200-mile trail: Mahoosuc Notch. Allow two to three hours to hike this stretch, merely a crack between mountains, where glaciers, for thousands of years, pushed rocks together into a massive playground.

Stop again in Strattan to visit the **20** **White Wolf Inn & Café**, home to the Wolfburger, considered by thru-hikers to be the best burger of the trail. A giant beef burger is piled high with veggies, cheese and cured meats – not for the faint of heart.

The **New England Forest Rally,** in Bethel and Newry (ME), is well worth a trip if you're in the area in early July. Part of the Rally America National Championship, the races feature European and American X-Game champions in souped-up cars that catch air as they whiz down rutted logging roads. Chat with famous drivers about their cars as you attend pre- and post-race celebrations at local ski lodges and watering holes.

Signs at either end of the next section of trail we're covering, known as the 100-Mile Wilderness, warn that unprepared hikers should not enter. They're not kidding: at 109.7 miles this stretch from Monson to Millinocket is the longest without a possibility of egress for food and shelter, but it's also one of the most rewarding sections of trail. You'll be alone, except for the occasional skinny, battered thru-hiker showing up at your campfire with tales as long as his beard. You should allow at least one (for experienced marathoners) to two (for rank amateurs) weeks for this section of trail.

6

Luckily, there is one point where you can get out in case of an emergency, Katahdin Ironworks Rd, where you can also find **㉑ Katahdin Ironworks State Historic Site**, a reminder of a time when blast furnaces and charcoal kilns smelted iron all day. The ironworks was built in 1843 and used for about 30 years, its proximity to natural resources being the secret of its success. Eventually, the costs of operating in such isolation made the facility unable to compete with foundries in Pennsylvania and other states and it shut its doors in 1890.

The northern terminus of the Appalachian Trail, Katahdin, was named by native Americans as K-taad-n, the "Greatest Mountain." Thoreau tried three times to climb its fish-hook peak, but never was able to, losing himself in the thick Maine woods. The 10.4-mile round-trip climbs 5200ft in 5 miles, the trail's steepest ascent. As you climb, you'll encounter iron bars drilled into the sides of rocks to help your ascent, thin layers of shadowed ice even in summer and hawks shrieking above you in an eggshell-blue sky.

THE GRAND CANYON IN MAINE?

Take Katahdin Ironworks Rd to visit **Gulf Hagas**, the "Grand Canyon of Maine." The most famous blue blaze along the Appalachian Trail is worth a trip in its own right. The gorge features a stunning 500ft drop studded with waterfalls over the course of its 5 miles. Carved over millions of years by water eroding the slate bedrock, the gulf is a National Natural Landmark and is surrounded by some of Maine's oldest white pines.

At 4000ft comes the Tableland, a flat stretch of tumbled stone that Thoreau described as "the raw materials of a planet, dropped from an unseen quarry… into the smiling and verdant plains and valleys of the earth." Baxter Peak, named after Maine's former governor, rises from the Tableland another 1000ft. Perched atop the mountain is a simple pyramid of wood, ubiquitous in photos posted all along the trail, photos of hikers marking the accomplishment of their adventure: the **㉒ Katahdin Summit**. The view from the isolated monolith is a cloth of dark-green spruce and fir, scattered with the undulant glitter of countless ponds and lakes.

Once the clouds have closed and if you feel particularly ambitious, hike down the backside of the mountain, the Knife Edge, a tumbled aggregation of loosely poised rocks that leads all the way back to the forest floor. Just don't plan on going down any stairs the next day. Then quaff a celebratory blueberry ale at the **㉓ Blue Ox Saloon** in nearby Millinocket and toast your success!

Melissa Jenks & Ray Bartlett

TRIP INFORMATION

GETTING THERE

From Hartford, follow Hwy 44 west for 50 miles, then drive south on Rte 126 for 2 miles to reach Falls Village.

DO

Hood Museum of Art

Excellent art museum connected to Dartmouth College. ☎ 603.646.2808; http://hoodmuseum.dartmouth.edu; Dartmouth College, Hanover, NH; admission free; ⏱ 10am-5pm Thu-Sat, Mon & Tue, 10am-9pm Wed, noon-5pm Sun

Jacob's Pillow Dance Festival

Named after a giant pillow-shaped boulder, this innovative festival challenges America's ideas about dance. ☎ 413-243-9919; www.jacobspillow.org; 358 George Carter Rd, Becket, MA; ⏱ Jun-Aug

Katahdin Ironworks State Historic Site

Step back into the past as you explore these well-preserved furnaces and ruins. ☎ 207-941-4014; www.state.me.us/doc/parks/index.html; Hogan Rd, Bangor, ME; admission free; ⏱ Memorial Day-Labor Day

Tanglewood Music Festival

Music lovers will enjoy lazing on the lawn at this summer retreat for the Boston Symphony Orchestra. ☎ 800-274-8499, 617-266-1200; www.bso.org; West St, Lenox, MA; lawn seats $17; ⏱ Jun 15-Aug 31

EAT

Four Aces Diner

An old railroad-car diner, this neighborhood joint offers delicious French Toast and "Eggs Benny." ☎ 603-298-6827; 23 Bridge St, West Lebanon, NH; mains $4-10; ⏱ 5am-8pm Tue-Sat, 7am-3pm Sun, 5am-3pm Mon

Inn at Long Trail

Beer connoisseurs will drink up at this Irish pub and B&B. ☎ 800-325-2540; www.innat longtrail.com; Sherburne Pass, 709 Rte 4, Killington, VT; dinner mains $4-10

Joe's Diner

Chat with locals about town gossip at this former haunt of Norman Rockwell. ☎ 413-243-9756; 85 Center St, Lee, MA; mains $3-15; ⏱ 5:30am-9pm Mon-Fri, 7:30am-3pm Sat, 7:30am-2pm Sun

Sunrise Diner

Sheffield's best, where those who know order the famous blueberry pancakes. ☎ 413-229-0263; 700 S Main St, Sheffield, MA; ⏱ 6am-7pm Mon-Fri, 6am-12pm Sat-Sun

White Hart Inn & Restaurant

A pleasant B&B, named after a previous public house located in Salisbury, England. ☎ 800-832-0041; www.whitehartinn.com; 15 Undermountain Rd, Salisbury, CT; dinner mains $10-34; ⏱ 7-10am, 11:30-3pm, 5-9pm

White Wolf Inn & Café

A weird and wonderful assortment of Maine beer and game are available at this beanery. ☎ 207-246-2922; www.thewhitewolfinn.com; Main St, Stratton, ME; mains $5-20; ⏱ 11am-8:30pm Thu-Mon, 4pm-8:30pm Wed; ⚇

SLEEP

Birdcage

This hiker hostel helps long-distance hikers clean up and rest after the exertions of their journey. ☎ 413-684-9770; 621 Main St, Dalton, NH; r by generous donation; ⏱ Mar-Oct

Hiker's Welcome Hostel

Former thru-hikers serve as your hosts at this gateway to the White Mountains. Linen is not provided, so bring your sleeping bag. ☎ 603-989-0040; www.hikerswelcome.com; 1396 Rte 25, Glencliff, NH; dm $15; ⏱ year-round

Lookout

This completely enclosed trailside cabin is situated 2500ft above an expansive view. ☎ 802-244-7037; Lookout Farm Rd, near Pomfret, VT; free; ⏱ year-round

Upper Goose Pond Cabin

Quiet and rustic AMC facility, nestled beside a gorgeous glacial lake. ☎ 413-243-0245; www.outdoors.org/lodging/cabins/; 125 Laurel St, Lee, MA; r incl breakfast by donation; ☾ Memorial Day-Labor Day daily, weekends spring & fall

Zealand Falls Hut

Protect the ecosystem and enjoy a hot bowl of soup as you support the AMC. ☎ 603-466-2727; www.outdoors.org/lodging/huts/; Zealand Notch, NH; dm AMC members/non-members $81/89; ☾ Jun-Oct 15

DRINK

Blue Ox Saloon

Only in Maine can you find a bar where the beer's always free: tomorrow. ☎ 207-723-OXEN; www.theblueoxsaloon.com; 61 Penobscot Ave, Millinocket, ME; ☾ 3pm-1am

Falls Village Inn & Tavern

Beautifully restored 19th-century establishment boasting period decor and delicious spaetzle. ☎ 860-824-4910; www.falls villageinn.com; 33 Railroad St, Falls Village, CT; mains $10-25; ☾ 11:30am-2:30pm & 5pm-10pm Wed-Sat, 11am-3pm & 5pm-8pm Sun

Long Trail Brewing Company

Vermont's most popular microbrewery offers tours and tastings of their bountiful beverages. ☎ 802-672-5011; www.longtrail .com; 5520 Hwy 4, Bridgewater Corners, VT; ☾ 10am-6pm daily

Woodstock Inn, Station & Brewery

This former railway station turned hotel boasts the trail's best breakfast and great hand-crafted brews. ☎ 603-745-3951, 800-321-3985; www. woodstockinnnh.com; 135 Main St, North Woodstock, NH; mains $4-23; ☾ 11:30am-10pm daily

USEFUL WEBSITES

www.appalachiantrail.org
www.nps.gov/appa

LINK YOUR TRIP

www.lonelyplanet.com/trip-planner

Food Trip: New England

WHY GO From fried clams and lobster to funky international dishes and freshly made desserts, New England has a plethora of places to tuck in your napkin, grab your fork, and dig into mouthwatering delectables. These top spots will have you drooling every time you park your car.

For many, New England is synonymous with seafood, and of course it is – where else can you find Maine lobster cooked to perfection or a bowl of chowder with meaty yet tender clams? Yet the true New England food experience goes beyond the simple stereotypes, revealing the rich history of these six states and celebrating the differences of the unique people and cultures that have collided here. French and Italians have influenced the cuisine, Native American recipes and traditions are still alive on the tongue much the way they were centuries ago, and Portuguese fishermen have brought their Old World heritage here to stay. This trip will not only take you on a journey over miles and across state lines but will also bring you back in time and across cultures. And while we've outlined some great places that are sure to please, don't be afraid to stop and smell what's cooking along the way…there's so much here that there's no way one trip could possibly uncover it all.

Start off in Boston in the North End, as close as some New Englanders will ever get to tasting Italy. The narrow streets are crammed with over 300 restaurants and Italian shops, and you'll likely see septuagenarians sitting outside on benches smoking their daily cigar as they chat in Italian. This is one of Boston's nicest neighborhoods, and with the new Rose Kennedy Greenway where the highway used to be, this area is prettier than ever. For something sweet, find **❶ Modern Pastry** (there are many imitations) on Hanover Street and prepare to wait in line (sometimes out the door) for one of their authentic Italian desserts.

TIME
2 – 3 days

DISTANCE
576 miles

BEST TIME TO GO
Jun – Sep

START
Boston, MA

END
Providence, RI

ALSO GOOD FOR

Rum baba, ricotta-cheese pie, and of course tiramisu are all popular, but for a bite of simple goodness try one of their cannolis. You can't go wrong here – the soft, creamy ricotta is sweetened just right, and on a hot summer day it's even better than ice cream. After a meal, a slow walk down Hanover Street to the waterfront, where you can watch ships entering the harbor at the mouth of the Charles River, can't be beat.

Even if you're not feeling bitter, why not drink something that is? ❷ **Harpoon Brewery** is within walking distance of the North End. Proud holders of Massachusetts Brewery Permit Number 1, Harpoon likes to let the world know that they started the brewing renaissance in Boston (not "the other" more famous Boston beer company). Of the many brews they produce, perhaps none is so well loved as their Harpoon India Pale Ale (IPA), 12 oz of golden pleasure that's become one of Boston's best-loved beers. IPAs were originally brewed by the British to stand up well in India, where troops needed something to boost morale in the sweltering heat. The bitterness of the hops is what makes the beer so refreshing on a hot day, especially in New England, which can sometimes feel like India when the temperature gets into the 90s. If you want something a little lighter ask if the Raspberry Hefeweizen is available – this wheat beer with just a hint of berry is oh-so drinkable.

After you've sobered up, meander northward to Londonderry in New Hampshire, where you can learn about and sample a different kind of fermentation:

yogurt. **❸ Stonyfield Farm** donates a percentage of its profits to charitable organizations, and is very active in supporting various New England community events. They also participate in a carbon offset program to help reduce the effects of CO_2 in the atmosphere. If a tasting leaves you wanting more, you'll find the farm's yogurts in New England supermarkets big and small – look for the cow on their distinctive containers.

Gourmands will want to experience the **❹ Dunaway Restaurant at Strawbery Banke** in Portsmouth, NH, where you can have what they term "rustic" foods but which to all others means "incredible." The executive chef apprenticed at the French Laundry, and as soon as you taste the food you'll know that was time well spent. Smoked Maine halibut, yellowfin tuna and lobster will please seafood lovers; the more adventurous eaters will want to try the barramundi with clams and prosciutto. It's part of Portsmouth's Strawbery Banke Museum (a 10-acre mix of period homes dating back to the 1690s), so you'll likely want to meander among the restored houses first – it's doubtful that our Puritan ancestors ever dined as finely as you will at the Dunaway, but one can bet that they would have wanted to.

IF IT LOOKS LIKE A CLAM BOX...

...it is one! You can't help but chuckle when you park here, since the building looks just like the take-out cardboard boxes you'll be ordering. For many Americans, a plate of hot, crispy, fried clams are what New England dining is all about. Happy to please, the **Clam Box** in Ipswich, MA, also offers scallops, oysters, shrimp, calamari, and a Fisherman's Platter that you'd better be really hungry for.

Sleep off the meal at the **❺ Sise Inn**, a beautiful 19th-century B&B just around the corner from the Dunaway that once belonged to a wealthy Portsmouth businessman. With polished butternut staircases and lots of light, the rooms here are airy, with big beds and lots of antique decorations and replicas. Incongruous but convenient wi-fi makes this a great stopping spot for anyone who needs to keep in touch with folks at home.

Duck into Maine and head for the **❻ A1 diner**. This classic Worcester Lunch Car has served the citizens of Gardiner since 1946, but don't go thinking it's just another run-of-the-mill greasy spoon. You'll also find noodle dishes in addition to the standard hamburgers and hot dogs, as well as the famous Bob's Biscuit, which goes for a hefty 1,000,000 dollars each. (That's what the menu says, anyway!)

Next, head south to Vermont, where among the maple trees and pumpkin farms you'll find **❼ Curtis' All American Barbecue Pit**, a world of smoky goodness that you can smell a mile away. Keep the windows rolled down and you won't even need to ask for directions – just follow your nose. This is a great pit stop – a barbecue pit, that is. Don't ask questions, don't look at the menu, just order some ribs and prepare to be amazed when you take the first bite. Curtis, a local legend, has been behind the smoker for almost 40 years. It's almost as much fun to watch as to eat: the whole place feels like a big 4th-of-July picnic with friends and family…and you don't have to worry about what to say to the in-laws. From the lines and the blissful expressions on the faces of the customers, you can tell that whatever his secret is, it's working.

DETOUR

Only 30 miles away in Chester, VT, the **Baba-a-Louis Bakery** gives a whole new meaning to the term "breaking bread." You'll find welcoming smiles, a very appreciative clientele, and artisan loaves that are well worth stopping for. Try to take time here and relax – the beautiful beams, lots of light, and enticing aromas all add to the experience. The cinnamon rolls are particularly scrumptious, the perfect complement to coffee as you head back out on the road.

Back into Massachusetts, this time to the ❽ **Lady Killigrew Cafe** in the Montague Bookmill, a beautiful restored building that once housed the area's only grist mill. This two-story café has huge windows overlooking a beautiful series of small waterfalls, as well as a great beer selection, cider from West County Cider, excellent coffee and staff who will make you feel like you own the place. Sit on the upper level and chat with the baristas, or snag a spot by the window and contemplate the world as the river gurgles and sings outside. With the bookstore right next door, the beautiful interior, and the view outside, you get the feeling that this is the kind of café Thoreau would come to if he were around today.

If a taste of the cider there has you craving more, try a visit to ❾ **West County Cider**. Apple pie gets all the publicity, but actually, few things are more American than apple cider. Freshly squeezed or fermented (that's "hard," in local lingo), apple cider is one of the many treats New Englanders look forward to each fall. In season, you can take a tour of the place, taste the samples on Cider Day (in November), and see first-hand how fall's apple harvest turns into nectar of the gods.

"This is the kind of café Thoreau would come to if he were around today"

Move on down to Hartford, CT, where ❿ **ON20** will dazzle and delight. This is a fancy spot where you pay for preparation and creativity, so don't expect giant portions plopped on the plate. Here, you'll see food treated as art – both in the culinary and the visual sense. If food could be framed, it's likely you'd see ON20's rillette of rabbit wrapped in bacon or the scallop-crusted sea bass hanging in a museum somewhere. It's worth noting that the chef (and restaurant) actively supports local farmers by assisting the Connecticut Farmland Trust, which helps to ensure the preservation of Connecticut farms, farmers, and local produce with a particular interest in family-owned farms. ON20's Noel Jones began working in French restaurants at age 14 and has since become one of Hartford's premier chefs – making this a spot where it's well worth the splurge.

Finish up this mouthwatering tour at the **11** **Bravo Brasserie** in Providence, RI. No taste is more quintessentially New England than fresh oysters on the half shell, and if you're going to have them anywhere, have them here. True connoisseurs forgo the cocktail sauce and just slurp them down as is. Whether or not you believe the rumor about them being an aphrodisiac, they're still euphorically good. If you're still in a seafood kind

CAFE LEBANON

Proving that dining in New England isn't all just fish and chips, the **Cafe Lebanon** (www.cafe lebanon.com) in Springfield offers wonderful Lebanese specialties in an atmospheric bar with low couches and dim light. You almost expect to see the Mediterranean Sea out the window. Don't miss the belly dancing shows – sensual, exotic and fun, they're a nice addition to an already excellent meal.

of mind, go for the pan-roasted cod, another New England tradition. Ease back on the long leather couches, enjoy the added sense of space that the mirrors lend the room, and toast the success of your New England food trip. It doesn't have to end, either…the road continues even if the page ends.
Ray Bartlett

TRIP INFORMATION

GETTING THERE
Boston and Providence are connected by I-93 and I-95.

DO
Harpoon Brewery
For many, Boston-brewed beer doesn't get better – see the production process and have a taste or two. ☎ 888-427-7666; www .harpoonbrewery.com; 306 Northern Ave, Boston, MA; tasting free; ☽ tasting 4pm Tue-Thu, 2pm & 4pm Fri, noon, 2pm, & 4pm Sat

Stonyfield Farm
Yogurt is the prime (but not the only) attraction at this eco- and socially conscious dairy in New Hampshire. ☎ 800-776-2697; www .stonyfield.com; 10 Burton Dr, Londonderry, NH; ☽ visitor center 9:30am-5pm Mon-Sat

West County Cider
Swing by here in autumn to see how apples turn into cider, and get tastes on Cider Day. ☎ 413-624-3481; 106 Bardwell's Ferry Rd, Shelburne, MA; www.westcountycider.com; ☽ tasting 10am-4:30pm Cider Day.

EAT
A1 Diner
Healthy noodles and the usual diner standbys at this classic spot. ☎ 207-582-4804; www .a1diner.com; 3 Bridge St, Gardiner, ME; breakfast from $2; ☽ 7am-8pm Mon-Thu, 7am-8:30pm Fri & Sat, 8am-1pm Sun

Bravo Brasserie
Elegant tavern-like setting, where mirrors and big windows enhance the sense of space. ☎ 401-490-5112; www.bravobrasserie.com; 123 Empire St, Providence, RI; mains $10-15; ☽ 11-1am Sun-Thu, 11-2am Fri & Sat

Curtis' All American Barbecue Pit
Sit down for a great "All American" meal. ☎ 802-387-5474; www.curtisbbqvt.com; 40 Old Deport Rd, Putney, VT; mains from $7; ☽ 10am-dusk Thu-Sun Apr-Oct

Dunaway Restaurant at Strawbery Banke
Some of the finest food on the planet in an atmospheric building; part of Strawbery Banke. ☎ 603-373-6112; www.dunaway restaurant.com; 66 Marcy St, Portsmouth, NH; mains from $20; ☽ 5:30-9:30pm Sun-Thu, 5-10pm Fri & Sat

Lady Killigrew Cafe
Café with a view of the river that's poetry perfect. ☎ 413-367-9666; www.theladykilli grew.com; 440 Greenfield Road, Montague, MA; meals from $7; ☽ 8am-11pm daily

Modern Pastry
Perfect Italian confections at a store that's been essentially the same since it was built. ☎ 617-523-3783; www.modernpastry.com; 257 Hanover St, Boston, MA; pastry from $3; ☽ 7am-10pm daily, hours vary seasonally

ON20
Lunch only at this upscale spot in Hartford, CT. ☎ 860-722-5161; www.ontwenty.com; 1 State St, 20th fl, Hartford, CT; prix fixe $35; ☽ 11am-close

SLEEP
Sise Inn
Nineteenth-century Victorian charm with new modern conveniences (including wi-fi!). ☎ 603-433-1200, 877-747-3463; www.sise inn.com; 40 Court St, Portsmouth, NH; r $119-279

USEFUL WEBSITES
www.ctfarmland.org

LINK YOUR TRIP

www.lonelyplanet.com/trip-planner

Seen Through the Eyes of an Artist

WHY GO For over four centuries, New England has provided artists with a brilliant palette of colors. Travel through this leafy realm and explore local museums, artists' studios, and the landscapes that inspired a canon of world-class art.

High in the hills of Vermont lies Bennington's triple threat – a museum, guild, and exhibition space. Spend a fast and furious morning getting a quick taste of what's to come. Have a glance at the ❶ **Bennington Museum**, which houses many works by Grandma Moses. After that, check out art in the making at ❷ **Bennington Potters**, where a group of local artisans maintain a strong tradition of local stoneware manufacturing that dates back to the 1700s. And before rolling down Rte 7 into Massachusetts, swing by the ❸ **Norman Rockwell Exhibition** to witness the compilation of more than 500 of Rockwell's *Saturday Evening Post* covers and prints.

Turn off the highway in Williamstown and stop at the ❹ **Clark Art Institute**. Robert Sterling Clark, a Yale engineer whose family had made money in the sewing machine industry, began collecting art in Paris in 1912. He and his wife eventually housed their wonderful collection in Williamstown in a white marble temple built expressly for this purpose. Mary Cassatt, Winslow Homer and John Singer Sargent represent the collection's contemporary American painting. From earlier centuries, there are works by Hans Memling, Jean Honoré Fragonard and Francisco de Goya. The Clark Art Institute's sister museum is the excellent ❺ **Williams College Museum of Art**. Around half of its 12,000 pieces comprise the American Collection, with works by notables including Edward Hopper and Grant Wood. The photography collection is equally strong, with representation by Diane Arbus, Man Ray and Alfred Stieglitz. The pieces representing ancient and medieval cultures are less numerous but equally distinguished. To find the museum, look for the huge bronze eyes embedded in the front lawn on Main St.

TIME
3 days

DISTANCE
620 miles

BEST TIME TO GO
May – Sep

START
Bennington, VT

END
Scarborough, ME

ALSO GOOD FOR

HISTORY &
CULTURE

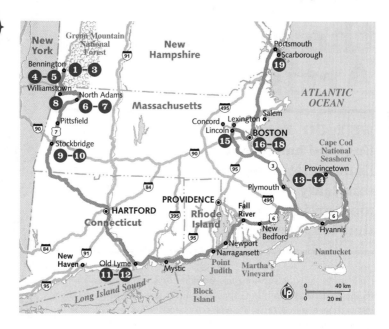

Down the road in North Adams, you'll find the rambling, 13-acre complex known as **6 MASS MoCA**. After the Sprague Electric Company packed up in 1985, more than $31 million was spent to modernize the property into the "largest gallery in the United States", which now encompasses 220,000 sq ft and over 25 buildings, including art construction areas, performance centers and 19 galleries. One gallery is the size of a football field, large enough to exhibit the work of Ann Hamilton and Tim Hawkinson. In addition to carrying the bread-and-butter rotation of description-defying installation pieces, the museum has evolved into one of the region's key venues for evening cabaret, documentary films, lectures and avant-garde dance performances. If you're peckish, pause for a quick nosh at one of MASS MoCA's two excellent eateries: Lickety Split (café-style food and coffee) and Café Latino (full-service restaurant and bar).

"One gallery is the size of a football field, large enough to exhibit the work of Ann Hamilton and Tim Hawkinson."

If you're completely engrossed by the area's never-ending collection of art, spend the night at **7 Porches**, whose new rooms combine well-considered color palettes, ample lighting and French doors into a pleasant sleeping experience. Thanks to a grant, it often puts up artists installing artworks at the museum. For something more bucolic, try the **8 Guest House at Field Farm**, which was once the country estate of Lawrence and Eleanore Bloedel, collectors of 20th-century art. Now run by the Trustees of Reservations, the 300-acre estate offers four miles of walking trails, tennis courts, and surprisingly modern rooms.

Rise with the rooster's crowing and head south along Hwy 7 until you arrive in Stockbridge. Take a good look down Stockbridge's wide Main St. Notice anything? More specifically, notice anything missing? Not one stoplight stutters the view, not one telephone pole blights the picture-perfect scene – it all looks a little too much like those wholesome Normal Rockwell paintings. It should come as no surprise, then, that Rockwell spent the last 25 years of his life living and working in this frightfully boring town. The **9 Norman Rockwell Museum** has the largest collection of the artist's original work and hosts exhibitions of other feel-good artists such as David Macaulay, of *The Way Things Work* fame. The grounds contain Rockwell's studio, which was moved here from his Stockbridge home. Before leaving little Stockbridge, follow MA 102 west of the town center and swing by **10 Chesterwood**, the former summer home of distinguished sculptor Daniel Chester French. His best-known oeuvre is the great seated statue of Abraham Lincoln at the Lincoln Monument in Washington DC. French's bevy of great public works (over 100 pieces, most of them monumental) earned him the big bucks, and opulent Chesterwood is a testament to his steady flow of cash. Most of the estate has remained unchanged, and visitors can ogle nearly 500 pieces of sculpture, finished and unfinished, in the barn-like studio.

EPHEMERAL ART

Held annually in mid-July on Revere Beach, just north of Boston's city center, the New England Sand Sculpting Festival (www.reverebeach partnership.com) showcases the talents of sculptors from all over the region. Contestants get 28 hours to spin 10 tons of quarried sand into their own ephemeral masterpiece. The results are shockingly amazing – past winners have created Shiva Natarajas and spaceships. Check it out before it gets washed away!

Head south on Hwy 7 then southeast Hwy 44 through Hartford to wind along the Connecticut River until it meets the sea at Old Lyme. In the 19th century, the mouth of the Connecticut River was home to some 60 sea captains. However, the area is best known as the center of the Lyme Art Colony, which embraced and cultivated the nascent American impressionist movement. Numerous artists including William Chadwick and Willard Metcalfe came here to paint and stayed in the mansion of local art patron Florence Griswold. Ms Griswold encouraged her artist friends to decorate her estate with murals (often in lieu of paying rent). Today the property has been preserved as the **11 Florence Griswold Museum** and features prominent impressionist and Barbizon paintings. A stay the **12 Bee & Thistle Inn**, a butter-yellow Dutch colonial farmhouse, makes it easy to understand from where the local artists drew their inspiration.

Flung all the way out on the curled tip of Cape Cod, the **13 Provincetown Art Association and Museum** celebrates the town's thriving art community. The gorgeous space boasts the works of over 500 artists who have found their inspiration on the Lower Cape. If you're feeling inspired yourself, PAAM offers a full agenda of workshops in painting, silk-screening, sculpting and other media throughout the summer, most lasting three to five days. If you're sticking around to get your hands dirty, spend your evenings at **⑭ Carpe Diem**. Sophisticated yet relaxed, the inn's rooms each involve a theme inspired by a different writer and the corner of the world from whence they came.

Wind your way back to the mainland and follow Rte 3, then I-95 until you reach the town of Lincoln. Here you'll find the magical **⑮ DeCordova Museum**, which encompasses 35 acres of green hills, and provides a spectacular natural environment for a constantly changing exhibit of outdoor artwork. Inside, the museum hosts rotating exhibits of contemporary sculpture, painting, photography and mixed media.

STOP! THIEF!

On March 18, 1990 two thieves disguised as police officers broke into the Isabella Stewart Gardner Museum in Boston. They left with nearly $200 million worth of artwork, including priceless pieces by Vermeer, Manet and Rembrandt. The crime was never solved. Mrs Gardner's will stipulated that the collection remain exactly as it was at the time of her death, so the walls where these paintings hung are barren.

In Cambridge, no entrance fees are necessary to experience MIT's insatiable appetite for modern architecture, but an **⑯ MIT Campus Tour** is probably a good idea. Tours depart from the lobby of Building 7 and crisscross the campus, stopping at architectural gems including the Chapel, the Infinite Corridor, Gehry's Stata Center and the Kresge Auditorium. Wander off on your own to check out the post-apocalyptic-looking dormitory designed by Stephen Holl, and Alvar Aalto's contribution to student life, Baker House.

The magnificent Venetian-style palazzo that houses the **⑰ Isabella Stewart Gardner Museum** was home to 'Mrs Jack' Gardner until her death in 1924. A monument to one woman's keen eye for exquisite art, the Gardner is filled with almost 2000 priceless objects, primarily European, including outstanding tapestries and Italian Renaissance and 17th-century Dutch paintings. The palazzo, with a four-story greenhouse courtyard, is in itself a masterpiece.

Finish your ultimate art tour at Boston's **⑱ Museum of Fine Arts**, whose highlight is undoubtedly its treasure trove of great American Art. There are also several dining options here if you need some sustenance. If time permits, a trip up to Winslow Homer's seaside cabin is the perfect coda after finishing your journey at the MFA. Located up the coast in Prouts Neck, near Scarborough, ME, the **⑲ Winslow Homer Studio** was recently acquired by the Portland Museum of Art, and once restorations are complete (sometime in 2009 or 2010) tourists will have the unique opportunity to visit the grounds that inspired his vivid oil paintings found in the MFA and beyond.

Brandon Presser

TRIP INFORMATION

GETTING THERE

From Boston follow I-93 north and head west along Rte 9 until you reach Bennington, Vermont.

DO

Bennington Museum

Offers an outstanding collection of early Americana including furniture, glassware, pottery, colonial paintings, dolls, military memorabilia, and the oldest surviving American Revolutionary flag. ☎ 802-447-1571; www.benningtonmuseum.com; 75 Main St, Rte 9, Bennington, VT; adult/child $8/7; ☷ 10am-5pm Thu-Tue; ♿

Bennington Potters

The artisans at this pottery are maintaining a strong tradition of local handmade stoneware manufacturing that dates back to the 1700s. Self-guided tours are available. ☎ 802-447-7531; www.benningtonpotters .com; 324 Country St, Bennington, VT; admission free; ☷ 9:30am-6pm Mon-Sat, 10am-5pm Sun; ♿

Chesterwood

This pastoral 22-acre country home was once owned by sculptor Daniel Chester French, and today it has been turned into a comprehensive museum featuring his works. ☎ 413-298-3579; www.chesterwood.org; 4 Williamsville Rd, Stockbridge, MA; adult/ child $12/5; ☷ 10am-5pm May-Oct

Clark Art Institute

A gem among US art museums, the institute has a vast collection of works accumulated by Robert Sterling Clark and his wife. ☎ 413-458-9545; www.clarkart.edu; 225 South St, Williamstown, MA; admission Jun-Oct $12.50, Nov-May free; ☷ 10am-5pm Tue-Sun Sep-Jun, daily Jun-Aug

DeCordova Museum

This campus of rolling hills hosts a constantly changing array of outdoor artwork. ☎ 781-259-8355; www.decordova.org; 51 Sandy Pond Rd, Lincoln, MA; adult/student $9/6; ☷ dawn-dusk

Florence Griswold Museum

The former core of American impressionist painting, the Florence Griswold estate is now a museum showcasing both impressionist and Barbizon works. ☎ 860-434-5542; www.flogris.org; 96 Lyme St, Old Lyme, CT; adult/child $8/4; ☷ 10am-5pm Tue-Sat, 1-5pm Sun

Isabella Stewart Gardner Museum

This stunning Venetian villa is a monument to one woman's taste for incredibly expensive art. ☎ 617-278-5166; www.gardnermuseum .org; 280 The Fenway, Boston, MA; adult/ child $10/free; ☷ 11am-5pm

MASS MoCA

An art-centric campus sprawling over 13 acres around downtown North Adams, which is around a third of the entire business district. ☎ 413-662-2111; www.massmoca.org; 87 Marshall St, North Adams, MA; adult/child $12.50/5; ☷ 10am-6pm Jul & Aug, 11am-5pm Wed-Mon Sep-Jun

MIT Campus Tour

These informative tours lead visitors through the campus as they learn about life at MIT as well as the university's interesting pieces of acquired art and architecture. ☎ 617-253-4795; www.web.mit.edu; Lobby 7, 77 Massachusetts Ave, Cambridge, MA; ☷ 9am-5pm; ♿

Museum of Fine Arts

A must on any art tour, this large museum in central Boston features an incredible number of masterpieces from America and beyond. ☎ 617-267-9300; www.mfa.org; 465 Huntington Ave, Boston, MA; adult/child $17/6.50; ☷ 10am-4:45pm Sat-Tue, 10am-9:45pm Wed-Fri

Norman Rockwell Exhibition

Exhibits 500 of Rockwell's *Saturday Evening Post* covers and prints. There is also a short film about the artist. ☎ 802-375-6423; Rte 7A, Arlington, VT; admission $1; ☷ 9am-5pm May-Oct, 10am-4pm Nov-Apr; ♿

Norman Rockwell Museum

This museum has the largest collection of Rockwell's original art and also hosts exhibitions of other wholesome, feel-good artists. ☎ 412-298-4100; www.nrm.org; Rte 183, Stockbridge, MA; adult/child $12/free; ⏱ 10am-5pm; ♿

Provincetown Art Association and Museum

This museum featuring loads of local talent is a must-see spot, especially after its recent renovation. ☎ 508-487-1750; www.paam .org; 460 Commercial St, Provincetown, MA; adult/child $5/free; ⏱ 11am-5pm Sep-Jun, extended hrs in summer

Williams College Museum of Art

Around half of its 12,000 pieces comprise the American Collection, with substantial works by such notables as Edward Hopper and Winslow Homer. ☎ 413-597-2429; www .wcma.org; Main St btwn Water & Spring Sts, Williamstown, MA; admission free; ⏱ 10am-5pm Tue-Sat, 1-5pm Sun

Winslow Homer Studio

This quiet seaside cabin once belonged to acclaimed New England artist Winslow Homer. ☎ 207-775-6148; www.portlandmuseum .org; Prouts Neck, Scarborough, ME; admission $10; ⏱ opening 2009/2010

SLEEP

Bee & Thistle Inn

This butter-yellow 1756 Dutch Colonial farmhouse makes it easy to see where the local artists' drew their inspiration from. ☎ 860-434-1667; www.beeandthistleinn.com; 100 Lyme St, Old Lyme, CT; d incl breakfast $130-200

Carpe Diem

Each room at this charming inn is inspired by a different writer and region of the world. ☎ 508-487-4242; www.carpediemguest house.com; 12 Johnson St, Provincetown, MA; r incl breakfast $155-255

Guest House at Field Farm

This quiet estate was built in 1948, in a spare, clean-lined post-WWII style on 300 acres of woods and farmland facing Mt Greylock. ☎ 413-458-3135; www.thetrustees.org; 554 Sloan Rd, Williamstown, MA; r incl breakfast $175-250;

Porches

Near MASS MoCA, the rooms at Porches combine well-considered color palettes, ample lighting and French doors into a pleasant sleeping experience. ☎ 413-664-0400; www .porches.com; 231 River St, North Adams, MA; r $155-235

USEFUL WEBSITES

www.mfa.org

LINK YOUR TRIP

www.lonelyplanet.com/trip-planner

MASSACHUSETTS TRIPS

Whatever kind of adventure you're looking for, chances are Massachusetts will have it right around the corner. With a beautiful coastline, beaches and bays, all the way out to the rolling, cow-dotted pastures and the gentle hills, Massachusetts won't disappoint. Boston, one of America's oldest and most interesting cities, provides the state with genuine diversity that you'll be hard-pressed to find elsewhere in New England. You can go from one world to another – a trendy Boston nightclub to a rural cow farm – on less than a tank of gas.

As you meander through some of America's richest history, take the time to muse about the state's literary and philosophical achievements at Author's Ridge in Concord or ponder the region's religious and social pioneers in the many churches

 PLAYLIST

Trips require the proper soundtrack, so roll down the windows and turn up the volume on these Massachusetts tunes. When you're in reach of Boston's radio waves, tune to commercial-free Boston College radio station WZBC (90.3FM):

- "Dirty Water," The Standells
- "Rock & Roll Band," Boston
- "Here Comes Your Man," Pixies
- "The Impression That I Get," The Mighty Mighty Bosstones
- "Sweet Emotion," Aerosmith
- "Get Me," Dinosaur Jr
- "The Outdoor Type," Lemonheads
- "Just What I Needed," Cars

and cemeteries. Chat with the characterful locals – they can help you out not just with directions and recommendations for the specialty dish at their local diner, but also with understanding what it means to be here. It's these moments that turn a list of stopping points into a memorable journey. What we cover here are only suggestions – we encourage you to break all the rules.

MASSACHUSETTS' BEST TRIPS

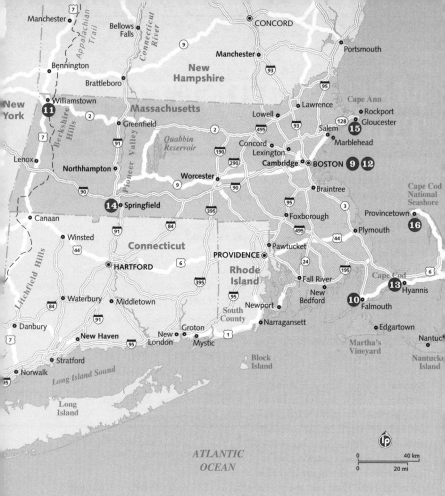

MASSACHUSETTS TRIPS

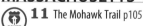
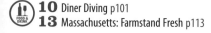

48 Hours in Boston

WHY GO From world-class cuisine and cobbled colonial lanes to vintage shopping and fanatical sports fans, Boston brews a colorful recipe for chaos. It'll take more than two days to crack Beantown's shell, but this sampler of sights and sounds is a wicked good way to get acquainted (or reacquainted) with the city.

TIME
2 days

BEST TIME TO GO
Year-round

START
Boston

END
Boston

ALSO GOOD FOR

HISTORY & CULTURE

While calculating how to best spend your 48 hours in Boston, start your day with a hearty breakfast and an uncanny mathematical phenomenon at ❶ **Paramount**, on Charles St. One of the top-rated brunch spots for many years and counting, this bustling little joint features delicious fruit spreads and fluffy French toast, but is perhaps best known for its bizarrely convenient seating rotations. Despite the crowded atmosphere, tables always seem to clear out by the time your eyes start searching for a place to rest your bottom. They call it a science. We're pretty sure it's good karma.

Bolster your early jolt of caffeine with a wobbly ride on the ❷ **MBTA** subway, known to locals simply as 'the T'. You'll hear the most perfect Bostonian accents as conductors announce upcoming train stations ("next stop *Pahk* Street!"). Boston's T is the country's oldest subway and has been in operation since 1897. New Charlie Cards (plastic swipe cards available from any uniformed employee) are rechargeable tickets that save passengers $0.30 per ride. The cards were named after poor old Charlie, a local legend made famous by the Kingston Trio; back in the old days you used to have to pay to get *off* the T and dear Charlie was stuck onboard forever because he couldn't pay the fare.

Exit the T at either Haymarket or State St Station for a leisurely stroll around the cheery marketplace of ❸ **Faneuil Hall**. Constructed in 1740 as a market and public meeting place, this brick colonial building

BEST TRIP

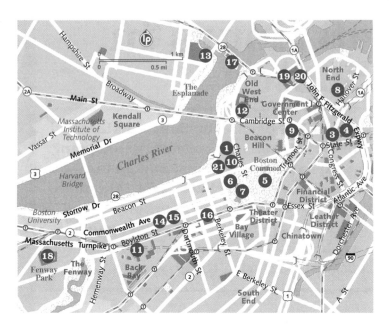

is topped by its signature grasshopper weather vane. Although the hall was supposed to be exclusively for local issues, the Sons of Liberty called many meetings here, informing public opinion about their objections to British taxation without representation. Three additional buildings in the back make up the bulk of the marketplace. Known as ❹ **Quincy Market**, these granite colonial structures were redeveloped in the 1970s into today's touristy, festive shopping and eating center with over 20 restaurants and 40 food stalls. Try out your Boston drawl as you order a hot bowl of clam *chowda* for lunch, or sample some of the other Boston staples such as baked beans or live lobster.

"Try out your Boston drawl as you order a hot bowl of clam chowda for lunch..."

After spending a disproportionate amount of money at one of the market's homemade-fudge stands, walk off your meal with a stroll through ❺ **Boston Common** and on to the ❻ **Public Garden**, a 24-acre botanical oasis of Victorian flowerbeds and weeping willows drooping over a lazy lagoon. Take a good look at the natural splendor while noting that in the 19th century this stunning garden was a tidal salt marsh (like the rest of Back Bay). For the quintessential Boston experience take a ride on the ❼ **Swan Boats**, a local tradition since 1877.

Ask anyone around town and they'll tell you that the ultimate Boston experience would be incomplete without venturing to the North End and eating at an Italian restaurant tucked away along one of the area's cobbled, Medieval-esque streets. The problem, however, is that there are so many great little family-owned joints to choose from and to make matters worse, Boston's other neighborhoods are speedily stocking up on their fair share of amazing eating establishments. To appease even the harshest of critics, save your trip to Little Italy for dessert at **8** **Mike's**, home of the world's most perfect cannoli. Try your best to ignore the bakery's gaudy decorative mix of mural-sized mirrors framed like Renaissance paintings and buzzing neon lights casting blinding rays upon sweet-toothed customers. If you can't resist the call of the cannoli until after dinner then pick one up on the go as you ponder the infinite dinner options around town. We suggest heading back to Beacon Hill to dine in the smooth, brick wine cellar at **9** **Grotto**, or at celebrity chef Todd English's yuppie pizza paradise **10** **Figs**, but why not stumble upon your own eatery that the guidebooks don't know about. After dinner head to the towering Prudential Center and take a ride all the way to the top for some cocktail clinking at the swank **11** **Top of the Hub**. Drink in the views of the twinkling city lights below while smooth jazz melts over the ivory piano keys in the corner.

As the evening winds down, make your way back to Charles St for some beauty sleep before another busy day tomorrow. For 140 years, those staying at 225 Charles St had to be dragged in kicking and screaming in order to spend the night. Today, the wretched Charles St Jail has been transformed into the luxurious **12** **Liberty Hotel**. The hotel's decor playfully references the building's prison past. The restaurant, Clink (chuckle chuckle), preserves some old observation cells and the exquisite lobby soars to a 90ft ceiling (it used to be an indoor exercise space). For views of Boston from across the river, try spending the night at **13** **Hotel Marlowe**. Although the abundance of sassy leopard prints is vaguely reminiscent of a '70s porno, the spicy decor will undoubtedly appeal to the retro swinger in all of us.

Start the morning with a designer breakfast at one of the chichi brunch spots along Boston's effortlessly quirky Newbury St. Afterwards, strut your stuff along the concrete catwalk while doing some serious window shopping, then skip the overpriced boutiques and try your luck at one of the colorful vintage shops. For browsers with an eye for fashion but without a pocketbook to

FREEDOM TRAIL

The best introduction to revolutionary Boston is the Freedom Trail. The redbrick path winds its way past 16 sites that earned this town its status as the cradle of liberty. The 2.5-mile trail follows the course of the conflict, from the Old State House, where Redcoats killed five men marking the Boston Massacre, to the Old North Church, where the sexton hung two lanterns to warn that British troops would come by sea. Visit the Boston Common information kiosk to pick up a free map or to hook up with a 90-minute guided tour led by the **Freedom Trail Foundation** (www.thefreedomtrail.org).

match, **14** **Closet, Inc** (and it does feel like some fashionista's overstuffed closet) is secondhand heaven. You'll never know what you're going to find at **15** **Second Time Around**, but you can be sure that it will have a designer label. Take a detour to Copley Sq and hit up **16** **Filene's Basement**, Boston's ultimate bargain bin. According to legend, the store's original owner, Mr Katz, planned to open a clothing store and decided that 'Feline's' would be an appropriately clever name for the shop. He hired an artist to create the store's front sign, but when the artist finished Mr Katz realized that he'd mixed up the 'i' and the first 'e', writing 'Filene's' instead. The name stuck and nowadays it's synonymous with great finds at great prices. The best part about Filene's is its unspoken longevity rule – items are automatically marked down the longer they remain in the store – so dig deep to find the real gems!

RED SOX NATION

First-time visitors to the Red Sox heartland always come away with some piece of memorabilia. If you're really smitten consider becoming an official member of the Red Sox fan club: check out www.redsox.com for more information. Famous fans include Matt Damon, Ben Affleck, Conan O'Brien, Steven Tyler, Rachael Ray and Steve Carell.

Try the immensely popular **17** **Duck Tours** for an abridged version of Boston's sights and history. Crafted from modified amphibious vehicles from WWII, the tour bus/boat splashes around the Charles River then takes to the city streets for a truly unique 90-minute tour.

Finish the day with an honest-to-goodness ballpark wiener at Fenway, home to the beloved **18** **Boston Red Sox**. Watching the rabid fans howl at their favorite players is way more fun than the actual game, but be warned: any back talk about the Sox or praise for the New York Yankees will be met with swift and severe punishment from vigilant devotees. If it isn't baseball season check out Boston's brood of die-hard fans cheering on the other local teams, like the **19** **Boston Bruins** or the **20** **Boston Celtics** (that's S-eltics, not K-eltics), who both play at Banknorth Garden.

After the game there's something that everyone's gotta do, no matter how touristy it may seem: have a drink where everybody knows your name. The Bull & Finch was an authentic English pub (dismantled in England, shipped to Boston and reassembled in a Beacon Hill townhouse). But that's not why hundreds of people descend on the place daily: the pub inspired the TV sitcom *Cheers* and has been thus renamed. Most visitors are disappointed that the interior of **21** **Cheers** bears no resemblance to the TV set. More importantly, tourists are the main clientele, so nobody knows your name (or anybody else's), although after five minutes you're almost guaranteed to hear a patron drunkenly humming the theme song under their breath and that's reason enough to visit.

Brandon Presser

TRIP INFORMATION

GETTING THERE
Start the trip in the heart of downtown Boston along Charles St near the Park St subway station.

DO
Boston Bruins
The Bruins, under the former star power of Bobby Orr and Ray Bourque, play ice hockey at Banknorth Garden. ☎ 617-624-1900; www.bostonbruins.com; Banknorth Garden, 150 Causeway St; ☷ mid-Oct–mid-Apr; ⚁

Boston Celtics
The Celtics, who've won more basketball championships than any other NBA team, play at Banknorth Garden above North Station. ☎ 617-523-3030; www.celtics.com; Banknorth Garden, 150 Causeway St; ☷ late Oct-Apr; ⚁

Boston Red Sox
The Sox play in Fenway Park, the nation's oldest and most storied ballpark, built in 1912. ☎ 617-267-1700; www.redsox.com; 4 Yawkey Way; tickets $18-55; ☷ early Apr-late Sep; ⚁

Closet, Inc
For shoppers with an eye for fashion but without the income to match. The Closet is a secondhand clothing store that carries high-quality items by acclaimed designers. ☎ 617-536-1919; 175 Newbury St; ☷ 9am-5pm Mon-Fri

Duck Tours
Ninety-minute narrated land and water tours of the Charles River and Boston using modified amphibious vehicles from WWII depart from the Prudential Center and the Museum of Science. ☎ 617-723-3825; www.boston ducktours.com; Prudential Center; adult /child $27/18; ☷ 9am-dusk; ⚁

Faneuil Hall
A brick colonial building topped with the beloved grasshopper weather vane. The hall has earned the nickname 'Cradle of Liberty' due to the heated political movements nurtured here during the American Revolution. ☎ 617-242-5642; www.faneuilhall.com; Congress & North Sts; admission free; ☷ 9am-5pm; ⚁

Filene's Basement
The granddaddy of bargain stores, Filene's Basement carries overstocked and irregular items at everyday low prices. ☎ 617-424-5520; 497 Boylston St; ☷ 9am-5pm Mon-Sat

MBTA
The MBTA operates the oldest subway in America, dating back to 1897. It is known locally as "the T." ☎ 617-222-3200; www.mbta .com; one ride $2; ☷ 5:30-12:30am; ⚁

Second Time Around
Come early and come often, because you never know what you're going to find, but you can be sure it will have a designer label. ☎ 617-247-3504; 219 Newbury St; ☷ 11am-7pm Mon-Fri, 10am-7pm Sat, 10am-6pm Sun

Swan Boats
A Boston tradition since 1877, the Swan Boats swim around the lazy lagoon in Boston's Public Gardens. ☎ 617-522-1966; www .swanboats.com; Public Garden; adult/child $3/2; ☷ 10am-4pm mid-Apr–mid-Sep; ⚁

EAT & DRINK
Cheers
However touristy it may seem, have a drink where everybody knows your name. ☎ 617-227-9605; 84 Beacon St; ☷ 11am-late

Figs
Figs is the brainchild of celebrity chef Todd English. Enjoy whisper-thin crusts topped with interesting exotic toppings. Case in point: The namesake fig and prosciutto with Gorgonzola. ☎ 617-742-3447; 42 Charles St; meals $15-30; ☷ lunch & dinner

Grotto
As romantic as it is charming, this cramped, brick wine cellar magically transforms into a

dim, candle-lit hideout for foodies. ☎ 617-227-3434; www.grottorestaurant.com; 37 Bowdoin St; meals $25-45; ⏱ 11:30am-10pm Mon-Fri, 5-10pm Sat & Sun

Mike's
A giant gaudy bakery in the heart of the Italian North End neighborhood. The cannolis are a must. ☎ 617-742-3050; www.mikespastry.com; 300 Hanover St; ⏱ 8am-9pm Sun-Thu, 8am-10:30pm Fri, 8am-11pm Sat

Paramount
The nexus of the universe's mathematical harmony, Paramount features excellent breakfast fare and a bizarre seating style. ☎ 617-720-1152; 44 Charles St; meals $8-30; ⏱ 7am-10pm Mon-Thu, 7am-11pm Fri, 8am-11pm Sat, 8am-10pm Sun; ♿

Quincy Market
This food hall is packed with restaurants and food stalls. Choose from chowder, bagels, Indian, Greek, baked goods and ice cream. ☎ 617-338-2323; cnr Congress & State Sts; meals $5-15; ⏱ 10am-9pm Mon-Sat, noon-6pm Sun; ♿

Top of the Hub
A brilliant place for bubbly overlooking the city. ☎ 617-536-1775; www.topofthehub .net; Prudential Center, 800 Boylston St; fixed menu $55; ⏱ 11:30am-1am Mon-Sat,11am-1am Sun

SLEEP

Hotel Marlowe
The spicy decor, including sassy leopard prints, will undoubtedly appeal to the retro swinger in all of us. ☎ 617-868-8000; www .hotelmarlowe.com; 25 Edwin H Land Blvd, Cambridge; r from $199; ♿ 🐾

Liberty Hotel
Once a dingy prison for common criminals, this hotel has been decorated playfully with its prison past in mind. Clink, the on-site restaurant, preserves some old observation cells and the lobby has a 90ft ceiling. ☎ 617-224-4000; www.libertyhotel.com; 225 Charles St; r from $375

USEFUL WEBSITES
www.boston.com
www.redsox.mlb.com

LINK YOUR TRIP
TRIP

www.lonelyplanet.com/trip-planner

Diner Diving

WHY GO Jump into the car, hit the gas, put in the American Graffiti soundtrack and prepare to gorge yourself at the quirkiest, funkiest, most retro diners Massachusetts has to offer. These favorites have weathered the decades and stand out as the best of the best.

Start your trip in Falmouth, home of the much loved, almost revered ❶ Betsy's Diner. Along with a funky old jukebox and other retro and vintage decor (pastel pink and white paint – think saddle shoes!), Betsy's has great fresh fish platters which some have been known to cross the bridges for, but everything's good here. After you're suitably stuffed you might need to make like a lounge lizard and lie in the sun at nearby ❷ Old Silver Beach – you may need days, even weeks, to digest all those calories.

If you're a glutton for more punishment, or simply a glutton, by dinnertime you'll be ready for ❸ John's Capeside Diner. It's no Worcester Lunch Car but with the friendly service, great plates of eggs and omelettes, and the local characters who eat here, you'll know this place holds its own against the best. The Capeside is right near the canal and you'll often hear the silverware-rattling rumble of the train as it goes by.

Head a little further down Rte 6A toward one of the Cape's best beaches, Sandy Neck, and spend the night at the ❹ Sandy Neck Motel, which doesn't have to pretend to be retro: It's been around for decades, long enough to be vintage in its own right. The motel offers simple rooms and a good location – most of the Upper Cape's dining and entertainment is within a 20-minute drive of here. Look for the gargantuan American flag out front, seemingly large enough to gift wrap one of the rooms.

TIME
2 days

DISTANCE
195 miles

BEST TIME TO GO
Year-round

START
Falmouth

END
Worcester

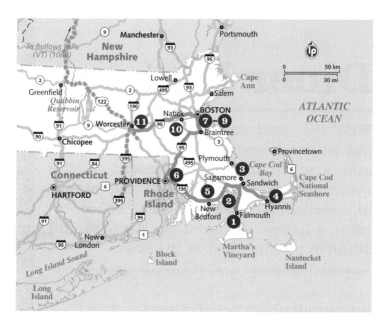

Now you're ready to set off for distant lands, or, in this case, New Bedford. Only an hour-long drive off-Cape, you'll find the **⑤ Shawmut Diner**, a movie-set-perfect classic diner easily recognizable by its signature Shawmut Indian sign; it's also on the National Register of Historic Places. Generations have grown up coming here, eating Portuguese specials that have hardly changed in decades. It's exactly the kind of place you'd expect to see a campaigning politician stopping by at to meet and greet. It's just got that feel – the rounded ceiling, the worn vinyl booths, the occasional celebrity or radio show host. The Shawmut is more than just a spot to grab a bite…it's an institution.

> "It's exactly the kind of place you'd expect to see a campaigning politician stopping by at..."

For some diner history from another institution, check out the **⑥ Culinary Arts Museum at Johnson & Wales University** in nearby Providence, just 30 minutes from the state line. In addition to viewing the world's largest collection of food preparation items (not all of which are on display), you can visit the diner museum, with display cases and information, much of it identical to the diners you'll have seen on this tour. Diners aren't just living history – you can eat there too!

Follow US-95 back up to Boston and drive into the fray. There're some great places to stay here, among them the **⑦ Midtown Hotel**, a self-proclaimed retro joint in Back Bay. It's one of the only spots in Boston where Fido is welcome and it has clean carpeted rooms, a pool and easy subway access. Alternatively, and *sans* Fido, try **8 Copley Inn**, tucked into the bustling Copley Sq on Garrison St, where you can warm up your leftovers in the kitchenettes, or at least store them in the refrigerator for midnight snacking. If you do stay in Boston you can park your car and take the subway for 30 minutes to the **9 Rosebud Diner** in Somerville, MA. This beautifully restored diner has common fare that's not for dieters – lots of fried fries and dripping meats – but for many it's a welcome escape from the shishifoofoo. The crowds *may* be partly due to the fact that there's a fully stocked bar – how convenient that you took the subway here instead of driving so you won't need a designated driver for the stumble home.

On the other side of Boston there's **10 Casey's Diner**, in Natick. This postage-stamp-sized diner deserves its place in history – just 10 stools have withstood the "taste" of time and owner Patrick Casey still dishes the

DETOUR **Miss Bellows Falls Diner**, in Bellow's Falls, VT, is a whopping two-hour trip from Worcester, but this historic landmark still sports original chrome, counters, floor and flavor. Ask for a "Bow Wow" (hot dog), a "Burn the British with extra cow paste" (English muffin with extra butter) or a few "life preservers" (doughnuts, as if anything could be further from the truth!). The Friday all-you-can-eat fish fry is one of the many reasons people keep coming back for more… and more…and more.

dogs like his great-grandfather did four generations ago. You can't go wrong if you get the "all-around," which to locals means a hot dog with onions, relish and mustard. Don't bother waiting for a seat – just do what most folks do and take your meal with you and sit on the hood of your car.

If you feel like exploring the more intellectual side of the diner experience, head out to the **11 Worcester Historical Museum**, which has exhibits about the birthplace of the diner's most famous icon, the Worcester Lunch Car. This impressive brick building also has rotating displays about a whole host of Worcester-related exhibits, as well as special events and collections.

Ray Bartlett

TRIP INFORMATION

GETTING THERE
Reach the Cape from Boston by following I-93 south to Hwy 3 to its terminus. Cross the Sagamore Bridge and you're good to go.

DO

Culinary Arts Museum at Johnson & Wales University
The world's largest collection of food-related items on display and yep, there's a diner exhibit. ☎ 401-598-2805; www.culinary .org; 315 Harborside Blvd, Providence, RI; adult/child $7/2; ☿ 10am-5pm Tue-Sun, closed major holidays & school holidays

Worcester Historical Museum
History of the city that gave birth to that wonder of wonders, the Worcester Lunch Car. ☎ 508-753-8278; www.worcesterhistory .org; 30 Elm St, Worcester; adult/child $5/free; ☿ 10am-4pm Tue, Wed, Fri & Sat, 10am-8:30pm Thu

EAT

Betsy's Diner
Beloved Betsy's serves up Falmouth's best breakfasts and great fried fish. ☎ 508-540-0060; 457 Main St, Falmouth; mains $15-20; ☿ 6am-8pm Mon-Sat, 6am-2pm Sun

Casey's Diner
Casey's may just be the world's tiniest diner, but that doesn't stop the crowds from squeezing in for the great chow. ☎ 508-655-3761; 36 South Ave, Natick; burgers from $3; ☿ 11:30am-8pm Mon-Fri, 11:30am-2pm Sat

John's Capeside Diner
Great food belies the shabby exterior and the train rumbling by, and service with a smile

makes your meal taste even better. ☎ 508-888-2530; 1025 Sandwich Rd, Sagamore, MA; mains $6-12; ☿ 5am-2pm Mon-Sat, 5am-1pm Sun

Rosebud Diner
A spot in Davis Sq that sports, among other things, a full bar instead of the '50s-era soda machine. ☎ 617 666-6015; 381 Summer St, Somerville; mains $5-15; ☿ 8am-11pm Sun-Thu, 8am-midnight Fri & Sat

Shawmut Diner
A time-honored icon that deserves its place in any Massachusetts diner compendium and which gently graces the National Register of Historic Places. ☎ 508-993-3073; 943 Shawmut Ave, New Bedford; mains $7-14; ☿ 5:30am-2:30pm Mon-Thu, 5:30am-8pm Fri, 5:30am-3pm Sat & Sun

SLEEP

Copley Inn
Has kitchenettes and is close to both Copley Sq and the subway. ☎ 617-236-0300; www .copleyinn.com; 19 Garrison St, Boston, MA; r $115-165

Midtown Hotel
Pets are welcome at this Back Bay hotel, with a pool, clean rooms and easy access to Boston. ☎ 617-262-1000, 1800-343-1177; www.midtownhotel.com; 220 Huntington Ave, Boston; r $250 🐾

Sandy Neck Motel
Cute rooms hidden behind what must be one of the world's largest American flags. ☎ 508-362-3992, 1-800-564-3992; www .sandyneck.com; 669 Rte 6A, East Sandwich; r $119-299

USEFUL WEBSITES
www.chowhound.com

LINK YOUR TRIP
www.lonelyplanet.com/trip-planner

The Mohawk Trail

WHY GO Though trade along this 66-mile route has gone from real furs to the faux kind, New England's oldest scenic highway holds sweet sweets, cozy B&Bs, spectacular scenery and even an emu or two... all part of the fun in this quick trip.

Once a trading route for the Mohawk tribe, fur trappers and explorers, the Mohawk Trail was the first scenic road in New England and is one of America's oldest byways. Take your time to explore this short stretch of history. Start at the eastern end of the trail with a gander at the ❶ **Chapin Library of Rare Books**, on the Williams College campus in Williamstown. Among the documents you'll find an original printing of the Declaration of Independence, the British retort and a host of other national treasures. The Chapin Library is in temporary quarters until 2011 due to renovations; however, the important documents are still viewable in the college's art museum. Among Williamstown's many lodging options is the ❷ **Northside Motel**, a big rambling colonial farmhouse with white clapboards, green shutters, a pool and a nest of cozy rooms inside.

Head along Rte 2 to nearby ❸ **North Adams**, an historical town with atmospheric brick warehouses and old industrial mills. Just past the center of town you'll find the turnoff for the ❹ **Natural Bridge State Park**. Once a marble quarry, this spot has a maze of bridges and walkways offering views of the only naturally eroded marble arch in the country and enough damp, clammy rocks to make you feel like you're in an adventure movie set.

Next, head up, up and away – past *the* ❺ **Hairpin Turn** to the ❻ **West Summit Overlook**, so high up you'll feel ready to circle like a condor up into the clouds. At the summit's ❼ **Wigwam and Western Summit** store, you can get gifts that range from corny to cute, but the biggest reason to stop is the fudge: rich, creamy and as good as it gets. Yum!

TIME
2 days

DISTANCE
65 miles

BEST TIME TO GO
May – Oct

START
Williamstown

END
After Erving

ALSO GOOD FOR

HISTORY &
CULTURE

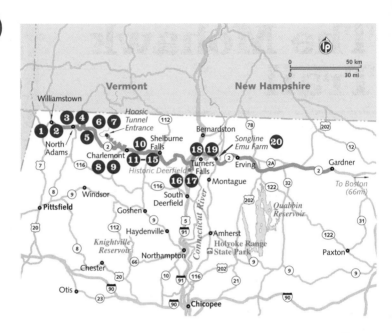

Descending back into the valley, on your right you'll pass the stately **8** **Hail to the Sunrise** statue in Mohawk Park and the **9** **Charlemont Federated Church** in (no surprise) Charlemont. The latter is a classic example of church architecture of the time and remains a community centerpiece centuries later.

If the spirit of adventure hits, try a river rafting trip with **10** **CrabApple Whitewater, Inc**, where you and up to five pals can whoop, holler and freeze your butt off as you head downstream. Depending on the location and the water level, trips can range from mild to I-need-to-change-my-shorts, so be ready to use that adrenalin rush.

The **Hoosic Tunnel**, started in 1851, runs for almost 5 miles and was the second-longest tunnel in the world at the time of its completion in 1875. Nicknamed the Bloody Pit for the number of (often gruesome) deaths during construction, it remains the longest tunnel in the eastern USA. The northern entrance is in North Adams, off an unmarked dirt road frequented by bear, deer and fishers.

ready to use that adrenalin rush.

Swing into sleepy lil **11** **Shelburne Falls** for a bite to eat or a stroll along the riverside, or join the kids swimming or playing on the riverbank. **12** **Mole Hollow Candle Factory**, over-looking the falls, offers old-fashioned dipped tapers in a variety of colors and sizes, including 100% beeswax and, for when that power outage leaves you with neither light nor food, *edible* soy. A little upstream you'll find the **13** **Bridge of Flowers**, where you can meander among blooms on this ex-trolley bridge. Since 1928 it has only been used for foot traffic and in 1929 fundraising allowed the town to transform the bridge into the blooming spectacle it is today, with on-going support and maintenance from the Shelburne Falls Women's Club.

Do not miss a bite to eat at ⑭ **Café Martin**, a lunch and dinner spot in the center of the main street. This casual, European-feel café is often packed with people waiting for the gourmet sandwiches, excellent soups and a variety of tasty main dishes. Don't be deterred – it's worth the wait. Across the street, ⑮ **Mocha Maya's Coffee House & Espresso Bar** has live music, free trade and organic cups o' Joe and open mic nights.

"…you can whoop, holler and freeze your butt off as you head downstream."

Continuing east, step back in time at ⑯ **Historic Deerfield**. Built hundreds of years ago when the Mohawk Trail actually had Mohawk tribe members on it, 13 of the houses here are in original condition – you can feel Hester Prynne's spirit peeking through a time-rippled windowpane. Don't miss the robin's-egg-blue house, the original color of the house of a well-to-do lawyer who wanted no doubts about which abode was his. The ⑰ **Visitors Center** in town can get you brochures, information on the living history demonstrations and help with lodging suggestions.

The flower-festooned gardens and stately bookshelf-lined rooms at the ⑱ **Poetry Ridge B&B** will force you to leave your stresses at the doorstep. Sip a cool julep in the afternoon on the verandah and watch the humming-birds, or play a round of billiards in the cellar. If time permits, head up to ⑲ **Poetry Ridge** itself and have your hat blown off as you admire the view. It's windy up here! A sonnet, anyone?

If someone on your souvenir list has everything and has seen it all, try giving them an emu steak to barbecue. ⑳ **Songline Emu Farm** has birdie bacon, steaks and other emu special-ties. It's worth just going out back and giggling at the funky birds themselves – you can almost hear the prehistoric-looking creatures, head cocked to the side, asking, "Hey, what are *you* looking at?".

GLACIAL EXOTICS

Just downstream from the Shelburne Falls dam is an exposed area of rock where you can see **Glacial Potholes**. Over time, small stones trapped in river currents ate away at the rock below, making remarkable holes and depressions – some are tiny, others are several feet in diameter. It's well worth taking the time to pick your way around and look at some as you contemplate what a few pebbles and a couple of centuries of rinsing can do.

From here, Rte 2, which from Montague to Harvard is called the Johnny Appleseed Trail, heads east into Boston. The lakes, marshes, swamps and forests along this route make for a leisurely trip before you hit the city suburbs.
Ray Bartlett

TRIP INFORMATION

GETTING THERE

To reach the western end of the Mohawk Trail in Williamstown from Boston, take Memorial Drive to Rte 2, then follow it for 60 miles (approximately one hour).

DO

Chapin Library of Rare Books

Houses American Revolution–era documents our Founding Fathers penned. Currently being remodeled but still open for viewing. ☎ 413-597-2462; www.williams.edu /resources/chapin; 26 Hopkins Hall Dr, Williamstown; admission free; ☺ 10am-noon & 1-5pm Mon-Fri

CrabApple Whitewater, Inc

Adrenaline flows faster than the river on these wild rafting trips down the Deerfield River. ☎ 413-625-2288, 1800-553-7238; www.crabapplewhitewater.com; 2056 Mohawk Trail, Charlemont; adult/child $87/69

Historic Deerfield

Centuries-old houses authentically restored, plus demos and living-history exhibits. ☎ 413-775-7214; www.historic-deerfield .org; 80 Old Main St, Deerfield; adult/child $14/5; ☺ 9:30am-4:30pm; ♿ ⊛

Natural Bridge State Park

USA's only natural marble arch and a stately old quarry. ☎ 413-663-6392; www.mass .gov/dcr/parks/western/nbdg.htm; McCauley Rd, off Rte 8, North Adams; parking $2; ☺ 9am-5pm Memorial Day-Columbus Day

Songline Emu Farm

Find facial creams, hair oil, birdie steaks and more at this farm for one of the world's funkiest fowls. ☎ 413-863-2700, 1866-539-2996; www.songlineemufarm.com; 66 French King Hwy, Gill; tours adult/child

$3/2; ☺ store noon-5pm Tue-Sat, tours on demand Apr 15-Oct 15; ♿

EAT

Café Martin

Scrumptious specialty soups, salads, sandwiches and mains in a shishifoofoo setting. ☎ 413-625-2795; www.cafemartin.wp.net; 24 Bridge St, Shelburne Falls; mains $15; ☺ 11am-3pm & 5pm-close Tue-Sun

Mocha Maya's Coffee House & Espresso Bar

Cups of great organic free-trade coffee in a hip, clean, classic coffeehouse. It sometimes stays open late for live music. ☎ 413-625-6292; www.mochamayas.com; 47 Bridge St, Shelburne Falls; mains $5; ☺ 6am-7pm Mon-Sat, 7am-6pm Sun

Wigwam and Western Summit

Mouthwatering fudge and gorgeous views from this up-in-the-clouds summit stop. ☎ 413-663-3205; www.thewigwam. net; 2350 Mohawk Trail, North Adams; ☺ 10:30am-6pm Tue-Sun, closed Dec 25-Jan 31

SLEEP

Northside Motel

Friendly, family-run inn with cozy rooms, a pool and a great Williamstown location. ☎ 413-458-8107; www.northsidemotel.com; 45 North St, Williamstown; r $79-129; ♿

Poetry Ridge B&B

Wonderfully restored old building, flower-festooned gardens and lots of light in this great stopover spot. ☎ 413-773-5143; www .rkotours.com; 55 Stone Ridge Lane, Greenfield; r $125-295

USEFUL WEBSITES

http://gorp.away.com

www.mohawktrail.com

www.lonelyplanet.com/trip-planner

LINK YOUR TRIP

Buried in Boston

WHY GO Ever want to see the ghost of Sam Adams or if Paul Revere is haunting the North End? No guarantees you'll see a spirit, but you can see some of Boston's oldest headstones in this cemetery trip that might just make you shiver if the moon is full.

This trip would ideally start at midnight when the moon is full, but truth be told, you won't see much in the dark and most of the attractions will be closed. Instead, start off with a nice cup of coffee at ❶ Caffé Vittoria, in the North End. Sip that latte and head to ❷ Copp's Hill Burying Ground, one of the oldest cemeteries in Boston, where you can hunt for bullet holes from the American Revolution in the headstones. What you won't see are gravestones for the African Americans who lived in Boston's "New Guinea" at the base of the hill, and are buried here in unmarked graves near Snowhill St.

Follow the Freedom Trail toward downtown and you'll soon come to King's Chapel, the oldest in Boston. Surrounded by the skyscrapers and buildings of downtown Boston is the ❸ King's Chapel Burial Ground, where, among other resting souls, you'll find William Emerson, father to the more famous Ralph Waldo, and Mary Chilton, who is thought to have been the first woman to land at Plymouth, when she was just 13.

Just around the corner on Tremont St you'll find the ❹ Granary Burial Ground, a beautiful cemetery with rows of chipped, time-worn headstones presided over by the matronly Park St Church. Here a little headstone hunting will reveal the final resting spots of a number of well-known Bostonians, including Paul Revere, Samuel Adams and John Hancock.

TIME
1-2 days

DISTANCE
35 miles

BEST TIME TO GO
May–Nov

START
North End, Boston

END
Waterfront, Boston

ALSO GOOD FOR

HISTORY & CULTURE

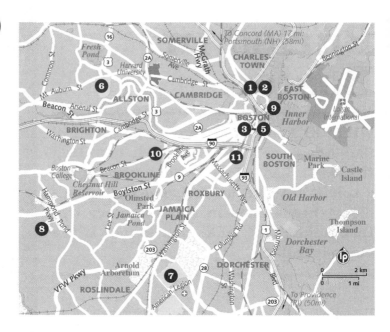

You can rest your feet, have a bite to eat or quaff a refreshing beverage where many of the folks whose gravesites you've seen surely dined. Open continuously since 1826 and thus Boston's oldest restaurant, the **5** **Union Oyster House** is nicely located right between the North End and Downtown. This

DETOUR Detour 20 miles out to Concord and you can stop in at **Sleepy Hollow Cemetery**…but don't go thinking you'll run into Ichabod Crane or anyone headless galloping around. Despite the identical names, this peaceful quiet spot isn't at all connected with the famous legend, which takes place in New York, near the Hudson River. Instead, here you'll find Author's Ridge, where Henry David Thoreau, Ralph Waldo Emerson, Louisa May Alcott and other famous authors lie.

venerable institution offers plenty of familiar modern items (including microbrews and Clams Casino) along with some quirky throwbacks to the Victorian era such as Indian pudding or oyster stew. The latter is an interesting, if a bit bland, taste of the 19th century.

Suitably stuffed, take a long walk or a short taxi ride up to Cambridge and find **6** **Mount Auburn Cemetery**, one of the most exclusive (read: expensive) spots in the country to be buried. Anyone interred here is in good company: numerous Harvard literati, eminent scholars and Boston Brahmin headed here when the dealing was done. This cemetery was the first in a movement of planned public open spaces and is now a National Historic Landmark. Indeed, with graceful walkways and gentle knolls, it seems more like a public park than a cemetery compared with the older cemeteries you've just visited – if it weren't for the somber marble monuments every few yards reminding you where you are. ❼ **Forest Hills Cemetery** is similarly scenic and was likewise designed not only with the dead but also the living in mind. Pass through the imposing stone entry gate and the place opens up – peaceful acres of grass, small hills, winding walkways and, of course, graves. Poets ee cummings and Anne Sexton are buried here, along with other notables such as playwright Eugene O'Neill.

The final stop in this cemetery whirl is the ❽ **Holyhood Cemetery**, where you'll find the parents of John F Kennedy, as well as the well-loved Arthur Fiedler, conductor of the Boston Pops Orchestra, and lesser-known but still loved Julius A Palmer, aid and friend to Hawaii's last queen, Lili'uokalani. The two lobbied President McKinley unsuccessfully for the return of sovereignty to the Hawaiian Kingdom after it was annexed by white plantation owners.

Return to Boston and reward yourself with a meal at ❾ **Sel de la Terre**, right on the waterfront. This wonderful French dining spot has local seafood and produce – it's a restaurant so good you'd expect to find it in Lyon rather than near the Boston Aquarium. In addition to excellent standards such as rib-eye steak or salmon, you can also find more unusual fruits of the sea such as monkfish, which is often discarded as worthless when caught in a net with haddock or cod. Using so-called "trash" fish takes pressure off the breeding stocks of traditional fish while exposing diners to new taste sensations.

TAPHOPHILIA TRIVIA

The "Winged Death's Head," an image of a skull with wings in the center frequently seen on gravestones, didn't mean the deceased was a member of a hellish motorcycle group. This symbol is interpreted today in many ways – from basic good luck to the totality and release of earthly shackles for a better world and it's likely it symbolized a range of things even back in the 1700s. Once a common motif, the Winged Death's Head eventually morphed into the far more photogenic but less death-related cherub.

When you're ready to turn in, head to the ❿ **Beech Tree Inn**, a friendly, tastefully decorated B&B near Coolidge Corner, steps away from the T and close to Holyhood Cemetery. This 19th-century Victorian-era home is intimate and cozy, with smallish but attractively furnished rooms – each has its own TV and there is wi-fi as well. The little patio beckons you to have a last cup of coffee before you turn in. For something more cosmopolitan, try the friendly ⓫ **Chandler Inn Hotel**, a boutique hotel with a nice bar-lounge on the 1st floor, perfect for tippling or meeting friends. Rooms have a stylish European feel – minimalist yet classy. Hit the pillow and prepare to snore.

Ray Bartlett

TRIP INFORMATION

GETTING THERE
Boston is one hour south of Portsmouth, NH, and one hour north of Providence, RI.

DO

Copp's Hill Burying Ground
Seventeenth-century cemetery right in the scenic North End, with American Revolution–era bullet holes in a few headstones. **cnr Hull & Snowhill Sts, Boston;** ⊙ 9am-5pm

Forest Hills Cemetery
Early cemetery designed as a public space, with lots of green trees and a castle-like entryway. ☎ 401-598-2805; www.foresthills cemetery.com; 95 Forest Hills Ave, Boston; ⊙ dawn-dusk

Granary Burial Ground
This spot has rows of orderly headstones and a monument to the parents of Benjamin Franklin. **Tremont St, Boston;** ⊙ 9am-5pm

Holyhood Cemetery
Pleasant spot and a good stop for Kennedy fans or Hawaiian history buffs. ☎ 617-327-1010; www.holyhood.com; 990 LaGrange St, West Roxbury; ⊙ dawn-dusk

King's Chapel Burial Ground
An old Boston burial ground that boasts, among others, the first gal to step ashore in Plymouth. **Tremont St btwn School & Park Sts;** ⊙ 9am-5pm

Mount Auburn Cemetery
These premium plots will set you back the cost of an education at the university across the street. ☎ 617-547-7105; www.mount auburn.org; 580 Mount Auburn St, Cambridge; ⊙ 8:30am-5pm Oct-Apr, 8:30am-7pm May-Sep

EAT

Caffé Vittoria
Get iced coffee in summer or *café corretto* (espresso with grappa) as a winter warmer. ☎ 617-227-7606; www.vittoriacaffe.com; 290-296 Hanover St, Boston; coffees $3; ⊙ 6am-midnight

Sel de la Terre
This not-so-rustic "rustic French" restaurant has great service and even better food. ☎ 617-720-1300; www.seldelaterre.com; 255 State St, Boston; mains $25-35; ⊙ 11am-11pm

Union Oyster House
Boston's oldest restaurant offers mains and desserts that hearken back to Victorian days. ☎ 617-227-2750; www.unionoysterhouse .com; 41 Union St, Boston; dinner mains $20-30; ⊙ 11am-9:30pm Sun-Thu, 11am-10pm Fri & Sat

SLEEP

Beech Tree Inn
In a quiet neighborhood, this cozy B&B has a convenient help-yourself breakfast included with your stay. ☎ 617-277-1620, 800-544-9660; www.thebeechtreeinn.com; 83 Long-wood Ave, Brookline; r $119-179

Chandler Inn Hotel
Friendly staff, small rooms but clean and nicely decorated. ☎ 617-482-3450, 800-842-3450; www.chandlerinn.com; 26 Chandler St, Boston; r $115-165

USEFUL WEBSITES
www.cityofboston.gov/parks/HBGI

LINK YOUR TRIP
TRIP
www.lonelyplanet.com/trip-planner

Massachusetts: Farmstand Fresh

WHY GO Had your fill of supermarket-prepared "food", cotton-flavored strawberries and mealy peaches? These farmers markets, recommended by the MA Department of Agriculture's David Webber, will inspire you to get back to the core of cookery – fresh produce, organic meats and the inspiration to do delicious things with them.

This trip is all about hunting and gathering. Whether you're holding a legendary dinner party, stocking the freezer for winter (mmm…soup), trying to go the healthy route, or wanting to steer away from chain megamarkets and support your local farmers, this trip takes you to the best spots to pick and choose the best products from the best farms.

"These are all top quality markets," Webber says. "But there are so many to choose from that it's difficult to list them all." First, he'd start off in Main St, Hyannis, on Wednesday. There are scores of fresh veggies from Cape growers, in-season produce, soaps and lotions – perfect for impressing your dinner guests when they visit to the bathroom. The ❶ Mid-Cape Farmers Market is Cape-only, save for certain preapproved prepared goods (such as jams or jellies…jam tarts for dessert, perhaps?), so you know that everything you see is fresh. Many Cape growers also offer organic foods. With all that dinner-party planning, it's time to treat yourself: get your ingredients at the market then cross Main St to the Village Green for a picnic lunch on the open green lawn among the winding pathways, with the town hall behind you overseeing it all.

On Thursday, Webber recommends hitting the ❷ Plymouth Farmers Market at Stephen's Field. Folk music and a plethora of choices mean you're best off meandering around for a bit prior to making your purchases. Among the more interesting options is worms – add them

TIME
5 days

DISTANCE
420 miles

BEST TIME TO GO
Wed – Sat,
May – Oct

START
Hyannis

END
Boston

113

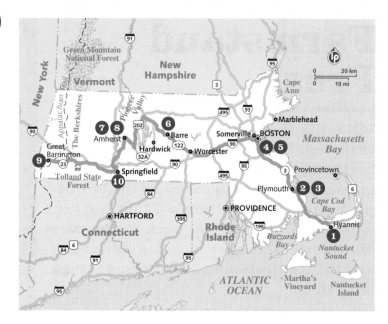

to your garden soil and flower boxes, or bake them into cookies for that schoolteacher you can't stand. You can't go wrong staying at the ❸ **Auberge Gladstone B&B**, only a 20-minute walk or a mere three-minute drive from the market, which offers several cozy rooms (including one in the attic), nice views of Cape Cod Bay and a Jacuzzi.

> *"…bushels of bright green cucumbers or rows of brilliant orange pumpkins make the Common come alive."*

In the big city it's easy to forget to slow down and smell the freshly baked artisan loaves. Take a stroll through the ❹ **Copley Square Farmers Market** in Boston, held on Tuesdays and Fridays. With ❺ **Trinity Church** looking on like a stately matron, the market has organic and sustainable farming produce, including a great variety of greens and herbs and fresh bread that begs you to bite into it. But try to resist: your purchases will make for a slow, relaxing evening of cooking and gorging.

Stop off in Barre on Saturday at the ❻ **Barre Farmers Market** in the Town Common, where you can get the usual produce and herbs. Buy some alpaca yarn and knit a sweater or hat to keep those cold Nor'easters at bay. Artists may want to bring a sketchpad: the bushels of bright green cucumbers or rows of brilliant orange pumpkins make the Common come alive.

Operating for more than five years, the Saturday ❼ **Amherst Farmers Market** is not to be missed. Set in the particularly quaint Amherst Village Common, this is the premier spot to snag and bag as much organic produce as you can; you'll also find organic meats such as lamb and pork and a host of other natural and sustainable items. Think of those dishes you've always meant to have a try at cooking – warming casseroles, rich *ragù*, roasts. Buy up big here then find a decent kitchen and have a cookfest.

If you're stuck for ideas of what to do with your purchases, seek inspiration at ❽ **Tabella Restaurant**, which is dedicated to small farms and local produce and even specifies which farm the ingredients have come from. Go on a Saturday and chances are that some of the ingredients were bought right there at the market you visited that afternoon. "Amherst is definitely a great one to include if you can," Webber recommends. "It's really one of the best. The produce is very high quality, with lots of organic [items]. The location by the Common in the town center is very quaint…".

BOSTON'S TOMATO FESTIVAL

City Hall Plaza can't get riper or juicier than it is during the **Annual Tomato Festival**, held every summer in late July or early August. No, you can't pelt the nearest politician, but you might be tempted to take a bite out of the succulent selections. Farmers and tomato fans from around the state come to see the cornucopia of heirloom, grape, beefsteak and more.

There are also some other Saturday options. Held at the old Great Barrington railroad station, the ❾ **Great Barrington Farmers Market** offers visitors a chance to sample the abundance of produce these beautiful mountains provide. There are lots of flowers, herbs, potted plants and perennials here – a visit gives the phrase "garden variety" a whole new meaning. Nothing run of the mill, just produce that's "Massachusetts grown…and fresher," as the slogan says. Grab some treats for the next stop on your trip, or invest in greening up your house with actual living things. A quaint notion, we know – just don't forget to water them!

In Springfield, ❿ **Naomi's Inn** has deliciously decadent rooms and pillows so plush you'll be begging for nap time – a perfect spot to stop overnight if you're too tired to head all the way back to

ASK A LOCAL

"It's hard work, but it ends up being inspirational. Seeing how much the produce is appreciated, seeing people come to purchase fresh vegetables and seeing new people understand all the variety that's available makes everything worth it. Customers tell me they didn't realize how different it tastes, or how many different kinds of fruits and vegetables there are. That's what farmers markets mean to me and why I keep farming."

Veronica Worthington, Mid-Cape Farmers Market, Hyannis

Boston. "Springfield [Tuesday] also has a great market," Webber adds. "Other suggestions are Hardwick [Sunday], Somerville [Wednesday] or Marblehead [Saturday]. This list represents some of the best markets in the state in terms of variety of offerings, or nice locations and exceptional market managers."
Ray Bartlett

TRIP 13

TRIP INFORMATION

GETTING THERE

From Boston, take I-93 south to RT-3, then US-6 to Exit 6 and follow the signs.

DO

Amherst Farmers Market

Big market in the historic Amherst Village Common, offering organic produce and a variety of organic meat cuts. ☎ 413-786-2335; www.farmersmarketamherst.com; 5 South Pleasant St, Amherst; ⏱ 7:30am-1:30pm Sat May 3-Nov 15

Barre Farmers Market

Alpaca yarn is an unusual item at this popular, friendly town market that's off the beaten path. ☎ 978-355-0140; www.barre farmersmarket.com; Town Common, Barre; ⏱ 9am-12:30pm Sat May-Oct

Copley Square Farmers Market

Bread and garden greens in a great downtown setting – pick up something yummy and eat it on the steps of nearby Trinity Church. **Copley Sq, Boston;** ⏱ 11am-6pm Tue & Fri May 20-Nov 25

Great Barrington Farmers Market

Great fruit 'n' veg straight from the garden – produce, flowers and herbs. **Former Railroad Station, Great Barrington;** ⏱ 9am-1pm Sat May 10-Oct 25

Mid-Cape Farmers Market

Cape Cod–only market in a central location where you can stock up on produce, veggies and other fresh foods. **232 Main St, Hyannis;** ⏱ 8am-noon Wed Jun 11-Sep 3

Plymouth Farmers Market at Stephen's Field

Popular spot for all the usual suspects and a few odd ones – such as worms. ☎ 508-732-9962; www.plymouthfarmersmarket.com; Stephen's Field, off Rte 3A, Plymouth; ⏱ 2:30-6:30pm Thu Jun 19-Oct 30

EAT

Tabella Restaurant

Only locally grown produce is served at this fine spot to wine and dine. ☎ 413-253-0220; www.tabellarestaurant.com; 28 Amity St, Amherst; mains $12-15; ⏱ 5:30-10pm Mon-Thu, 5:30-11pm Fri & Sat, 5:30-9pm Sun

SLEEP

Auberge Gladstone B&B

The cozy rooms here include a Jacuzzi and are a mere meander from the Plymouth Farmers Market. ☎ 508-830-1890; www.auberge gladstone.com; 8 Vernon St, Plymouth; r $125

Naomi's Inn

Opulent yet comfortable, Naomi's is a plush escape that will leave you well rested come the morn. ☎ 413-732-3924, 1-888-762-6647; www.naomisinn.net; 20 Springfield St, Springfield; r $135

USEFUL WEBSITES

www.massfarmersmarkets.org
www.mass.gov/agr/massgrown/farmers
_markets.htm

LINK YOUR TRIP   www.lonelyplanet.com/trip-planner

Book Hunting in the Pioneer Valley

WHY GO Nestled along the fertile banks of the Connecticut River are the state's best secondhand bookstores, as well as some great spots for a bite or an overnight stay. Search for something special to read out loud on the road.

Book hunting is hungry work, so let's take care of that first at ❶ **Donut Dip**, an independent doughnut shop in West Springfield. Come in as early as 3am for soft, chewy doughnuts or the popular apple fritter (large enough to split). Take something for the road, then head for ❷ **Sage Books** in Southampton. Housed in a delightful home complete with front porch and flower garden, with books neatly arranged by section on floor-to-ceiling shelves, walking in here feels like stepping into a children's library, where everything is neatly placed – even the cats seem to know exactly where they are supposed to be. There's something for everyone here and don't forget to find the plate of homemade cookies to munch on as you find some reading matter for the road.

Keep going on Rte 10 until you hit ❸ **Northampton**. With its wide streets and cluster of shops, there's plenty to see and do here for anyone, even those who aren't book inclined. Bookworms will want to seek out ❹ **Raven Used Books**, which has all sorts of bibliographic goodness, set out in long shelves across an L-shaped basement in a brick building. This shop specializes in academic and scholarly works, among others, and is also a central part of the Northampton community – it's not unlikely that you'll see a tattooed bicycle courier politely stepping aside to let someone in a tweed jacket and khakis get to the book he needs. Right nearby, ❺ **Pride & Joy** offers gay- and lesbian-related items, including books, literature and postcards, and is a source of info about Northampton gay and lesbian events.

When you start getting hunger pangs, cross the street and find ❻ **Lhasa Café**, a wonderful little Tibetan restaurant where you'll dine

TIME
2 days

DISTANCE
54 miles

BEST TIME TO GO
May – Oct

START
West Springfield

END
Bernardston

HISTORY & CULTURE

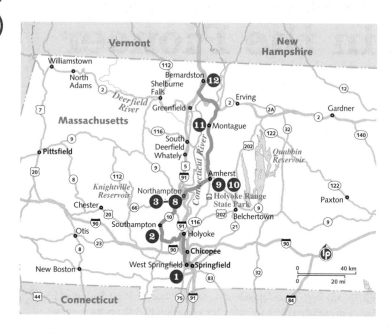

beneath a panoramic photo of the café's namesake that's so large you'll almost feel like you've landed in Tibet. You'll want to spend time reading the menu here; don't be afraid to ask questions. Of the many options you can sample here, perhaps the most authentic Tibetan fare is yak, offered in a variety of ways. The *momo* (pot-sticker-type dumplings) are fantastic. *Bocha*, a salty and buttered Tibetan chai-like drink is unusual. Served hot, it's not really the best drink option for a summer afternoon. For that, you'll want to make your way to ❼ **Ben & Bill's Chocolate Emporium**, a few stores down, where a large, malty, perfect frappe will soothe and satisfy. You can pick up other sweets here too: the ice cream and chocolates are all handmade and just stepping inside this narrow, dark store will make you want a sample.

> **DETOUR** Step back to childhood with a trip to the **Eric Carle Museum of Picture Book Art**, in Amherst, MA. Who doesn't remember *The Very Hungry Caterpillar* and other wonderful tales? This new museum has a history of this well-loved illustrator, numerous galleries of his and other artists' work including that of much-celebrated Maurice Sendak, an art studio where future illustrators can master the craft of the crayon and a café where weary parents can soothe souls and soles. Ready for a Wild Rumpus, anyone?

The ❽ **Hotel Northampton**, right in the center of town, is a fancy spot in a neat old building with lots of air and glass. Rooms vary substantially but your best bet is to ask for one of the two double-balcony queen rooms. These rooms have an outside balcony overlooking the street and an inside balcony that opens into the glassed-in entrance to the lobby. Even from the street, the artfully arranged bottles of liquor in the tavern and café seem to beckon passersby to come inside, shed the worries of the day and sip something soothing in the warm afternoon sunlight.

Cross over the Connecticut River and meander into Amherst, where you'll find the aptly named **9 Amherst Books**, a new-and-used bookstore with three floors to linger on. Feel free to scan the shelves, plop down in a comfortable chair, or pick up art cards and postcards to send home. Stay at the snug, artfully restored **10 Allen House Inn**, where you'll find rooms with wonderful Victorian clutter, period wallpaper and many fine antiques. The beds are soft and springy and many rooms have long gilded mirrors and so many elegant touches that it's not hard to imagine that Emily Dickinson might be sleeping in the next room or come walking down the dark stairway, pen and paper in hand.

> *"...it's not hard to imagine that Emily Dickinson might be sleeping in the next room..."*

The **11 Montague Bookmill**, located in a wonderful old mill building, is now a used bookstore, coffeehouse and café. The dusty wooden floors, narrow stairways tucked in the back and wide planking all serve as reminders of the building's industrial past. The soothing sounds of the river waft in through the windows, sunbeams dance upon the shelves, and the staff are happy to both help and let you browse in uninterrupted leisure.

MEETINGHOUSE BOOKS

Meetinghouse Books (www.meetinghouse books.com) in South Deerfield is one of those classic bookstores, with cardboard boxes splitting at the seams and towering piles of books. The high ceilings are a reminder of the building's previous life as a chapel, and the air is redolent with the smell of well-thumbed pages. It's a great spot to find rare and out-of-print items, or to chat with the owners. Check out the prints and engravings and pat a cat before you leave. Call ahead in the dead of winter (January to February) before swinging by.

Finish off with a stop at **12 Bernardston Books** in Bernardston, housed in a garage on a shaded lawn at the back of the owner's house, where books on history in general and military history specifically are the primary focus. It's a good spot to come when you know exactly what you're looking for and calling first is recommended. Hours vary – don't be afraid to knock on a few doors if you have to.

Ray Bartlett

HISTORY & CULTURE

TRIP INFORMATION

GETTING THERE
From Boston, follow I-90 west for three hours until you hit Springfield.

DO

Amherst Books
Primarily new books in a nice, clean, comfortable spot in central Amherst. ☎ 413-256-1547, 800-503-5865; www.amherstbooks.com; 8 Main St, Amherst; ☉ 6:30am-9pm Mon-Sat, 6:30am-5pm Sun

Bernardston Books
Offers a variety of historical books out of a garage, with an emphasis on military history. ☎ 413-648-9864; www.abebooks.com/home/bernbook; 219 South St, Bernardston; ☉ 9am-5pm

Montague Bookmill
An old mill building infused with new life as a bookstore, café and coffeehouse. The river setting is perfect for a long, slow browse. ☎ 413-367-9206; www.montaguebookmill.com; 440 Greenfield Rd, Montague; ☉ 10am-6pm Mon-Wed, 10am-8pm Thu-Sun, hours vary seasonally

Pride & Joy
Gay and lesbian books, cards, fiction and souvenirs at this Northampton store. ☎ 413-585-0683; www.nohoprideandjoy.com; 20 Crafts Ave, Northampton; ☉ 10am-6pm Mon-Wed, 10am-9pm Thu-Sat, noon-6pm Sun, hours vary seasonally

Raven Used Books
A basement taken up by long shelves that never have a chance to collect dust. ☎ 413-584-9868; www.ravenusedbooks.com; 4 Old South St, Northampton; ☉ 10am-9pm Mon-Thu, 10am-10pm Fri & Sat, 11am-7pm Sun

Sage Books
Freshly baked cookies and cute cats make browsing here a pleasure. ☎ 413-527-7703; www.sagebks.com; 220 College Hwy (Rte 10), Southampton; ☉ noon-5pm Tue, Wed & Fri, noon-9pm Thu, 10am-5pm Sat

EAT

Ben & Bill's Chocolate Emporium
Homemade and oh-so-delicious, this chocolate and ice-cream parlor won't disappoint. ☎ 413-584-5695; www.benandbills.com; 141 Main St, Northampton; cones from $3; ☉ 11am-9pm; ⚒

Donut Dip
Freshly baked and tender, you won't find these doughnuts sitting around for long before they're grabbed, dunked and devoured. ☎ 413-733-9604; 1305 Riverdale Rd, West Springfield; doughnuts from 90c, 6 doughnuts $5.89; ☉ 3am-midnight; ⚒

Lhasa Café
Wash down yak meat with some *bocha* and you'll swear you're in Tibet. ☎ 413-586-5427; www.lhasacafe.com; 159 Main St, Northampton; mains from $10; ☉ noon-3pm & 5-9:30pm Mon-Thu, noon-10pm Fri & Sat, noon-9:30pm Sun

SLEEP

Allen House Inn
Emily Dickinson would surely approve of this beautifully restored Victorian. ☎ 413-253-5000; www.allenhouse.com; 599 Main St, Amherst; r $75-195

Hotel Northampton
Grand ole hotel in the town center with interesting history and two funky, double-balconied rooms. ☎ 413-584-3100; www.hotelnorthampton.com; 36 King St, Northampton; r $210-450

USEFUL WEBSITES
www.mariab.org
www.valleyvisitor.com

LINK YOUR TRIP

www.lonelyplanet.com/trip-planner

Cape Ann Curiosities

WHY GO Don't think Cape Ann is just widow's walks and long-dead sailing lore. One of New England's most vibrant fishing towns, an artist colony, pumpkin beer, purebred hot dogs and even a town that went – literally – to the dogs all await Cape Ann visitors.

Start this trip in scenic ❶ **Gloucester**, one of New England's oldest and most authentic fishing ports. It's a pretty place to walk around and early birds will want to bring their cameras – few sights are more classic New England than that of a rusted, battered fishing boat cutting its way through the mist-kissed, glassy water as it leaves the harbor. The fishing industry may be in dire straits, but it hasn't lost any of its romance or allure. If it's hot out you can cool down with a decidedly chilly ❷ **Cape Pond Ice** tour, which still operates today as Gloucester's only ice supply. Tour the frigid premises (bring your coat, brrr!), see the ice sculptures, pick up a T-shirt (à la Bugsy in *The Perfect Storm*) or just marvel that ice can be measured by the ton.

Just around the corner is the ❸ **Cape Ann Brewing Company**, where you can take a tour, have tastes or snag a growler of your favorite ale to pass around at the campfire. This is a casual place where you'll be able to chat with the brewmaster if you want to, while sitting at the curved, natural wood bar that echoes the deck of a sailing vessel of old. The Fisherman's India Pale Ale (IPA) is a very solid competitor for the "other" Boston-area IPA. In season, try the pumpkin brew or any of the other varietals.

If ales tire, try wh-ales: ❹ **7 Seas Whale Watching** runs daily out to Stellwagen Bank National Marine Sanctuary, famous for humpback, minke and finback whales. Right whales are rare but in 2008 were seen here in record numbers. The biggest question on most travelers'

TIME
2 days

DISTANCE
25 miles

BEST TIME TO GO
May – Sep

START
Gloucester

END
Essex

ALSO GOOD FOR

HISTORY &
CULTURE

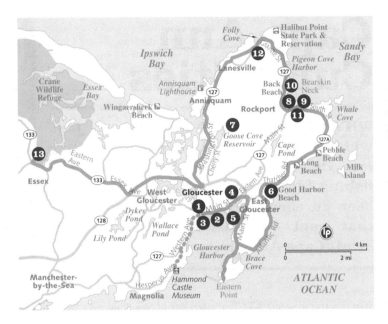

minds is "Will we see whales?" and the good news is that, excepting certain conditions, you will almost always spot a cetacean and usually the encounters are so close you may wish you had a bigger boat. Unlike many whale tours where you chase down migrating whales as they head to other places, at Stellwagen Bank the whales have stopped for active feeding. Sometimes they're all around the boat, but even if you're not close enough to smell their (foul, fishy) breath, you'll be near enough to get good glimpses. Behaviors to watch for are spy hopping (when the whale sticks its head out of the water and looks around, like a 50-ton bowling pin floating in the water), feeding (usually done by blowing a ring of bubbles to surround the sand eel prey, then lunging through the middle) or breaching (when the whale jumps out of the water). Few maritime sights can equal the awe of a 50-ton whale lifting itself entirely out of the water and then sending up a mountain of spray. The only real killjoy is fog – when it's foggy you'll be able to hear the whales, but rarely see them.

Landlubbers may prefer to wander over to the ➎ **Rocky Neck Artists' Colony**, one of America's oldest, where Winslow Homer, among numerous others, found solace and inspiration in this area's unique vistas, rocky crags, boats and pilings, and weathered Cape-style houses. No matter what the season, you'll find artists busy at their easels, framing their unique glimpses of this area and fleshing out their vision in many different mediums. This is one spot where you'll want to just follow your own aesthetic muse as you meander through the various galleries – take your time, talk with the artists and note how each medium, be it acrylic, oil, watercolor, pencil or film, changes the portrayal of the subject matter as much as the artist's individual vision does. As well as checking out the galleries, follow the road all the way out to the end of the point for several particularly scenic views, some of Rocky Neck and the colony, others of the harbor and the fishing boats. If you find yourself not wanting to leave this creative hub, the colony offers efficiencies right on the water, some with decks overlooking the water. The units are rustic, with beams in the ceilings harking back to the buildings' heritage as sail lofts. The colony site also has an abandoned (until recently) paint factory that will hopefully be preserved as a local landmark. This beautiful old building is visible even from the other side of the harbor:

DETOUR ▸ **Hammond Castle**, on the outskirts of Gloucester, is well worth a quick visit if you're looking for something out of the ordinary. Built during the late 1920s by eccentric inventor John Hays Hammond Jr, the Hammond Castle is complete with secret passages, optical illusions (the pool always looks deeper at the other end) and subterranean rooms to deter spying. Gardens, lookout towers, an armory and even a dungeon add to this faux Renaissance castle's ambience.

look for the brick-red, swaybacked old warehouse with white block letters on it. It serves not only as a beacon for returning fishers, but also as a roost for numerous seagulls and cormorants, who freely decorate it with their own form of paint.

The ❻ **Vista Motel**, slightly out of town, is right on the water, offering gorgeous water views. Rooms have refrigerators but not much else; however, few spots can beat the Vista for dawn walks along the seashore or a quiet cocktail sipped as the sun goes down.

Once you've seen whales, you're ready for dogs: ❼ **Dogtown**, a vast conservation area filled with hiking trails, forests, swamps and plenty of mosquitoes. The best access is via Cherry St, but there are a number of other entrances as well. This wacky spot literally went to the dogs – as sailors lost their lives at sea or were unable to return to their pets, the number of stray dogs in the area increased. Widows often fed the dogs or kept animals as protection and when they passed away, these semiferal animals shared the abandoned settlement with vagabonds and "witches." Eventually even these human inhabitants left. Buildings crumbled and were reclaimed by the forest. Now it is pristine conservation land, with rambling old rock walls with a foundation or two serving as the only visible reminders that this was once an actual town. As you wander through the trails, keep an eye out for any of the three dozen Babson Boulders inscribed with various mottos and sayings, such as "Truth" or "Keep Out of Debt". Commissioned by wealthy Roger Babson, these carvings provided out-of-work stonecutters with jobs during the Great Depression. The boulders, called glacial erratics by geologists, were placed here during the last ice age – as the ice melted, the trapped rocks and boulders within were deposited in piles, forming land masses (such as Cape Cod, in southern Massachusetts) or merely making the land untillable, as in Cape Ann.

After you've visited Dogtown, you might be oddly in the mood for Rockport's ❽ **Top Dog**, a hot-dog stand of international repute, where you can sample "Purebreds," "Bloodhounds" or even "Golden Retrievers" (as well as other "breeds") to the tune of a few George Washingtons. For dessert, breakfast or just a snack for the road, hit ❾ **Helmut's Strudel**, nearby, for light, crispy apple-filled phyllo bliss. Artists should check out ❿ **Motif #1**, a famous red-clapboard fisher's shack with a few tasteful lobster buoys that's right across from the pier. The former studio of painter John Buckley in the 1930s, this classic structure has formed the foundation of art and art history classes for decades.

At ⓫ **Seven South Street Inn** in Rockport you'll find antique glass in the windows (the kind with the warps and air bubbles in it), hundreds of years of history, incredibly sweet service from the owners and staff and ever-changing four-course gourmet breakfasts that have won regional awards and much acclaim. Rooms here vary in size, from cozily cramped to luxuriously spacious, but all are done tastefully, with floral patterns and a country style that will make you feel at home. Within walking distance from the center of Rockport, this is a perfect stopping place if you're ready to take a rest from the road.

"...the Paper House…will leave you wondering about the difference between determination and utter madness."

Following Rte 127, the next stop is the ⓬ **Paper House**, a sight that will leave you wondering about the difference between determination and utter madness. With walls, furniture and even the fireplace made of shellacked newspaper (about 100,000 newspapers were used), this abode is about as odd as can be. At first glance it's hard to even realize it's made of paper – it looks more like some kind of quilted cardboard. Only when you get right up close will you see the newsprint visible beneath the layers of long-brown shellac, which were originally merely going to be the insulation. Part of the fun is getting close enough to read the actual newsprint, which details the curiosities of the 1920s when the house was made. The grandfather clock is made using newspapers from every state (there were only 48 back then) with the various capitals clearly visible in the rolls. Though the fireplace is actually a real, usable (brick) fireplace that's been coated with paper, it goes without saying that this is a nonsmoking establishment.

Follow Rte 127 to Rte 128 and then turn on 133, passing some beautiful wave-slapped coves, rocky bluffs and weathered clapboard houses, and arrive at the **⑬ Essex Shipbuilding Museum**. Exhibits range from displays of the various shipbuilding tools to photographs of yesteryears' launchings. Amazingly enough, among the hundreds of successful launchings there were always a few that didn't quite go the way the builders had planned: a few newly christened vessels made it only as far as the end of the launching scaffold before capsizing. Ouch.

Ray Bartlett

TRIP INFORMATION

GETTING THERE
Reach Cape Ann from Boston on I-93 north to I-95/MA-128, then follow Rte 128 to Gloucester. The trip takes approximately 40 minutes.

DO

7 Seas Whale Watching
Head for Stellwagen Bank and its cetacean wonders – sunny days mean you'll almost always spot a whale. ☎ 978-283-1776, 888-283-1776; www.7seas-whalewatch.com; 63 Rogers St, Gloucester; tours adult/child $42/26; ⏱ tour times vary seasonally

Cape Ann Brewing Company
Beautiful malted barley combines with…oh, just go have a pint for yourself. Better yet, grab a growler. ☎ 978-281-4782; http://capeannbrewing.com; 27 Commercial St, Gloucester; admission free; ⏱ noon-6pm Thu-Sat & Mon

Cape Pond Ice
Ice makes the fishing world go round and you can see the process on this chill-filled tour. ☎ 978-283-0174; www.capepondice .com; 104 Commercial St, Gloucester; tours adult/child $10/6; ⏱ store 7:30am-4:30pm Mon-Fri, 7:30am-3pm Sat, 7am-noon Sun & holidays, tours 9:30am, 11am & 2pm Mon-Sat, 11am or by appointment Sun & holidays

Essex Shipbuilding Museum
Lots of history under the bow at this somber yet interesting museum. ☎ 978-768-7541; www.essexshipbuildingmuseum.org; 66 Main St, Essex; adult/child $7/6; ⏱ 10am-5pm Wed-Sun Jun-Oct, 10am-5pm Sat & Sun Nov-May

Paper House
Few sights are stranger than the paper house – built almost entirely from shellacked newspapers. ☎ 978-546-2629; www.paperhouse

rockport.com; 52 Pigeon Hill, Rockport; admission $1.50; ⏱ Apr 1-Oct 31

EAT

Helmut's Strudel
Flakey strudel worthy of the Old World and perfect for recharging the batteries, served in a teeny café near the water. ☎ 978-546-2824; 49 Bearskin Neck, Rockport; mains $3-10; ⏱ 7am-6pm daily Apr-Sep, 7am-6pm Sat & Sun Oct-Mar

Top Dog
Have your dog and eat it too at this hot-dog palace where you can order any "breed" you like. ☎ 978-546-0006; www.topdogrockport.com; 2 Doyles Cove Rd, Rockport; mains from $2.75; ⏱ 11am-4pm Mon-Thu, 11am-7pm Fri-Sun May–mid-Oct

SLEEP

Rocky Neck Artists' Colony
The colony offers rustic efficiencies right on the water. There's an additional charge of $15 for stays of less than three nights. ☎ 978-283-1625; www.rockyneckaccommodations.com; 43 Rocky Neck Ave, Gloucester; efficiencies per night $79-128, per week $450-700

Seven South Street Inn
Sweet staff and comfortable coziness at a well-located 300-year-old inn. The breakfasts can't be beat. ☎ 978-546-6708; www.sevensouthstreetinn.com; 7 South St, Rockport; r $94-189

Vista Motel
Has views of the ocean appropriate to the name, plenty of rooms and decent prices. ☎ 978-281-3410; www.vistamotel.com; 22 Thatcher Rd, Gloucester; r $75-150, efficiencies $85-180

USEFUL WEBSITES
www.capeannchamber.com

LINK YOUR TRIP

www.lonelyplanet.com/trip-planner

Pilgrims & Puritans

WHY GO Got a hankering to meet a Pilgrim in person, see Plymouth Rock, climb up the Pilgrim monument, learn about the Salem witch trials or see where much of this country's history began? Head to these museums and monuments that keep the memory of our earliest ancestors alive.

TIME
2 days

DISTANCE
269 miles

BEST TIME TO GO
Apr – Nov

START
Provincetwon

END
Boston

Start your trip in Provincetown, where the Pilgrims ended their journey across the Atlantic. Most people don't know that months before the "official" landing on Plymouth Rock, the Pilgrims arrived in Provincetown with the intention of making that their settlement. Despite the protected harbor and good fishing, they were unable to find a good source of reliable freshwater and so they headed off to Plymouth. The ❶ **Pilgrim Monument & Provincetown Museum** is a great way to look at the view, but you can dig deeper into the area's history at ❷ **Expedition Whydah** museum on Fisherman's Wharf, where you can see the oldest datable pirate gold ever found. The infamous *Sam Bellamy* sank in Wellfleet waters in 1717 and it wasn't until underwater archaeological explorer Barry Clifford came along that the wreck was uncovered.

Next, head for Sandwich along Route 6A, the ❸ **Old King's Highway**. Once a horse and buggy route, this winding road is still one of the Cape's prettiest. When you reach quaint Sandwich, one of the Cape's oldest towns, stretch your legs by stopping in at the ❹ **Brown Jug**, where you can get freshly made wraps, sandwiches, cookies and – as the name implies – even a bottle of wine with which to wash it down. With the waterwheel at the old mill, the white clapboard houses and the swans on the pond, the center of Sandwich is as pretty as a Cape Cod town can be. Those looking to stay overnight can step back into the 1850s at the ❺ **Isaiah Jones Homestead B&B**. While there are modern touches, you'll appreciate being surrounded by antiques

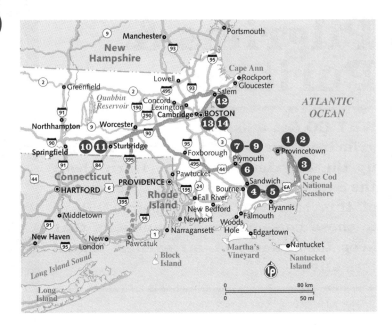

not unlike what was used when the house was built. The fireplace in the parlor, the beautiful stairway, four-post beds and a big garden out back are all good reasons to stay here.

While you're in Sandwich, check out the **6** **Aptucxet Trading Post Museum Complex** in nearby Bourne, believed to be the oldest remains of a Pilgrim building ever found. Although the simple, unpainted, clapboard structure standing today is a replica built on the original foundation, it's still possible to imagine Pilgrims, Wampanoag and Dutch coming here to barter for goods, seeds, tools and food.

Now you're ready to leave the Cape and head to **7** **Plimoth Plantation**, one of the best and biggest living history museums. Wander through the settlement, scratch the baby pigs and watch pottery- or barrel-making demonstrations. Some of the activities are even hands on – feel free to help weed a garden or try your hand at planing planks with a handmade chisel. It's a big place, so budget at least half a day here – there's a lot to see. Once you enter, the main attraction is the series of buildings in the Plimoth Village. Each house has a different function and these are tied to very real people who lived in the settlement shortly after the Pilgrims arrived. It's both fun and educational to chat with them and realize how many modern conveniences they had to do without. If you ask them what time it is, they won't look down to their wristwatch. Instead, they'll study the sky a moment and give you a pretty good estimate based on the position of the sun. Kids especially will be surprised at how well the actors play their various roles. Overnight programs for kids go even further – you dress, eat and sleep like the early settlers did.

Don't miss the Native American settlement and demonstrations too – they're off a side path near the inlet. Dressed in moccasins and a loincloth, a Wampanoag tribe member will guide you through the traditional *wetu,* or dwelling, and explain or demonstrate everything from hide-tanning to making a fire without matches or a lighter. It's worth noting that (unlike the Plimoth settlement) these are not actors – they're Native Americans who take pride in the fact that their ancestors, unlike the Pilgrims, have lived here for over 10,000 years.

When you've had your fill of Plimoth Village it's time to pay your respects at **8** **Plymouth Rock**. There are actually two – one that's outside in the approximate location where the Pilgrims might have stepped and another in the **9** **Pilgrim Hall Museum**. The former is a glacial erratic that sits surrounded by grates to deter pranksters, painters and those looking for a souvenir. You can get a good look at it and take pictures from about 10ft away. But if that has you longing for a closer encounter, you can actually touch a piece of it at the museum along with a number of other Pilgrim artifacts. There's a large collection of samplers (those "Home Sweet Home" cross-stitch things) as well as various chairs, all of which seem to perfectly fit the Puritan ideal: they look punishingly painful to sit in for any length of time. One wonders what the average Pilgrim would have done if confronted with a La-Z-Boy Recliner? Whether a gift from God or sin of the Devil, there were no such luxuries when our forefathers arrived.

> **DETOUR** See the other side of the story with a three-hour round-trip detour to Pawcatuk, CT, where you can visit the **Mashantucket Pequot Museum & Research Center** (www.pequotmuseum.org). Find out how Native Americans arrived on the continent, how they lived, how they made shelters or found food and what the arrival of white settlers meant to the various tribes. The museum also covers significant modern events, such as land grants and official tribal recognition.

"One wonders what the average Pilgrim would have done if confronted with a La-Z-Boy Recliner?"

For more information and a similar experience, head out to **10** **Old Sturbridge Village** where you'll find reenactments of military battles, lots of hands-on demos such as churning butter into cream and even some odd things such as Hawaiian dance, brought along with Hawaiian patchwork quilts to Boston by sailors who stopped in Hawaii en route to Asia and the spice lands. Old Sturbridge Village and Plimoth Plantation are similar in that they're both dedicated to preserving the past and to educating present visitors through interactive exhibits. Here, too, character actors will let you inquire about what life was like at the time their characters were alive. Yet, whereas the Plimoth Plantation brings that particular settlement alive, Old Sturbridge Village has a bigger, broader agenda – bringing to life the entire era. Don't miss the horse-drawn apple cider mill. Cider, the hard (many say the good) stuff, was an integral part of early settler life and where there wasn't a river or stream to do the dirty work, horses had to. Another interesting highlight is the printer's shop, where you can see how early books and flyers were made with hand-set type – either metal or wood. Inking was a dirty, sometimes dangerous process – linseed oil was mixed with soot, applied to the type and cleaned off later with lye, which is highly caustic and can burn or blind. Injuries were common and, of course, the cures weren't what they are today.

Lay thee down to sleep at ⑪ **Copper Lantern Motor Lodge**, a clean spot not far away. You'll have a choice of kitchenette rooms or normal ones in a rust-red building that looks a bit like a country farmhouse. What's best about this place is the view – acres of rolling farmland and a glassy pond that will beckon you to step outside and go for an amble before turning in for the night amid the luminescent flicker of the fireflies.

Rise and shine and head for the ⑫ **Salem Witch Museum**. If you're finding it hard to not start reciting lines from Monty Python in the accent of John Cleese or Eric Idle, you'll start sobering up when you realize that something as seemingly innocuous as wearing a red dress might have gotten you hanged if you were in Salem at just the wrong time. About 180 people in this close-knit community were accused of being witches – men and women, outsiders and up-standing society members. Most of the accusers were young girls who, researchers believe, may have been afflicted with hysteria or possibly poisoned by ergot fungus present in the grain they ate. It's easy to chuckle at the various life-size dioramas depicting the chronology of what happened there, yet as the museum makes clear, the phenomenon of

SANDWICH GLASS

Thanks to easy access to silica from the quartz sand on its beaches, the town of Sandwich quickly became a leader in the world of glass. The **Sandwich Glass Factory** was one of the first to mass-produce pressed glass; its saucers and candlesticks are now prized heirlooms. Sandwich remains a spot for many working glassblowers. At **McDermott Glass Studio** (www.mcdermottglass.com) you can watch glass being blown and perhaps pick up a souvenir for someone special.

witch hunts, whether actual or figurative, is an all-too-easy, all-too-human and uncomfortably ubiquitous reality. Part of coming here means coming to grips with the disturbing fact that, far from being an isolated event in the distant past, the counterparts of witches and persecutors still exist in many forms today.

Finish the trip with a stop at Boston's ⓭ **Old South Meeting House**, one of the few buildings in that part of the city spared by the Great Fire of 1872, which miraculously stopped right before consuming this Boston landmark. Originally built in 1729 as a Puritan meeting house, its true claim to fame is its role as the gathering spot for colonists who started the Boston Tea Party. It's a simple spot still much used and much loved today, functioning as a gathering place and a public space. Also spared was the ⓮ **Jacob Wirth Restaurant**, on Stuart St, Boston's second-oldest restaurant that's still in operation today. Note the gold-lettered sign and the 19th-century facade – not much has changed since its heyday in the late 1800s. The menu, however, has kept up with modern times. Among other options, you can choose from an international, very cosmopolitan, very modern selection of imported beers and microbrews. Thank goodness the uptight Puritans' Temperance Movement never quite got off the ground. Cheers!

Ray Bartlett

TRIP INFORMATION

GETTING THERE
From Boston, take I-93 south to RT-3, then follow RT-6 to Provincetown.

DO

Expedition Whydah
Learn about Barry Clifford's first salvage success before finding the *Titanic*. ☎ 508-487-8899; http://whydah.com; Fisherman's Wharf, Provincetown; adult/child $8/5; 🕑 10am-5pm May, Sept & Oct, 10am-8pm Jun-Aug

Old South Meeting House
This Puritan meeting house was the sole survivor of Boston's Great Fire. ☎ 617-482-6439; www.oldsouthmeetinghouse.org; 310 Washington St, Boston; adult/child $5/1; 🕑 9:30am-5pm Apr 1-Oct 31, 10am-4pm Nov 1-Mar 31

Old Sturbridge Village
Authentic dress and character actors bring the Puritan era to life. ☎ 508-347-3362; www.osv.org; 1 Old Sturbridge Village Rd, Sturbridge; adult/child $20/6; 🕑 9:30am-5pm, hours vary seasonally; ♿

Pilgrim Hall Museum
Fondle a piece of the rock that started it all. ☎ 508-746-1620; www.pilgrimhall.org; 75 Court St, Plymouth; adult/child $7/4; 🕑 9:30am-4:30pm Feb-Dec

Pilgrim Monument & Provincetown Museum
Where the Pilgrims first landed before Plymouth stole the spotlight. ☎ 508-487-1310; www.pilgrim-monument.org; High Pole Hill Rd, Provincetown; adult/child $7/3.50; 🕑 9am-5pm Apr 1-Jun 14 & Sep 16-Nov 30, 9am-7pm Jun 15-Sep 15

Plimoth Plantation
Living history demos bring us back to when the Pilgrims lived here. ☎ 508-746-1622; www.plimoth.org; 137 Warren Ave, Plymouth; adult/child from $24/14; 🕑 9am-5:30pm late Mar-Nov; ♿

Salem Witch Museum
Exhibits about witches old and new, then and now. ☎ 978-744-1692; Washington Sq North, Salem; www.salemwitchmuseum.com; adult/child $8/5.50; 🕑 10am-5pm Sep-Jun, 10am-7pm Jul & Aug

EAT

Brown Jug
Everything you could want in a café – clean, courteous, delicious food and wine as well. ☎ 508-888-4669; www.thebrownjug.com; 155 Main St, Sandwich; sandwiches from $6.50; 🕑 7am-8pm Mon-Thu, 7am-8:30pm Fri & Sat, 8am-1pm Sun

Jacob Wirth Restaurant
The second-oldest restaurant in Boston, with a 19th-century storefront and great beer selection. ☎ 617-338-8586; www.jacobwirth.com; 31-37 Stuart St, Boston; lunch from $8, dinner from $15; 🕑 11:30am-8pm Mon & Sun, 11:30am-10pm Tue-Thu, 11:30am-midnight Fri, 11:30am-11pm Sat

SLEEP

Copper Lantern Motor Lodge
Kitchenette-equipped rooms close to Old Sturbridge Village. ☎ 508-867-6441; www.copperlanternmotorlodge.com; 184 West Main St, West Brookfield; r $58-82; ♿

Isaiah Jones Homestead B&B
Victorian B&B within walking distance of most of Sandwich's delights. ☎ 508-888-9115, 800-526-1625; www.isaiahjones.com; 165 Main St, Sandwich; r $200-275

LINK YOUR TRIP
www.lonelyplanet.com/trip-planner

TRIP
15 Cape Ann Curiosities p121

Day Trips from Boston

Take a break from Boston with a few quick escapes to Provincetown, Salem, Tanglewood and Lexington, where you'll be able to take in the wonders of Massachusetts not found in the big city.

PEABODY ESSEX MUSEUM, SALEM

The Peabody Essex Museum (PEM; www.pem.org) is almost as much of a treat to look at as to look in. Housed in its new building, the museum has a premier collection – ranging from fine paintings and prints to curious items from the Boston–Asia sea-trading days. Not to be missed are the Hawaiian items, including the statue of the god Ku. One of the more interesting features is the collection of entire homes that have been painstakingly re-created to enable viewers to see not just objects under glass, but entire rooms and houses. The Yin Yu Tang House is particularly special – a Chinese merchant's domicile that you can walk around in (advance reservations required). Like Boston's Museum of Fine Arts (MFA), the PEM is a massive museum and you'll want to allow plenty of time for exploring. If you have some time to spare, the Salem Witch Museum is a good option too. **Take the Newbury/Rockport MBTA commuter line to Salem and you'll be an easy five-minute walk from the PEM. If you're driving, take Rte 1A up the coast from Boston.**

See Also **TRIPS 8 & 16**

TANGLEWOOD

Tanglewood, the Boston Symphony Orchestra's summer home since the 1930s, is a wonderful way to catch up on culture while you're traveling. It's nearly synonymous with great concerts, but there are a host of other activities as well, ranging from jazz festivals to food and wine events, cooking classes, music seminars and more. There are numerous buildings on this campus that you'll want to peek at, such as the Ozawa Music Hall, but the fields and forests will beckon you to get a take-out sandwich and a beverage, find yourself a nice spot for a picnic, then relax and listen for snippets of music. Check the Boston Symphony Orchestra website, www.bso.org, then click on the Tanglewood link prior to coming to find out about the latest events. There is always something special going on. **Take the I-90 from Boston to Exit 2 and follow the signs.**

LEXINGTON

For the historically inclined, a zip out to Lexington makes a great day trip and will show you one of the best known battlegrounds of the Revolutionary War. The Minute Man National Historical Park, with its rolling pastures, placid river and quaint (reconstructed) North Bridge, seems so peaceful that it's hard to imagine that on April 19, 1775, one of the key battles in the American Revolution began just down the road from here, at Lexington's Battle Green, and ended up in this space as the British were chased from the Battle Green and fired upon along Battle Rd. More importantly, it's still unclear whether the Minutemen or the British troops fired what is thought to be the first shot of the American Revolution, one that would free the United States from British taxation and tyranny and change the course of history for the next 200 years. It was not a particularly bloody battle, nor was it one where a decisive victory was made, but it was the tipping point for these two warring nations. **Lexington is best reached by car, following I-93 north to RT-128 south, then take RT-225 into Lexington. Signs mark the way to the battlefield.**

PROVINCETOWN

Skip the city and skip the traffic by taking the ferry to Provincetown for the day. This is a full day trip, with the ferry taking 1½ to three hours, depending on which one you take. You disembark in the center of flamboyant P-town (as it's nicknamed) where you'll have easy access to everything this crazy town has to offer. MacMillan and Fisherman's Wharves offer whale watches, fishing trips and lip-smacking good fried seafood (don't miss Joe's, right on Commercial St). Those who want to delve deeper can check out the Crown and Anchor, where the much-loved Painted Ladies (you guessed it, not ladies at all) perform sold-out drag-impersonation shows. The world's oldest datable pirate gold is on display at the Expedition Whydah museum, along with numerous other artifacts from underwater archaeologist Barry Clifford's first big treasure find (the second was, of course, the *Titanic*). **Catch the ferry in Boston at the World Trade Center, reachable via the subway's Silver Line. In Provincetown, the ferry leaves from its slip on MacMillan Wharf, with the ticket office on Commercial St, across from Standish St.**

Ray Bartlett   See Also **TRIP 20**

CAPE COD AREA TRIPS

Ah, old Cape Cod. Nearly everyone, it seems, has an opinion about this enchanted and legendary stretch of land: it's too crowded; it's not like it used to be; you should have been here 20 years ago. But regardless of what those who've come before might have to say, the good news is this: genuine American magic happens everywhere on this remote and arm-shaped peninsula, each and every day of the year.

And where exactly might "everywhere" be? It might be in the clubs of Provincetown, where the energy is often so thick you can almost reach out and touch it. Or maybe on the early morning ferry to Martha's Vineyard, or during a midwinter walk on Monomoy Island, or perhaps during a quiet drive down the Old King's Hwy, past pilgrim churches and sea captains' houses.

And as for how the magic of Cape Cod will touch you, well…who can

PLAYLIST ♫♪ Crank that Upper East Side Soweto to 10, tighten your whale belt and get your head in the game, Cape Cod–style:

- "Cape Cod Kwassa Kwassa," Vampire Weekend
- "New England," Jonathan Richman and the Modern Lovers
- "Cape Cod Girls," Baby Gramps
- "Is This Love?" Carly Simon
- "Nantucket," Jonathan Geer
- "Walcott," Vampire Weekend
- "Blow the Man Down," Gale Huntington
- "Old Cape Cod," Patti Page

say? But here's the point: for those of you able to look past the summer crowds and the touristy schmaltz, it's out there, somewhere on old Cape Cod, east of America. Go find it.

CAPE COD'S BEST TRIPS

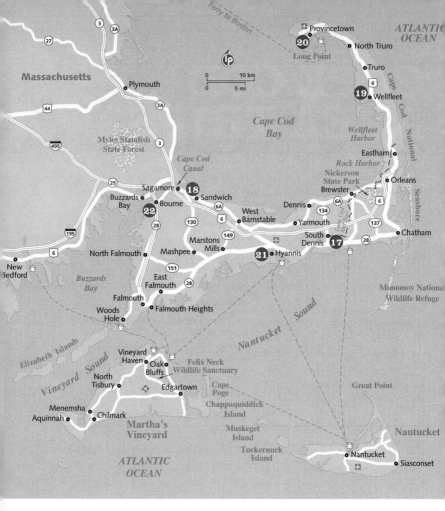

CAPE COD AREA TRIPS

Cape Cod Rail Trail

WHY GO Kvetching about the Cape's overdevelopment has lately become something of a local cliché. But spend a leisurely afternoon cycling among the pine woods and cranberry bogs of the 22-mile Cape Cod Rail Trail and you'll almost certainly discover the simple and unadulterated aesthetic that led you here in the first place.

TIME
1 day

DISTANCE
22 miles

BEST TIME TO GO
Apr – Nov

START
South Dennis

END
Wellfleet

It certainly doesn't take a guidebook writer to explain the huge popularity of the Cape Cod Rail Trail, a paved bicycle path that winds its way across 22 miles of calming natural beauty. Locals and visitors alike have been walking, biking and even horseback riding back and forth along this stretch of the former Boston-to-Providence railroad corridor since 1978, when the trail's first section was finally paved. Over the following three decades the trail was slowly lengthened and nonconnecting extensions were added in other villages. Hopefully, say Rail Trail enthusiasts, it will one day be possible to cross all of Cape Cod on just one bike path.

For the time being, however, most cyclists begin their Cape Cod exploration at the trailhead in South Dennis. Conveniently enough, that's also the location of the popular **1** **Barb's Bike Shop**. Barb's has half a dozen different bicycles for rent by the hour or the day, including tandems, beach cruisers and kids' bikes. You can also pick up in-line skates, maps and gear. (Helmets are loaned free with every rental.)

As you begin to pedal, keep your eyes peeled for the small, still bodies of water on your left and right. Known locally as "kettle ponds," they were formed by the massive retreating glacier that covered much of New England thousands of years ago. Even today, the kettle ponds still offer potable water.

BEST TRIP

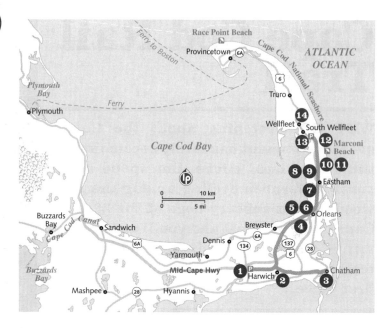

Before long you'll encounter the bike rotary, where the trail forks. Head to the right and continue on for just over a half-mile, where Rte 124 crosses the trail. Follow Rte 124 to the right as well and you'll soon find yourself at the **② Harwich Historical Society Museum**, an old Doric-style schoolhouse built in 1844 and originally used as a seminary. Two hundred years worth of Harwich town history is preserved inside. Certainly one of the most fascinating permanent exhibits for visitors is the museum's extensive documentation of the cranberry industry, which had a very different reputation during the Cape's earliest days to what it has now. The harvesting itself, for instance, was physically demanding to the extreme and was mostly the responsibility of migrant laborers. Today, of course, those very same wet and marshy cranberry bogs are something of a tourist attraction for visitors from all over the world. In fact, as you cycle through Harwich after leaving the museum, keep your eyes peeled for the idyllic bogs that border the rail trail. Works by the prolific Cape Cod painter Charles Cahoon, grandson of a well-known Harwich cranberry grower, can also be seen at the museum. Other unusual exhibits include a genuine gunpowder house used during the American Revolution, as well as a restored outhouse from the late 1800s. Amateur historians are welcome to thumb through the museum's impressively well maintained genealogical collection.

If you're now feeling particularly adventurous and up for a bit of high-end shopping, continue along the trail until the pavement ends and the rugged dirt path begins. The tony downtown area of ❸ **Chatham** is just 2 miles away; you'll find everything from exclusive boutique shopping to trendy restaurants to irresistible ice-cream and candy shops here.

But if off-road biking isn't what you're after, don't sweat it: simply pedal back to the bike rotary, hang a right and before you know it you'll be surrounded once again by kettle ponds and salt marsh grasses waving in the wind. Immediately after making your way through the Rte 6A underpass, you'll be inside the Cape's much-admired ❹ **Nickerson State Park**. This 1961-acre wilderness is dominated by lush pine and oak forests and has 13 miles of hiking and biking trails. Don't make the mistake of simply passing through the park; instead, take an hour to ride alongside Cliff Pond, or to slowly stroll and watch the bird life at Higgins Pond in the park's eastern

MORE CAPE COD BIKE TRAILS

If you've covered the Rail Trail back and forth but aren't quite ready to stop riding, you're in luck: The Cape is rich in walking and biking trails, including many paths that have been freshly paved. Pick up a Cape Cod road and bicycle map, which can be purchased at almost any of the bike-rental shops in the area – the Rubel map is a local favorite.

You'll find trails worth traversing in Provincetown, Falmouth, Dennis and even on Martha's Vineyard and Nantucket.

end. Bird-watchers often find their work cut out for them in Nickerson Park. Canada geese, hawks, owls, woodpeckers, warblers, wrens, finches, larks and ospreys are just some of the feathered fowl known to populate this corner of the Cape. You're likely to see the widest variety and largest number of bird species throughout autumn, although the summer migratory season can also be good.

You'll almost certainly be ready for a well-deserved break after leaving Nickerson Park, so it's a good thing the compact and quaint center of ❺ **Orleans** is just a short ride away. It's nearly impossible to miss the town's ❻ **Hot Chocolate Sparrow Café**, which was one of the first local shops to jump on the espresso bandwagon. It's still a Cape favorite today and for good reason: the building is huge, with one counter for the candies and chocolates that are prepared in-house and another for the coffee and espresso bar. If you're in a hurry, just grab a soft-serve cone at the outdoor window, which faces the Rail Trail. You'll also find two bike-rental shops nearby, which might come in handy if you've managed to get a flat.

By the way, if you happen to be staying at the ❼ **HI-Mid Cape Hostel** in Eastham, you're almost home. Simply jump back on the trail heading north, but slow down once you've crossed the Rte 6 overpass. Go left at the bulletin board, which sits immediately after the overpass and then follow the signs. One of only three hostels on the Cape (Truro and Provincetown have the others), HI-Mid Cape was specifically designed with nature-lovers in mind. The

Rail Trail, of course, is just a quick pedal away. And thanks to an impressive collection of bird feeders and bird baths, the hostel grounds seem to attract an endless parade of colorful wildlife. While you're there, borrow one of the house's free boogie boards and head to the seashore, or ask about the hostel's guided kayak trips.

For those of you who picked up a few thousand extra calories in Orleans, it's time to head north toward the **8** **Salt Pond Visitors Center** in Eastham. A superb museum with whaling displays and an educational film series, this is a can't-miss stop for anyone interested in sea life, or for that matter, any of the Cape's natural resources. The center also offers occasional lectures and guided walks. To get there, go right on Locust Rd, which intersects the trail, and then follow the signs.

And what if the cinnamon bun you gobbled down at Hot Chocolate Sparrow didn't exactly fill you up? You might consider making a pit stop at the award-winning **9** **Arnold's**, where the Wellfleet oysters and fried clams will at least give your exhausted body a much-needed gift of protein. Arnold's is an easy 1-mile pedal north of the visitors center and it sits right alongside the trail.

Once you've made it to Arnold's, you'll be perfectly situated to make a run for the **10** **Cape Cod National Seashore**. Stretching from Provincetown's Race Point Beach in the north and well past Nauset Beach in Orleans, a whopping 44,600 acres of seashore land have been legally protected from development since 1961. This is good news, of course, for the native wildlife that must either relocate or die every time a new oceanfront resort rises from the sand. But it's also good news for the earth itself: the Cape's seashore, as it happens, is home to a number of exceedingly rare plant communities and marine ecosystems. It was President John F Kennedy, by the way, who introduced the legislation that created the National Seashore.

CAPE COD PATHWAYS

For more than 15 years now, Cape Cod has been home to an active community of walking enthusiasts who've been working to create a network of trails that will one day stretch from Provincetown all the way to Falmouth and Bourne. The trails are collectively known as Cape Cod Pathways and on the organization's website, at www.capecodcommission.org/pathways, you'll find a series of Cape-wide walking routes complete with detailed instructions.

A healthy 1.5-mile trek stands between you and the next destination, Nauset Light Beach (go east on Brackett Rd, left on Nauset Rd, then right on Cable Rd). This trek's eventual reward will be not just the low-rolling surf and pillowy sand, but also the **11** **Nauset Beach Lighthouse**. If you've got a camera handy, this is the time to use it: of all the breathtaking lighthouses on Cape Cod, the 48ft-high Nauset Light, made of cast iron and listed on the National Register of Historic Places, is said to be the most photographed.

From here on, it's just you, the quiet buzz of nature and the rest of the trail. You may have noticed how the woodsy geography of the trail became much more salty and dominated by plant life after leaving Nickerson State Park. You'll experience more of the same all the way to South Wellfleet, where the paved portion of the Rail Trail comes to an end. If you're up for a bit of post-trip sightseeing, hang a right onto Lecount Hollow Rd, which sits at the end of the paved path, and follow it to land's end, also known as **⑫ Lecount Hollow Beach**. If the weather's just so, you'll probably see a few surfers out on the waves.

"Of all the Cape's breathtaking lighthouses, Nauset Light is said to be the most-photographed."

You may also notice a small cluster of shops at the end of the paved trail. They sit right along Rte 6 and that's where you'll spot the **⑬ South Wellfleet General Store**, perfect for stocking up on provisions. The store's finest feature, a deli counter called Behind the Tides, is tucked away in the back. Order a fatboy sandwich and don't miss the locally brewed Beanstock Coffee.

Beanstock started its life as a modest café inside the **⑭ Inn at Duck Creeke**, a classic New England–style B&B and one of the most popular in Wellfleet, a traditional Cape village that lately has become something of an artists' retreat. Just a mile away from the Atlantic and midway between Provincetown and Orleans, the Inn at Duck Creeke consists of three different historic dwellings and two restaurants. Just like the rest of downtown Wellfleet, and for that matter the rest of the Cape, it somehow manages to be both elegant and eccentric at the same time.

Dan Eldridge

TRIP INFORMATION

GETTING THERE
From Hyannis take Rte 28 east to Rte 134 north. Continue north for 1.5 miles to the South Dennis trailhead.

DO

Barb's Bike Shop
A wide variety of bicycle and in-line skate rentals, conveniently located at the trailhead. ☎ 508-760-4723; www.barbsbikeshop.com; 430 Rte 134, South Dennis; per day bikes/skates $24/15; ⊙ 8:30am-6:30pm; ⧉

Cape Cod National Seashore
Protected beachfront and woodlands running alongside the Cape's Atlantic coast. ☎ 508-349-3785; www.nps.gov/caco; pedestrians, motorcycles and bikes $3, cars $15; ⊙ parking lots 6am-midnight; ⧉ ⧉

Harwich Historical Society Museum
Over 200 years of Harwich history on display. ☎ 508-432-8089; www.harwichhistorical society.org; 80 Parallel St, Harwich; adult/child $3/free; ⊙ 1-4pm Thu-Sat Jun 26-Oct 11

Nauset Beach Lighthouse
Take a tour through this cast-iron lighthouse, supposedly the most photographed on the Cape. ☎ 508-240-2612; www.nausetlight .org; Cable Rd at Ocean View Dr, Nauset Beach; admission free; ⊙ call for tour schedule

Nickerson State Park
Find yourself pleasantly lost amid Nickerson Park's 1961 woodsy acres, complete with hiking trails and the Cape's unusual kettle ponds. ☎ 508-896-3491; www.mass .gov/dcr/parks/southeast/nick.htm; Rte 6A, Brewster

Salt Pond Visitors Center
A seashore museum complete with in-the-know staffers who sometimes offer trip-planning suggestions. ☎ 508-255-3421; www.nps.gov/caco; Doane Rd, Eastham; admission free; ⊙ 9am-4:30pm; ⧉

EAT

Arnold's
Come hungry for some of the Cape's best fried clams, or make a pit stop for homemade ice-cream. ☎ 508-255-2575; www .arnoldsrestaurant.com; 3580 State Hwy (Rte 6), Eastham; meals $10-40; ⊙ 11:30am-9pm

Hot Chocolate Sparrow Café
Stop off for ice cream, espresso drinks or a staggering array of hand-dipped chocolate candy. ☎ 800-922-6399; www.hotchoco latesparrow.com; 5 Old Colony Way, Orleans; ⊙ 6:30am-11pm Mon-Sat, 6:30am-8pm Sun

South Wellfleet General Store
An olde-timey general store with a surprisingly high-quality deli tucked inside. ☎ 508-349-2335; 1446 Rte 6, South Wellfleet; sandwiches $7.50; ⊙ 8am-6pm

SLEEP

HI-Mid Cape Hostel
Relax near the garden or mingle with backpackers at this ecofriendly hostel. ☎ 508-255-2785; www.usahostels.org/cape/himc; 75 Goody Hallet Dr, Eastham; dm $35, r $128-175; ⊙ late May-early Sep

Inn at Duck Creeke
Sleep tight in one of three Yankee-style B&B buildings and dig in at one of the popular on-site eateries. ☎ 508-349-9333; www .innatduckcreeke.com; 70 Main St, Wellfleet; r $90-135

USEFUL WEBSITES
www.capecodbikeguide.com
www.cctrails.org/bike.htm

LINK YOUR TRIP

www.lonelyplanet.com/trip-planner

TRIP
19 Clam Diggin' the Cape p147
22 Antiquing the Cape p161
39 Tip to Tail by Bike & Rail p259

Cape Cod & Nantucket Architecture

WHY GO In this distinguished corner of New England, homes with notable history and architecture can be spotted in nearly every neighborhood. But what about getting inside for a look around? Well, that's another story altogether. It's also exactly why we created this trip.

TIME
3 days

DISTANCE
150 miles

BEST TIME TO GO
Jul – Nov

START
Sandwich

END
Truro

ALSO GOOD FOR

OUTDOORS

When it comes to exploring the most important homes on Cape Cod and the islands, or for that matter the rarest or just unique homes, the question is where to start. Some architecture enthusiasts may prefer to simply wander, spotting a clapboard here and a Colonial Revival Cape there. (To recognize an original Cape Cod–style structure, imagine how a young child usually draws a house. *That's* an original Cape Cod.)

In the Upper Cape, one of the most architecturally stunning places to stay is the ❶ **Belfry Inn & Bistro**, a collection of three separate structures in Sandwich. Ask for a room in the Painted Lady, a phenomenally renovated Victorian, or the Abbey, a former chapel with a number of rooms featuring striking stained-glass windows with religious themes. The Belfry is also home to a contemporary American eatery where the majority of produce on offer is purchased from local farms.

❷ **Yarmouth** draws history buffs and historic-home aficionados from all over New England. One of its most-visited homes is the ❸ **Edward Gorey House** in Yarmouth Port, where the legendary illustrator of ghoulish children's books lived for the last 14 years of his life. Gorey was often described as living in a "macabre yet merry world," and indeed, the same descriptor could easily be applied to his 200-year-old house, filled as it is with unsettling original art and odd personal effects.

Also in Yarmouth Port is the fabled ❹ **Winslow Crocker House**, a shingled Georgian-style structure built in the late 1700s. More than a

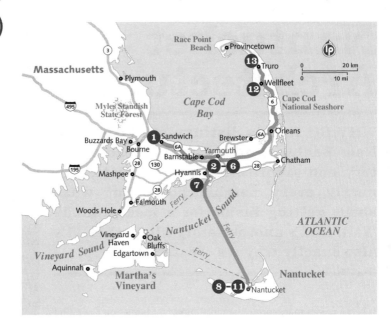

century after its creation, the house was occupied by Mary Thacher, a direct descendent of Yarmouth's town founder. Not only did Thacher move the house from West Barnstable to its present location, she also brightened the rooms with what is today a very valuable antique and furniture collection.

TRANSFIGURATION ARCHITECTURE

The **Church of the Transfiguration** in Orleans, with sculpted bronze doors and interior columns, is a house of worship for an unconventional religious organization known as the **Community of Jesus**. The Community asserts its nondenominational status, although some locals think of it more as a cult.

Religious arguments aside, however, this is certainly one of the most creatively designed churches on the Eastern Seaboard. Don't miss the opportunity to view its mosaic processional path and contemporary frescoes.

Fans of maritime culture should visit the Greek Revival–style ❺ **Captain Bangs Hallet House Museum**. This is the only sea captain's home on Cape Cod open to visitors on a regular basis; the interiors of others may be viewed only on occasional walking tours. Built in 1840, the house's rooms have been decorated by the Historical Society of Old Yarmouth to reflect what a wealthy captain's house would have looked like in the mid-to-late 1800s.

Finally, while touring the stretch of Rte 6A in Yarmouth Port known as ❻ **Yarmouth Captains' Mile**, don't forget to keep a watchful eye out for the area's 53 remaining sea captains' homes. The houses are each marked by black-and-gold plaques featuring a ship's silhouette.

If you've kept a steady pace thus far, you've probably earned yourself a drink. But first, it's necessary to make one more journey – to the nearby island of Nantucket. Head to the ferry docks of Hyannisport and hook up with **7 Hy-Line Cruises**, which offers surprisingly fair rates to the island. Most people leave their vehicle in the paid parking lot here, but Steamship Authority can transport vehicles. Both companies also travel to Martha's Vineyard.

Upon docking in **8 Nantucket**, take a stroll along the cobblestone Main St in the historic downtown district, where old-style lamps still illuminate the streets at night. Of course, when it comes to Nantucket, "historic" is a relative term – this is an island with more buildings on the National Register of Historic Places than any city, town or borough in the entire state of Massachusetts. Nantucket also boasts one of the country's largest concentrations of pre–Civil War houses: more than 800 still exist, many of which can be seen near the harbor in Nantucket town, which is also home to an incredible collection of captains' homes from the 18th and 19th centuries. Check out www.nha.org for tour information.

CAPE COD'S HUMBLE ROOTS

It's easy to forget that throughout much of its relatively short life, Cape Cod was a poor and humble place. The homes of its late-18th-century inhabitants, for instance, were built by hand with native wood. According to area historians, only one such house still exists. Known as the **Harris-Black House**, it's a simple half-Cape consisting of just one room.

Sitting alongside the house is the handsome 18th-century **Higgins Farm Windmill**. Both structures reside on Rte 6A in West Brewster.

Make your way to the gorgeously pastoral headquarters of **9 Cisco Brewers**. Just 3 miles from the Broad St ferry depot and not far from Cisco Beach, the company was once Nantucket's solitary craft-beer brewer. **10 Nantucket Vineyard** is operated by the same organization and is situated on essentially the same plot of land. Tours of the winery, the vineyard and the brewery must be booked in advance, but visitors are always welcome to join a tasting session or visit the gift shop. Those with a taste for the harder stuff will no doubt appreciate a visit to the **11 Triple Eight Distillery**, a super-premium vodka, rum and gin producer, also operated by the Cisco family.

Soak up some of the afternoon's alcohol with a plate of locally grown protein and healthy carbs; the liberal-leaning villages of the Outer Cape are known for having an abundance of high-end contemporary restaurants. You'll find some of the Cape's finest creatively prepared seafood at the **12 Wicked Oyster** in Wellfleet, which sits inside a converted wooden house complete with rare, foot-wide floorboards known as king's boards. Also try one of Truro's newest contemporary spots, **13 Blackfish**, which is operated by the Wicked Oyster's former head chef. After just one season in business, locals and critics alike proclaimed Blackfish's changing seasonal menu among the Cape's finest.

Dan Eldridge

HISTORY & CULTURE

TRIP INFORMATION

GETTING THERE
Sandwich is located off Rte 6 in the Cape's northwestern corner, just a stone's throw from mainland Massachusetts.

DO
Captain Bangs Hallet House Museum
A luxuriously outfitted sea captain's home. ☎ 508-362-3021; www.hsoy.org; 11 Strawberry Lane, Yarmouth Port; adult/child $3/0.50; ⊙ tours 1pm, 2pm & 3pm Thu-Sun

Edward Gorey House
Exhibits and personal artifacts offer a glimpse inside the late illustrator's curious mind. ☎ 508-362-3909; www.edwardgoreyhouse .org; 8 Strawberry Lane, Yarmouth Port; admission $5; ⊙ 11am-4pm Wed-Sat, noon-4pm Sun

Hy-Line Cruises
Take the slow boat to Nantucket or Martha's Vineyard. ☎ 800-492-8082; www.hy-line cruises.com; 220 Ocean St, Hyannis; Nantucket adult/child return $45/26, one-way $22.50/13; ⊙ departs Hyannis 9:20am, 1:30pm & 6:10pm Jun 21-Sep 1

Winslow Crocker House
A prime example of Cape Cod architecture c 1780, with an early American antiques collection inside. ☎ 617-227-3957; www .hsoy.org; 250 Rte 6A (Old King's Hwy), Yarmouth Port; admission $4; ⊙ 11am-5pm 1st & 3rd Sat Jun-Oct 15

EAT
Blackfish
This gastropub is among the trendiest fine-dining options in the Outer Cape. ☎ 508-349-3399; 17 Truro Center Rd, Truro; mains $19-33; ⊙ from 5pm

Wicked Oyster
Toothsome classic contemporary mains and high-end seafood. ☎ 508-349-3455; 50 Main St, Wellfleet; mains $9-26; ⊙ 7am-2pm & 5:30-10pm Thue-Tue, 7am-2pm Wed

DRINK
Cisco Brewers
Nantucket's first craft-beer brewery is known for its pale ales and light lagers. Tours are by appointment only. ☎ 508-325-5929; www .ciscobrewers.com; 5-7 Bartlett Farm Rd, Nantucket; ⊙ 10am-6pm Mon-Sat

Nantucket Vineyard
Tastings feature 10 wines produced here; tours are by appointment only. ☎ 508-325-5929; www.nantucketvineyard.com; 5-7 Bartlett Farm Rd, Nantucket; ⊙ 10am-6pm Mon-Sat, noon-5pm Sun

Triple Eight Distillery
Part of Nantucket's Cisco family, this premium distiller produces an award-winning cranberry vodka. Stop by for samples. ☎ 508-325-5929; www.888distillery.com; 5-7 Bartlett Farm Rd, Nantucket; ⊙ 10am-6pm Mon-Sat

SLEEP
Belfry Inn & Bistro
Call it a night inside a former chapel, a towering Victorian or a Federal-style building. ☎ 508-888-8550; www.belfryinn .com; 8 Jarves St, Sandwich; r $125-310; ⊙ year-round

USEFUL WEBSITES
www.capecodlife.com
www.nantucket.net

LINK YOUR TRIP
www.lonelyplanet.com/trip-planner

Clam Diggin' the Cape

WHY GO For my money, there is simply no person, place or thing more symbolic of lazy Cape Cod summers than the ubiquitous roadside clam shack. To be certain that your own seafood memories were sufficiently unique, we invited Taylor Brown, a professional clam digger, to share some of her local favorites.

For those of you about to dig deeply into the Cape's incredibly varied clam-shack scene, here's something important to keep in mind: just about everyone you meet – especially the locals – will have a different opinion about which shacks are the best and which are the worst and why. They'll tell you that for the best lobster roll you'll have to go here and for the freshest scallops you'll have to go there. But that isn't necessarily a bad thing, because along the way you'll have undoubtedly traveled to untouristed corners of the Cape – tiny villages, say, or hidden back roads – that you wouldn't otherwise have stumbled across.

But if you simply don't have the time, or the inclination, to sample fried foods at dozens of different roadside shacks, you might want to make your way to ❶ **Wellfleet**, says Brown. An especially picturesque little town in the Outer Cape, Wellfleet is known not only for its famous oysters, but also for its respected art scene. In the summer, nearly two dozen of the town's galleries hold open receptions on Saturday evenings. Along the highway just north of town you'll find ❷ **Moby Dick's Restaurant**, a must-visit seafood spot if ever there was one. You may see one of the owners going from table to table here, checking up on guests. And be sure not to miss the impressively broad collection of novels and other books in which the eatery has made appearances.

Head toward the village's center, Brown advises, if you'd rather try ❸ **Mac's Seafood**, an eclectic shack known for serving breakfast

TIME
2 days

DISTANCE
100 miles

BEST TIME TO GO
Jun – Aug

START
Wellfleet

END
Woods Hole

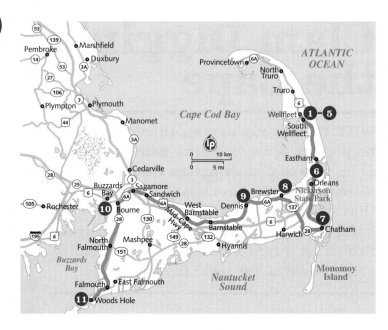

food, Tex Mex–style burritos and even sushi. Be sure not to confuse it with the nearby Mac's Shack, however, which is actually a high-end restaurant. The shack you're looking for is right on the Wellfleet Town Pier, where the view itself is enough to make you a repeat customer. Of course, if that should happen, you'll need a place to sleep; naturally, you'll also want to stay true to this trip's maritime theme, in which case we'd like to suggest the Victorian ④ **Stone Lion Inn**, an exquisitely renovated sea captain's home. Families have been known to rent the inn's on-site cottage, which offers more of an apartment-living experience.

EAT LOCALLY, THINK GLOBALLY

Spend enough time eating your way through the villages of Cape Cod and you're almost certain to catch wind of the increasingly popular "locavore" movement, which encourages people to eat more locally grown and locally produced foods. The majority of the Cape's finest eateries, in fact, are very serious supporters of environmentally sustainable food production. To find area restaurants that are in on the trend, visit www.ediblecapecod.com and www.capecod clash.org.

Now that you've set up camp, you'll probably want to meet the locals and nowhere in Wellfleet is that a more enjoyable experience than at the Bombshelter, a basement bar that sits directly underneath the distinctive ⑤ **Bookstore & Restaurant**. A longtime neighborhood favorite, this eclectic eatery serves clam-shack-style grub in a decidedly unpretentious setting. And yes, there really is a used bookstore inside.

Head south to the town of Orleans for your next stop, ⑥ **Sir Cricket's Fish 'n Chips**. This may be a simple strip-mall clam shack, but be sure to take a close look at your seat before sitting on it – you'll find a minimural of a Cape Cod celebrity there. Sir Cricket's, by the way, is famous not only for its fish, but also its fried oysters.

Children are sure to be amused by the sights of the Chatham Fish Pier, where you may just run into Taylor Brown herself – she digs for clams there a few times a week. ⑦ **Nickerson Fish & Lobster** is one of the pier's main attractions and you'll have a tough time finding seafood fresher than this. Look closely and you may spot Brown hauling her morning's catch through the back door.

The ⑧ **Cape Cod Museum of Natural History** may well prove to be an important stop on your clam-shack trip. That is, assuming you'd like to learn something about the underwater universe that's provided sustenance to Cape Cod for so many years. This museum has always been a big hit with the kids and it has the added advantage of being directly on Rte 6A. You'll find

WHAT'S W.H.A.T.?

At some point during your exploration of the clam shacks and seafood eateries in Wellfleet, you're almost certain to pass by a ramshackle, flat-topped building with the word "W.H.A.T." spelled out in large billboard-style letters on its roof. This is the original home of the **Wellfleet Harbor Actors Theater**.

In 2007 the company saw its public profile raised considerably after the opening of a $6.8-million state-of-the-art facility next to the local post office. Thankfully, W.H.A.T. chose not to shutter this original rustic location and even today, the 90-seat structure plays host to some of the Cape's most impressively pioneering theater.

not just endless miles of antique shops on this historic road, but also a number of old-school roadside clam shacks, such as ⑨ **Captain Frosty's**, where lobster rolls and soft-serve ice cream can be enjoyed on a shaded back patio.

Incidentally, a road trip along the length of Rte 6 will also reveal a wealth of classic shacks, many of them not mentioned in this trip. The food may not always be top-notch at these establishments, although the campy roadside architecture generally is. Start at the aforementioned Moby Dick's in Wellfleet then continue south and then west until you've had your fill.

If you'd like just a bit more education in your diet, you've got two fantastic choices in the Upper Cape. There's the ⑩ **National Marine Life Center** in Buzzards Bay, where sick and injured sea animals who've gotten lost in the mazelike geography of the Cape's bays and inlets are nursed back to health. Alternately, make your way to the ⑪ **Woods Hole Science Aquarium**, where a vast array of marine animals is waiting patiently to be poked, prodded and petted by sea-life lovers just like yourself.

Dan Eldridge

FOOD & DRINK

TRIP INFORMATION

GETTING THERE
To reach the village of Wellfleet, simply hop on Rte 6 east from anywhere in the upper- or mid-Cape.

DO

Cape Cod Museum of Natural History
Explore 17,000 sq ft of flora and fauna, including interactive kids' exhibits. ☎ 508-896-3867; www.ccmnh.org; 869 Main St (Rte 6A), Brewster; adult $8, child 3-12 $3.50; 🕑 9:30am-4pm; 🚻

National Marine Life Center
A cutting-edge marine-life rehabilitation warehouse with an exhibit center. ☎ 508-743-9888; www.nmlc.org; 120 Main St, Buzzards Bay; admission free; 🕑 10am-5pm late May-early Sep

Woods Hole Science Aquarium
Kids are thrilled by the hands-on exhibits here, while adults appreciate the educational displays. ☎ 508-495-2001; aquarium.nefsc.noaa.gov; Albatross St at Water St, Woods Hole; admission free; 🕑 11am-4pm Tue-Sat; 🚻

EAT

Bookstore & Restaurant
Not technically a clam shack, but with its used bookstore and kick-ass underground bar, the Bombshelter, who cares? ☎ 508-349-3154; www.wellfleetoyster.com; 50 Kendrick Ave, Wellfleet; mains $9-23; 🕑 8am-10pm

Captain Frosty's
Right on historic Rte 6A, the captain is famous for his lobster rolls and the lightly breaded fish-and-chips. ☎ 508-385-8548; www.captainfrosty.com; 219 Main St (Rte 6A), Dennis; mains $9-19; 🕑 11am-9pm

Mac's Seafood
Easily the Cape's most creative clam shack (try a burrito or a sushi roll!) and certainly the best view. ☎ 508-349-0404; www.macsseafood.com; Wellfleet Town Pier; mains $9-23; 🕑 7:30am-10pm

Moby Dick's Restaurant
A can't-miss Cape Cod tradition, this is a smart choice for families with kids. ☎ 508-349-9795; www.mobydicksrestaurant.com; 3225 Rte 6, Wellfleet; mains $8-20; 🕑 11:30am-10pm; 🚻

Nickerson Fish & Lobster
Cape seafood doesn't get much fresher than at Nickerson, a clam shack right on the Chatham Fish Pier. ☎ 508-945-0145; Shore Rd, Chatham Fish Pier; mains $10-19; 🕑 9am-6pm

Sir Cricket's Fish 'n Chips
Even better than the fried oysters and fish sandwiches here are the chairs, all uniquely illustrated by local artist Dan Joy. ☎ 508-255-4453; 38 Rte 6A, Orleans; mains $10-18; 🕑 11am-8pm

SLEEP

Stone Lion Inn
Stay in this renovated, Victorian-style sea captain's home, right in central Wellfleet. The on-site cottage is perfect for families. ☎ 508-349-9565; www.stonelioncapecod.com; 130 Commercial St, Wellfleet; r $140-200

USEFUL WEBSITES
www.ediblecapecod.com
www.shellfishing.org

LINK YOUR TRIP
www.lonelyplanet.com/trip-planner

A Culture Vulture in Provincetown

WHY GO Provincetown has always been an unusually creative sort of place. For decades, both the gay community and the artistically inclined have been drawn by P-Town's seemingly irresistible pull. Consider this trip your opportunity to celebrate a truly extraordinary and open-minded corner of the country.

If you've ever spent an afternoon people-watching at a sidewalk café in Provincetown, you've probably asked yourself some variation of the question nearly every visitor to P-Town eventually contemplates: "How did this far-away village, which was once little more than a modest fishing and whaling outpost, become the odd and extraordinary place it is today?"

The answer's quite simple, really: it all started back in the summer of 1899, when a man by the name of Charles Hawthorne came to Provincetown and opened the Cape Cod School of Art. This was the first institution in the country to focus primarily on the "plein air" style of painting, meaning "open air" or "outdoor". Over the next 15 years, a handful of art teachers flocked to Provincetown and set up shop, with literally hundreds of students following. By the summer of 1916, the mainstream media had taken notice. The *Boston Globe* even ran a story about the emerging scene, titled "Biggest Art Colony in the World at Provincetown." Thanks in large part to that simple headline, this once-quiet community at the very tip of Cape Cod has been a creative person's mecca ever since.

Of course, there's much more to the story than just that. If you're at all interested in digging deeper, consider joining a ❶ **Historic Walking Tour of Provincetown**. It's one of the simplest and most enjoyable ways to wrap your head around the history and culture that transformed

TIME	2 days
DISTANCE	35 miles
BEST TIME TO GO	Jun – Sep
START	Provincetown
END	Truro

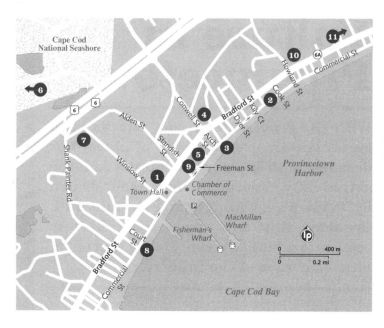

Provincetown into its current incarnation. The two-hour tour happens every Tuesday at 9am during the months of July and August, so take care to schedule accordingly. During the 2-mile trek, you'll learn about the town's venerable history as a magnet for right-brained creative types. You'll also hear about the whaling and fishing industries that dominated P-Town long before that first painter's easel was ever planted in the sand.

Speaking of easels, it should be noted that Hawthorne's painting school eventually came to be known as the Hawthorne School of Art. And although the studio itself still stands at 29 Miller Hill Rd and was even added to the National Register of Historic Places in 1978, it was up for sale at the time of writing and in danger of being torn down by developers. So unless you're an independently wealthy supporter of the arts, make your way instead to Hawthorne's other major P-Town contribution: the ❷ **Provincetown Art Association and Museum (PAAM)**, which is located on the main drag of Commercial St.

> "…learn about the town's venerable history as a magnet for right-brained creative types."

Established in 1914, the exhibition of local artists' work has always been PAAM's primary raison d'être. Essentially a historical record of the many important artists who've passed through the Outer Cape, you'll find a relatively even mix of impressionist, modernist and even contemporary work in the galleries. Check the museum's event schedule to see if any music, dance or spoken word performances are happening. And don't miss the gift shop's impressive collection of art books.

You won't find an on-site café at PAAM. But if it's empty calories and caffeine you're after, hang a right when exiting the museum and go about seven blocks down Commercial St toward the ❸ **Wired Puppy**, an exquisitely designed European-style coffee shop popular with P-Town's gay and lesbian crowd. Extra points if you manage to escape without picking up a dozen Wired Puppy T-shirts, ball caps, backpacks, coffee mugs and refrigerator magnets.

Now that you're properly caffeinated and fully rested, it's time for – what else? – more art! The ❹ **Fine Arts Work Center (FAWC)** is your next stop. Just a block and a half up from the café, FAWC is something of a boarding house for promising young artists and writers, 20 of whom spend seven entire months immersed in their creative work. Sounds like a pretty sweet deal, huh? Thankfully, the community benefits from this arrangement as well: during the busy summer season, events such as readings, slide shows, film screenings and exhibitions are scheduled nearly every night of the week. Even better, all events are free, although donations are encouraged.

OUTERMOST PUBLIC RADIO

As you drive north through the Outer Cape toward Provincetown, fiddle a bit with your car stereo and see if you can't tune into **WOMR 92.1FM**, a noncommercial public radio station that broadcasts from the east end of P-Town. The programming quality falls somewhere in between that of NPR and a free-form university station. You'll hear everything from obscure jazz to community news to nationally syndicated shows.

To access NPR coverage in other corners of the Cape, tune into **WCAI 90.1FM**.

Travelers on a shoestring budget will undoubtedly also benefit from a stay at the ❺ **Pilgrim House Hotel**, just a couple minutes' walk from FAWC. In fact, unless you're prepared to do a night or two in a dorm-room bunk bed, it doesn't get much cheaper than this in Provincetown proper. And while the Pilgrim House is certainly no Four Seasons, it's more than adequate. You won't be at a loss for excuses to celebrate, either: the lesbian-friendly Vixen Nightclub is right downstairs (ask for a top-floor room if you plan to retire early) and the appropriately named Bacchanal Wine Bar, complete with a little outdoor balcony, is off the hotel's lobby.

Provincetown's boisterous party atmosphere doesn't necessarily appeal to everyone. That goes double for travelers who've come to the Cape especially for its peace and quiet. And therein lies the rub of securing proper accommodations in P-Town: what if the only lapping you care to hear at night is that of the nearby ocean waves? Furthermore, what if you're not made of money? In that case, your best bet may be the ❻ **Race Point Lighthouse**, or to be more specific, the restored Keeper's House or the truly secluded Whistle House. Both sit within a stone's throw of the lighthouse itself, which is located way out on the Cape Cod National Seashore, and they're both operated somewhat like a B&B. (At Whistle House you have the place to yourself, whereas a 'keeper family' occupies the 1st floor of the other house.) Guests at tranquil Race Point claim to have seen whales, dolphins and seals during previous stays.

For those of you who'd prefer to stay a little closer to the action but don't mind roughing it just a bit, there's always the **❼ Outermost Hostel**, a cluster of bunk-bed-filled cabins in a garden setting. Aside from being the only hostel in P-Town, this is also the only independently owned hostel on Cape Cod, so expect a party atmosphere. If the place is fully booked, your nearest hostel option is the HI-Truro house on Truro's North Pamet Rd.

DETOUR Just 6 miles south of Provincetown's business district and conveniently located right on Rte 6, the family-owned **Truro Vineyards of Cape Cod** offers visitors the only opportunity to stop at a winery and enjoy a tasting while on the Outer Cape. Guided tours of the vineyard, including a restored 1830s farmhouse, take place at 1pm and 3pm daily during the summer season. To find Truro Vineyards, keep an eye out for the big wine barrel sitting atop a tower.

Regardless of where you've chosen to pass the night, you've still got to eat. If the crowds are out in full force, settle in at **❽ Bubala's by the Bay**, a trendy, longtime favorite among locals and tourists alike. You've got double the entertainment options here: dine on the heated outdoor patio and watch the people-parade as it marches down Commercial St or simply take in the astonishing bay view.

If you're looking for something a bit less fashionable but twice as eccentric, you're looking for **❾ Napi's Restaurant**, which is right in the heart of town, and not far from Pilgrim House Hotel. Napi's likes to call itself Provincetown's most unusual restaurant, which may very well be the case. The dining room is simply flooded with creative energy, including stained glass, unusual antiques and an incredible brick mural by local artist Conrad Malicoat. The food has its own eccentric flavor; if there's an obscure international dish you've been craving, there's a decent chance you'll find it on the menu here.

RESPECT YOUR ELDERS

Tennessee Williams and **Norman Mailer**, both of whom were long-time Provincetown residents, are but two of the hugely influential writers whose names will forever be tied to this small corner of New England. Fittingly, both men are honored annually with festivals; both happen at the beginning of autumn. Visit www.twptown.org and www.normanmailersociety.com for details.

After dinner, of course, it's time for a bit of entertainment. Considering P-Town's history as the birthplace of American theater, not to mention its reputation for attracting up-and-coming talent, you never know who you'll see on the boards at ⑩ **Provincetown Theater**. After all, the town's original theater company, the Provincetown Players, was formed by none other than Eugene O'Neill and Susan Glaspell back in 1916. Provincetown is also where the playwright Tennessee Williams found fame.

If you're not staying the night in Provincetown, you might want to consider stopping by the ⑪ **Truro Center for the Arts at Castle Hill** on your way out of town. Driving away from Provincetown, it's on the left-hand side of Rte 6. Truro Center offers an incredibly wide array of arts instruction courses, so even if you're only planning to be in town for a day or two, it's still smart to look over the online catalog. Lectures, concerts, festivals and other artist appearances are scheduled here throughout the summer as well.

DETOUR If a visit to Provincetown's stunning Pilgrim Monument leaves you aching for more historical sky-high views, simply take a 5-mile detour back down Rte 6. Just across the highway from Truro Vineyards is where you'll find the **Cape Cod Highland Lighthouse**, referred to locally as **Highland Light**. Sitting just a few hundred feet from a craggy cliff and an observation deck, this is the oldest and tallest lighthouse on the Cape.

Dan Eldridge

TRIP INFORMATION

GETTING THERE

From anywhere on the Cape, hop on Rte 6 East and get comfortable – it's a long haul. Signs point to Provincetown's business district.

DO

Fine Arts Work Center

This fellowship center for young artists and writers has a jam-packed summer schedule of readings, screenings and exhibitions. ☎ 508-487-9960; www.fawc.org; 24 Pearl St, Provincetown; $5 donation; ☽ events at 7pm

Historic Walking Tour of Provincetown

Learn about P-Town's historic architecture and about its popularity among artists and writers. ☎ 508-487-1310; www.ptownchamber.com /todo.html; Pilgrim Monument & Provincetown Museum, High Pole Hill Rd; tour $5; ☽ 9am Tue Jul & Aug

Provincetown Art Association and Museum

Nearly 2000 works by hundreds of important Provincetown artists. ☎ 508-487-1750; www.paam.org; 460 Commercial St, Provincetown; admission $5; ☽ 11am-8pm Mon-Thu, 11am-10pm Fri, 11am-5pm Sat & Sun

Provincetown Theater

Celebrate P-Town's status as the birthplace of modern American theater by taking in a play, a dance performance or a concert. ☎ 508-487-9793; www.newprovincetown players.org; 238 Bradford St, Provincetown; ☽ year-round

Truro Center for the Arts at Castle Hill

Hosts frequent exhibitions, lectures, concerts and more. Check online for the current schedule. ☎ 508-349-7511; www.castlehill.org; 10 Meetinghouse Rd, Truro; ☽ 9am-5pm Mon-Fri

EAT & DRINK

Bubala's by the Bay

A funky P-Town favorite for 15 years now. Go for the stunning bay views and unbeatable people-watching. ☎ 508-487-0773; www .bubalas.com; 183-185 Commercial St, Provincetown; mains $9-22; ☽ 11am-11pm

Napi's Restaurant

A broad offering of international dishes. Parking in the rear! ☎ 800-571-6274; www.napis -restaurant.com; 7 Freeman St, Provincetown; mains $15-26; ☽ 11am-4:30pm & 5-10pm

Wired Puppy

A sleek specialty espresso café with free wi-fi, in-the-know baristas and merchandise for sale. ☎ 508-487-0017; www.wiredpuppy .com; 379 Commercial St, Provincetown; ☽ 6am-7pm Sun-Thu, 6am-9pm Fri & Sat

SLEEP

Outermost Hostel

Five dorm-style cabins make up this "cottage colony," adequately tucked away from the madness of Commercial St. ☎ 508-487-4378; www.outermosthostel.com; 28 Winslow St, Provincetown; dm $25; ☽ May-Oct

Pilgrim House Hotel

P-Town's cheapest hotel, with an on-site wine bar, is smack-dab in the center of the action. ☎ 508-487-6424; www.thepilgrim house.com; 336 Commercial St, Provincetown; r $99-149

Race Point Lighthouse

Stay in a restored, 1950s-era Keeper's House, literally at land's end. Daily transport provided. ☎ 508-487-9930; www.racepoint lighthouse.net; Race Point Lighthouse, North Truro; r $155-185; ☽ May-Oct 13

USEFUL WEBSITES

www.goptown.com
www.provincetown.com

LINK YOUR TRIP

www.lonelyplanet.com/trip-planner

Meet the Kennedys

WHY GO The Kennedy connection to Cape Cod dates all the way back to the 1920s. That was when Joseph Kennedy, the family patriarch, purchased a summer home in Hyannisport. This trip will look at the many decades worth of Kennedy clan history from a multitude of perspectives, each one unique.

The Kennedys: America's first and only royal family.

It's one of America's classic affirmations, cited repeatedly in the media. So often is it mentioned that to many of us, regardless of political leanings or knowledge, it seems indisputable. And yet inside the relatively small, modest galleries of the ❶ **JFK Hyannis Museum**, such grandiosities seem meaningless. The museum concentrates solely on the family's Hyannis story, told for the most part through a series of oversized photographs. Maybe it's the diminutive size of the museum, or of Hyannis itself, that lends it such an intimate and affectionate feel.

Perhaps even more intimate and certainly more solemn, is the ❷ **JFK Memorial** in West Hyannisport, right on the town harbor and a short drive from the museum. The memorial is a large circular fountain sitting in front of a stone wall, upon which a bas-relief of JFK's profile has been carved. The inner harbor is a quiet and peaceful place, ideal for reflection. A ❸ **Korean War Memorial** with plaques featuring the names of local fallen soldiers can be seen in the adjoining Veterans Park.

Join one of the narrated ❹ **Olde Barnstable Trolley Tours**, which acts not only as a mobile history lesson, but also as an area shuttle. Most trolley tour guides are well versed in Hyannis' celebrity-rich history, as well as Kennedy lore. Tickets can be purchased right at the JFK Museum; the trolley picks up and drops off passengers there as well.

TIME
2 days

DISTANCE
125 miles

BEST TIME TO GO
Jun – Sep

START
Hyannis

END
Martha's Vineyard

ALSO GOOD FOR

CITY

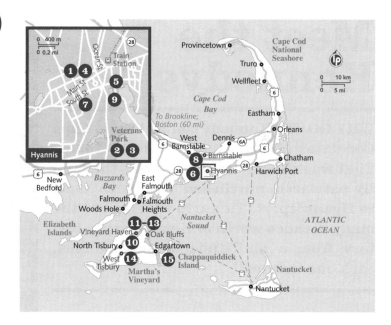

Hyannis, of course, has more to offer than just the Kennedy Circuit, although some of its most popular tourist draws would have attracted the interest of JFK himself. The ⑤ **Cape Cod Maritime Museum**, on the town marina, comprehensively documents the Cape's maritime culture and history. The museum also sponsors frequent lectures and other events on or near the marina, including boatbuilding demonstrations. The ⑥ **Four Seas Ice Cream** shack in nearby Centerville, meanwhile, was said to be JFK's favorite place to pick up a cone. The shop even famously provided the peach ice-cream at Caroline Kennedy's wedding rehearsal dinner.

> "…Centerville… was said to be JFK's favorite place to pick up a cone."

If it's genuine, Kennedy-specific minutiae you've come to Hyannis for, there's plenty worth your attention. Visit the ⑦ **St Francis Xavier Roman Catholic Church**, where various members of the Kennedy family have been known to worship. Arnold Schwarzenegger was officially admitted to the clan after being wed to Maria Shriver at St Francis in late April of 1986. An overnight stay at the ⑧ **Cape Codder Resort**, where guests can at least *live* like a Kennedy, is good too. With its over-the-top amenities – an on-site Beach Plum Spa and an 8200-sq-ft indoor wave pool suitable for kids – the resort can feel more like a compound than a hotel. You'll also be close to the downtown Hyannis action.

Speaking of compounds, the answer is "no." The question, which probably every local in Hyannis has been asked at least a time or two, has to do with the location of the famed Kennedy compound and whether or not it's accessible to outsiders. There are, however, a number of **9** **Hyannisport harbor cruises** leaving from the Ocean Street Dock and most take visitors as near to the compound as possible. Hy-Line Cruises is one of the more popular operators, but everyone has their favorite; be sure to ask specific questions about what your cruise will include before purchasing tickets.

For a lengthier and quite possibly more memorable maritime experience, head back to the Hyannisport Dock for a round-trip ticket to the island of **10** **Martha's Vineyard**. This is a casual and exceedingly laid-back sort of place, although because of its popularity as a vacation retreat among high-ranking politicians, including some US presidents, it's often incorrectly assumed to have a straitlaced atmosphere. T-shirts and shorts, however, are fine on the Vineyard. Open-air seafood eateries such as **11** **Coop de Ville**, or locals-only snack shops such as **12** **Skinny's Fat Sandwiches**, are some of the most popular and consistently packed spots.

That's not to suggest the blue-blood lifestyle isn't available for those who want it. Restaurants such as the highly regarded **13** **Sweet Life Café**, where contemporary mains come with locally grown ingredients, are relatively easy to find. The island hotel scene, unfortunately, is a bit different. Unless you've made advance reservations at **14** **HI-Martha's Vineyard**, the island's solitary hostel, expect to pay an often staggering amount for the most ordinary accommodations.

For a significantly darker view of Kennedy clan history, Vineyard visitors can travel to the far-eastern end of **15** **Chappaquiddick Island**, where Dike Rd becomes Dike Bridge. The body of water underneath it, Poucha Pond, is where the infamous and tragic Chappaquiddick incident involving Ted Kennedy and Mary Jo Kopechne took place in the summer of 1969.
Dan Eldridge

ASK A LOCAL

"Sometimes I go to **Veterans Park** just to walk around – just to clear my head and do nothing, because it can be so quiet and peaceful out here. I can sit and watch the boats for hours. It's really my own style of meditation, I guess. I think there's something sacred about the ocean. It can change your entire attitude, just watching it and doing nothing and saying nothing."
Gary Rodriguez, Hyannis

DETOUR

The **John F Kennedy Presidential Library & Museum** (just off the I-93 near Boston), designed by IM Pei, is home to an astonishing and inspiring collection of Kennedy-related archives, including 400,000 photographs and 70,000 volumes of printed matter.

In suburban Brookline, where the family lived throughout much of JFK's boyhood, JFK's mother restored the family home (in 1967) at 83 Beals St to resemble the house JFK grew up in and it's now open for tours. There are also ranger-led tours of the surrounding neighborhoods for serious Kennedy enthusiasts.

TRIP INFORMATION

GETTING THERE

Hyannis is in the Mid-Cape and south of Rte 6, approximately where Rte 132 and Rte 28 meet.

DO

Cape Cod Maritime Museum

Immerse yourself in the Cape's storied maritime culture, just steps from the marina. ☎ 508-775-1723; www.capecodmaritimemuseum.org; 135 South St, Hyannis; adult/child $15.50/8; ☺ 10am-4pm Tue-Sat, noon-4pm Sun; ♿

Hyannisport harbor cruises

This one-hour boat trip floats directly past the Kennedy compound. ☎ 800-492-8082; www.hylinecruises.com; 220 Ocean St, Ocean Street Dock, Hyannis; adult/child $15.50/8; ☺ every 75min 10am-7pm; ♿

JFK Hyannis Museum

The Kennedy clan's Hyannis years are documented in artful photographs and a short film. ☎ 508-790-3077; www.jfkhyannismuseum.org; 397 Main St, Hyannis; admission $5; ☺ 9am-5pm Mon-Sat, noon-5pm Sun

Olde Barnstable Trolley Tours

Tour Barnstable, Hyannis and Centerville in style, all while learning about area history and secrets. ☎ 508-771-8687; www.oldebarnstabletrolley.com; 397 Main St, Hyannis; adult/child $10/5

St Francis Xavier Roman Catholic Church

The Kennedy family has been known to worship here. ☎ 508-775-0818; www.stfrancishyannis.org; 347 South St, Hyannis; ☺ mass 7am Mon-Fri, mass at 7am, 9am & 11am Sun

EAT

Coop de Ville

Fried seafood and chicken wings in a casual, open-air setting. A true Vineyard tradition. ☎ 508-693-3420; www.coopdevillemv.com; Dockside Marketplace, Oak Bluffs Harbor; mains $9-20; ☺ 11am-10pm; ♿

Four Seas Ice Cream

JFK's favorite snack shop even provided the ice cream for Caroline Kennedy's rehearsal dinner. ☎ 508-775-1394; www.fourseasicecream.com; 360 South Main St, Centerville; mains $7-12; ☺ 9am-9:30pm summer

Skinny's Fat Sandwiches

Thanks to the use of local ingredients, you won't find a fresher or more toothsome take-out sandwich shop anywhere on the island. ☎ 508-693-5281; 12 Circuit Ave, Vineyard Haven; mains $7-12; ☺ 10am-midnight

Sweet Life Café

Enjoy garden dining and all-local produce at this fine seafood restaurant. ☎ 508-696-0200; www.sweetlifemv.com; 63 Circuit Ave, Oak Bluffs; mains $32-44; ☺ 5:30-10pm

SLEEP

Cape Codder Resort

Dive into the indoor wave pool and indulge at the on-site spa. ☎ 508-771-3000; www.capecodderresort.com; 1225 Iyannough Rd (Rte 132), Hyannis; r from $250; ♿

HI-Martha's Vineyard

Conveniently located along a bike path, this simple saltbox structure was the country's first hostel. ☎ 508-693-2665; www.usahostels.org/cape/himv; Edgartown-West Tisbury Rte 525, Vineyard Haven; dm $30-35, r $150-200; ☺ mid-May–mid-Oct

USEFUL WEBSITES

www.jfkhyannismuseum.org
www.jfklibrary.org

LINK YOUR TRIP

www.lonelyplanet.com/trip-planner

Antiquing the Cape

WHY GO With more opportunities for antique shopping than anywhere else in the Northeastern United States, it's no wonder so many serious shoppers come to Cape Cod armed with little more than an Amex card and a map of the Old King's Hwy. This is what the ancient art of buying and selling is really all about.

It's quite likely that Cape Cod wouldn't be the top-notch antiquing destination it is today if it weren't for the historic rural road known as the Old King's Hwy. We'll explore this 34-mile road, technically known as Rte 6A. But for the time being, let's start our trip where the two-lane byway begins. That would be the town of Bourne, which has the distinction of sitting closer to mainland Massachusetts than any other town on the Cape. Bourne is also home to an unusual open-air museum known as the ❶ **Aptucxet Trading Post Museum Complex.**

Built by the Pilgrims for the purpose of trading with the Dutch and Native Americans, the trading post itself is the main draw here. The replicated structure you'll encounter was built in the 1920s, after two archaeologists used antique maps to successfully discover the original foundation. Also on the complex grounds is the Grey Gables Railroad Station, which served as a private stop for President Grover Cleveland, who kept a summer home in Bourne.

The historic town of Sandwich is your next stop. Even if you don't happen to be an admirer of antique or stained glass, you'll almost certainly still be fascinated by the recently renovated ❷ **Sandwich Glass Museum.** Show up by 3pm to see the glass-blowing demonstrations.

Also in Sandwich is another must-see attraction, the ❸ **Heritage Museums and Gardens.** Antique-auto fans will make a beeline for

Sidebar

TIME
2 days

DISTANCE
60 miles

BEST TIME TO GO
Jun – Sept

START
Bourne

END
Wellfleet

ALSO GOOD FOR

ROUTE

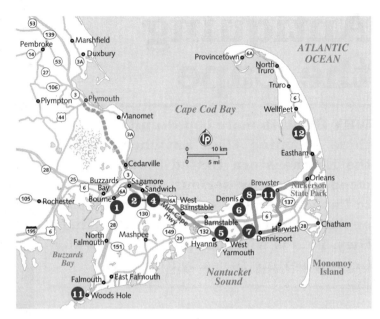

the Shaker round barn, with its jaw-dropping collection of pristine old autos. At the Art Museum here you'll find an antique, hand-carved carousel. The on-site American History Museum is known for its impressive collection of military antiques and miniatures.

Should you decide to pass the night in Cape Cod's oldest town, the **4 Dan'l Webster Inn and Spa** will be right up your alley. It's been accommodating travelers, in one form or another, for 300 years. When it's time to take supper at the Dan'l Webster, you've got a total of four dining rooms to choose from, serving both traditional and contemporary cuisine.

No matter where you rest your head, you'll want a good night's sleep before descending upon the **5 Antiques Center of Yarmouth** and the **6 Antiques Center of Cape Cod**, located in nearby Dennis. Both are home to dozens of antique dealers hawking every odd collectible you can fathom and some you probably can't. If you only have time to choose one, head straight to Dennis, where some of the finest regional collectibles in New England are up for sale.

Before you max out the credit card and head back to the highway, stop by the ever-popular **7 Dick & Ellie's Flea Market**, also in the Dennis area. Given the confluence of wealth and advanced age in this part of New England, thrift stores and used markets here are often taken seriously by collectors. At Dick & Ellie's you'll also see clothing and boutique-style accessories that are essentially brand-new. This is a community market, in other words, where you're sure to uncover crafts that aren't on sale anywhere else.

Once you've worked up an appetite, head back up to Rte 6A to **8 Brewster**. Aside from the seemingly endless string of high-quality antique shops lining both sides of the Old King's Hwy there, you'll also find the casual but hugely popular **9 Brewster Fish House**. New Englanders have been known to travel seriously long distances to take a meal at the fish house, where the relaxed atmosphere belies the restaurant's innovative seafood and wine menus.

DETOUR Often referred to as America's Hometown, the historic city of **Plymouth** sits just 20 miles north of Sandwich. Plymouth's first-rate antiquing opportunities are a perfect excuse to pull out the pocketbook after leaving the Aptucxet Trading Post Museum Complex.

Head first to the intersection of Court, Main and North Sts, where you'll find two competing antique malls: the **Plymouth Antiques Trading Company** and **Main Street Antiques**. Both are home to nearly 100 independent dealers.

If you'd rather sit down to supper in your Sunday finest, look for the **10 Bramble Inn & Restaurant**, where it's possible to stay the night in one of five country-inn-style guest rooms. As for the dining, you'll wonder if you've accidentally wandered into a private Cape Cod residence. The eclectic but traditionally American four-course menu here is prix fixe, although it changes so regularly you'll probably never see the same item twice.

If you find yourself reluctant to leave the Cape, visit the colony of cottages known as **11 Linger Longer by the Sea** along the Brewster seafront. Specifically designed for long stays and perfect for families, the atmosphere in the private apartments here is serene and comfortably homey.

Those of you staying within the reaches of the Outer Cape will have a much easier time giving the credit cards a workout at the **12 Wellfleet Flea Market**. Come nightfall, this patch of earth is home to the only operational drive-in movie theater on

ASK A LOCAL "When you think about how old most of the population is out here and the insane amount of money that's here, you realize this pretty much has to be one of the best thrifting spots in the country. I don't go to the flea markets very often, but every single time I do, I find so much incredible stuff and I always end up spending way more money than I meant to."
Anne Bennett, Falmouth

the Cape. Arrive early enough on the weekend, though, and you'll wonder if half of New England has arrived with you. And just think: this is the same stretch of land described in Thoreau's time as "bare and wind-swept." Makes you wonder where they did their shopping, doesn't it?
Dan Eldridge

TRIP INFORMATION

GETTING THERE
Bourne sits right at the entrance of Cape Cod and very near the mainland part of Massachusetts that locals refer to as "off Cape."

DO

Antiques Center of Cape Cod
With over 250 dealers located in a former lumber yard, this is the Cape's largest antique center. ☎ 508-385-6400; www.antique centerofcapecod.com; 243 Rte 6A, Dennis; ⊗ 10am-5pm Mon-Sat, 11am-5pm Sun

Antiques Center of Yarmouth
Over 100 dealers in this irresistibly cluttered building offer everything from antique jewelry to collectible firearms. ☎ 508-771-3327; www.antiquescenterofyarmouth.com; 325 Rte 28, West Yarmouth; ⊗ 10am-5:30pm

Aptucxet Trading Post Museum Complex
Explore a Pilgrim-Dutch trading post replica, a Dutch-style windmill and more. ☎ 508-759-8167; www.bournehistoricalsoc.org; 24 Aptucxet Rd, Bourne; adult/child $4/2; ⊗ 10am-4pm Tue-Sat, 2-5pm Sun; ⬧

Dick & Ellie's Flea Market
Antique jewelry and housewares are among the treasures you'll spot here. ☎ 508-394-6131; www.dickandellies.com; Theophilus Smith Rd at Rte 134, Dennis; adult/child $12/6; ⊗ 8am-5pm Thu-Sun; ⬧

Heritage Museums and Gardens
A hand-carved carousel, antique toys and automobiles and three American art museums. ☎ 508-888-3300; www.heritagemuseums andgardens.org; 67 Grove St, Sandwich; adult/child $12/6; ⊗ 10am-5pm Apr-Oct; ⬧

Sandwich Glass Museum
Collectors can learn about the historical town of Sandwich and its worldwide contribution to the glass industry. ☎ 508-888-0251; www.sandwichglassmuseum.org; 129 Main St, Sandwich; adult/child $5/1.30; ⊗ 9:30am-5pm Apr-Dec

Wellfleet Flea Market
Up to 300 vendors hawk their wares on the grounds of a drive-in theater. ☎ 866-696-3532; www.wellfleetcinemas.com/flea_mar ket.htm; 51 Rte 6, Wellfleet; admission per car $1-3; ⊗ 8am-3pm Wed, Thu, Sat & Sun Jul & Aug, 8am-3pm Sat & Sun Sep- Jun

EAT

Bramble Inn & Restaurant
An historic 1860s home with five artful dining rooms and an eclectic menu. Reservations required. ☎ 508-896-7644; www.brambleinn .com; 2019 Main St (Rte 6A), Brewster; mains $18-34; ⊗ dinner

Brewster Fish House
Popular with locals, this fine-dining fresh seafood spot is decidedly casual. ☎ 508-896-7867; 2208 Main St (Rte 6A), Brewster; mains $15-25; ⊗ 11:30am-9:30pm

SLEEP

Dan'l Webster Inn and Spa
Cape Cod's oldest inn, located on the site of a historic tavern, has been serving travelers for 300 years. ☎ 508-888-3622; www.danlweb sterinn.com; 149 Main St, Sandwich; apartments/cottages from $175/235

Linger Longer by the Sea
This complex of beachfront cottages is perfect for families and extended stays. ☎ 508-896-7714; www.lingerlongerbythesea.com; 261 Linnell Landing Rd, Brewster; apartments /cottages from $175/235; ⬧

USEFUL WEBSITES
www.antiquecenterofcapecod.com
www.ccada.com

LINK YOUR TRIP
www.lonelyplanet.com/trip-planner

RHODE ISLAND TRIPS

Saturday Night Live fans around the world will never forget the husky, middle-aged voice of one effervescent Linda Richman. Played by Mike Myers, this bouffant-wearing New Yorker was a hilarious tribute to his Jewish mother-in-law.

She would ramble on about weighty subjects such as Barbra Streisand tearjerkers ("her voice, it's like buttah!") and would subsequently become verklempt. Unable to continue her show, she would ask the audience for a moment to collect herself, offering them an earth-shattering statement to ponder: "Talk amongst yourselves… I'll give you a topic: Rhode Island is neither a road nor an island. Discuss." And discuss we did.

Turns out the state's official name isn't even Rhode Island! The smallest member of the union actually has the longest official moniker: the State of Rhode Island and Providence Plantations.

This quirky, pinprick-sized state is full of other bizarre factoids: "Awful

PLAYLIST 🎵 OK, you'll have driven through the entire state by the fifth track, but these songs, either sung in Rhode Island or performed by former Rhode Islanders, are worth the $0.99 download on iTunes:

- "Psycho Killer," Talking Heads
- "April in Paris" (Live, Newport 1957), Ella Fitzgerald
- "Here It Goes Again," OK Go
- "Swingin'," Blu Cantrell
- "St Patrick's Gay Parade," Arab on Radar
- "Trouble in Mind," (Live, Newport 1960), Nina Simone
- "Stay," Lisa Loeb
- "The Impression That I Get," The Mighty Mighty Bosstones
- "Indian Lake," The Cowsills

Awfuls" are actually quite good, "coffee milk" is even better and locals *drink* "cabinets" instead of storing their cups in them.

If this all sounds like gibberish to you, then you clearly haven't spent enough time in Rhode Island.

 ## RHODE ISLAND'S BEST TRIPS

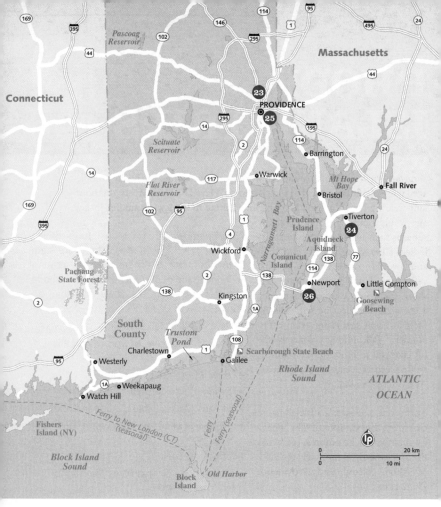

RHODE ISLAND TRIPS

Providence Arts & Culture

WHY GO Like a cat with nine lives, Providence always manages to scratch its way back from the brink of extinction. The city's current incarnation seems to be its most promising; come check out the hipster art scene that chills out amid a colorful gridiron of well-preserved colonial architecture.

TIME
2 – 3 days

BEST TIME TO GO
Year-round

START
Providence

END
Providence

ALSO GOOD FOR

HISTORY & CULTURE

Providence. The name sounds so biblical. "Thou shalt not covet thy neighbor's wife…in Providence…?". Despite its godly connotations, Providence was actually founded by a religious outcast from Boston. Roger Williams was deemed a ne'er-do-well for his strong opinions regarding the separation of government and religion and was promptly booted from the Massachusetts Bay Colony. After purchasing a tract of land from the Narragansett Indians, Williams set up shop along the bay as the go-to place for religious exiles. The face of little Providence changed after the American Revolution when maritime endeavors were replaced with manufacturing and loads of European immigrants joined the descendants of the original dissenters. After many decades of dramatic booms and busts (in which there were more "busts" than "booms"), the city entered its self-proclaimed renaissance with the help of some investors and has since been on a slow-but-steady path to reclaim its original identity as a haven for free thought.

Today, the city's undeniable artsy vibe is largely due to the omnipresence of RISD, one of the top design schools in the nation. From public statuary to film performances to indecipherable screen-printed flyers stapled to College Hill telephone poles, RISD oozes its smooth coolness all across the small cityscape. From mummies to Matisse, the standout collection of the ❶ **RISD Museum** includes 19th-century French paintings, medieval and Renaissance works and examples of 19th- and 20th-century American painting, furniture and decorative

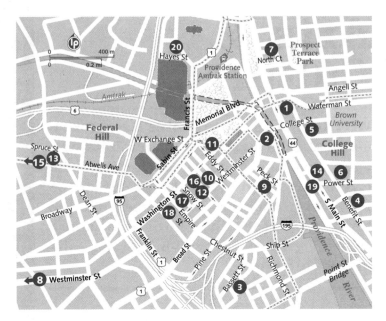

arts. The 1st floor is a temporary exhibition area, which usually takes an ubermodern twist. When we visited, the space was devoted to a meditation on Styrofoam. If you want to take a masterpiece home with you, head to **2** **RISD|works**, down the street. This funky shop-and-showcase displays an assortment of goods (jewelry, photographic prints, flatware, coffee tables and children's books) made by faculty and alumni.

Place your newly purchased Eames-inspired desk chair in the back of your car and reward yourself with a quick hop over to the "downtown" side of the river for lunch. Obscured by a jungle of crimson brick warehouses, **3** Cav continues our artsy theme with a creative menu of international flavors. However, the restaurant's biggest draw is undoubtedly the decor. Like a giant *vide grenier,* Cav is stuffed brim to bow with forgotten heirlooms (and everything is for sale!) – as soon as you walk in you'll wonder, "Did *Amelie* explode in here?".

> *"...as soon as you walk in you'll wonder, "Did* Amelie *explode in here?".*

After lunch, retrace your steps back across to College Hill to absorb the flavor of Providence's rich colonial past reflected in the multihued 18th-century houses lining **4** **Benefit Street**. These lovely gestures of colonial design are, for the most part, private homes. Benefit St is a fitting symbol of the Providence renaissance, rescued by local preservationists in the 1960s from misguided urban-renewal efforts. Check out the clean Greek Revival lines of

William Strickland's 1838 **5 Providence Athenaeum**. Plaster busts and oil paintings abound in the spaces not occupied by the dusty leather tomes. Edgar Allan Poe was a regular and often courted ladies here. Also in the neighborhood is the brick **6 John Brown House**, which John Quincy Adams called the "most magnificent and elegant mansion that I have ever seen…on this continent." If you find yourself sharing the sixth president's sentiment, then book a room at the similarly stately **7 Old Court**, a buxom manor house along Benefit St.

For dinner, sneak away from the city center and try a local chow spot fiercely hidden away from prying visitors. **8 El Rancho Grande** sits on the west side of the Huntington Expressway, making it the ultimate cheap taco joint for people in the know. The fresh Mexican fare is simply out of this world and the astonishingly cheap prices will make you feel like you were invited over to your *abuelita*'s house for some homemade *mole*. Wash down your burrito with a few drinks at **9 Red Fez**, in the heart of downtown "PVD". Head upstairs and brood with your beer under the dim red lights along with dozens of RISD hipster types clad in plaited hair, go-go boots and an ironic Mickey Mouse T-shirt cut up into a million pieces and resewn in some nightmarish fashion. If you really want to fit in, bring a pad of paper and a pen and start intensely doodling random nonsense. If it's not too late, try stopping by **10 Xxodus Café** for some live music. The space belongs to the Providence Black Repertory Company (Black Rep), the anchor of Providence's thriving community of black artists. Check out the website for up-to-the-minute performance listings.

OPEN HOUSE

Every year at the beginning of June, the Providence Preservation Society coaxes wealthy local homeowners into opening their doors to the public for a weekend entitled the **Festival of Historic Homes** (www.ppsri.org). Around a dozen colonial houses are selected each year and the $35 ticket grants you glimpses of lavish interior design, priceless heirlooms and fabulous refurbishments.

For those who weren't too keen on staying at the colonial-themed Old Court, try the **11 Providence Biltmore** downtown. The granddaddy of Providence's hotels, the Biltmore behemoth dates back to the 1920s. The lobby is a bit of a throwback to flapper times, with twisting staircases and bejeweled chandeliers. Snag a room on one of the top floors for privileged views of the city's architectural gems below. **12 Hotel Providence** is another local fave, sporting lavish interiors with chic furnishings designed by an RISD professor.

Disregard everything your mother taught you and start your second day off with dessert at **13 Pastiche**. Awash in soothing colors and warmed by a fire in winter, this wee patisserie deserves every bit of its local reputation as the top spot for high-quality confections.

If the weather looks a bit grim, plunk yourself down at ⑭ **Cable Car** for a round of cappuccinos followed by whatever indie film they're showing in the back. If you're lucky, a local character (and chronic customer) might grace you with a creepy rendition of "Teddy Bears' Picnic" before the movie starts. When the weather isn't being its usual unpredictable self, head to the ⑮ **Steel Yard** to witness Providence's urban renaissance in motion. Tours are available at 1pm on Wednesdays and Fridays and they're a fantastic way to learn about the city's continuous attempt to morph urban decay into an appealing community for creative types. In addition to the tours, there are events and lectures, and for those sticking around town there are courses and volunteer opportunities.

WATERFIRE

The brainchild of artist Barnaby Evans and an attempt to resuscitate Providence's urban appeal, WaterFire (www.waterfire.com) is an outdoor art installation consisting of 100 bonfires blazing in the center of the city's snaking river. Sure, the canned Enya music and overbearing scent of charred wood can be a bit much, but the carnival-like atmosphere and riverside gondola rides create a truly memorable and romantic evening. WaterFire occurs about a dozen times between May and October and begins at dusk.

Break for lunch at ⑯ **Local 121**, another new establishment helping to blaze the gentrification trail in the city's older, more run-down industrial districts. For dessert, grab a vegan cookie at the anchor of Providence's progressive arts scene, ⑰ **AS220** (pronounced "A-S-two-twenty"), and stick around to check out the rotating exhibits of local art, installations and live performances in the evenings.

Dinner at ⑱ **Bravo** is a must. The scrumptious steak *au poivre* is tops, but you can't go wrong with anything on the menu. Bravo's highlight is the freshly baked baguettes, which emit thick plumes of steam as you crack them open to slather on your butter. ⑲ **L'Elizabeth** is a great spot for after-dinner drinks; don't let the *l'apostrophe* fool you – the only thing "French" is the winelist. This quirky, antique-clad realm is a great place to

GALLERY NIGHT

Held every third Thursday evening of the month between March and Novermber, Gallery Night (www.gallerynight.info) is a fantastic (and free!) event in which over two dozen galleries open their doors to the public.

relax and chat with friends over a bottle of smooth red wine. The large throne-like chairs each have unique ornamentation yet they all seamlessly blend together. Only the strange, tiled ceiling feels cheap and out of place; this mismatched design detail makes for great conversation fodder.

Stop by ⑳ **Temple Downtown** for one last hurrah. The city's original Masonic lodge is now a shmansy nightclub covered in graffiti murals from the public artist who used to tag the derelict building before it became hip.

Brandon Presser

TRIP INFORMATION

GETTING THERE
From Boston's city center head south along I-93 and after 15 miles merge onto I-95 to complete the remaining 33 miles to Providence's gridiron downtown.

DO
AS220
The anchor of Providence's progressive arts scene offers rotating exhibits of local art, installations and live performances in the evenings. ☎ 401-831-9327; www.as220 .org; 115 Empire St; admission free-$10; ⊙ from 3pm

Cable Car
A great retreat for a rainy day, Cable Car is an indie movie theater with threadbare couches and a messy coffee shop. ☎ 401-272-3970; www.cablecarcinema.com; 204 S Main St; tickets $8.50; ⊙ from 7:30am

John Brown House
A monument to stately colonial architecture; described by John Quincy Adams as the "most magnificent and elegant mansion...on this continent." ☎ 401-273-7507; www.rihs .org; 52 Power St; adult/child $8/4; ⊙ tours 1:30pm & 3pm Tue-Fri, morning tours Sat Apr-Dec

Providence Athenaeum
Leather tomes, plaster busts and oil paintings compete for space in Edgar Allan Poe's old stomping ground. ☎ 401-421-6970; www .providenceathenaeum.com; 251 Benefit St; admission free; ⊙ 9am-7pm Mon-Thu, 9am-5pm Fri & Sat, 1-5pm Sun

RISD Museum
An excellent university art collection featuring impressionist paintings, classical Greek and Roman art and modern designs by cutting-edge artists. ☎ 401-454-6500; www.risd.edu/museum; 224 Benefit St; adult/child/student/senior $8/2/3/5; ⊙ 10am-5pm Wed, Thu, Sat & Sun, 10am-8pm Fri; ♿

RISD|works
A veritable design showcase unto itself, this little shop displays an assortment of goods made by faculty and alumni. ☎ 401-277-4949; www.risdworks.com; 20 North Main St; ⊙ 10am-6pm Mon-Sat; ♿

Steel Yard
Learn about the city's continuous attempt to morph the urban decay into an appealing community for creative types. ☎ 401-273-7101; www.thesteelyard.org; 27 Sims Ave

EAT
Bravo
A laid-back brasserie, Bravo dishes up top-notch French cuisine (scrumptious steak au poivre, freshly baked baguettes) that will transport you directly to Paris. ☎ 401-490-5112; www.bravobrasserie.com; 123 Empire St; mains $8-18; ⊙ 11am-1am Sun-Thu, 11am-2am Fri & Sat; ♿

Cav
Stuffed with forgotten heirlooms, this restaurant's decor draws the patrons (and everything is for sale!). ☎ 401-751-9164; www.cavrestaurant.com; 14 Imperial Pl #101; ⊙ 11:30am-10pm Mon-Thu, Sat & Sun, 11:30am-1am Fri; ♿

El Rancho Grande
The fresh Mexican fare here is out-of-this-world. Incredibly cheap prices will make you feel like you were invited over to your *abuelita*'s house for some homemade *mole*. ☎ 401-275-0808; www.elranchogrande restaurant.com; 311 Plainfield St; dinner mains $3-15; ⊙ 8am-10pm; ♿

Local 121
A newer establishment helping to blaze the gentrification trail in the city's older, more run-down industrial districts. ☎ 401-274-2121; www.local121.com; 121 Washington St; dinner mains $11-24; ⊙ 5-10pm Mon, noon-3pm & 5-10pm Tue-Thu, noon-3pm & 5-11pm Fri, 5-11pm Sat, 5-9pm Sun; ♿

TRIP
23
CITY

Pastiche

A teeny patisserie that has earned a reputation in town as the city's best spot for sweets. ☎ 401-861-5190; www.pastichefinedesserts.com; 92 Spruce St; ⊗ 8:30am-11pm Tue-Thu, 8:30am-11:30pm Fri & Sat, 10am-10pm Sun; ♿

DRINK

L'Elizabeth

Don't let the *l'apostrophe* fool you, the only thing French about this place is the wine list. ☎ 401-861-1974; www.l-elizabeth.com; 285 Main St; ⊗ 3pm-12am Sun-Tue, 3pm-1am Wed-Sat

Red Fez

Head upstairs and brood with your beer under the dim red lights along with dozens of RISD hipster types clad in plaited hair, go-go boots and an ironic Mickey Mouse T-shirt cut up into a million pieces and resewn in some nightmarish fashion. ☎ 401-272-1212; 49 Peck St; ⊗ 4pm-1am Tue & Wed, 4pm-2am Thu-Sat

Temple Downtown

The city's original Masonic lodge has since been turned into a clubbing hot spot covered in graffiti murals from the public artist who used to tag the derelict building before it became hip. ☎ 401-919-5050; www.temple-downtown.com; 120 Francis St; cocktails $7; ⊗ noon-1am Mon & Sun, 6pm-1am Tue-Sat

Xxodus Café

This space belongs to the Providence Black Repertory Company (Black Rep), the anchor of Providence's thriving community of black artists. ☎ 401-351-0352; www.blackrep.org; 276 Westminster St; ⊗ from 8pm

SLEEP

Hotel Providence

A popular choice for visitors in the city center. The rooms were designed by a professor at RISD. ☎ 401-861-8000; www.hotelprovidence.com; 311 Westminster St; r from $199

Old Court

Well-positioned among the historic buildings of College Hill, this 3-story 1863 Italianate home has worn wooden floors, old fireplaces and stacks of charm. ☎ 401-751-2002; www.oldcourt.com; 144 Benefit St; r $185

Providence Biltmore

The granddaddy of Providence's hotels, the Biltmore dates to the 1920s. ☎ 410-421-0700; www.providencebiltmore.com; 11 Dorrance St; r from $179; ♿

USEFUL WEBSITES

www.artinruins.com
www.providenceri.com

LINK YOUR TRIP

www.lonelyplanet.com/trip-planner

Rhode Island: Roads & Islands

WHY GO After traveling along the state's scenic roads and visiting the jagged islands floating in the Narragansett Bay, you will understand why Rhode Island got the honor of being called the Ocean State over all the other coastal states in the union.

TIME
2 – 4 days

DISTANCE
120 miles

BEST TIME TO GO
May – Sep

START
Providence

END
Westerly

ALSO GOOD FOR

Tackle your first stretch of road early in the morning and take Rte 114 out of Providence and down along the eastern arm of Narragansett Bay. On the north stretch of Rte 77, you'll find gray-shingled ❶ **Evelyn's**, a traditional roadside eatery in Tiverton from another era. Park on the crushed-shell driveway and eat amazing lobster rolls. The joint sits next to a blue inlet with a handful of bobbing dinghies. After a quick nosh, continue on to Little Compton. Here large wood-framed homes become older, grayer and statelier just as an increasing number of stone walls crisscross the green landscape. If you found Tiverton appealing, you'll probably wet yourself at the classic sight of the village's ❷ **Common** with its white-steepled church and graveyard. Park the car and wander the sweet colonial streets or make a beeline for the seashore to test the waters at ❸ **Goosewing Beach**. Lovely, remote, ocean-facing Goosewing is the only good public beach in Little Compton. Access can be a bit tricky due to an ongoing wrangle between the town and the Nature Conservancy so it's best to park at ❹ **South Shore Beach** and walk across a small tidal inlet.

Next, head along scenic Rte 24, and as you pass the churning water on both sides, you'll arrive on Aquidneck Island, home to the East Coast's original lap of luxury, ❺ **Newport**. Although not technically a road, Newport's infamous seaside footpath, the ❻ **Cliff Walk**, is a 3.5-mile walk featuring dramatic sea-swept cliffs on one side and uber-opulent mansions on the other. The path begins off Memorial Blvd just west of Easton's Beach and goes south and then west to the

BEST TRIP

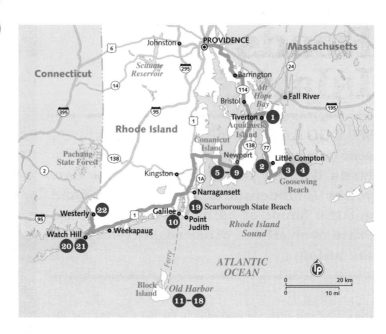

intersection of Bellevue and Coggeshalls Aves. For views of the island and the surrounding bay, take a boat ride with **7** **Classic Cruises of Newport** and hop aboard the *Rum Runner II,* a Prohibition-era bootlegging vessel, as it takes you past mansions and former speakeasies. For those interested in a road tour rather than an island tour, sign up with **8** **Newport History Tours**. Guides will take you on a walk of Historic Hill, where you will learn about Newport's colorful past, which was once referred to as "a sewer of religious contagion" by Cotton Mather.

Before heading across the Narragansett Bay and Conanicut Island, stop at **9** **Salvation Café** for a light bite and a beer. Combining an outdoor Tiki lounge, corduroy couches, Formica tables and wood-paneled walls, this joint is a stylish spot for a relaxed snack sans the busloads of tourists. Pull into the quiet fishing town of Galilee and end the evening at the popular **10** **Fishermen's Memorial State Campground**.

In the morning, take the passenger boat from Galilee and make your way down to Block Island. From the deck of the summer ferry, you'll see a cluster of mansard roofs and gingerbread houses rising picturesquely from the commercial village of Old Harbor, where little has changed since about 1895. Yes, they've added lights and toilets, but – especially if you remain after the departure of the masses on the last ferry – the scale and pace of the island will seem distinctly premodern. During off-season, the island landscape has the spare, haunted feeling of an Andrew Wyeth painting, with stone walls demarcating centuries-old property lines and few trees to interrupt the ocean views. During these quieter months the island's population dwindles to a few hundred folks.

Block Island's attractions are simple: long stretches of bleach-blonde sand punctuated by the odd towering shaft of steel with a searchlight on top. The best way to explore the rugged islet is by bike or by foot. Dozens of outfitters will try to hook you up with some wheels right when you alight; try ⑪ **Island Moped & Bike Rentals** for specialized brand hybrids. Most islanders resent the noise and hazards caused by the many tourists on mopeds, so you'll get friendlier greetings (and exercise) if you opt for a bicycle.

Before hitting the dunes, stock up on carbs at the ⑫ **Post Office Bagel Shop**. Order at the counter and grab a seat on the umbrella-shaded patio. Don't miss the warm, homemade granola bars crammed with toasted oats, coconuts and pumpkin seeds. Pack a picnic for lunch from the assorted items at ⑬ **Block Island Grocery**, the island's largest market, and head to ⑭ **Block Island State Beach**.

For dinner, venture into Old Harbor for plates full of freshly caught fish at ⑮ **Eli's**. The dining room is cramped, crowded and casual with lots of pine-wood and a bit of well-conceived art, but patrons rarely notice the ambience as they are too busy gorging on fresh fillets of sea bass and tarts crafted from local berries.

1 IF BY LAND, 2 IF BY SEA

If you're circumnavigating the Ocean State, why not help out Mother Nature and use Rhode Island's handy brigade of public transportation? By land, you'll find one sturdy option that zig-zags around the state: **RIPTA** (www.ripta.com). Those traveling by sea have two choices: you can hop on the **RIPTA ferry** from Providence to Newport and take the **Interstate Navigation** (www.blockislandferry.com) when traveling from Newport to Block Island.

In the evening, check into one of the many quaint cottagelike inns that dot the rocky shore. Camping is unfortunately prohibited on the island and although there are around three dozen B&Bs, it's still best to book ahead and keep spontaneity for other parts of the trip. With its high Victorian "widow's walk" turret and small but lushly furnished guest rooms, the ⑯ **Hotel Manisses** combines sophistication with Block Island's relaxed brand of country charm. Check with the reception for additional private-cottage rental opportunities around the island. The ⑰ **Blue Dory Inn**, with its 14 small rooms, is a cozy place at the edge of Old Harbor overlooking a stretch of beach. The style is decidedly Victorian with abounding doilies, flowery bedspreads, cheesy room names and the smell of freshly baked cookies wafting through the air. At the ⑱ **Surf Hotel** you'll find yourself in the center of the Old Harbor main-drag bustle while also taking in the serene ocean views out the windows on the other side. You'll find multiple porches on several levels – one of which dramatically juts out into the harbor – and a rooftop cupola. The overly cluttered lobby contains a jumble of taxidermy, dark Victorian furniture, busy wallpaper and people playing Scrabble.

If time permits, lather, rinse and repeat yesterday's activities. If not, take a morning ferry back to the mainland at Point Judith and continue west along Hwy 1 toward the Connecticut border. ⓳ **Scarborough State Beach** is the quintessential Rhode Island beach, considered by many to be the best beach in the state. A massive, castlelike pavilion, generous boardwalks, a wide and long beachfront and great predictable surf make Scarborough extra special. Grab an umbrella, a blanket and four rocks – that's all you'll need for this leg of the trip. Not much beats a well-chosen section of sand on a sunny August day in South County. The sandy shore extends virtually uninterrupted for several dozen miles and much of it is open to the public. Some beaches teem with thousands of well-oiled young bodies, while others are more subdued, where visitors can thin themselves into relative privacy across a long landscape. Follow the scenic Hwy 1 along the coast and select your very own slice of sand.

RAILS TO TRAILS

The old industrial train tracks that scar Rhode Island's verdant countryside are gradually being transformed into scenic bike routes along the coast and throughout the inner part of the state. Check out www.dot.state.ri.us/bikeri /bikepathfuture/htm for more information on how to scope out these rail trails.

In the afternoon travel the last scenic stretch of road along Hwy 1A to the state's extreme western edge. Itty-bitty Watch Hill sits on a slender spit just beyond Westerly and a stone's throw from Connecticut next door. Head into the town center for provisions and let the kids get distracted at the ⓴ **Flying Horses Carousel**, one of the country's oldest carousels still in operation. The horses are suspended by chains rather than poles, giving the illusion that the equines are actually airborne. Stop for sandwiches at ㉑ **Bay St Deli** and pack a sunset picnic to take to the beach nearby. The road ends 5 miles outside Watch Hill (near the beach town of Weekapaug) at ㉒ **Grandview B&B**.

Brandon Presser

"Grab an umbrella, a blanket and four rocks – that's all you'll need..."

TRIP INFORMATION

GETTING THERE

From Boston, follow I-95 down to Providence and Rte 114 along the eastern coast of the Narragansett Bay.

DO

Classic Cruises of Newport

Runs excursions on the *Rum Runner II*, a Prohibition-era bootlegging vessel. The narrated tour will take you past mansions and former speakeasies. ☎ 401-847-0299; www.cruisenewport.com; Bannister's Wharf, Newport; adult/child $18/12; ☉ mid-May–mid-Oct

Flying Horses Carousel

The Flying Horses is an antique carousel at the end of Bay St dating back to 1883. Riders must be under the age of 12. **Bay St; rides $1;** ☉ 11am-9pm Mon-Fri, 10am-9pm Sat & Sun; ⚐

Goosewing Beach

A beautiful and secluded stretch of sand just beyond Little Compton. Access is limited so it is best to park at South Shore Beach and walk. ☎ 401-635-4400; Little Compton; ☉ dawn-dusk

Island Moped & Bike Rentals

An outfitter on Block Island specializing in all sorts of wheels for rent. ☎ 401-466-2700; Chapel St, Old Harbor, Block Island; bike per day/week $20/35, moped per day $115; ☉ 9am-6pm; ⚐

Newport History Tours

Guided tours of Historic Hill. Periodically, the society offers African-American and religious heritage tours, where you'll learn why Cotton Mather called Newport "a sewer of religious contagion." ☎ 401-846-0813; www.newporthistorical.org; Newport; tours $8; ☉ 10am Thu-Sat May-Sep

Scarborough State Beach

Rhode Island's best-known beach, Scarborough (often called "Scarboro") features wide dunes and plenty of space to spread out. ☎ 401-789-2324; www.riparks.com; 870 Ocean Rd, Narragansett; RI resident/nonresident parking $6/12; ☉ 9am-6pm May-Aug

South Shore Beach

A pleasant and populated beach in Little Compton with plenty of parking. ☎ 401-635-9974; Little Compton; parking $10; ☉ dawn-dusk; ⚐

EAT

Bay St Deli

Stop by this deli for takeout, prepared items and specialty sandwiches such as roast beef and Muenster cheese on pumpernickel, or a wrap of tabbouleh, cucumber, tomato and sprouts. ☎ 401-596-6606; 112 Bay St, Watch Hill; sandwiches $6-9; ☉ 8am-8pm

Block Island Grocery

The largest market on the island selling lots of alcohol and snacks. ☎ 401-466-2949; Ocean Ave, Old Harbor, Block Island; ☉ 8am-10pm

Eli's

Locally caught sea bass specials (tender fillets over scallions, grapes and beans) taste so fresh and mildly salty and sweet that their memory will haunt you for weeks. Seriously. ☎ 401-466-5230; Chapel St, Old Harbor, Block Island; meals $21-40; ☉ from 5:30pm

Evelyn's

A traditional roadside eatery plucked from another era. ☎ 401-624-3100; 2335 Main Rd, Tiverton; fish $5-18; ☉ 11:30am-8:30pm Wed-Mon early Apr-Sep

Post Office Bagel Shop

Order at the counter and grab a seat on the umbrella-shaded patio. Fine sandwiches are served on bagels and sourdough, though the top-shelf baked sweets should grab your eye. ☎ 401-466-5959; Bridgegate Sq, Old Harbor, Block Island; mains $2.50-9; ☉ 6:30am-3pm

Salvation Café

Combining an outdoor Tiki lounge, corduroy couches, Formica tables and wood-paneled walls, this bar and restaurant is a good place for a hipster drink. ☎ 401-847-2620; www.salvationcafe.com; 140 Broadway St, Newport; mains from $5; 🕙 5-11pm

SLEEP

Blue Dory Inn

With 14 small rooms, this cozy place sits at the edge of Old Harbor overlooking a stretch of beach. There's a great porch to take in the views while nibbling on freshly baked cookies. ☎ 401-466-5891; www.blockislandinns.com; Dodge St, Old Harbor, Block Island; r $225-325

Fishermen's Memorial State Campground

This campground is so popular that families often return year after year to the same site. There are only 180 campsites so it's wise to reserve early. ☎ 401-789-8374; www.riparks.com; 1011 Point Judith Rd (Rte 108), Galilee; tent sites RI residents/nonresidents $14/20

Grandview B&B

Within the town limits of Westerly, yet close to the beach town of Weekapaug, this modestly furnished guesthouse boasts a stone porch and a knowledgeable proprietor full of friendly tips about the area. Charming as the place is, rooms in the front catch a bit of traffic noise. ☎ 401-596-6384; www.grandviewbandb.com; 212 Shore Rd (Hwy 1A), Westerly; r $90-120

Hotel Manisses

With its high Victorian "widow's walk" turret and small but lushly furnished guest rooms, the Manisses combines sophistication with Block Island's relaxed brand of country charm. ☎ 401-466-2421; www.blockislandresorts.com; Spring St, Old Harbor, Block Island; r $220-370

Surf Hotel

A classic 19th-century hotel. One side faces the bustle of Old Harbor's main drag, the other turns toward the ocean. The cluttered lobby contains a jumble of taxidermy, dark Victorian accoutrements, busy wallpaper and people playing Scrabble. ☎ 401-466-2241; Dodge St, Old Harbor, Block Island; r $200, with shared bathroom $110-150

USEFUL WEBSITES

www.goblockisland.com
www.southcountyri.com

LINK YOUR TRIP

www.lonelyplanet.com/trip-planner

Wacky Tacky Rhode Island

WHY GO While driving between Massachusetts and Connecticut, many speed demons might not realize they've passed through an entire state. However, those who stop for a closer look will uncover a treasure trove of useless oddities and factoids that are somehow only salient in a state the size of a pinprick.

Any themed road trip in teeny Rhode Island, be it history or schlock, would only take three or four hours – one wrong turn and, oops, you're in Massachusetts! So, we've decided that for this trip, all you drivers must swap your Toyota Prius for pedals. Yes, that's right folks: leave your car in the driveway, it's time to blow the dust off your bicycle. This transport switcheroo will hopefully keep wayward wanderers from sneaking off to one of Rhode Island's bigger neighbors. And, of course, there's nothing wrong with "going green" and giving a shout out to our melting polar ice caps. Heck, if global warming continues, our poor little Ocean State is gonna get even smaller!

For those of you who don't have your own wheels – nice try, we're not letting you off the hook – there are plenty of places around Providence that offer daily rentals. Try ❶ Providence Bicycle on Branch Ave, or ❷ East Providence Cycle in (yeah, you guessed it) East Providence. If you can't snag a tandem, then at least score a ride sporting one of those cheesy wicker baskets dangling off the front – that'll really set the tone for our crap-tacular adventure.

The first stop on our tacky trek is the ❸ Culinary Arts Museum at Johnson & Wales University on Harborside Blvd in Providence. A shrine to Rhode Island's kitschy yesteryears, the museum features 25,000 sq ft of gallery space stuffed with everything dining-related, from presidential tea sets to diner memorabilia.

TIME
1 – 2 days

DISTANCE
40 miles

BEST TIME TO GO
Apr – Oct

START
Providence

END
Newport

ALSO GOOD FOR

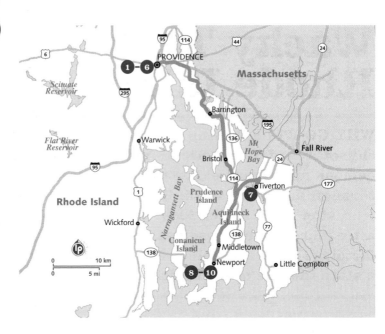

If the kitchen gadgets and recipe tomes got your tummy in a grumble, then hop back on your wheels and pedal down toward City Hall. A local institution, the infamous **4** **Haven Bros Diner** is the ultimate joint for anyone

"...one wrong turn and, oops, you're in Massachusetts! "

who wants to pack an artery. Housed in a shiny steel truck, this heart-attack-on-wheels parks along Washington St every afternoon around 4:30pm and dishes out the calories until the wee hours of the morning. For a place with a bit more atmosphere (and by atmosphere we mean crayon doodles, cereal boxes and curling, faded pictures taped to the walls). try

5 Louis', Brown University's favorite greasy spoon, serving breakfast to bleary-eyed students while random fits of classical music waft through the air.

While the diner is Rhode Island's most familiar contribution to America's lunching lexicon, the wee state has an entire repertoire of bizarre recipes known only to its residents. Quench your thirst with a frosty plastic cup of frozen lemonade at **6** Del's on Wickenden St (or at one of the 20 other locations within the state's borders). For years this franchised refreshment stand has been trying to establish its product as Rhode Island's beverage of choice, but the state legislature put the kibosh on these dreams by naming coffee milk the Official State Drink. This simple concoction of milk and coffee syrup is available almost everywhere, but it's best savored after an arduous bike ride down to Tiverton's historic four corners. Here you'll find **7** Gray's Ice Cream, a Rhode Island institution. Enjoy your coffee milk with a couple of scoops of out-of-this-world ice cream made daily at the on-site dairy. Choose from over 40 flavors including Butter Krunch, Ginger, Frozen Pudding and Peach Brandy.

Capitalize on your sugar rush and cycle down to posh Newport. Skip the usual mansion tour and head to ❽ **Aardvark Antiques**, home to the ultimate collection of unnecessary displays of wealth. Aardvark is like an orphanage of unwanted objets d'art – think giant copper seahorses, to-scale replicas of Michelangelo's *David* and fountains decked with satyrs spewing water from their mouths (and other less appropriate areas). Next, head to Touro Park to discover Newport's most bizarre and underrated attraction, the ❾ **Old Stone Mill**. New England's version of Stonehenge takes the form of a circular shaft squatting atop several stout legs. The function of the collection of stones is unclear, which has prompted conspiracy theorists and local nutjobs to spread the rumor that the structure is over 1000 years old. Although carbon-14 dating has proven that the "mill" was not in fact built during Viking times, this bizarre tower does account for the prominence of Viking-named companies in Newport.

DETOUR The union's tiniest state is home to the world's biggest pest – no, not Regis Philbin – **Nibbles Woodaway**, an enormous blue termite, which sits on the roof of New England Pest Control in Providence. The wire-mesh behemoth is exactly 928 times the size of the actual six-legged critter. Check out this infamous novelty item from I-95, or if you want a closer look, the pest control center sits on O'Connell St just south of the city center.

At the end of the day, do not pass go, do not collect $200 – go directly to jail, the ❿ **Jailhouse Hotel**, that is. This charming hotel, with its classical facade, was once the spot in town where drunks and derelicts spent the night. Today, guests have to fork over big bucks to sleep behind bars. But don't worry, the entire building has been completely redone – the strategically placed wrought-iron barricades are only used for show.

Brandon Presser

TRIP INFORMATION

GETTING THERE
Jump on I-95 from Boston and head south to the heart of downtown Providence.

DO
Aardvark Antiques
An orphanage of unwanted objets d'art — think giant copper seahorses and to-scale replicas of Michelangelo's *David*. ☎ 401-849-1591; www.aardvarkantiques.com; 9 JT Connel Hwy, Newport; ◷ 9am-5pm Mon-Sat

Culinary Arts Museum & Johnson & Wales University
A shrine to Rhode Island's kitschy yester-years, this museum features 25,000 sq ft of gallery space stuffed with everything from presidential tea sets to diner memorabilia. ☎ 401-723-4342; www.culinary.org; 315 Harborside Blvd, Providence; adult/child $7/2; ◷ 10am-5pm Mon-Sat

East Providence Cycle
A top spot in Providence to pick up a set of wheels. ☎ 401-434-3838; www.eastprovidencebicycle.com; 414 Warren Ave, Providence; ◷ 9am-6pm Mon, 9am-8pm Tue-Fri, 9am-5:30pm Sat, 11am-5pm Sun; ♿

Old Stone Mill
A strange ring of stones that was perhaps constructed before Western colonization. ☎ 401-846-1398; Touro Park, Providence; ◷ dusk-dawn; ♿

Providence Bicycle
A friendly shop offering bike rentals. ☎ 401-331-6610; www.providencebicycle.com; 725 Branch Ave, Providence; ◷ 9:30am-8pm Mon-Thu, 9:30am-6pm Fri, 9:30am-6pm Sun, shorter hours in winter; ♿

EAT
Del's
This franchised lemonade stand serves up its signature recipe of frozen lemons. There are over 20 locations throughout the state. ☎ 401-621-7974; www.dels.com; 227 Wickenden St, Providence

Gray's Ice Cream
A Rhode Island institution serving out-of-this-world ice cream made daily at an on-site dairy. Choose from over 40 flavors, including Butter Krunch, Ginger, Frozen Pudding and Peach Brandy. ☎ 401-624-4500; www.graysicecream.com; 16 East Rd, Tiverton; ice cream $3-5; ♿

Haven Bros Diner
This is the ultimate joint for anyone who wants to pack an artery. Housed in a shiny steel truck, this heart-attack-on-wheels parks along Washington St every afternoon around 4:30pm and dishes out the calories until the wee hours of the morning. Washington St, Providence; meals $5-10; ◷ 4:30pm-4am

Louis'
Brown University's favorite greasy spoon serves breakfast to bleary-eyed students while random fits of classical music waft through the air. ☎ 401-861-5225; 286 Brook St, Providence; breakfast $3-7; ◷ 7am-3pm; ♿

SLEEP
Jailhouse Hotel
This charming hotel, with its classical facade, was once the spot in town where drunks and derelicts spent the night. Today, guests have to fork over big bucks to sleep behind bars. ☎ 800-427-9444; www.jailhouse.com; 13 Marlborough St, Newport; r from $150

USEFUL WEBSITES
www.dot.state.ru.us/bikeri
www.quahog.org

LINK YOUR TRIP
TRIP

www.lonelyplanet.com/trip-planner

Mansions of Newport

WHY GO Newport became synonymous with luxury centuries before the Hamptons turned into a veritable celeb safari. We got the inside scoop from Kimberley Keefe, a Cliff Walk resident (her exact address is classified information, of course) and assembled the ultimate peek at the lifestyles of the rich and famous.

TIME
2 – 3 days

BEST TIME TO GO
Jun – Aug

START
Newport

END
Newport

ALSO GOOD FOR

CITY

Opulent Newport's beginnings were humble. After thousands of years as a favored spot for indigenous tribes, ships full of sunburned Europeans came through to set up shop. The bay overflowed with floppy fish and the shores proved remarkably arable. British colonists constructed a small port and the surrounding pastures echoed with the baa-ing of their grazing sheep. Bolstered by a sudden boom in the shipping industry, little Newport quickly earned its spot on the map as foreign funds turned the harbor haven into the fourth-richest town in a newly independent America. As long-distance transportation rapidly modernized, wealthy entrepreneurs quickly turned to Newport for relaxing escapes from the smoke stacks and city smog. Year after year wealthy American families would purchase generous parcels of land and erect a testimony to their overflowing wealth in the form of a sumptuous summer mansion. Ritzy, lantern-lined Bellevue Ave was the heart of the action – freshly minted debutants would flit down the street scoping out potential suitors while swapping calling cards and tea-party invitations. As capitalist kings competed for the unofficial crown, these new estates became increasingly over the top; Italianate palazzos were mimicked, French châteaux reproduced inch-by-inch and English manors cloned from steeple to cellar.

Known locally as the most "liveable" mansion, the ❶ Elms is the perfect place to kick off a mansions tour. The stately, square retreat was designed to mimic Château D'Asnières near Paris. The original

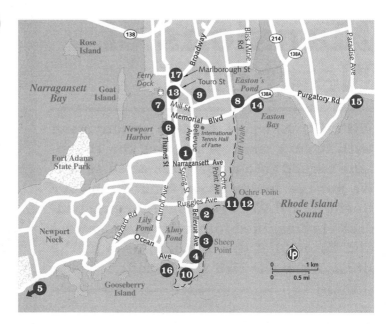

owners earned their fortune in coal mining and a special train was built to lug coal from a storage garage into the house. Opt for a "behind-the-scenes" tour, which will have you snaking through the basement operations, servants' quarters and up onto the roof. Along the way you'll learn about the activities of the army of servants and the architectural devices that kept them hidden from those swirling port glasses in the formal rooms. After the tour relax in the lavish gardens, which feature symmetrical flower beds focused around spouting fountains.

Further down Bellevue Ave stands the impressive ❷ **Rosecliff** estate. Stanford White designed this behemoth to look like the Grand Trianon at Versailles and its palatial ballroom (Newport's largest) and landscaped grounds quickly became the setting for some truly enormous parties. Houdini even entertained at one. Rosecliff was built for Mrs Hermann Oelrichs, an heiress of the Comstock Lode silver discovery. If the building seems oddly familiar during your visit, that might be because it has appeared in films such as *The Great Gatsby* and *True Lies*. In June the property hosts an impressive flower show.

Our third stop along Bellevue Ave is the aptly named ❸ **Marble House**, whose foyer is constructed entirely from imported Italian marble. After uttering an unavoidable "blech!" while staring at the garish composition of colors, take a moment to appreciate just how much work (and money) it took to lug these hulking chunks of rock across the Atlantic. As you wind your way through the mansion, the focus thankfully shifts away from marble and centers on replicas of regal furniture. Taking cues from the French court, the Versaillaise decor flows from room to room, each one a meditation on a different theme. The Gold Room and the Gothic Room are our favorites. Before leaving the grounds, don't forget to check out the bright red and green Chinese Teahouse, perched on a seaside cliff. It provides an odd contrast to the stern gray stone of the Marble House's exterior.

If you have the energy to tackle one more mansion before the end of the day, make it **4** **Belcourt Castle**, also along opulent Bellevue Ave. From the exterior, this elegant Louis XIII–style hunting lodge seems rather similar to the other displays of wealth along the shoreline; however, a peculiar floor plan lurks behind the ornate facade. The original design scheme featured but a single bedroom and the entire first floor was designed for the owner's beloved horses. Luxurious interior stables accommodated 30 coaching horses, each with their own monogrammed satin sheets. When Mr Belmont's dearest horse passed away, he had the brown beast stuffed and mounted in his study. It seems like Catherine the Great wasn't the only one with a bizarre horse fetish…

> **DETOUR**
>
> For a delightful tribute to 19th-century leisure sports, check out the **International Tennis Hall of Fame** (www.tennisfame.com). The grass courts are set up according to the parameters of the uber-elitist "court tennis" – the precursor to the modern-day game. If you brought your whites (and your wallet), it's just a $90 swipe of a credit card for 90 glorious minutes of volleying and pseudo-snobby guffawing. An annual tournament takes the town by storm in July, with an accompanying induction of star athletes into the illustrious hall of fame.

Take a break from clicking your camera at objets d'art and head to **5** **Brenton Point Park** at the serene southern tip of the island. A favorite local hangout, this rocky outcropping is a great place to go fly a kite (in the literal sense) and fiery sunsets are particularly stunning. As the harbor lights start to flicker on, stroll down **6** **Thames Street** (which is pronounced phonetically, unlike London's river) browsing the colorful mosaic of boutiques. When hunger strikes, head to Bannister's Wharf to tempt your tastebuds at **7** **Black Pearl**. A great spot to *sea* and be seen, this local treasure serves a mouthwatering assortment of surf and turf to locals, tourists and the occasional celebrity.

"…Catherine the Great wasn't the only one with a bizarre horse fetish…"

Grab a spot on the wood-planked patio and slowly spin your chardonnay as sparkling white sailboats idly bob beside your wrought-iron table.

If all of the opulence ogling has left you a little jealous, then book a room at the **8** **Chanler** – a stunning property rivaling the grandeur of the mansion-museums seen earlier in the day. The estate's 20 rooms are nothing short of regal, offering sweeping views of the sea from beyond the elaborate window treatments. Butlers are at your disposal to chauffeur you to the beach of your choosing, where they will set up pillows and a picnic under the cool shade of a canvas beach umbrella. But here's the catch: if you have enough money to stay at the Chanler, then you probably already own a Newport mansion. **9 Hotel Viking** is a solid second choice if you don't want to auction off your kids on eBay to catch 40 winks.

Start your second day with a wander around **10 Rough Point**, whose splendid gardens are reason enough to fork over the hefty entrance fee. Built for the Vanderbilt clan in 1889, the stunning property mimics the classical English manorial style and sits on a rocky escarpment jutting out into the waves. Later purchased by tobacco baron James B Duke, the mansion fell into the hands of Duke's only daughter, Doris (aged 13 years), who gave the estate to the Newport Restoration Society upon her death. Today, the property features much of Doris Duke's impressive art holdings, including medieval tapestries, furniture owned by French emperors, Ming dynasty ceramics, paintings by Renoir and Van Dyck, and an army of mannequins displaying eight decades worth of bizarro couture. Outside, the exotic green grounds overflow with exotic flowers and even more exotic creatures – zebras have been known to clomp around.

ALL THAT JAZZ

If corsets, fake British accents and teacup poodles aren't your thing, then the annual **JVC Jazz Festival** might coax you into visiting Newport. Held on a mid-August weekend, this big-ticket event draws top performers like Ella Fitzgerald, Aretha Franklin, Miles Davis, Herbie Hancock, John Coltrane and Nina Simone. Events usually take place at the Newport Casino and Fort Adams State Park.

Just when you thought it couldn't get better than silk kimonos and African equines, the **11 Breakers** blows the Dukes' estate out of the water. Newport's crème de la crème is a sweeping 70-bedroom Italian Renaissance mega-palace inspired by 16-century Genovese palazzos. Richard Morris Hunt did most of the legwork, though he imported craftspeople from around the world to perfect the sculptural and decorative program. The on-site **12 Stable & Carriage** has been transformed into a museum about the Vanderbilt family (one of whom still lives on the palace's top floor). Scores of heirlooms are on display and captions detail the sumptuous lifestyle of one of America's wealthiest families at the turn of the 20th century.

Stop for a spicy noontime fajita at **13 Brick Alley Pub** and wash it down with a shot of sea salt along the crowded dunes at **14 First Beach**. An antique, Coney Island–style carousel is a great distraction, as is the small aquarium. Those in search of bigger waves and a little more seclusion will prefer **15 Second Beach**, a mere three-minute drive up the road.

Before retreating back to Newport's town center for a savory dinner, have a quick peek at **16 Bailey's Beach Club**, one of the most exclusive societies in America. This veritable WASP nest occupies a private slice of bleach-blonde sand and guards its members' list so tightly that A-listers who are deemed to be "too gaudy" are rejected... After watching through the window as American aristocrats nibble foie gras and clink their champagne glasses, you will undoubtedly work up an appetite for your own upscale repast. Try the **17 White Horse Tavern**, on Marlborough St, for an elegant evening amid soft lantern lighting. Founded by a pirate in 1687, this gambrel-roofed tavern is one of the oldest establishments in America. Although eye patches and powdered wigs have been gradually swapped for collared shirts and blazers (a "business casual" dress code is strictly enforced), the lovely dining room is still very much a step back in time (but watch your footing – the floorboards are very uneven!).

CLIFF WALK

A narrow footpath snaking 3.5 miles along a churning sea, the Cliff Walk is a fine excuse for exercise and offers an abridged version of the Newport mansions tour. The bustle of beach traffic slowly fades away as you make your way south along the trail. Descend the "40 Steps" stone staircase to uncover dramatic cliffs to your left and a backdrop of robber-baron-era mansions to the right.

Brandon Presser

HISTORY & CULTURE

TRIP INFORMATION

GETTING THERE
From Providence follow Rte 114 along the eastern shores of Narragansett Bay until you reach little Newport, 30 miles away.

DO
Belcourt Castle
A stunning seaside castle with a bizarre horse history. ☎ 401-846-0669; www.belcourt castle.com; 657 Bellevue Ave; ☒ 10am-4pm

Breakers
Newport's crème de la crème is a rambling Italianate palace with 70 stunning bedrooms. ☎ 401-847-1000; www.newportmansions .org; 44 Ochre Point Ave; adult/child $16/4; ☒ 9am-6pm mid-Apr–Jan, 10am-5pm Sat & Sun Jan–mid-Apr; ⬚

Elms
This stunning château-inspired mansion boasts a memorable garden decked with exotic flora and fauna. ☎ 401-847-1000; www.newport mansions.org; 367 Bellevue Ave; adult/child $11/4; ☒ 10am-6pm mid-Apr–Jan, 10am-5pm Sat & Sun Jan–mid-Apr; ⬚

Marble House
Built for a Vanderbilt in 1892, this gaudy mansion blinds eyes with colorful marble and flamboyant Versaillaise furniture. ☎ 401-847-1000; www.newportmansions.org; 596 Bellevue Ave; adult/child $11/4; ☒ 10am-6pm mid-Apr–Jan; ⬚

Rosecliff
A French-style estate with an immense ball-room made famous by Hollywood. ☎ 401-847-1000; www.newportmansions.org; 548 Bellevue Ave; adult/child $11/4; ☒ 10am-6pm mid-Apr–Jan; ⬚

Rough Point
Another Vanderbilt property, Rough Point features breathtaking grounds and takes its design cues from the traditional English manor. ☎ 401-849-7300; www.newport restoration.com; 680 Bellevue Ave; admission $25; ☒ 10am-2:40pm Tue-Sat mid-Apr–early Nov; ⬚

EAT
Black Pearl
A popular spot for visiting celebrities, Black Pearl's patrons will have a hard time deciding what's better: the food or the views. ☎ 401-846-5264; www.blackpearlnewport.com; Bannister's Wharf; ☒ noon-1am

Brick Alley Pub
This fully fledged restaurant serves up a tasty assortment of steaks, salads and fajitas. ☎ 401-849-6334; 140 Thames St; ☒ 11:30am-10pm

White Horse Tavern
Founded by a pirate in 1687, this lovely, lantern-lit tavern is one of the oldest restaurants in America. ☎ 401-849-3600; www .whitehorsetavern.com; 26 Marlborough St; ☒ from 11:30am

SLEEP
Chanler
A stunning, sumptuous retreat that rivals the grandeur of the mansion museums. ☎ 401-847-1300; www.thechanler.com; 117 Memorial Blvd; d from $395

Hotel Viking
A luxurious manor featuring gushing curtains and four-poster beds. ☎ 401-847-3300; www.hotelviking.com; 1 Bellevue Ave; d from $249

USEFUL WEBSITES
www.gonewport.com
www.newportmansions.org

LINK YOUR TRIP
www.lonelyplanet.com/trip-planner

CONNECTICUT TRIPS

Spend a few days exploring the tangle of two-lane country roads that seem to cover Connecticut's every inch then make your way through a rural town or two: you'll probably find yourself mulling over a number of age-old Connecticut questions.

For instance, how is it possible that every neat-and-tidy country village here seems to be more historically important than the one you passed 5 miles back? And why is it that every picture-perfect country farm appears more aesthetically pleasing than the next?

I'm exaggerating, of course. And yet the Constitution State does seem to have a knack for taking your breath away at the most unexpected of moments. Like when you bump into a Hollywood celebrity at a corner coffee shop. Or discovering an unassuming French bistro in the middle of nowhere and then learning that its owner is one of the country's most innovative young chefs.

 PLAYLIST Who says Connecticut doesn't swing? Dig this playlist and get yourself in a Constitution State of mind.

- "The Connecticut Peddler," Jim Douglas
- "Connecticut," Judy Garland and Bing Crosby
- "Pennsylvania 6-5000," Spring Heeled Jack
- "Yankee Doodle," Boxcar Willie
- "Connecticut Fun," Punkestra
- "Connecticut," Government Issue
- "Million Dollar Legs," The Outlaw Four
- "The Wives are in Connecticut," Carly Simon

In other words, Connecticut is surprisingly different from the image you probably have in your mind. But why not take a quick trip and discover that for yourself?

 BEST TRIPS

CONNECTICUT TRIPS

Route 169: The Quiet Corner

WHY GO Is the New England of your imagination a pastoral and rustic place, yet in a sophisticated and shabby-chic sort of way? If it is, you'll almost undoubtedly find yourself equally captivated and charmed by the small northeastern block of Connecticut known as the Quiet Corner.

Take a look at the state of Connecticut on a map of America, then compare its size to the massive blocks of country surrounding it: Massachusetts, New York, Pennsylvania. Connecticut seems to be such a tiny place—almost insignificant. And of course, the corner of the state covered by this trip is even smaller still: just the modest strip of land running along the Quinebaug and Shetucket Rivers. And yet the Last Green Valley, as the area is also known, still manages to envelop more than 1000 sq miles—certainly not an unsubstantial plot, by any estimation.

Thank goodness, then, for Connecticut state road Rte 169, 32 miles of which have been designated a National Historic Highway. The route's historic stretch begins in the considerably urban area of Norwich, although a quick drive east along Rte 165 to bucolic **1** **Preston**, which was established as a farming community in the late 1600s, will get the day off to an appropriately relaxed start. After strolling through town, head north along Jewett City Rd to a long-time local favorite, **2** **Buttonwood Farm Ice Cream**. Along with sugar-free options, this natural farm creamery offers fresh homemade ice cream, yogurt and sorbet.

Just a bit further north, in the town of Canterbury, is the **3** **Prudence Crandall Museum**. This was New England's first upper-crust school for black women, or "little misses of color," as they were known. Crandall had to fight long and hard before being legally allowed to educate minorities in the 1830s.

TIME
3 days

DISTANCE
90 miles

BEST TIME TO GO
Aug – Nov

START
Norwich

END
Woodstock

ALSO GOOD FOR

HISTORY & CULTURE

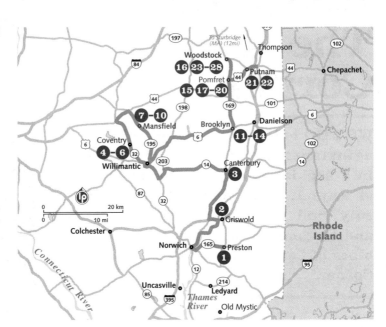

Take Rte 14 west, then Rte 32 into ❹ **Coventry**, the hometown of Connecticut's celebrated Civil War hero Nathan Hale. After being pegged as a spy by the British, who then hanged him at the age of 21, it was Hale who famously regretted that he had but one life to lose for his country. The hugely popular ❺ **Nathan Hale Homestead** was this young hero's family home and it succeeds in giving visitors a good idea of what domestic life was like for our nation's very first citizens. The ❻ **Strong-Porter House Museum**, where Nathan Hale was born, is nearby. The farmhouse here was built sometime around 1730 by Hale's great uncle.

> "...appreciating the bucolic ambience is just as popular as stopping off at roadside ice-cream stands."

Make your way next to ❼ **Mansfield**, where the country's first silk mill was built and where both the buzz saw and the screw auger were invented. Mansfield is also home to the ❽ **Gurleyville Gristmill**, which is the only stone mill of its type in the state. Grinding equipment from the 1830s can also be seen. Trekkers should take note that a portion of the ❾ **Connecticut Blue-Blazed Nipmuck Trail** can be picked up at the gristmill. If you'd rather contemplate public transportation, the open-air ❿ **Connecticut Eastern Railroad Museum** is a unique way to get up close and personal with railroading technology.

Head east once again, this time toward the regally pastoral community of ⓫ **Brooklyn**. You're now in a part of the Quiet Corner where driving slowly and simply appreciating the area's bucolic ambience is just as popular an activity as museum-going, or stopping off at roadside ice-cream stands. Try to bear in mind, however, that local drivers are probably going somewhere specific; slowly pulling onto the road's shoulder and letting faster drivers pass is an appreciated practice in these parts.

A visit to Brooklyn's ⑫ **Meadow Stone Farm Shoppe** is always a worthwhile diversion, no matter what your age. Nearly everything traded here, from the goat's milk and cheeses to the specialty skin care products, was produced either right on the farm or with farm materials. On your way out, don't forget to give a hearty wave to the critters who so selflessly contributed to your new soaps and shampoos. Next, make a stop at the ⑬ **Creamery Brook Bison Farm**, another educational and amusing animal attraction. A number of different farm tours are offered here, although the most popular, a 45-minute wagon ride, is something akin to a Quiet Corner safari and will likely get you much closer to a buffalo herd than you ever imagined possible.

A-MAIZE-ING!

Beginning as early as mid-July, an astonishing number of life-size, interactive **corn mazes** begin cropping up on farms throughout New England. Some are small and cutely kid-sized, while others, like **Davis' Mega Maze** in Sterling, MA, can take up to six hours to complete.

In the Quiet Corner, the best mazes are at **Preston Farms** in Preston, **Quintessential Gardens** at Fort Hill Farms in Thompson and at the **Nathan Hale Homestead** in Coventry. For a more comprehensive list, visit www.thelastgreenvalley.org and www.visitthelastgreenvalley.info.

To learn more about what life was like here during the republic's first few decades, stop off at the ⑭ **Brooklyn Historical Society Museum**, which is essentially a tribute to the life of Israel Putnam. Putnam was a local Revolutionary War general and is still known for his Battle of Bunker Hill command, "Don't fire until you see the whites of their eyes."

Drive north along Rte 169 toward the village of ⑮ **Pomfret**. Along with the nearby town of ⑯ **Woodstock**, this is where many Quiet Corner visitors choose to base themselves. A number of impressively expansive colonial homes have been converted into luxurious inns here; for more accommodation options, see this chapter's Connecticut Wine Trail trip.

The 1885 Queen Anne Victorian that houses ⑰ **Celebrations Inn**, a standard country B&B with a wide range of rooms, is also something of a meeting place for the surrounding area's artistic community. The onsite art gallery features the work of more than 50 local artists and artisans.

The ⑱ **Chickadee Cottage B&B** is ideal for extended stays. Guests who choose the typical B&B experience will appreciate their interactions with Chickadee's very gracious hosts, although it's possible to stay in a more secluded cottage instead. Walking trails are nearby and there's a pond on the premises. The

19 **Inn at Tonmar** is another area favorite and for good reason: perched on a hilltop and overlooking town, this antique farmhouse with perennial gardens and surrounding stone walls represents quintessential New England. The nearby **20** **Vanilla Bean Café** has long been a neighborhood favorite, both for its bistro-casual dining atmosphere and the occasional live music and art shows.

Minutes away on Rte 44 is **21** **Putnam**, known for its antique stores. Even window shoppers get a kick out of the **22** **Great Atlantic Company**, which, given its ambitiously cluttered collection of odd treasures, could just as easily be a museum. As you drive north toward Woodstock along Rte 169, look out for the beautifully preserved **23** **Roseland Cottage Bowen House**. This incredible Gothic Revival – the exterior is pink and it has a private bowling alley – was the summer home of Henry Bowen, a local who made his fortune in New York. The **24** **Quasset School** is another unusual example of historic New England life. That's especially true for the third-grade students who spend one week each year experiencing life in the 19th century first-hand.

> **ASK A LOCAL**
>
> "When I go out, I usually go to **JD Cooper's**. It's a sports bar, but with a really different vibe and really good food. It's not a touristy place, either – it's where the people who live here go to drink after work and on the weekends. By the way, everyone here just calls it Cooper's."
>
> *Brittany, Putnam*

With plenty of farms and vineyards in the Quiet Corner, eating and drinking are both relatively serious pursuits here. To investigate this yourself, start at the considerably modest **25** **Sweet Evalina's Stand**, a local pizza and ice-cream favorite, and then push on to **26** **Taylor Brooke Winery** to tour the grounds and taste the seasonal vintages on offer. Next, get into the spirit of backbreaking manual labor at **27** **Woodstock Orchards** by picking your own apples and berries and then kick back with a cool glass of cider.

> **DETOUR**
>
> If you've had more than your fill of vineyard tours and wine tastings but still want to knock back a drink or two, cross over the CT state line and drive the 10 or so miles to the all-American **Pioneer Brewing Company** in Fiskdale, MA. A number of lovingly hand-crafted brews are on tap inside the Pioneer's Stein Hall, where souvenirs and seasonal fruit are also on offer.
>
> If you've got children in tow, try the Hyland Orchard and Brewery in nearby Sturbridge, MA. There's a petting zoo and wagon rides for the kids and a brewery tour for the grown-ups.

And conveniently enough, neither the learning nor the exploring needs to end during a stay at the **28** **Elias Child House B&B**, a stately Colonial from the 18th century. You can enjoy hearth-cooking demonstrations here and wander the estate's 47 acres, which include hiking trails. In other words, you'll have plenty of opportunities to reflect upon the incredible amount of vital American history you've been exposed to over the past few days.

Dan Eldridge

TRIP INFORMATION

GETTING THERE
To reach Norwich, where Rte 169 begins, take US-395 north from New London, or Rte 2 east from Hartford.

DO

Brooklyn Historical Society Museum
American Revolution hero General Israel Putnam is remembered here. ☎ 860-774-7728; www.brooklynct.org; 25 Canterbury Rd (Rte 169), Brooklyn; admission free; ☽ 1-5pm Wed & Sun Jun-Sep

Connecticut Eastern Railroad Museum
Located where the Columbia Junction Freight Yard once sat, this open-area museum sits right on the tracks. ☎ 860-429-9023; www.joshualandtrust.org/gristmill.html; Stone Mill Rd, Mansfield; admission free; ☽ 1-5pm Sun May-Oct

Great Atlantic Company
Pomfret is well known for its affordable and high-quality antique shops; this well-stocked store is one of the best. ☎ 860-428-3439; www.putnumantiques.com; 58 Pomfret St, Putnum; ☽ 10am-5pm

Gurleyville Gristmill
The only original stone gristmill in Connecticut, located on the 5.5-acre Michael's Preserve. ☎ 860-429-9023; www.joshualandtrust.org/gristmill.html; Stone Mill Rd, Mansfield; admission free; ☽ 1-5pm Sun May-Oct

Meadow Stone Farm Shoppe
Purchase honey, goat milk and skin care products, all made right on the farm. ☎ 860-617-2982; www.meadowstonefarm.com; 199 Hartford Rd, Brooklyn ☽ 1:30-6:30pm Thu & Sat; ♿

Nathan Hale Homestead
Connecticut's official State Hero spent most of his young life on this 400-acre farm. ☎ 860-742-6917; www.ctlandmarks.org/hale.php; 2299 South St, Coventry; adult/child $7/4; ☽ 11am-4pm Wed & Fri-Sun

Prudence Crandall Museum
Learn about Connecticut's State Heroine and the bigotry she battled in the educational system. ☎ 860-256-2800; www.cultureandtourism.org; 1 South Canterbury Rd, Canterbury; adult/child $3/2; ☽ 10am-4pm Wed-Sun Apr-Dec

Quasset School
For one week each year, this one-room schoolhouse is still used by area children. ☎ 860-928-9175; www.townofwoodstock.com; Frog Pond Rd, Woodstock; admission free; ☽ 1-4pm Sun Jul-Aug; ♿

Roseland Cottage Bowen House
Proof that wealthy Americans had fancy summer homes even in the mid-1800s. ☎ 860-928-4074; www.historicnewengland.org; 556 Rte 169, Woodstock; admission $8; ☽ tours hourly 11am-4pm Wed-Sun Jun–mid-Oct

Strong-Porter House Museum
The birthplace of Nathan Hale is now a museum with occasional historic exhibitions. ☎ 860-742-9025; www.coventrythistoricalsociety.org; 2382 South St, Coventry; admission free; ☽ noon-3pm Sun Jun-Oct

Woodstock Orchards
A popular "pick your own" farm known for its apples and blueberries. The fresh cider is also a big draw. ☎ 860-928-2225; 494 Rte 169, Woodstock; ☽ 9am-6pm Aug-May; ♿

EAT & DRINK

Buttonwood Farm Ice Cream
Some of the very best homemade ice cream, yogurt and sorbet. ☎ 860-367-4081; www.buttonwoodfarmicecream.com; 471 Shetucket Turnpike; Griswold/Jewett City; snacks $2-7; ☽ 1-8pm Mon-Fri, noon-8pm Sat & Sun; ♿

Creamery Brook Bison Farm
Meet the buffalos on a wagon tour, then purchase their relatives' flesh. Ring ahead for tour schedules. ☎ 860-779-0126; www.creamerybrookbison.net; 19 Purvis Rd, Brooklyn; tours adult/child $7/5.50; ♿

Sweet Evalina's Stand

No longer just a stand, the meatball sandwiches, pizza and ice cream here reign supreme! ☎ 860-928-4029; 688 Rte 169, Woodstock; mains $6-17; ☽ 7am-8pm Mon-Thu, 7am-9pm Fri & Sat, 8am-8pm Sun

Taylor Brooke Winery

Say hello to Zima the Wine Dog in between tastings and winery tours here. ☎ 860-974-1263; www.taylorbrookewinery.com; 848 Rte 171, Woodstock; ☽ 11am-6pm Fri, 11am-5pm Sat & Sun

Vanilla Bean Café

Lunch, dinner, art and espresso. ☎ 860-928-1562; www.thevanillabeancafe.com; cnr Rtes 44, 169 & 97, Pomfret; mains from $9; ☽ 7am-3pm Mon & Tue, 7am-8pm Wed & Thu, 7am-9pm Fri, 8am-9pm Sat, 8am-8pm Sun

SLEEP

Celebrations Inn

This Queen Ann Victorian houses a B&B, a wonderful art gallery featuring local work and a gift shop. ☎ 860-928-5492; www.celebrationsinn.com; 330 Pomfret St (Rte 169), Pomfret; r from $105

Chickadee Cottage B&B

The spacious Carriage House here has its own deck and separate entrance; great for long stays. ☎ 860-963-0587; www.chickadeecottage.com; 70 Averill Rd (Rte 44), Pomfret; r $120

Elias Child House B&B

Once a Colonial-era mansion, this B&B has original walk-in hearths and beehive ovens. ☎ 860-974-9836; www.eliaschildhouse.com; 50 Perrin Rd, Woodstock; r $115-149

Inn at Tonmar

An antique farmhouse with wi-fi and a wonderful view of Pomfret, aka Antique Country. ☎ 860-974-1583; 55 Babbitt Hill Rd, Pomfret; r $110; ⊛

USEFUL WEBSITES

www.thelastgreenvalley.org
www.visitthelastgreenvalley.info

LINK YOUR TRIP

www.lonelyplanet.com/trip-planner

Connecticut Wine Trail

WHY GO With meandering wine trails on both sides of the state, Connecticut has established itself as a serious wine-growing region. During our vineyard explorations, we talked with PBS's Chef Harry, of "Chef Harry and Friends." With his wife, Laurie, he runs Heritage Trail, a winery in the region known as the Last Green Valley.

TIME
3 days

DISTANCE
350 miles

BEST TIME TO GO
Jul – Nov

START
Shelton

END
Pomfret

ALSO GOOD FOR

As any travel writer worth their salt will tell you, the most memorable journeys begin before you actually reach your destination – they begin in the mind. So with that said, let's consider a bit of advice from Chef Harry himself – a big part of the wine trail fun is squeezing in visits to as many wineries as possible. Just check www.ctwine.com when you're planning your trip: there may have been recent changes to the trail.

Get your trip in the Constitution State off to a positive start at ❶ Jones Family Farm & Winery, a seasonal "pick your own" farm with an on-site tasting barn and an educational kitchen. Jones is known for using only grapes from its own vineyard or other local vineyards, and as a result the family's dessert and fruit wines are simply luscious. The vineyard's founder and resident winemaker, Jamie Jones, is now the sixth generational member of his family to operate the farm.

Head northwest to enjoy a lazy outdoor picnic at ❷ DiGrazia Vineyards. Guided tours of the winery begin every 20 minutes during the weekend. Even better is the reassuring fact that you likely won't walk away feeling guilty for overindulging: the resident winemaker, Dr Di-Grazia, has been actively involved for years in the development of wines with high antioxidant counts. DiGrazia is perhaps best known, however, for its very clean, crisp wines, which the doctor often sweetens with a touch of local fruit and honey.

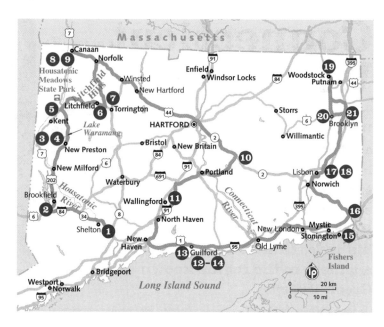

Check in early at New Preston's ③ **Hopkins Inn**, where visitors have been con-templating the northern shore of tranquil Lake Waramaug for more than 150 years. The inn is perched ever so slightly above the lake, with a view to the Berk-shire foothills. There's an Austrian restaurant on-site and across the driveway is the must-visit ④ **Hopkins Vineyard** winery. Along with the aforementioned DiGrazia Vineyards, Hopkins is a CT Wine Trail old-timer, planting its first vines back in 1979, just one year after the Connecticut Winery Act was passed, which permitted commercial wineries to exist. If you're in the mood for a bite and itching to explore the surrounding towns, head to Kent and ⑤ **Doc's Trat-toria & Pizzeria**, an Italian bistro with ten different specialty pizzas.

Definitely don't pass up a visit to the ⑥ **Haight-Brown Vineyard**, which was Connecticut's first legally established winery when it opened in 1978. Not only is it possible to taste 11 different vintages here, but also when you're fin-ished, the Haight-Brown folks will loan you a pair of muck boots – the better for getting up close and personal with their vines and crops, of course.

Further north in the Litchfield Hills is one of the trail's newer additions, the ⑦ **Connecticut Valley Winery**. One of his local favorites, Chef Harry says that CVW has very quickly become one of the area's most popular growers.

Of course, Connecticut's newer farms are generally the exception to the rule. Take, for instance, ⑧ **Land of Nod Winery** in New Canaan: resting in the foothills of the Berkshires, this winery is housed on 200 acres of nationally recognized bicentennial farmland. An almost unbelievable nine generations have done business here. And within easy walking distance on Lower Rd is the old **9** **Beckley Iron Furnace**, a 40ft blast furnace that was closed in 1919. Now on the National Register of Historic Places, it's known as the state's only industrial monument.

This is also where the trip's western part comes to a close, so unless you have plans to check out the wineries in New Hartford or Simsbury (refer to the Connecticut Wine Trail brochure, available at www.ctwine.com), it's time for a cross-state road trip. Drive southeast toward Hartford and then transfer to Rte 2, which leads almost directly to **10** **Priam Vineyards**, well known in this part of the state for of-

DON'T FORGET YOUR PASSPORT

You'll probably hear something about the Connecticut Wine Trail's **Passport Program** within your first few vineyard visits. But if not, simply request a passport from any winery employee and ask them to stamp it as well.

Here's how it works: request a "stamp" from each winery you visit. After collecting 14 stamps, surrender the passport to anyone behind the counter. There's an annual passport draw and prizes are dutifully awarded. Former grand prize winners have enjoyed wine country tours in Western Europe.

fering a sophisticated yet unpretentious wine country experience. Priam is also one of Chef Harry's favorite Connecticut wineries, and he also recommends visiting the seasonal farmers market located in the vineyard above the winery's parking lot. There, visitors can select fresh fruits and other local goodies for an impromptu picnic. For those less ambitious visitors, he says, several area restaurants will deliver lunch or dinner to the winery's patio. If that's your plan, ask a Priam employee for recommendations.

Drive south to **11** **Gouveia Vineyards** next. This stone and old timber winery churns out an award-winning cabernet franc—one of the only red grape varieties that can actually flourish in the cool Connecticut climate. Just a bit further south in the historic town of **12** **Guilford** is another one of Chef Harry's all-time favorites, **13** **Bishop's Orchards Winery**, where he suggests scheduling a little extra time than you normally might. Bishop's is much more than just a winery—it's also a "pick your own" farm, where berries, peaches, pears, apples and pumpkins can be picked from June through October. If you happen to have kids along for the ride, they'll get a kick out of the llamas, alpacas and grazing goats. Take a drive into Guilford before moving on and pay a visit to the **14** **Henry Whitfield State Museum**. Designated a National Historic Landmark in 1997, this Colonial Revival stone house is the state's oldest abode. Exhibits explore the lifestyles of New England colonists.

15 **Stonington Vineyards**, located deep in Connecticut's southeastern corner, is known as the state's premiere producer of fine table wines. Ask them how it's done any day of the week at 2pm by joining an educational tour. **16** **Jonathan**

Edwards Winery is a quick drive away in North Stonington and, according to Chef Harry, in-the-know locals often pick up lunch at a take-out bistro or general store along the way. The winery's 48-acre estate overlooks the Atlantic Ocean, making midday or afternoon picnics particularly stunning.

If you'd prefer to have someone else take care of the cooking, point your nose toward the scenic and historic Rte 169 and travel to the small town of Lisbon.

WHO NEEDS A GPS?

It's worth bearing in mind that nearly every Connecticut winery is tucked far into the pastoral countryside and down a series of often unmarked country roads. Finding your way can sometimes be a challenge.

But not to worry: if you'd like to plan your expedition in even greater detail than this trip allows, visit www.ctwine.com, where you can download a PDF version of the very useful Connecticut Wine Trail brochure. Every winery and vineyard in the brochure comes complete with very specific driving directions.

The updated and newly reconstructed **17 Heritage Trail Vineyards** awaits you there, as does Chef Harry himself. He purchased the vineyard with his wife Laurie and added a restaurant in the summer of 2008. The area's passionate locavore community will be pleased to learn that locally grown and produced food will dominate Harry's menu: an assortment including smoked trout raised on their own spring-fed pond, smoked meats, thin-crust pizzas and grilled veggies. At the time of writing they had not yet opened for business.

Don't be surprised, by the way, if this particular corner of Connecticut entices you to stick around for a bit longer than you intended. If you do begin to get the urge, shacking up at the **18 Lonesome Dove B&B**, a squeaky-clean inn popular with honeymooning couples, will put you within the general vicinity of the Mystic area, as well as the Foxwoods and Mohegan Sun casinos. The **19 Inn at Woodstock Hill**, on the other hand, is great for those interested in a more countrified and pastoral experience. The main building is an absolutely sprawling 19th-century manor house and the estate covers 19 rolling acres in total.

"Experience a hayride around the farm before being serenaded by acoustic guitarists during dinner."

One of the most sought-after dining experiences in this part of the state takes place on the back patio of Pomfret's **20 Sharpe Hill Vineyard**, which is so popular locally that you might not get a seat without advance reservations, even on a weekday. After all, it's worth remembering that eating well is taken quite seriously in this corner of Connecticut. Which is part of the reason Chef Harry insists that a visit to Brooklyn's **21 Golden Lamb Buttery** is "an absolute must." You'll experience a hayride around the farm before being serenaded by acoustic guitarists during dinner. Casual conversation and good wine are shared around liberally. And appropriately enough, the night doesn't end, believe it or not, until the candles burn out.

Dan Eldridge

TRIP INFORMATION

GETTING THERE
From New York, take I-95 north to Bridge-port, then take Rte 25 north to Rte 111 to Rte 110. Follow signs from there. From Hartford, take I-84 west to Waterbury, then take Rte 8 south to Rte 34 north to Rte 100.

DO

Beckley Iron Furnace
View the ancient remnants of Connecticut's short-lived steel industry during a visit to this 40ft blast furnace. www.beckleyfurnace.org; 140 Lower Rd, East Canaan; admission free

Bishop's Orchards Winery
Pick your own fruit at this superb farm, then sample fruit wine in the tasting room. ☎ 866-224-7467; www.bishopsorchards winery.com; 1355 Boston Post Rd., Guilford; ☾ 10am-7pm Mon-Sat, 11am-6pm Sun; 🚻

Connecticut Valley Winery
This fairly recent addition to the wine trail is quickly becoming a local favorite. ☎ 860-489-WINE; www.ctvalleywinery.com; 1480 Litchfield Turnpike (Rte 202), New Hartford; ☾ noon-5pm Sat & Sun

DiGrazia Vineyards
Owned by a semiretired area doctor, high antioxidant wines are produced here. Try the blueberry dessert wine. ☎ 203-775-1616; www.digrazia.com; 131 Tower Rd, Brook-field; ☾ 11am-5pm daily May-Dec, Sat & Sun Jan-Apr

Gouveia Vineyards
Visitors enjoy watching the sun set on the outdoor balcony at this friendly farm. Picnick-ing is encouraged. ☎ 203-265-5526; www .gouveiavineyards.com; 1339 Whirlwind Hill Rd, Wallingford; ☾ 11am-8pm Fri & Sat, 11am-6pm Sun

Haight-Brown Vineyard
The state's oldest winery, with a rustic yet sophisticated tasting room. Great photo opportunities with a massive wine barrel!

☎ 860-567-4045; www.haightvineyards .com; 29 Chestnut Hill Rd, Litchfield; ☾ noon-6pm Thu-Sun

Henry Whitfield State Museum
Connecticut's oldest house and New England's oldest stone house is now a time-capsule museum. ☎ 203-453-2457; www .whitfieldmuseum.com; 248 Old Whitfield St, Guilford; adult/child $4/2.50; ☾ 10am-4:30pm Wed-Sun Apr-Dec

Hopkins Vineyard
With a fantastic tea and gift shop, even teetotalers will be entertained. ☎ 860-868-1768; www.hopkinsvineyard.com; 25 Hopkins Rd, New Preston ☾ daily May-Dec, Fri-Sun Jan & Feb, Wed-Sun Mar & Apr

Jonathan Edwards Winery
This former dairy farm boasts a California-style tasting room inside a New England barn. ☎ 860-535-0202; www.jedwardswinery .com; 74 Chester Main Rd., North Stonington; ☾ Wed-Sun 11am-5pm, tour at 3pm daily

Jones Family Winery
Families with young children are warmly welcomed by generous hosts at this pick-your-own farm. ☎ 203-929-8425; www .jonesfamilyfarms.com; 606 Walnut Tree Hill Rd, Shelton; ☾ 11am-5pm Fri-Sun May-Nov; 🚻

Land of Nod Winery
Visit this bicentennial farm in March to see pure maple syrup cranked out in the sugar-house. ☎ 860-824-5225; www.landofnod winery.com; 99 Lower Rd, East Canaan; ☾ 11am-5pm Fri-Sun Apr-Nov

Priam Vineyards
This winery took home 24 international competition medals in its first two years of business. Guided tours available. ☎ 860-267-8520; www.priamvineyards.com; 11 Shailor Hill Rd, Colchester; ☾ 11am-5pm Fri-Sun Mar-Dec

Stonington Vineyards
Just minutes from Mystic, European-style table wines are popular here, as are impromptu vineyard picnics. ☎ 860-535-1222; www

.stoningtonvineyards.com; 523 Taugwong Rd, Stonington; ⏰ 11am-5pm; tours 2pm

EAT

Doc's Trattoria & Pizzeria
Enjoy traditional Italian entrees or specialty pizza while dining outdoors. ☎ 860-927-3810; www.docstrattoria.com; 9 Maple St, Kent; mains $12-26; ⏰ noon-3pm Tue-Sat, 5-9pm Tue-Thu, 5-9:30pm Fri-Sat, 1-8pm Sun

Golden Lamb Buttery
Possibly the state's most remarkable fine-dining concept, including hayrides and lingering, casual conversation. ☎ 860-774-4423; www.thegoldenlamb.com; 499 Wolf Den Rd, Brooklyn; dinner prix fixe $75 (excl drinks); ⏰ Tue-Sat noon-2:30pm, Fri-Sat 7pm

Heritage Trail Vineyards
Say hello to PBS's Chef Harry, who operates the restaurant while his wife runs the winery. ☎ 860-376-0659; www.heritagetrail.com; 291 North Burnham Hwy, Lisbon; mains $12-20; ⏰ Tue-Sun 11am-6pm

Sharpe Hill Vineyard
Make reservations in advance for the outdoor gourmet restaurant here; it's considered one of the area's best. ☎ 860-974-3549; www.sharpehill.com; 108 Wade Rd, Pomfret; mains $24-35; ⏰ 11am-5pm Fri-Sun

SLEEP

Hopkins Inn
Situated right next to the winery and perched high enough above Lake Waramaug to make for stunning views. ☎ 860-868-7295; www.thehopkinsinn.com; 22 Hopkins Rd, New Preston; r $110-215

Inn at Woodstock Hill
An absolutely stunning 19th-century manor house with stone walls, perennial flowers, four-post beds – the works. ☎ 860-928-0528; www.woodstockhill.net; 94 Plaine Hill Rd, Woodstock; r $160-260

Lonesome Dove B&B
Close to Mystic and Stonington and with a certified National Wildlife Backyard Habitat to boot! ☎ 860-859-9600; www.lonesomedovebnb.com; 332 South Burnham Hwy, Lisbon; r $129-179

USEFUL WEBSITES
www.ctwine.com
www.ctwine.net

LINK YOUR TRIP

www.lonelyplanet.com/trip-planner

OFFBEAT

Quirky Connecticut

WHY GO With an unusual museum or landmark in nearly every town, Connecticut is nothing if not eclectic. After all, where else can you see a Temple of Trash one day and the gravesites of Tiny Tim and PT Barnum the next, with side trips to Easter Island and the world's largest casino?

TIME
5 days

DISTANCE
250 miles

BEST TIME TO GO
Jun – Sep

START
Middlebury

END
Greenwich

ALSO GOOD FOR

ROUTE

Take our word for it: you're going to need all the energy you can muster to make your way through this trip, which begins in the popular seaside town of Mystic, then passes through the capital city of Hartford before heading west to New Haven, and eventually into the upscale bedroom community of Greenwich.

And that's exactly why we're recommending you start your journey in Mystic itself. Or, to be a bit more specific, at ❶ **Mystic Pizza**, where the classic romantic comedy of the same name was filmed in the late 1980s. We found the restaurant's signature blend of cheeses melted atop fluffy, pastry-like crust to be more than worthy of the hype.

Naturally, you'll need to be appropriately rested as well, which is something that can be easily accomplished at the ❷ **Mermaid Inn of Mystic**. The Victorian-style B&B comes complete with glamorous yet subtle touches everywhere, like the Italian granite baths in each room and the mermaid murals by local artist Jennifer Wolcin.

Once you're properly situated with room and board, you'll want to prepare yourself mentally for the thrills and indulgences of the area's two gambling casinos, both owned and operated by Native American tribes. There's something slightly ridiculous about them, with clashing gewgaws and decorations everywhere. At ❸ **Foxwoods Resort & Casino**, said to be North America's largest gambling hall, it's possible to enjoy a meal

BEST TRIP

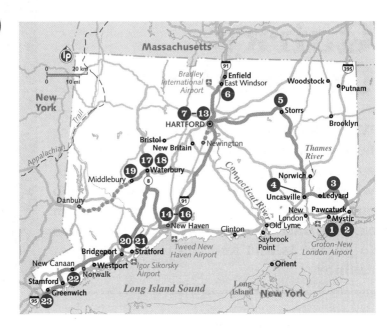

at any of the casino's gourmet restaurants, experience a pedicure at the spa and enjoy shopping at one of the many upscale boutiques. A similar experience can be had at ❹ **Mohegan Sun**, a nearby casino that offers an eclectic hodge-podge of contemporary Native American décor. Art aficionados should take special care not to miss the spectacular, 25ft Dale Chihuly glass sculpture here.

Next, head to the rather unusual ❺ **Ballard Institute & Museum of Puppetry** in Storrs. BIMP, as it's referred to by in-the-know locals, preserves and showcases an impressive collection of puppets from around the world, and offers yearly puppet performances, research and other educational opportunities.

"...leave the Trash Museum with a commitment to reduce postconsumer waste."

Travel next to the small town of East Windsor. This is where the wonderful ❻ **Connecticut Trolley Museum** lies in wait. A highlight of every visit to the museum, founded in 1940 by the very stoic-sounding Connecticut Electric Railway Association, is the three-mile journey around the facility itself, which takes place in a genuine old-school streetcar.

The capital city of ❼ **Hartford**, a half-hour drive south of the trolley museum, is an absolute boon to odd-Americana fanatics. In fact, one of our all-time favorites, the state-operated ❽ **Trash Museum**, is located here. This actual recycling facility plays double duty as an educational public resource and you'll likely find yourself captivated by the modern technology associated with garbage removal and disposal today. You may even find yourself leaving the museum, as we did, with a renewed commitment to reduce postconsumer waste and increase recycling within your own household.

For those of you planning to stick around for a while in the capital city, your quirky housing options, unfortunately, are somewhat limited. Very near to the top of the heap, however, is the ❾ **Mark Twain Hostel**, a rather grand Victorian building in the city's upscale West End district. On the opposite end of the accommodation spectrum is the downtown area's ❿ **Goodwin Hotel**. Consistently named Hartford's best hotel, the building's mid-19th-century exterior strongly belies the interior of its suites and guest rooms, decorated with boutique hotel–style detail. The appropriately named JP Morgan Suite was once the wealthy financier's home.

The ⓫ **Mark Twain House & Museum** is easily one of Hartford's most-visited attractions. The idiosyncratic humorist lived in the 19-room Victorian mansion from 1874 to 1891, and today the house boasts an impressive

> **ASK A LOCAL**
>
> Yale is the biggest reason people come to New Haven and I think people have some crazy ideas about what it's like. And then they get here and it's not really what they expected. But still, there are so many new galleries and new shops and even new restaurants, too. It seems like someone is always talking about a new place that just opened.
>
> *Leah, New Haven*

library and rotating exhibits dedicated to the author's legacy. Located near to Twain's former digs is the ⓬ **Harriet Beecher Stowe Center**. In addition to celebrating the life and work of the renowned author of *Uncle Tom's Cabin,* the Victorian Gothic Revival home also includes a library featuring Stowe's original correspondence and manuscripts of her work.

Before leaving Hartford, check out what is possibly the city's quirkiest attraction, the ⓭ **Museum of Natural & Other Curiosities**. Not unlike the famously bizarre Museum of Jurassic Technology in Los Angeles, this particular display is meant to pay homage to the unusual and often misleading museum collections of the 17th and 18th centuries. On display here, for instance, are such curiosities as a two-headed calf, a Siamese pig fetus and the horn of a unicorn.

⓮ **New Haven**, a 45-minute drive from central Hartford, is our next destination. Thanks largely to the presence of Yale and its especially moneyed underclassmen, the city can certainly boast of its impressive contemporary-dining scene. Without doubt, one of more unusual area eateries is ⓯ **116 Crown**, a can't-miss cocktail bar with futuristic design elements and cave-like cushioned booths. The cocktail menu here, full of obscure liquors and odd concoctions, is worth the trip by itself. Also in New Haven and also rather unusual is ⓰ **Gastronomique**. Not much larger than a walk-in closet, the concept here is French take-out cuisine at prices the average college student can actually afford.

A 45-minute drive north of New Haven along Rte 8 will lead you to Connecticut's singular **17 Timexpo Museum**, which, yes, actually is the corporate museum of the well-known timepiece manufacturer. Sounds about as much fun as a nail in the eye, doesn't it? But somehow, the exhibits in this old brass mill building succeed in being both educational and attention-grabbing. One floor is dedicated to the memory of Thor Heyerdahl, the Scandinavian adventurer and author of *Kon-Tiki*, who happened to be a close friend of Timex's CEO. As something of a tribute to Heyerdahl's worldwide explorations, a huge replica of an **18 Easter Island Moai statue** has been installed on the museum's lawn.

Heading briefly west on I-84 will take you to the neighboring town of Middlebury, home to the **19 Golden Age of Trucking Museum**. A meticulously restored big-rig rests in front of the building's main entrance, while the museum itself is absolutely packed with antique trucks, the vast majority being of the 16-wheel variety. There's an odd assortment of antique work vehicles as well, including a fire truck and an ambulance.

Rejoin Rte 8 and head toward Bridgeport, a city that circus enthusiasts may recognize as the hometown of America's original practitioner of guerrilla marketing, PT Barnum. Naturally, Bridgeport is also the location of the **20 Barnum Museum**. Be prepared to be absolutely awestruck by the museum's massive collection of Barnum circus memorabilia, which includes a preserved slice of Tom Thumb's wedding cake. The museum's oldest artifact and perhaps its most popular is a 4000-year-old Egyptian mummy known only as Pa-Ib. As you exit the museum, ask a docent for printed directions to **21 Mountain Grove Cemetery**, where Barnum and Tom Thumb are buried.

DETOUR The "Disneyland of dairy stores," **Stew Leonard's** is a family-owned grocery chain known for its mechanical chorus of singing animals: crowing roosters, cows who praise the store's milk and eggs in song. Petting zoos have appeared outside the stores and occasionally employees roam the isles wearing animal or banana costumes. Stores can be found in Danbury, Newington and Norwalk (CT) and Yonkers (NY).

Make your way further west to the estate of another unusually prolific American, architect Philip Johnson. The **22 Philip Johnson Glass House** is located on a 47-acre estate that was once home to the hotly debated architect. Though Johnson's work has been frowned upon by some critics for his refusal to design in any one particular style, the estate has become so popular that reservations must be made well in advance.

And if you want to enjoy the lifestyle of Philip Johnson, spoil yourself at the **23 Delamar on Greenwich Harbor**. With spectacular views, beds covered in fine Italian linens, and deep cast-iron baths, the Delamar serves as the epitome of Greenwich style. And take it from us: there isn't anything quirky about that!

Dan Eldridge

TRIP INFORMATION
GETTING THERE

DO

Ballard Institute & Museum of Puppetry
An unusual collection of puppets from around the world. ☎ 860-486-4605; www.bimp .uconn.edu; UConn Depot Campus, 6 Bourn Pl, Storrs; admission free; ☾ noon-5pm Fri-Sun, Apr 27-Nov 30

Barnum Museum
A comprehensive look at the famed circus master's life, right in his own hometown. ☎ 203-331-1104; www.barnum-museum .org; 820 Main St, Bridgeport; adult/child $7/4; ☾ 10am-4:30pm Tue-Sat, noon-4:30pm Sun; ♿

Connecticut Trolley Museum
Enjoy trolley rides at this streetcar history museum. ☎ 860-627-6540; www.ct-trolley .org; 58 North Road, East Windsor; admission adult/child $8/5 ☾ 10am-4pm Mon & Wed, 10am-8pm Fri, 10am-5pm Sat, noon-5pm Sun

Foxwoods Resort & Casino
The country's largest casino, featuring gaming, shopping, dining and entertainment on the Mashantucket Pequot reservation. ☎ 860-312-2000; www.foxwoods.com; 39 Norwich-Westerly Rd, Ledyard; casino admission free; ☾ noon-midnight

Golden Age of Trucking Museum
A sizable collection of big-rigs, antique fire trucks, ambulances, tractors and more. ☎ 203-577-2181; www.goldenagetruck museum.com; 1101 Southford Rd, Middlebury; adult/child $8/5; ☾ 10am-4pm Tue-Sat, noon-4pm Sun

Harriet Beecher Stowe Center
Former home of the *Uncle Tom's Cabin* author, with exhibits and a research library. ☎ 860-522-9258; www.harrietbeecher stowecenter.org; 77 Forest St, Hartford; tours adult/child $8/4; ☾ 9:30am-4:30pm, Mon-Sat, noon-4:30pm Sun

Mark Twain House & Museum
Tour the idiosyncratic author's home and its on-site museum. Lectures and performances happen often. ☎ 860-247-0998; www.mark twainhouse.org; 351 Farmington Ave, Hartford; adult/child $14/8; ☾ 9:30am-5:30pm Mon-Sat, noon-5:30pm Sun

Mohegan Sun
A gloriously obscene example of casino ostentation, complete with a three-story crystal mountain. ☎ 860-885-2956; www .mohegansun.com; 1 Mohegan Sun Blvd, Uncasville; admission free; ☾ 24hr

Mountain Grove Cemetery
Pay your respects at the final resting places of PT Barnum, Tom Thumb and more than 80 Civil War veterans. ☎ 203-336-3579; 215 Dewey St, Bridgeport; ☾ 8:30am-4pm Mon-Fri

Museum of Natural & Other Curiosities
Examine a two-headed calf and other natural oddities in this 18th-century-style museum setting. ☎ 860-522-6766; www.ctosh.org; 800 Main St, Hartford; adult/child $6/3; ☾ 11am-5pm Mon-Fri

Philip Johnson Glass House
Take a once-in-a-lifetime tour of this legendary modernist-architecture landmark. ☎ 203-966-8167; www.philipjohnsonglass house.org; 199 Elm St, New Canaan; tours by reservation $25-40

Timexpo Museum
The history of the Timex watch is explored in surprisingly fascinating detail. Look for the life-sized Easter Island head. ☎ 203-755-8463; www.timexpo.com; 175 Union St, Waterbury; adult/child $6/4; ☾ 10am-5pm Tue-Sat

Trash Museum
Gawk at the Temple of Trash and watch real recycling in action from a viewing platform. ☎ 860-757-7764; www.crra .org; 211 Murphy Road, Hartford; admission free; ☾ 10am-4pm Wed-Fri, 10am-2pm Tue; ♿

EAT AND DRINK

116 Crown
One of New Haven's hippest and most elegant cocktail bars in the Ninth Sq. ☎ 203-777-3116; www.116crown.com; 116 Crown St, New Haven; cocktails from $7; ⊙ 4pm-2am Fri & Sat, 4pm-1am Tue-Thu & Sun

Gastronomique
Quirky French take-out with soups, sandwiches, brunch and raw food. The menu changes seasonally. ☎ 203-776-7007; www.thegastro.com; 25 High St, New Haven; mains $6-17; ⊙ 10am-9pm Mon-Sat

Mystic Pizza
If you've seen the movie, try a slice of this modest shop's surprisingly toothsome pizza. T-shirts and touristy gewgaws abound. ☎ 800-536-3700; www.mysticpizza.com; 56 West Main St, Mystic; mains $6-18

SLEEP

Delamar on Greenwich Harbor
Sink into slumberland at this waterfront luxury boutique hotel, which has been called one of the world's finest. ☎ 203-661-9800; www.thedelamar.com; 500 Steamboat Rd, Greenwich; r $369-1,600

Goodwin Hotel
Downtown Hartford's finest digs, popular with business types, comes complete with the style and attitude of a boutique hotel. ☎ 860-246-7500; www.goodwinhotel.com; 1 Haynes St, Hartford; r from $209; ⊛

Mark Twain Hostel
A friendly couple runs this old Victorian hostel, which could use a solid dusting, in the West End area. ☎ 860-523-7255; 131 Tremont St, Hartford; dm/r $27/43

Mermaid Inn of Mystic
This 1843 Victorian Italianate, luxurious yet still homey, is outfitted with unusual murals throughout. ☎ 877-692-2632; www.mermaidinnofmystic.com; 2 Broadway Ave, Mystic; r from $140

USEFUL WEBSITES
www.roadsideamerica.com/location/ct
www.visitconnecticut.com

LINK YOUR TRIP   www.lonelyplanet.com/trip-planner

Lower River Valley

WHY GO Look closely enough at the many proud legends of Connecticut's River Valley and you'll find that the history you uncover is in some ways the collective tale of America, distilled to its very essence. This region, once a serious economic contender, was vital to the growing strength of a new empire.

TIME
2 days

DISTANCE
70 miles

BEST TIME TO GO
Sep – Nov

START
Old Lyme

END
Hartford

ALSO GOOD FOR

HISTORY & CULTURE

Begin your journey at the must-see ❶ **Florence Griswold Museum** in Old Lyme. The grounds are popularly known as the birthplace of American impressionism, and the story of how that came to pass is a shining example of American ingenuity and free-market entrepreneurship in action. Late in the 19th century, homemaker Florence Griswold was in dire financial straits. After making the brave decision to open her house to boarders, a successful landscape painter arrived. He soon decided the area's bucolic surrounds were the ideal location for a new American art colony and hundreds of artists heeded his call. Griswold's home became known as the Lyme Art Colony, and a number of the impressionist works produced there are still considered some of the movement's most important.

The Griswold home, unfortunately, is no longer taking boarders, although Old Lyme's ❷ **Bee & Thistle Inn** most certainly is. Located on a sprawling, five-acre property that borders the Lieutenant River, each guest room here is uniquely designed and features fine linens, beautifully restored antiques and all the finishing touches you'd expect in an elegant New England country home. And as proof positive that the arts are still alive in the River Valley, the inn offers a seasonal schedule of arts festivals and evening readings by local authors.

Cross the Connecticut River to reach ❸ **Old Saybrook**, the oldest town on the Connecticut shoreline. Because of its strategic location at

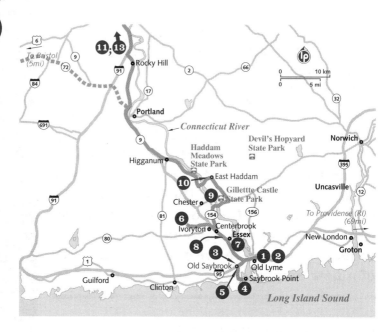

the river's entrance to Long Island Sound, Old Saybrook was an economically vital locale during the first few decades of European colonization. The Dutch West India Company, in fact, had ambitious plans to lay claim to Saybrook Point, but ultimately the English took it for themselves and then constructed a fort on the premises. ❹ **Fort Saybrook Monument Park** is now a popular tourist attraction with arguably the area's best view of the sound. A series of storyboards describe the fort's history in detail.

"The area's bucolic surrounds were the ideal location for a new American art colony"

Afterwards, grab lunch or a midafternoon snack at Old Saybrook's ❺ **Paperback Café**, an eclectic local favorite that feels something like a writer's study, or perhaps a library, and where conversations between diners often jump from table to table.

Just a short distance north in the small village of Ivoryton, the sophisticated ❻ **Copper Beech Inn** awaits. Generally agreed upon as the Lower River Valley's very finest country inn, each elegantly outfitted guestroom in this restored 1890 property comes complete with period antiques and Asian carpets.

And although the Copper Beach is indeed well known for its on-site gourmet restaurant—an AAA four-diamond rated restaurant, no less—you may want to hold off on that experience until tomorrow morning's breakfast and instead head out for a late evening dinner at ❼ **Gabrielle's**, an upscale American bistro in Essex. Located in a restored Victorian house, and with a front porch designed to resemble a gazebo, the restaurant's approach is to serve ingredients that are both extremely fresh and extremely local. Go for the goat cheese salad, accentuated with the tang of pistachio crisps and balsamic vinegar, or try one of the gourmet thin-crust pizzas, which are perfect for sharing.

You'll find the 1892 **8** **Essex Steam Train and Riverboat** station nearby. There, you can purchase a ticket for a narrated expedition aboard an authentic, coal-powered steam locomotive and a Mississippi-style riverboat known as the *Becky Thatcher*. The entire trip takes 2½ hours. Unique themed events happen often aboard the train and the riverboat, so be sure to take a close look at the upcoming schedule.

After arriving back at Essex Station, drive 5 miles north along Rte 154 until you're able to cross the Connecticut River. You'll arrive at the **9** **Gillette Castle State Park**, where, as its name suggests, the park's castle is the main draw. Built for eccentric actor and playwright William Gillette, who famously portrayed Sherlock Holmes on the silver screen, the stone castle has a decidedly medieval style. It's perched on a hill within a 120-acre estate where visitors can enjoy walking trails, a goldfish pond and stone-arch bridges.

DETOUR ➤ Growing tired of the non-stop, museum-style tourism so popular in this part of New England? Consider giving your grey matter the day off at **Lake Compounce**, a 332-acre theme park in Bristol that has seen $50 million in upgrades over the past decade. The park opened more than 150 years ago and today features four roller coasters, dozens of rides and the biggest water park in Connecticut. From Old Lyme, take Rte 9 to Rte 72. Watch for signs as you approach Bristol – the drive takes about an hour.

After a bit of exploring or dining in downtown **10** **East Haddam**, which is found just north of the park, prepare for a slightly longer expedition to the historic district of **11** **Old Wethersfield**. Sitting just south of Hartford, Wethersfield is known as a living New England village. It's an actual residential community, in other words, and it's been almost perfectly preserved for 375 years. You might think of it as a populated open-air museum—the polar opposite of the Disney-owned community of Celebration, Florida. You'll find hundreds of architecturally historic homes here, as well as a number of museums. The best way to get your bearings, however, is to start at the **12** **Wethersfield Museum and Visitors Center**.

And if you have time to pop into Hartford before calling it a day, check out the **13** **City Steam Brewery Café**, where an actual steam method is used during the craft-brewed production process. The brewery is housed inside an old Hartford department store and the sandwiches and finger foods here are the perfect accompaniment to a bitter ale or a few pints of the café's finely crafted lager.

Dan Eldridge

TRIP INFORMATION

GETTING THERE
Old Lyme is located where the Connecticut River and the Long Island Sound meet. Take exit 70 going in either direction on I-95.

DO
Essex Steam Train and Riverboat
Tour the River Valley aboard an authentic steam locomotive and a triple-decker, Mississippi-style riverboat. ☎ 860-767-0103; www.essexsteamtrain.com; 1 Railroad Ave, Essex; train & boat adult/child 2-11 $26/13, train adult/child 2-11 $17/9; ⏰ 11am-3:30pm; ♿

Florence Griswold Museum
Griswold's art colony, now a museum, is regarded as the birthplace of American impressionism. ☎ 860-434-5542; www.flogris.org; 96 Lyme St, Old Lyme; adult/child $8/4; ⏰ 10am-5pm Tue-Sat, 1-5pm Sun

Fort Saybrook Monument Park
Storyboards walk visitors through this former British outpost at the mouth of the Connecticut River. ☎ 860-395-3152; Saybrook Point, Rte 154, Old Saybrook; admission free; ⏰ dawn-dusk

Gillette Castle State Park
The granite castle here was once home to eccentric film sensation William Gillette. ☎ 860-526-2336; www.friendsofgillettecastle.org; 67 River Rd, East Haddam; castle admission $5/2; ⏰ 8am-dusk

Wethersfield Museum and Visitors Center
Exhibits, brochures and local information make this a wise first stop in Wethersfield. ☎ 860-529-7161; www.historicwethersfield.org; 200 Main St, Wethersfield; adult/child under 16 $3/free; ⏰ 10am-4pm Mon-Sat, 1-4pm Sun

LINK YOUR TRIP

EAT
City Steam Brewery Café
Formerly a department store, this multilevel microbrewery has weekend comedy shows and a bistro-style menu. ☎ 860-525-1600; www.citysteambrewerycafe.com; 942 Main St, Hartford; mains $15-25; ⏰ 11:30am-10:30pm Mon-Thu, 11:30am-midnight Fri & Sat

Gabrielle's
An upscale, contemporary restaurant featuring country French cuisine; operated by a graduate of the New York Restaurant School. ☎ 860-767-2440; www.gabrielles.net; 76 Main St, Essex; mains $12-28; ⏰ 11:30am-2:30pm & 5-9pm Mon-Fri, 5-9:30pm Sat, 11am-3pm & 5-9:30pm Sun

Paperback Café
Soups, salads, wraps, espresso drinks and the best breakfast for miles around. ☎ 860-388-9718; 210 Main St, Old Saybrook; mains $4-12; ⏰ 7am-4pm Mon-Thu, 7am-9pm Fri & Sat, 8am-4pm Sun

SLEEP
Bee & Thistle Inn
An unequivocally charming B&B with award-winning dining, located on five acres along the Lieutenant River. ☎ 860-434-1667; www.beeandthistleinn.com; 100 Lyme St, Old Lyme; r $190-275

Cooper Beech Inn
Even Ralph Lauren would feel at home in this incredibly sophisticated country inn, complete with a gourmet French restaurant. ☎ 888-809-2056; www.cooperbeechinn.com; 46 Main St, Ivoryton; r $295-375

USEFUL WEBSITES
www.visitctriver.com
www.ctrivervalley.com

www.lonelyplanet.com/trip-planner

New Haven Arts & Galleries

WHY GO With its proximity to overpriced New York and its creative college-town atmosphere, New Haven is quickly becoming known for its raw, uncorrupted artistic talent. Silas Finch, a self-taught sculptor who builds disturbing and unclassifiable creations with mostly found metal objects, helped us discover the true heart of the city's contemporary art scene.

TIME
3 days

DISTANCE
10 miles

BEST TIME TO GO
Jun – Oct

START
New Haven

END
New Haven

ALSO GOOD FOR

According to sculptor Silas Finch, who rents a studio in the heart of New Haven's up-and-coming ❶ **Ninth Square** neighborhood, the wisest way to approach a New Haven art tour is to begin at ❷ **Artspace**, a nonprofit volunteer-run gallery. Not only is Artspace an enthusiastic supporter of both contemporary art and the surrounding community, but, as Finch explains, there's also a huge selection of flyers and postcards there advertising other galleries, or the occasional obscure art event.

But before heading out in search of the city's lesser-known art gems, hang a left out of the gallery and walk one block toward the ❸ **Lot**, an unusual out-of-doors project organized by Artspace. The Lot is, in fact, a small lot. It also sits directly behind a public bus stop and features a rotating series of contemporary paintings and installations, some with overt political overtones.

Head west on Chapel St to discover the nearby ❹ **Hope Gallery and Tattoo Studio**. According to Finch, Hope's three resident artists are celebrated throughout the contemporary art world as much for their painting acumen as for their skill with the tattoo iron. And as its name implies, the Hope Studio is also an art gallery in its own right. Every wall inside is home to a wildly divergent medley of the sort of lowbrow art featured in such magazines as *Juxtapoz,* and popularized in part by such painters as Robert Williams and Mark Ryden.

BEST TRIP

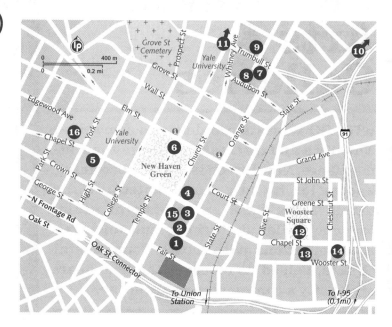

Make tracks to Audubon St next, but first, it's time for a quick bite. Of course, this being intellectual New Haven, we'll be dining at the ❺ **Atticus Bookstore Cafe**, which is indeed a full-service restaurant inside a bookstore. But unlike the coffee shop at your hometown chain bookstore, Atticus has a well-deserved reputation for delivering freshly made and high-quality soups, salads and desserts. The emphasis is clearly on snacks and small bites, however, giving those with particularly large appetites a good excuse to sample even more of the menu.

Make your way through the urban park known as ❻ **New Haven Green** as you head to the ❼ **Audubon Arts District**, which consists of the wide block laid out between Church and Orange Sts. Check out the galleries at ❽ **Creative Arts Workshop** first. CAW operates as both a cultural resource center for the community and an art school, and exhibitions can be viewed in two separate spaces. The two-floor Hilles Gallery is by far the more prestigious of the two. The equally contemporary ❾ **John Slade Ely House**, which had the proud distinction of being New Haven's only legitimate arts center when it opened in 1961, sits right across the street.

A bit further north on State St is the ever-popular ❿ **City Gallery**, an artist-run cooperative. "It's just an awesome space," says Finch. "When you have a show there, they almost make it feel like it's your own gallery." Indeed, the space measures 675 sq ft in total; new shows open once a month. Less than 2 miles north is the fascinating **⑪ Eli Whitney Museum**, where a number of the legendary cotton gin inventor's discoveries are on display.

Travel to the **⑫ Wooster Square** area next. Just east of downtown, this neighborhood is historically Italian, and aside from its healthy art scene, visitors and locals alike arrive in droves for the celebrated pizzerias. Indeed, some critics have hailed them America's finest. Head to **⑬ Frank Pepe Pizzeria Napoletana**, known locally as "Pepe's," for a slice of the Neapolitan-style "apizza" that is distinctive to southern Connecticut and especially New Haven.

⑭ Fuel Coffee Shop is something of a neighborhood hangout for Wooster Square's creative set. Organized art events take place occasionally and the espresso drinks are generally considered to be among New Haven's very best. Silas Finch is particularly fond of Fuel's commitment to local artists. Halfway through a recent exhibition there, the producers of the A&E Channel's *Flip This House* stopped by for a latte and ended up buying half his work.

To see a few examples of Finch's work, head back downtown to **⑮ Foster's Restaurant**, where "eclectic American" dishes are on offer. The eatery's chef and namesake, David Foster, commissioned Finch to create a handful of his unparalleled elephant sculptures for the restaurant's dining room.

And when it finally comes time to call it a night at some point during your arty rambles, you won't have far to stumble if you're staying at the **⑯ Duncan Hotel**, which is perhaps better known for its almost shockingly low rates than for, say, superior service. Still, the staff at the Duncan is friendly enough and, unlike the vast majority of New Haven's higher-priced chain hotels, this place definitely has character, albeit in a *Barton Fink* sort of way. But after all, this trip is about discoveries. So tuck in for the night and get busy dreaming. You've got another big day ahead.
Dan Eldridge

THE CITY AS A STUDIO

It's no secret that at any given time in New Haven, scores of talented artists are hard at work in their private studios. In fact, for all we know, the next Tracey Emin or Damien Hirst might be banging away in the building next door. Wouldn't it be interesting to see inside those workspaces, just for a quick look around?

During the annual **City-Wide Open Studios** event, hosted by Artspace, it's possible to do just that. CWOS usually takes place in autumn; visit Artspace (www.artspacenh.org) for details.

ARTS & IDEAS IN ELM CITY

For well over a decade now, thousands of inquisitive and intelligent art enthusiasts have gathered in New Haven each June to enjoy a month-long series of music and dance events, lectures, live theater and more. Known as the **International Festival of Arts and Ideas**, this far-reaching fête of all things cultural and creative showcases artists and performers from well over 20 countries. Perhaps even more exciting is the fact that 85% of the events on offer are entirely free of charge.

TRIP
31

HISTORY &
CULTURE

TRIP INFORMATION

GETTING THERE
New Haven sits conveniently on I-95, right on the Long Island Sound, in the approximate center of Connecticut's south coast.

DO

Artspace
One of New Haven's leading contemporary art galleries, Artspace also organizes a number of community-oriented art events. ☎ 203-772-2709; www.artspacenh.org; 50 Orange St; admission free; ☼ noon-6pm Tue-Thu, noon-8pm Fri & Sat

City Gallery
This relatively new addition to the NH arts scene is a 16-member coop with twelve shows per year. ☎ 203-782-2489; www.city -gallery.org; 994 State St; admission free; ☼ noon-4pm Tue-Sun

Creative Arts Workshop
This educational art center has classes for kids and adults, plus two on-site galleries. ☎ 203-562-4927; www.creativeartswork shop.org; 80 Audubon St; admission free; ☼ 9:30am-5:30pm Mon-Fri, 9am-noon Sat; ♿

Eli Whitney Museum
The inventor of the cotton gin led an incredibly full life. Learn about it here. ☎ 203-777-1833; www.eliwhitney.org/index2.htm; 915 Whit- ney Ave, Hamden; admission free; ☼ noon- 5pm Wed-Fri, 11am-4pm Sat, noon-5pm Sun

Hope Gallery and Tattoo Studio
Get that tatt you've always wanted, and then dig on the lowbrow paintings. ☎ 203-752- 0564; www.hopegallerytattoo.com; 817 Chapel St, Suite 2F; admission free; ☼ noon-8pm Mon-Sat

John Slade Ely House
Connecticut artists only are featured in the eight galleries of this converted Elizabethan building. ☎ 203-624-8055; www.elyhouse .org; 51 Trumbull St; admission free; ☼ 11am-4pm Wed-Fri, 2-5pm Wed-Fri

EAT AND DRINK

Atticus Bookstore Cafe
Fresh sandwiches and soups of exceptionally high quality are the draw at this downtown café. ☎ 203-776-4040; 1082 Chapel St; snacks $2-6; ☼ 8am-midnight

Foster's Restaurant
This contemporary bistro is proof positive that NH's foody scene has officially arrived. ☎ 203-859-6666; www.fostersrestaurant .com; 56-62 Orange St; mains $17-28; ☼ 11:30am-2:30pm & 5-10pm Mon-Thu, 11:30am-2:30pm & 5-11pm Fri, 5-11pm Sat

Fuel Coffee Shop
New Haven's requisite hipster café, featuring free-trade beans and vegetarian finger food. ☎ 203-772-0330; myspace.com/fuelcoffee shop; 516 Chapel St, Wooster Sq; snacks $2-4; ☼ 6:30am-5pm Mon-Fri, 8am-5pm Sat-Sun; 🌱

Frank Pepe Pizzeria Napoletana
Try a New Haven–style "apizza" at the his- toric shop where the beloved foodstuff was invented. ☎ 203-865-5762; www.pepes pizzeria.com; 157 Wooster St, Wooster Sq; mains $6-22; ☼ 4-10pm Mon, Wed & Thu, 11:30am-11pm Fri & Sat, 2:30-10pm Sun

SLEEP

Duncan Hotel
Don't expect to hear downtempo in the lobby; this is (affordable) hotel living of the quirky and eccentric sort. ☎ 203-787-1273; 1151 Chapel St; r from $60

USEFUL WEBSITES
www.newhavenarts.org
www.infonewhaven.com

www.lonelyplanet.com/trip-planner

LINK YOUR TRIP

Maritime Connecticut

WHY GO Thankfully for those of us with a serious interest in America's crucially important maritime history, the state of Connecticut offers untold opportunities to learn more. Visit world-class research museums, inspect a genuine tall ship, or even take to the high seas yourself on a luxury cruise or an educational trip.

Here's an always-amusing experiment: mention your upcoming Connecticut vacation to friends and family and then wait for the inevitable response. Chances are good it'll sound something like this: "What is there to do in Connecticut?"

For starters, there's the irresistible maritime town of ❶ **Mystic**, an historic shipbuilding hub since the 1600s. And yet the town wasn't famously associated with sailing and sea culture – at least not in the American public consciousness – until 1929, when Mystic's Museum of America and the Sea, as ❷ **Mystic Seaport** is commonly known, opened its doors to the world. Mystic Seaport is also referred to as a "living history maritime museum," and for those of you preparing to embark on an exploration of the state's sea culture, a gentle word of warning is probably in order: you're not likely to discover a more engaging maritime experience anywhere else on the entire eastern seaboard.

The seaport's dozens of acres are filled with much more than average museum exhibits. Climb aboard genuine tall ships, discover a recreated 19th-century seafaring village, become immersed in maritime art and literature – you could stay here for a week straight if you really wanted to and let's face it, if you're on this trip, you probably do.

When it comes time to search out sustenance in Mystic, consider leaving the downtown crowds behind and dining instead at ❹ **Rice**

TIME
5 days

DISTANCE
85 miles

BEST TIME TO GO
Jun – Aug

START
Mystic

END
New Haven

ALSO GOOD FOR

OUTDOORS

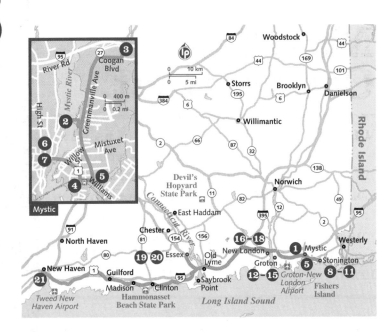

Spice Noodles, next to the old train station. Southeast Asian fare is given a unique fusion twist here, with fresh and local seafood. You'll also be just a few minutes from the ❺ Inn at Mystic, where Bogart and Bacall spent their honeymoon. Choose from four separate accommodations here, including a colonial revival mansion.

Interested in being closer to the action? Try downtown Mystic's ❻ Steamboat Inn, which sits atop the Mystic River. It's just a pebble's toss from the historic ❼ Mystic Drawbridge, which is still raised every hour for passing ships.

If you're looking for something outside the clamor of town, however, pay a visit to the nearby village of ❽ Stonington. With its all-American fairytale streets and its impeccably restored examples of colonial and federal architecture, this small waterfront community seems to have materialized out of an American history book. On foot, stroll the length of the village's main drag, ❾ Water Street, which is rich in eateries and antique shops. And on your way to tiny ❿ DuBois Beach, where in 1814 the town miraculously defended itself against the British in the Battle of Stonington, stop off at the ⓫ Old Lighthouse Museum. Inside, you'll learn about the proud, patriotic history of the surrounding area.

Next, take a drive to the nearby town of ⓬ Groton, popularly known as the "Submarine Capital of the World." Visit the ⓭ Submarine Force Museum and its more than 80,000 historical military artifacts. This is the only museum of its kind operated by the US Navy and for anyone interested in underwater warfare, it's an impressive display. Many visitors head directly outside, where it's possible to board the ⑭ **USS Nautilus,** famous (or infamous, depending on your point of view) for being the world's first nuclear-powered sub. Turn right out of the museum's parking lot and follow the signs to the nearby ⑮ **Submarine Veterans of WWII Memorial.** A placard informs visitors that the memorial is "Dedicated to our shipmates on eternal patrol."

The town of ⑯ **New London** sits just across the Thames River from Groton. It's home to the prestigious ⑰ **US Coast Guard Academy**, which welcomes the public to tour its grounds and its official training vessel, the tall ship *Eagle*. Both the Cadet Memorial Chapel and the academy's on-site museum are popular draws as well.

OCEANIC EDUCATION

If you're traveling with kids who happen to be showing a genuine interest in marine life, consider booking them – and possibly yourself – on one of the many educational cruises organized by **Project Oceanology** (www.oceanology.org). Headquartered at the University of Connecticut's Avery Point Campus (I-95, Exit 87), Project O describes its mission as "nurturing interest and enthusiasm for science and our planet's environment." The group achieves this aim by taking adults, students and children out on the ocean for up-close-and-personal adventures.

After a few days of being surrounded by seaworthy ships, you certainly won't be blamed for developing a bad case of itchy feet. Assuming you find yourself yearning to sail, head to the docks of New London's City Pier, where the ⑱ **Mystic Whaler Dinner Cruise** departs every few days in the summer season for extravagant lobster cruises, as well as a bevy of other edible oceanic adventures. Or, for a maritime experience even a dyed-in-the-wool landlubber could appreciate, make your way west to the state's Lower River Valley region and decamp to the historic town of ⑲ **Essex**, home to the ⑳ **Connecticut River Museum**. Here you'll learn about the long and often complicated history of the river, the regional shipbuilding industry and even the state's crucial steamboat service that once operated between Hartford and New York.

"You certainly won't be blamed for developing a bad case of itchy feet"

Lastly, for a completely different perspective on maritime history in the region, pick up the Amistad Trail in New Haven. Carrying 53 African slaves bound for Cuba, the ship *Amistad* landed here and after a landmark court case in which former US president John Quincy Adams argued for their liberation, the slaves were freed and opted to return home. The bronze ㉑ **Amistad Memorial** that sits outside New Haven's City Hall is just one of the trail's 60 statewide locations, all of which played an important part in the African-American quest for freedom. To discover the rest, visit www.visitconnecticut.com/amistad.htm.
Dan Eldridge

TRIP INFORMATION

GETTING THERE
From Boston to Mystic, it's a two-hour drive down I-95. From Hartford, shoot down Rte 2, then I-395 S.

DO
Connecticut River Museum
Learn about the mighty Connecticut River itself and those who've lived and worked around it. ☎ 860-767-8269; www.ctrivermuseum.org; 67 Main St, Essex; adult/child $8/5; ⊗ 10am-5pm, Tue-Sun

Mystic Seaport
America's museum of the sea features genuine tall ships and a recreated seaport village. ☎ 203-852-0700; www.mysticseaport.org; 75 Greenmanville Ave (Rte 27), Mystic; adult/child $18.50/13.00; ⊗ 9am-5pm; ♿

Old Lighthouse Museum
Six rooms worth of exhibits on the area inside a stone lighthouse near the sea. ☎ 860-535-1440; www.stoningtonhistory.org; 7 Water St, Stonington; adult/child $4/2; ⊗ 10am-5pm May-Oct

Submarine Force Museum & USS Nautilus
Climb aboard the world's first nuclear-powered submarine. View military submarine exhibits, some interactive. ☎ 860-343-0079; www.ussnautilus.org; 1 Crystal Lake Rd, Groton; admission free

US Coast Guard Academy
Tour the grounds of this prestigious military academy, where 1000 cadets train annually.

☎ 860-444-8511; www.cga.edu; 15 Mohegan Ave, New London; adult/child $23/17; ⊗ 9am-5pm

EAT
Rice Spice Noodles
Enjoy innovative and contemporary Thai food with fresh and local ingredients at Mystic's trendiest Southeast Asian café. ☎ 860-572-8488; 4 Roosevelt Ave, Mystic; mains $6-24; ⊗ 11am-3pm & 5-9:30pm

Mystic Whaler Dinner Cruise
Enjoy day-sailing adventures or lobster dinner cruises aboard a genuine tall ship. Reservations required; call for the schedule. ☎ 860-447-1249; www.mysticwhaler.com; City Pier, New London; lobster cruise adult/child $80/40

SLEEP
Inn at Mystic
Chose from four separate buildings, including a mansion, at this famous inn where Bogart and Bacall spent their honeymoon. ☎ 860-536-9604; www.innatmystic.com; 3 Williams Ave, Mystic; r $115-295

Steamboat Inn
Watch tugboats and pleasure craft float past your window at this perfectly intimate inn. Downtown Mystic's only waterfront accommodation. ☎ 860-536-8300; www.steamboatinnmystic.com; 73 Steamboat Wharf, Mystic; r $200-300

USEFUL WEBSITES
www.mystic.org
www.ctrivermuseum.org

LINK YOUR TRIP
www.lonelyplanet.com/trip-planner

Litchfield Hills Loop

WHY GO Arriving in northwestern Connecticut, you'll first notice the landscape looking like something out of an old movie. From the quiet country roads to the still and peaceful river streams, life seems to happen at a slower pace here. In fact, it's worth bearing in mind the local tourism board's one-word slogan: unwind.

TIME
3 days

DISTANCE
75 miles

BEST TIME TO GO
Sep – Nov

START
New Milford

END
Woodbury

As far as real-estate agents and state planners are concerned, the Litchfield Hills region is *huge*. It technically stretches as far south as Danbury—or even Ridgefield, depending on who you ask—and as far east as Bristol. The western and northern borders are conveniently provided by the states of New York and Massachusetts respectively.

Something you may soon notice, however, is that the expanse of country covered in this trip is a bit less ambitious. We've stuck to a fairly well-defined route, but by no means are you required to do the same. In fact, getting lost in the seemingly endless web of two-lane country roads is something of a rite of passage for visitors around here. It's also a big part of the fun because, after all, you never can tell what surprises might be waiting for you right around the next bend. Maybe it's a jaw-dropping view of the Housatonic River or a covered bridge. Maybe it's a rickety old general store with the very best deli sandwich you've ever tasted in your life. The point is, this part of the country encourages and rewards ex ploration, so don't ever hesitate to dive right in.

As far as we're concerned, though, the perfect Litchfield loop always kicks off in the historic downtown area of ❶ **New Milford**. Head directly to the boutique bonanza that is Bank St, where it's possible

BEST TRIP

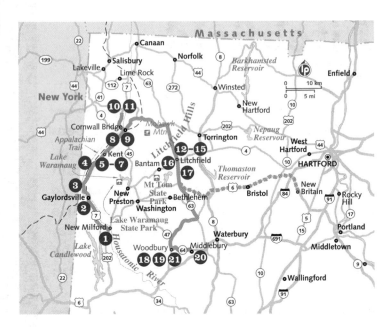

to fill up on coffee, pick up a few Lonely Planet guides, buy a new suite of designer living-room furniture and then get a tattoo to commemorate your trip. Or not.

And after a Bank St shopping spree, there is perhaps no better way to get into a Litchfield Hills frame of mind than by hopping on the Ethan Allen Hwy (Rte 7) and heading north. The mighty Housatonic River runs directly alongside the road for a good portion of this stretch, and with the overgrown shrubbery and endless clusters of trees, the scenery here is just unreal. You'll probably

"Getting lost in the web of country roads is a rite of passage for visitors here."

see vegetable or fruit stands outside big red barns, and there's decent antique shopping in ❷ **Gaylordsville**, a town you'll most certainly miss if you happen to be blinking. Continue on to the covered ❸ **Bull's Bridge**, where getting out of the car and stretching your legs is highly recommended. There's a recreational area here perfect for hiking, and in fact the ❹ **Appalachian Trail** runs right through it.

The town of ❺ **Kent** is your next stop, and for anyone planning to complete this loop in one day, a friendly warning is in order: it's uncommonly easy to loose all track of time while browsing through the boutique shops here, most of which close around 6pm. The best meal in town is on the main drag as well; at the ❻ **Fife 'n Drum Restaurant & Inn**, which, as the name suggests, will happily put you up for the night as well.

Just down the road is the unusual yet still fascinating ❼ **Sloane-Stanley Museum**, which features an extensive collection of antique tools owned by Eric Sloane, a highly regarded local painter of pastoral New England landscapes. A reconstructed version of Sloane's studio has been erected here and some of his original work can be seen. An industrial museum, featuring steam and gas tractors and other examples of antique agricultural machinery, is right next door.

Continue meandering north; about 5 miles out of Kent is an entrance to ❽ **Kent Falls State Park**, where a quarter-mile-long trail winds above and behind the cascading waterfall. The trail is easy enough to traverse and it affords a series of wonderfully varying views along the way.

Another 4 or 5 miles lead you into the village of Cornwall Bridge, where the luxurious ❾ **Breadloaf Mountain Lodge & Cottages** sit directly across Rte 7 from a small corner of Mohawk Mountain State Park and the Housatonic River. Get into the spirit of the outdoors by eschewing the main lodge and going for one of the cottages instead. They're all equipped with gas fireplaces.

"horse-drawn carriages slowed down to a steady trot, allowing their hidden passengers a bit of alone time"

Still further north on Rte 7 is the town of ❿ **West Cornwall**, which is worth a quick look. There's a small business district with cafés and a few interesting shops, including a photography gallery and a good barbeque restaurant. In order to reach the town, you'll have to pass through the lengthy ⓫ **West Cornwall covered bridge**. This particular bridge is so long, in fact, that it became known as the "Kissing Bridge," because horse-drawn carriages were able to slow down to a steady trot inside, thus allowing their hidden passengers a brief bit of alone time. That's hot!

You'll need to turn around at some point and pass through the covered bridge again in order to get onto scenic Rte 128. It's a fairly long haul to Rte 63 south, which leads directly to the town common in ⓬ **Litchfield**.

There's much to see and do in Litchfield, and because it has one of the largest business districts in the area, it's surprisingly common to spot A-list celebrities out on the town. ⓭ **West Street Grill** is a good option for star-spotting, and the pasta and contemporary bistro-style cuisine is consistently brilliant. For something a bit more low-key, try the nearby ⓮ **Bohemian Pizza**. With its college dorm–style interior design, you might not expect much, but the specialty pies here are absolutely worth the fuss. There's an attached bar that draws a mixed crowd of young artsy types and blue-collar locals.

Another consistently popular draw is the ⓯ **Tapping Reeve House and Law School**, which in 1773 became this country's very first law school, eventually graduating over 100 members of Congress. Through interactive areas and role-playing games, visitors are encouraged to explore not just the exhibits but also the lives and minds of early 19th-century students.

Less than 2 miles away is the grandly Colonial **16 Litchfield Inn,** where pets are welcome and every room has a TV and a private bath. Hanging out in the on-site pub and restaurant is a great way to meet some of the other guests in the nearly three-dozen rooms here.

Before taking your leave of Litchfield, swing by one of the area's more unusual attractions, the **17 Lourdes in Litchfield Shrine Grotto.** Along with a gift shop and a designated picnic area, there's a reproduction of France's Lourdes grotto here, as well as the Stations of the Cross. This is also a popular religious pilgrimage site from May through October and liturgies are sometimes given right at the grotto; call for a schedule of upcoming services.

H.O.R.S.E. OF A DIFFERENT COLOR

The **Humane Organization Representing Suffering Equines (H.O.R.S.E.)** is a truly unique nonprofit organization based in the town of Washington, in the Litchfield Hills. Neglected and physically abused horses are nursed back to their old selves here by a team of volunteers. It's possible for out-of-towners to feed the horses and even tour the facility on relatively short notice, although anyone interested in volunteering—even for just a day—should give the good folks at H.O.R.S.E. a couple of days' notice. Give 'em a call at (860) 868-1960, or visit www.horseofct.org for more detailed information.

To choose your next destination, grab a pencil and a decent map of Connecticut. Draw a triangle by connecting the towns of Litchfield, New Milford and Woodbury. Inside that triangle are a number of interesting small towns worth a visit and enough winding and scenic country roads to keep you busy for a week. There's a winery and the gorgeous Lake Waramaug in New Preston, not to mention a slew of B&Bs and country inns. There's an historic garden on Bethlehem's Main St North. And in Washington, you can feed horses at a nonprofit rescue organization (see boxed text, "H.O.R.S.E. of a Different Color".) So pick a place that looks unusual and head out for an afternoon drive.

When you're ready to move on, head to the town of **18 Woodbury,** which is often referred to as the antiques capital of Connecticut. Most tourists, however, come for a look at the **19 Glebe House Museum & the Gertrude Jekyll Garden,** which is known as the birthplace of the Episcopal Church in America. The country's first Episcopal Bishop, John Marshall, lived there in the late 1800s, and today, the restored house stands as a near-perfect replica of the original. The plans for the garden surrounding the house were drawn by Gertrude Jekyll, a legendary English landscape designer who created the still-popular cottage style of gardening.

A quick drive down Rte 64 east will take you past **⑳ Quassy Amusement Park**, a 20-acre park abutting Lake Quassapaug that's perfect for young kids. Don't expect to find any terrifying steel roller coasters, though. The vibe is much more about antique carousels, paddle boats and deep-fried junk food.

To put the perfect cap on your evening, experience the pleasure of truly artful food preparation at the **㉑ Good News Cafe**, which has been named one of America's best restaurants by Zagat's. Chef Carole Peck, in fact, is often referred to as the Alice Waters of the East Coast. As for her food, it's generally considered to be inventive and exciting, but not in a pretentious or off-putting sort of way.

DETOUR

Creative people and artistic influences can be found almost anywhere in Connecticut. When it comes to the pictures that hang on people's walls, however, it's certainly easier to find Currier & Ives around these parts than, say, Warhol or Rothko.

For an artistic change of pace, visit the **New Britain Museum of American Art**, where the collection includes more than 1,500 works by Sol LeWitt, a New Britain native. The **Aldrich Contemporary Art Museum** houses a screening room, a sound gallery, and a performance space.

Peck also procures most of her food locally and perhaps because of that, she's become known for changing her menu entirely with each season. She's even claimed that no two visits to the restaurant will ever be the same. That sounds like a pretty smart business model to us. And when you think about it—the four seasons, the changing colors, the towns that grow or shrink with each passing year—it also sounds a whole lot like New England.

Dan Eldridge

TRIP INFORMATION

GETTING THERE
From New Haven, take I-95 toward Norwalk then transfer to Rte 7 north.

DO

Glebe House Museum & the Gertrude Jekyll Garden
An 18th-century farmhouse once inhabited by Woodbury's first Episcopal priest. ☎ 203-263-2855; www.theglebehouse.org; 49 Hollow Rd, Woodbury; adult/child $5/2; ⏰ 1-4pm Wed-Sun May-Oct

Lourdes in Litchfield Shrine Grotto
Light a candle for world peace at this 35-acre shrine, modeled after France's Lourdes grotto. ☎ 860-567-1041; 56 Montfort Rd, Litchfield; admission free; ⏰ dawn-dusk; ♿

Quassy Amusement Park
A wooden roller coaster, kids' rides and paddle boats. ☎ 203-758-2913; www.quassy.com; 2132 Middlebury Rd (Rte 64), Middlebury; per ride $3; ⏰ 11am-8pm Sun-Thu, 11am-10pm Fri & Sat Memorial Day-Labor Day

Tapping Reeve House and Law School
Experience 19th-century school life through interactive exhibits. ☎ 860-567-4501; www.litchfieldhistoricalsociety.org; 82 South St, Litchfield; adult/child $5/3; ⏰ 11am-5pm Tue-Sat, 1-5pm Sun mid-Apr–Nov; ♿

Sloane-Stanley Museum
An impressively large collection of tools belonging to famed American painter Eric Sloane. ☎ 860-927-3849; 31 Kent-Cornwall Rd, Rte 7, Kent; adult/child $4/2.50; ⏰ 10am-4pm Wed-Sun mid-May–Oct)

EAT & DRINK

Bohemian Pizza
Specialty pizzas in an ubercreative environment, with a neighborhood hipster bar attached. ☎ 860-567-3980; myspace.com/bohemianpizzaanddittos; 342 Bantam Rd, Rte 202, Litchfield; mains $12-19; ⏰ 11:30am-9pm Mon-Thu, 11:30am-10pm Fri & Sat, 11:30am-8pm Sun

Fife 'n Drum Restaurant and Inn
Kent's favorite restaurant and probably its best. ☎ 860-927-3509; www.fifendrum.com; Rte 2, Kent; mains $20-37; ⏰ 11:30am-3:30pm Mon, Wed & Thu-Sat, 5:30-9:30pm Mon, Wed & Thu, 5:30-10:30pm Fri, 5:30-10:30pm Sat, 3-8:30pm Sun

Good News Cafe
A regular award winner, where the food is inventive without being pretentious. ☎ 203-266-4663; www.good-news-cafe.com; 694 Main St South, Woodbury; mains $18-29; ⏰ 11:30am-10pm Mon & Wed-Sat

West Street Grill
A trendy contemporary bistro known for its fusion food and celeb-spotting possibilities. ☎ 860-567-3885; www.weststreetgrill.com; 43 West St, Litchfield; mains $22-37; ⏰ 11:30am-3pm & 5:30-9pm Mon-Thu, 11:30am-4pm & 5:30-10:30pm Fri & Sat

SLEEP

Breadloaf Mountain Lodge & Cottages
With the Housatonic at its doorstep, this is the inn of choice for nature enthusiasts. ☎ 860-672-6064; www.breadloafmountainlodge.com; 13 Rte 7, Cornwall Bridge; r $115-325

Litchfield Inn
An elegant Colonial inn with cable, wi-fi, restaurant and a baby grand. ☎ 860-567-4503; www.litchfieldct.com; 432 Bantam Rd (Rte 202), Litchfield; r $170-310; ♿

USEFUL WEBSITES
www.ctvisit.com
www.litchfieldhills.com

www.lonelyplanet.com/trip-planner

LINK YOUR TRIP

VERMONT TRIPS

For anyone who appreciates slow-paced meandering and nonstop scenic beauty, Vermont is a road-tripper's paradise. The Green Mountain State has an eclectic allure, offering outdoor adventure, vibrant local arts, photogenic villages, great locavore eating, a palpable pride in its rural heritage, and America's highest per capita concentration of microbreweries and covered bridges.

Throughout the state, stubborn mountain ridges make straight-line driving impossible, yet this enforced lack of predictable 65mph efficiency makes for an ever-present sense of adventure and discovery as you zigzag through one of America's most uniformly bucolic landscapes.

Travelers invariably notice something different when they cross the

PLAYLIST Set the scene with this Vermont playlist, featuring everything from Phish to local blues and bluegrass artists:

- "Farmhouse," Phish
- "Down from Canada," Patti Casey
- "Nothing But the Water," Grace Potter & the Nocturnals
- "Moonlight in Vermont," Willie Nelson
- "When I Leave Winooski," Rebecca Padula
- "O My Star," Anais Mitchell & Rachel Ries
- "George," Richard Ruane & Michael Chorney
- "Whatever Makes You High," The Doughboys

Vermont state line. For starters, there's the total lack of billboards. All businesses – from the humblest mom-and-pop to the mightiest McDonald's – are allowed to advertise only on understated black-and-white signs. Vermont also provides uniquely fertile ground for creative thinkers. Wherever you go, independent-minded people – from small-scale farmers to artists building 20ft puppets – have brought personal passions to fruition and integrated them into local communities, reinvigorating Vermont's traditional small town culture even as they create new reasons for outsiders to visit.

VERMONT'S BEST TRIPS

VERMONT TRIPS

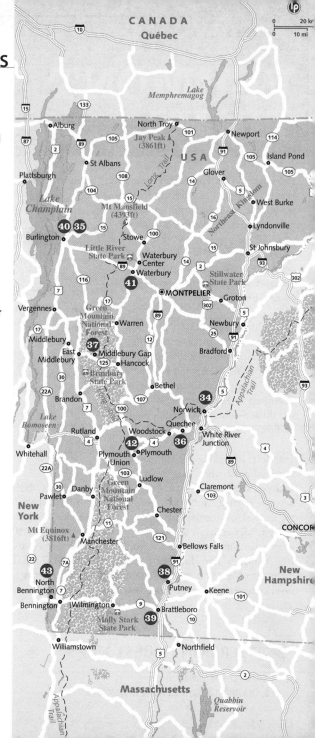

Vermont Backroads Ramble

WHY GO Vermont is filled with entrancingly picturesque spots: historic villages seemingly frozen in time, narrow mountain passes crossed by dirt roads, expanses of farmland stretching out to lush maple-covered mountains, swimming holes at the foot of waterfalls and atmospheric old general stores. How do you find these places? Read on...

Warning: this trip is full of curves, backtracking and dirt roads. Promise: this trip is fun and is intended to capture the spirit of meandering backroad adventure that makes Vermont so addictive to spontaneous-minded explorers.

Get your motor running at ❶ **Dan & Whit's General Store** on Main St, Norwich, just off I-91. As its motto says, "If we don't have it, you don't need it." It's fun catching snippets of local conversation while wandering the aisles loading up on pretrip provisions and pondering whether you really need that poison-ivy soap, hockey stick or "Doe in Heat" scent.

From here, you're perfectly poised to take the "old highway" (Hwy 5) north along the Connecticut River. Nowadays neglected by tourists in favor of high-speed I-91, Hwy 5 is well worth driving. You'll lose a few mph but gain the opportunity to appreciate small towns such as Bradford and Newbury. In the former, check out ❷ **Perfect Pear**, a café built inside a historic grist mill; its stone terrace overlooking the Waits River makes a perfect lunch spot.

As you wend your way north, pretty views of the river's lazy curves and New Hampshire's White Mountains begin to unfold around every bend. Leave the river at Barnet, following Bimson Dr toward West Barnet and climbing into the charmed high pasturelands surrounding ❸ **Peacham**,

TIME
4 days

DISTANCE
325 miles

BEST TIME TO GO
May – Oct

START
Norwich

END
Norwich

ALSO GOOD FOR

HISTORY & CULTURE

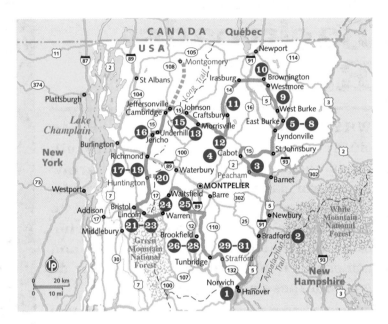

one of Vermont's most beautifully sited towns. Originally a stop on the historic Bayley-Hazen Military Rd – intended to help Americans launch a sneak attack on the British during the Revolutionary War – Peacham today retains a lost-in-time quality, its sleepy main street virtually devoid of commerce but affording pastoral views over the surrounding countryside. Take a self-guided walking tour using the free brochure from the town library, or browse the antiques and handicrafts over a cup of coffee at the Peacham Corner Guild.

Head over the mountains on unpaved Mack Mountain Rd – it's a right fork off Church St opposite Peacham's very picturesque cemetery and town historical society. Seven miles out, a quick jog left on Hwy 2 brings you to a second dirt road, Danville Hill Rd, which stays up high before plunging dramatically into the lush valley that serves as home to ❹ **Cabot Creamery**. Despite its nation-wide distribution network, Cabot remains basically true to its roots as a New England dairy cooperative. Its half-hour tour gives you a look at the cheese-making process (not to mention high-tech machinery painted like Holsteins), after which you can pig out to your heart's content in the sample room.

Chart a zigzag course along Rte 232, Rte 15, Hwy 2 and I-91 into Lyndon-ville. After an optional stop to savor 75c microbrew samples at ❺ **Trout River Brewery**, climb Darling Hill Rd and feast on the amazing vistas from the 500-acre farm surrounding ❻ **Wildflower Inn**, a family resort that lets out all the stops. Amenities include a petting barn, an outdoor hot tub and swimming pool and miles of hiking trails. The inn's trails represent only a small fraction of the 100-mile **7 Kingdom Trails Network**. This dream come true for hikers, mountain bikers and cross-country skiers relies on an innovative arrangement whereby local landowners make their land publicly accessible for recreation year-round and users pay a fee. Maps are available at Kingdom Trails headquarters in nearby East Burke. While there, poke your head into the **8 Bailey's & Burke General Store**, a perennial favorite for pre- and post-trip snacking.

Point your compass 16 miles north, following Burke Hollow Rd and Rte 5A to **9 Lake Willoughby**. Here the dramatic granite escarpments of Mt Pisgah and Mt Hor frame one of the north country's prettiest lakes, complete with swimming beach at its northern end. Hikers can climb Mt Pisgah via the trail at the lake's southern edge for stunning aerial views. A few miles further on, west of the junction of Rte 5A and Rte 58, is another sleeping beauty, the historic town of Brownington, whose well-preserved but little-visited **10 Old Stone House Museum** is just one of many lovely 19th-century buildings reposing under the shade of

MONTGOMERY'S COVERED BRIDGES

A 20-mile detour north from Jeffersonville via Rte 108, 109 and 118 takes you to the covered bridge capital of Vermont. In an idyllic valley at the confluence of multiple watersheds, the twin villages of Montgomery and Montgomery Center share seven spans crisscrossing the local rivers. Especially beautiful – though challenging to find – is remote **Creamery Bridge** just off Hill West Rd, which straddles a waterfall with a swimming hole at its base.

equally ancient maple trees. The museum pays tribute to educational trailblazer Alexander Twilight, America's first African-American college graduate, who built Brownington's boarding school and ran it for decades.

A short jog west on Rte 58, followed by a southbound stint on Rte 14, brings you to Craftsbury, where the community-owned **11 Craftsbury General Store** makes killer mac'n'cheese and showcases everything from local honey to handmade clothing and furniture in its Vermont Local Products section. Craftsbury also has its own extensive network of trails and is a big center for outdoor pursuits year-round.

Segue from Rte 14 to Rte 15 just east of Wolcott and look for the **12 Fisher Covered Railroad Bridge** on your left as you head westward. This century-old span, with its cupola designed as an outlet for steam locomotives' smoke, is among the last covered railroad bridges in America still in regular use.

Continue along the verdant Lamoille River valley into Morrisville, whose convoluted main street leads to the **13 Bee's Knees**, a great eatery with tables on the sidewalk and live music almost nightly. A few miles further west, pull in at the **14 Governor's House**, former mansion of 19th-century Vermont governor Carroll Page. It's one of those amazingly ornate places that makes people say, "Wish I could stay there." Well, in this case, you can. Jane Austen junkies, take note: the hotel occasionally hosts Austen weekends, complete with carriage rides, book discussions and afternoon teas.

A few miles down the Lamoille River, the town of Johnson radiates with the energy of artists and writers from around the world, who receive grants to spend four to 12 weeks at the **15** **Vermont Studio Center**, the largest artist-in-residence program in the United States. Regular readings, talks and a gallery space open to the public provide a glimpse of what all those artists are up to.

Continue along Rte 15 toward Jeffersonville and Cambridge. Here at the base of the 4393ft Mt Mansfield are some of Vermont's most awe-inspiring vistas. After a scenic detour onto Pleasant Valley Rd south of Cambridge, rejoin Rte 15 in Underhill and follow it west to Jericho, where the ultra-photogenic **16** **Old Red Mill** sits astride the Browns River gorge. Inside the mill, a nice display of Vermont crafts shares space with a free museum showcasing the captivating microphotography of native son "Snowflake" Bentley, who provided groundbreaking evidence that no two snowflakes are created equal. Out back, the Browns River Trail traverses a soft carpet of evergreen needles to a little sandy beach with big boulders and a deep pool for swimming.

Follow Lee River Rd to the pretty town green in Jericho Center, then continue south on Browns Trace Rd into Richmond, a small town that has done a remarkable job of preserving its village feel, despite the encroachment of Burlington's suburbs and a major interstate highway just west. Heading south along Bridge St, **17** **On the Rise Bakery** is a good place to soak up some of this community spirit over a sandwich before crossing the Winooski River to the early-19th-century **18** **Old Round Church**, one of Vermont's most unique structures. The graceful 16-sided edifice, used by multiple congregations over the years, is as elegant inside as out.

"While you're picking, guitarists may be pickin' and grinnin'."

The main road curves south of the Round Church toward Huntington. Around the 3-mile mark, in July and August, it's well worth checking in at **19** **Owl's Head Blueberry Farm**, a scenic spot to pick your own blueberries. While you're picking, don't be surprised to see local guitarists pickin' and grinnin' – the farm hosts biweekly concerts each summer to keep everyone smiling.

Between the towns of Huntington and Huntington Center, enter a gorgeous valley presided over by Vermont's most distinctively shaped peak, **20** **Camel's Hump** (it actually looked like a sleeping lion to early French explorers – so feel free to zoomorphize it any way you like).

Continue toward Bristol along Huntington Rd, Gore Rd, Rte 17 and Rte 116, then turn east (left) onto Lincoln Gap Rd just north of Bristol and begin climbing to the highest (and arguably most beautiful) pass in the Green Mountains. On a sunny day, just a few hundred yards up the road, parked cars along the right-hand side will alert you to the presence of ㉑ **Bartlett Falls**, where the New Haven River's raging waters cascade into a natural swimming hole flanked by cliffs that make a popular jumping-off point for local youths.

After a dip, continue eastward on Lincoln Gap Rd, which narrows and steepens noticeably beyond the town of Lincoln, culminating in a 24% grade. Shortly before ㉒ **Lincoln Gap**, a quarter-mile-long trail on the left leads steeply up to a granite outcropping with fantastic views over the Greens, while at the summit itself the Long Trail offers a couple of nice day-hiking options, including the 5-mile round-trip to the top of 4006ft Mt Abraham.

DETOUR The distinctive form of **Camel's Hump** is a familiar image to Vermonters – its silhouette is visible on the Vermont state quarter, from suburban Burlington and along I-89. Yet it remains one of the state's wildest spots, the only significant Vermont peak not developed for skiing. From Huntington Center, head east 3 miles, dead-ending at the trailhead for the 6-mile Burrows–Forest City loop to the summit. After climbing through forest, the final ascent skirts rock faces above the treeline, affording magnificent views.

Hang on to your hat for the roller-coaster ride into Warren. Lincoln Gap Rd dead-ends into Rte 100, which you follow left for five seconds before jogging right onto Covered Bridge Rd. Cross the bridge onto Warren's Main St and make a beeline for the ㉓ **Warren Store**, hands down one of Vermont's most appealing general stores. Residents and tourists alike flock to this animated community hangout with wavy 19th-century floors, a deli serving gourmet sandwiches and pastries, an upstairs store full of carefully chosen jewelry, toys, clothing and knickknacks, and a pretty sundeck overlooking the sculpted granite rocks near the headwaters of the Mad River.

From Warren, turn east (uphill) on Brook Rd, which climbs into high country commanding exquisite views over the upland fields and mountains. About 5 miles north, as the road begins descending toward Waitsfield, the ㉔ **Inn at Round Barn** is sure to catch your attention. It's a 19th-century house surrounded by ponds, trails, high pastureland and a magnificent old barn that hosts everything from opera to theater. As a member of the Vermont Fresh Network, the inn sources ingredients for its breakfasts from local farms.

And now for some one-of-a-kind covered bridge fun! Drive down into Waitsfield and follow Rte 100 north to Moretown, where signs on the right steer you onto mostly unpaved Moretown Mountain Rd. Nine miles along, just before entering the town of Northfield, you'll cross not one but ㉕ **three** covered bridges in a row within a span of two-tenths of a mile, a concentration equalled nowhere else in the state.

From Northfield zigzag your way southeast to Williamstown via Rte 12 and Rte 64. After plunging southward on Rte 14 through Williamstown Gulf (a gulf, in Vermont parlance, is a low pass between watersheds), turn west onto Rte 65 toward the little town of Brookfield. Brookfield's biggest claim to fame is the ㉖ **Brookfield Floating Bridge** (intermittently closed to vehicles but always open to pedestrians and fishermen) . Built on floating pontoons across glassy Sunset Lake, it's the only span of its kind east of the Mississippi and one of Vermont's most photographed spots. Overlooking the lake, ㉗ **Ariel's Restaurant & Pond Village Pub** is one of the most highly regarded eateries in the state, renowned for its $20 prix-fixe three-course dinner on Sundays. When you're done eating, waddle on over to ㉘ **Green Trails Inn**, a comfortably refurbished B&B run by cookbook author Jane Doerfer.

Backtrack to Rte 14 and continue south through classic Vermont farm country, with big barns and covered bridges flanking the roadway. Just past the town of East Randolph, follow the signposted dirt road southeast to Tunbridge, especially worth visiting in mid-September during the Tunbridge World's Fair.

Continuing east, take Strafford Rd 8 miles into ㉙ **Strafford**, another picture-postcard village with a steepled 19th-century meetinghouse at the end of its graceful town green. On a hot day, it's worth detouring east onto Old City Falls Rd (named for Strafford's original town site). Just after crossing a bridge, look on your left for the sign indicating ㉚ **Old City Falls**, a sylvan swimming hole tucked into a deep river gorge accessed by a switchbacking forest path. Back in town, the 19th-century pink gingerbread museum on your left is the ㉛ **Morrill Homestead**, former home of Justin Smith Morrill, a blacksmith's son who left school at age 15 due to his family's poverty. Eventually becoming a US Senator, Morrill spearheaded the Land Grant Acts that made college learning affordable for millions of Americans.

TUNBRIDGE WORLD'S FAIR

September visitors to central Vermont shouldn't miss the Tunbridge World's Fair, an annual celebration of Vermont rural culture that has run continuously since 1867. Once home to gambling, drinking and burlesque shows, the fair has a more wholesome reputation nowadays, but farmers still lead their oxen to drink from the river as they might have done a century ago. For a uniquely Vermont experience, try the maple cotton candy and the apple Creemees (Vermont's semiofficial name for soft-serve ice cream).

A final scenic meander follows Rte 132 through the pretty town of South Strafford and rejoins Hwy 5 near Norwich, where you can pick up I-91 or start charting a new backroads adventure of your own.

Gregor Clark

TRIP INFORMATION

GETTING THERE

From Boston, take I-93 to I-89 to I-91 northbound. At Exit 13 (Norwich), take Hwy 5 northbound to Main St, Norwich.

DO

Cabot Creamery

This high-tech factory in a pastoral setting makes Vermont's most famous cheddar. ☎ 888-792-2268; www.cabotcheese.com; 2878 Main St, Cabot; tours $2; ⏰ 9am-5pm Jun-Oct, 9am-4pm Nov-May; ⛲

Kingdom Trails Network

This vast network of trails is the best way to explore the Northeast Kingdom's rural landscape. ☎ 802-626-0737; www.kingdomtrails.org; Main St, East Burke; ⏰ 8am-5pm Sun-Thu, 8am-6pm Fri & Sat; ⛲

Morrill Homestead

Vermont's first National Historic Landmark tells the inspiring tale of Morrill's crusade to bring college education to the masses. ☎ 802-765-4484; www.morrillhomestead.org; Morrill Hwy, Strafford; tours $5; ⏰ 11am-5pm Sat & Sun Memorial Day-Columbus Day

Old Red Mill

"Snowflake" Bentley's ice crystal photos are remarkable and the view of the falls is a Vermont classic. ☎ 802-899-3225; www.jerichohistoricalsociety.org/mill.htm; Rte 15, Jericho; admission free; ⏰ 10am-5pm Mon-Sat, 1-5pm Sun

Old Round Church

One of Vermont's most beautiful historic buildings sits tranquilly by the Winooski River only 2 miles from the interstate. ☎ 802-434-2556; www.oldroundchurch.com; Bridge St, Richmond; admission free; ⏰ Jun-Oct

Old Stone House Museum

Four floors of history are packed into this lovely old building. ☎ 802-754-2022; www.oldstonehousemuseum.org; 109 Old Stone House Rd, Brownington; adult/child $5/2; ⏰ 11am-5pm Wed-Sun mid-May–mid-Oct

Owl's Head Blueberry Farm

Harvest berries to live music at scenically located Owl's Head. ☎ 802-434-3387; www.owlsheadfarm.com; 263 Blueberry Farm Rd, Richmond; ⏰ 5pm-dusk Tue & thu, 10am-dusk Wed, 9am-4pm Fri-Sun mid-Jul–late Aug; ⛲

Vermont Studio Center

America's largest artist- and writer-in-residence program hosts rotating shows throughout the year at its Red Mill Gallery. ☎ 802-635-2727; www.vermontstudiocenter.org; 80 Pearl St, Johnson

EAT

Ariel's Restaurant & Pond Village Pub

Brookfield's acclaimed restaurant overlooks the famous floating bridge and Sunset Lake. ☎ 802-276-3939; www.arielsrestaurant.com; 29 Stone Rd, Brookfield; mains $13-28; ⏰ 6pm-close Wed-Sun May-Oct

Bailey's & Burke General Store

The popular deli here draws cyclists exploring the nearby Kingdom Trails Network. ☎ 802-626-9250; www.baileysandburke.com; Main St, East Burke; ⏰ 8am-7pm Sun-Thu, 8am-8pm Fri & Sat

Bee's Knees

Local organic ingredients, vegan and veggie options and regular live music make this a local favorite. ☎ 802-888-7889; www.thebeesknees-vt.com; 82 Lower Main St, Morrisville; ⏰ 6:30am-10pm Tue-Fri, 8am-10pm Sat & Sun

Craftsbury General Store

This store is a true community endeavor, displaying local arts and crafts and serving tasty deli treats. ☎ 802-586-2811; 118 S Craftsbury Rd, Craftsbury; ⏰ 6am-7:30pm Mon-Sat, 7am-6pm Sun

Dan & Whit's General Store

Norwich's classic general store claims to have everything under the sun – and it does!

☎ 802-649-1602; www.danandwhits.com;
319 Main St, Norwich; ⊗ 7am-9pm

On the Rise Bakery

Beyond the delectable baked goods, On the Rise wins points for its wood-fired pizzas and local microbrews. ☎ 802-434-7787; www .ontherisebakery.net; Bridge St, Richmond; ⊗ 6am-6pm Mon & Tue, 6am-10pm Wed-Sat, 6am-2pm Sun

Perfect Pear

This old grist mill with a pretty river view serves contemporary American cuisine. ☎ 802-222-5912; www.theperfectpearcafe .com; 48 Main St, Bradford; mains $7-20; ⊗ 11:30am-3pm & 5-8:45pm Tue-Sat, 5-8:45pm Sun

Warren Store

Tourists and locals alike congregate on the front porch, the deck and the creekside steps at this laid-back, eclectic store. ☎ 802-496-3864; www.warrenstore.com; Main St, Warren; sandwiches $5-8; ⊗ 8am-7pm

DRINK

Trout River Brewery

Sample a few 75c beers and try the smoked trout pizza Friday and Saturday nights. ☎ 802-626-9396; www.troutriver brewing.com; Hwy 5, Lyndonville; pizzas from $11; ⊗ 5-8:30pm Fri & Sat

SLEEP

Governor's House

Former Vermont governor Carroll Page's late-19th-century mansion is now an atmospheric B&B with period details and spacious grounds. ☎ 802-888-6888; www.onehun dredmain.com; 100 Main St, Hyde Park; r $95-265

Green Trails Inn

In the heart of pretty Brookfield village, providing easy access to the restaurant and pub across the street. ☎ 802-276-3412; www .greentrailsinn.com; 24 Stone Rd, Brookfield; r $95-135

Inn at Round Barn

One of Vermont's prettiest inns boasts a historic round barn set amid ponds and high meadows. ☎ 802-496-2276; www.theround barn.com; 1661 E Warren Rd, Waitsfield; r $165-315

Wildflower Inn

With a 500-acre backyard and views that won't quit, the Wildflower rates among New England's family friendliest inns. ☎ 800-627-8310, 802-626-8310; www.wildflower inn.com; 2059 Darling Hill Rd, Lyndonville; r $125-460; ♿

USEFUL WEBSITES

www.511vt.com
www.eotsweb.org/forecasts.php

LINK YOUR TRIP   www.lonelyplanet.com/trip-planner

TRIP
36 Cider Season Sampler p243
39 Tip to Tail by Bike & Rail p259

King-Sized Fun in the Queen City

WHY GO With 40,000 residents, Burlington would barely pass for a small town in some states, but Vermonters consider it a veritable hub of cosmopolitan life. With its pretty lakefront and pedestrian-friendly downtown, the Queen City is an engaging place with a low-key, friendly buzz and sophisticated without losing its smaller-town flavor.

TIME
2 days

BEST TIME TO GO
Jun – Oct

START
Burlington

END
Burlington

ALSO GOOD FOR

If Burlington is the Queen City, Lake Champlain is surely its crown. A great way to start the day is by the waterfront at the ❶ Skinny Pancake, one of Burlington's local feel-good stories. What started as a Church St food cart began doing such a brisk business that in 2006 it moved operations to a permanent restaurant on the lakeshore. With outdoor tables and a spacious interior, the new restaurant cranks out crepes tasty enough to please the discerning palates of visitors from Montréal and Quebec City, not to mention the loyal locals. Regionally sourced classics such as Vermont Apples and Cabot Cheddar share the menu with creative alternatives including the Love Maker – Nutella, strawberries and whipped cream (watch out, if you add bananas it becomes the Heart Breaker!). Another local alternative, if you're here on a Saturday, is the ❷ Burlington Farmers Market, held from 8:30am to 2pm in City Hall Park, a big green space in the heart of downtown.

Having properly broken your fast, it's time to hit Burlington's great lake. Champlain isn't quite as big as the *real* Great Lakes, but it's hard not to be impressed by the sight of its sparkling waters backed by New York's Adirondack Mountains.

Nature lovers, or those interested in green architecture, will definitely want to explore the ❸ ECHO Aquarium & Science Center, a water-

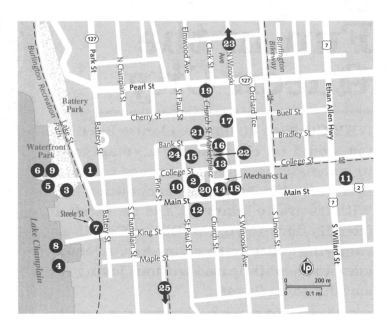

front science museum LEED-certified for its state-of-the-art environmentally friendly design. It has a moderate-sized aquarium featuring local fish, a resource room and a science lab for students of the lake, and plenty of exhibits about Lake Champlain, including one devoted to its famous monster, Champ. Down the lake a piece, on Perkins Pier, you can pay homage to a small Champ monument, then take to the waves for a sighting of your own in a kayak or canoe from ❹ **Waterfront Boat Rentals**.

"…a waterfront location and crepes tasty enough to please the discerning palates of visitors from Quebec."

Other environmentally friendly ways to explore the lake include sailing and biking. In summer ❺ **Whistling Man Schooner** sails three times daily from the ECHO museum, with an especially beautiful dusk run. Experienced skippers can take the tiller themselves at ❻ **Winds of Ireland**, which rents sailboats by the day or half-day down at the Burlington Boathouse north of Main St. Landlubbers will likely prefer pedaling along the lakeshore with the help of a rental bike from ❼ **Local Motion**, a cycling-advocacy group whose trailside center sits astride the 12-mile waterfront Island Line Trail, tracing the edge of Lake Champlain. The center stocks a wide variety of maps and brochures on topics of interest to cyclists.

Those with an aversion to self-propulsion can instead cross the lake by ferry. Departing from the King St dock, ❽ **Lake Champlain Ferries** offers crossings to Port Kent, New York, every hour or two between 9am and 6pm, while the **9** **Spirit of Ethan Allen** runs circle tours for pretty much every taste, from the basic narrated trip around the lake to Rum and Reggae or Lobstah-on-the-Lake cruises.

For lunch, grab a wood-fired pizza and a Zero Gravity home brew at **10** **American Flatbread**, then check into your room (and maybe take an afternoon catnap) at **11** **Lang House B&B**, conveniently located just up Main St from downtown.

Nighttime is the right time to check out Burlington's vast (for Vermont) entertainment offerings. High-caliber music, dance and theater, including local acts as well as those from as far away as China and Africa, are on display most weekend nights at the **12** **Flynn Center for the Performing Arts** on Main St. Bars such as the **13** **Daily Planet**, **14** **½ Lounge** and **15** **Green Room** are popular not only for their drinks but also for their good food and ever-so-

ASK A LOCAL

"For a different take on Burlington, head to the South End where you can pick up gourmet wines and cheeses from **Fresh Market** or browse in the **Lamp Shop**, full of vintage lamps and flea-market finds. In Fall, there's also the **South End Art Hop** each year, one weekend chock-full of art displayed in crazy nooks and crannies. And don't miss **Oakledge Park** – great for sunsets or for diving off the rocks into Lake Champlain."
David Alles, Duxbury, VT

cool vibe. Or, for a nonalcoholic nightcap, hunker down cross-legged on the cushions behind the beaded curtain at **16** **Dobra Tea**, the lone US franchise of a Czech-based teahouse chain, where you can sample a dizzying array of teas from around the world.

Next morning, brave the lines (it's really worth it!) for Burlington's best breakfast at **17** **Penny Cluse**. Everything is made fresh and those weary of New England diner fare will appreciate the zingy N'awlins and southwestern twists to some dishes – especially recommended are the *chiles rellenos,* surely the best this side of Lake Champlain, if not Las Cruces. If pastries and cakes are more your thing, head for **18** **Mirabelles**. A glance in the display case will let you know what most people come here for, although the café's traditional egg-and-bacon specials are pretty tempting in their own right.

A few paces away, Burlington's commercial and social hub is the **19** **Church Street Marketplace**, an attractive multiblock pedestrian zone lined with shops, food carts, street musicians and climbing rocks popular with young children. Near the foot of the pedestrian zone, the **20** **Firehouse Center for the Visual Arts** operates a contemporary arts gallery featuring Vermont artists as well as those from further afield.

Further up the street, on a hot day, don't miss two very popular local businesses guaranteed to cool you down: **㉑ Lake Champlain Chocolates** makes killer chocolate ice cream, along with specialty truffles and other chocolatey goodies, while **㉒ Rookie's Root Beer Stand**, staffed by cofounder-owner Jenny Rooke, serves up a lightly carbonated blend of wintergreen, sassafras, licorice root and Bourbon vanilla, sweetened only with molasses and turbinado sugar. (She'll gladly show you samples of the ingredients from her root collection.)

THE LOVABLE LAKE MONSTER

Dinosaur relic or Ice Age proto whale? Tree trunk? Really really big fish? Lake Champlain's legendary sea monster, Champ, has long fascinated local residents. Known to the Abenaki as Tatoskok, Champ was also sighted by French explorer Samuel de Champlain. Indulge your curiosity at the Champ display in Burlington's ECHO museum, or – for a more dependable sighting – attend a Vermont Lake Monsters baseball game, where a lovable green-costumed Champ mascot dances on the dugout roof between innings!

Another shining example of Burlington's livable and environmentally friendly nature is the **㉓ Intervale**, a cluster of small organic farms lining the verdant banks of the Winooski River a mile northeast of downtown. Follow Winooski and Riverside Aves to Intervale Rd, then descend into a small paradise of greenery, where you can shop for gardening supplies, see the city's community vegetable garden, pick your own berries at Adam's Berry Farm, ride or hike along the network of riverside trails or simply escape the urban "jungle" for an hour or two.

For a farewell meal, it's hard to beat the exquisite Chinese food at **㉔ Single Pebble**. Like Skinny Pancake, this place got its start as a humble food cart. Now occupying an old New England home whose red-painted door frames and paper globe lanterns have convincingly morphed it into a cozy Asian-vibed eatery, Single Pebble delights vegans and vegetarians with its varied menu. Portions are large, intended to be eaten family style, and each item is brought directly from the wok to the table the minute it's cooked.

BURLINGTON'S FESTIVALS

Burlington is a city that knows how to have fun. Three of the best festivals are: **First Night Burlington** (www.firstnightburlington.com), an alcohol-free New Year's Eve celebration with lots of kids' activities and fireworks over the lake; the **Vermont Brewers Festival** (www.vermontbrewers.com) in July at Waterfront Park, where you can taste Burlington's own fabulous Switchback Ale and dozens of other Vermont microbrews; and the **Discover Jazz Festival** (www.discoverjazz.com), which fills the streets with music in late May/early June.

Alternatively, if you're leaving town early and have your own wheels, you can squeeze in a visit to the **㉕ Magic Hat Brewery**, just a few miles south of town on Hwy 7, for a few free tastes and Vermont microbrew souvenirs before hitting the interstate or the airport.

Gregor Clark

TRIP INFORMATION

GETTING THERE
From Boston, take I-93 northbound to I-89. At Vermont Exit 14 (Burlington), follow Hwy 2 westbound, which becomes Burlington's Main St.

DO

ECHO Aquarium & Science Center
Right on the waterfront, this aquarium and science museum focuses on Lake Champlain's ecosystem. ☎ 802-864-1848; www.echovermont.org; 1 College St; adult/child $9.50/7; ⏱ 10am-5pm; ♿

Firehouse Center for the Visual Arts
The gallery at Burlington's community art center specializes in contemporary art. ☎ 802-865-7166; www.burlingtoncityarts .com; 135 Church St; ⏱ noon-5pm Tue-Thu & Sun, noon-8pm Fri, 9am-8pm Sat

Flynn Center for the Performing Arts
Downtown Burlington's premiere venue for live music, dance and theater, which take place on its main stage and the more intimate FlynnSpace. ☎ 802-863-5966; www .flynncenter.org; 153 Main St; ♿

Lake Champlain Ferries
The cheapest way to tour Lake Champlain is the one-hour ferry crossing to Port Kent, New York. ☎ 802-864-9804; www.ferries. com; King St Dock; round-trip $9.30; ⏱ late May–mid-Oct

Local Motion
Bike rentals adjacent to Burlington's lakefront recreation path. ☎ 802-652-2453; www.localmotion.org; 1 Steele St; adult/child/tandem bikes per day $28/22/50; ⏱ 9am-6pm Jul & Aug, 10am-6pm May, Jun, Sep & Oct; ♿

Spirit of Ethan Allen
Burlington's biggest cruise ship offers a variety of themed cruises around Lake Champlain. ☎ 802-862-8300; www.soea .com; Burlington Community Boathouse, College St; narrated cruises adult/child $11/5; ⏱ May-Oct

Waterfront Boat Rentals
On the lakeshore just south of Main St, Waterfront rents canoes and kayaks. ☎ 802-864-4858; www.waterfrontboatrentals.com; Perkins Pier; canoes/kayaks/double kayaks per hr $15/12/16; ⏱ 10am-dusk May-Oct

Whistling Man Schooner
The most affordable way to sail Lake Champlain; BYO food and drink. ☎ 802-598-6504; www.whistlingman.com; College St; 2hr sails adult/child $35/20; ⏱ May-Oct

Winds of Ireland
Rent a sailboat for eight to 12 people, with or without a captain. ☎ 802-863-5090; www .windsofireland.net; Burlington Community Boathouse, College St; sailboats per day $430-900, captain per hr $25

EAT

American Flatbread
The Burlington branch of Vermont's favorite wood-fired, locally sourced pizzeria also brews excellent beer. ☎ 802-861-2999; www.flatbreadhearth.com; 115 St Paul St; flatbreads $7.30-18; ⏱ 5-10pm Mon-Thu, 11:30am-2:30pm & 5-11pm Fri-Sun

Daily Planet
With its interior solarium, local artwork, great bar snacks and salads, full meals and memorable martinis, Daily Planet's appeal is wide-ranging. ☎ 802-862-9647; www .dailyplanet15.com; 15 Center St; ⏱ 4pm-late

Green Room
With comfy couches and an artsy lounge vibe, this casual chic hangout serves late-night drinks and fabulous "small plate" dinners. ☎ 802-651-9669; www.greenroomvt .com; 86 St Paul St; mains $7-15; ⏱ 5pm-2am Mon-Sat

Lake Champlain Chocolates
Pop in for chocolate truffles, hot chocolate or ice cream while strolling the Church St pedestrian mall. ☎ 802-862-5185; www .lakechamplainchocolates.com; 65 Church St; ⏱ 10am-8pm Mon-Thu, 10am-9pm Fri & Sat, 11am-6pm Sun

Mirabelles
Renowned for everything from croissants to wedding cakes to tasty breakfasts, Mirabelles is a popular Main St fixture. ☎ 802-658-3074; www.mirabellescafe.com; 198 Main St; ⊙ 7am-5pm Mon-Fri, 8am-5pm Sat, 8am-2:30pm Sun

Penny Cluse
From gingerbread pancakes to zydeco eggs, Penny Cluse puts a new spin on breakfast. ☎ 802-651-8834; www.pennycluse.com; 169 Cherry St; mains $7-10; ⊙ 6:45am-3pm Mon-Fri, 8am-3pm Sat & Sun

Single Pebble
This exceptional, vegetarian-friendly Chinese eatery serves everything the minute it comes out of the wok. ☎ 802-865-5200; www.asinglepebble.com; 133 Bank St; mains $15-20; ⊙ 11:30am-1:45pm & 5pm-late Mon-Fri, 5pm-late Sat & Sun

Skinny Pancake
Creative crepes served on the waterfront, plus regular folk and fondue nights. ☎ 802-540-0188; www.skinnypancake.com; 60 Lake St; mains $6.50-9; ⊙ 8am-2:30pm Mon, 8am-9pm or later Tue-Sun

DRINK

½ Lounge
Good things come in small packages: this diminutive yet sophisticated bar makes the best drinks in town. ☎ 802-865-0012; 136½ Church St; ⊙ 4pm-2am Tue-Sat, 5pm-2am Sun & Mon

Dobra Tea
A chilled-out place to savor teas from around the world, plus couscous and other simple snacks. ☎ 802-951-2424; www.dobratea.com; 80 Church St; ⊙ 11am-10pm Mon-Thu, 11am-11pm Fri & Sat, noon-10pm Sun

Magic Hat Brewery
With 48 taps and a penchant for creative experimentation, Magic Hat is just plain fun. ☎ 802-658-2739; www.magichat.net; 5 Bartlett Bay Rd; ⊙ 10am-6pm Mon-Sat, noon-5pm Sun

Rookie's Root Beer Stand
In good weather, Burlington's homegrown root-beer company operates a cart on pedestrianized Church St, in front of Boutilier's Art Supply. 98 Church St; ⊙ May-Oct

SLEEP

Lang House B&B
Between downtown and the University of Vermont campus, this pleasant B&B is a short walk from everything. ☎ 877-919-9799; www.langhouse.com; 360 Main St; r $145-245

USEFUL WEBSITES
www.sevendaysvt.com

LINK YOUR TRIP   www.lonelyplanet.com/trip-planner

Cider Season Sampler

WHY GO Vermont is radiantly beautiful in harvest season, its farmstands overflowing with fresh produce and leaves just showing the first hints of color. With fresh-pressed cider, pick-your-own berries, countless craft breweries and a burgeoning locavore movement creating partnerships between farms and restaurants statewide, late summer in Vermont is an epicure's delight.

When most people think Vermont food, the first image that comes to mind is those two ex-hippies on the pint-sized ice-cream carton. Sure, no foodie's trip to Vermont would be complete without a visit to Ben & Jerry's Waterbury factory, but these days the real excitement is happening on the farms and in the zillion locavore restaurants sprouting like mushrooms around the state. Vermont chefs, farmers and communities have begun to work together in mutually supportive ways, revitalizing local economies as they create a dynamic new food culture that values freshness and celebrates the state's long-standing agricultural tradition.

A perfect place to start appreciating Vermont's penchant for locally grown food is the ❶ **Farmer's Diner** in Quechee. This epicenter of the locavore movement is the brainchild of Tod Murphy, who years ago envisioned a restaurant that would buy direct from farmers, similar to what happened in his grandmother's day. Today roughly 65% of the diner's menu is sourced within a 70-mile radius. A board above the counter proudly lists dozens of ingredients and their origins: chicken from Misty Knoll, yogurt from Butterworks Farm, bacon from Vermont Smoke and Cure. Whatever you do, don't miss the incredible milkshakes made with ice cream from Strafford Creamery!

TIME
3 – 4 days

DISTANCE
275 miles

BEST TIME TO GO
Aug – Oct

START
Quechee

END
Norwich

ALSO GOOD FOR

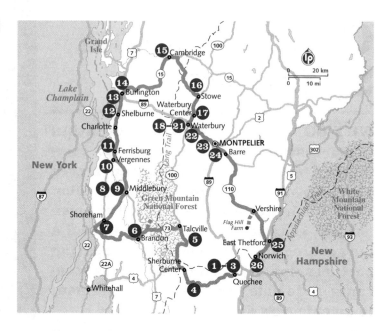

Work off those slabs of locally sourced bacon with a hike to the bottom of **2 Quechee Gorge**, which some have nicknamed Vermont's Grand Canyon. It's a few thousand feet too shallow to compete with the Arizona version, but the 15-minute descent through pine forest is beautiful, following a trail on the south side of Hwy 4. Park at the gorge visitor center, half a mile west of the diner.

Next, it's on to **3 Simon Pearce** in downtown Quechee, sited in an old woolen mill cantilevered out over the Ottauquechee River, with views of a raging waterfall and a covered bridge. Pearce, an Irish glassblower, immigrated to Quechee in 1981, drawn by a vision of running his entire operation self-sufficiently with hydro power. Three decades later, he has built a small empire, with his flagship Quechee store displaying two floors of pottery and glassware and offering glassblowing demonstrations daily. When lunchtime (or brunchtime on Sundays) rolls around, angle for a window seat at the riverview restaurant upstairs, where you can drink from Pearce-made stemware and enjoy specialties such as sesame seared chicken or field greens salad with Vermont-blue or goat cheese.

Following the Ottauquechee a few miles upstream along Hwy 4, stop in at the **4 Long Trail Brewing Company**, Vermont's number-one producer of craft beer. On a sunny day, it's delightful to sit in its riverside beer garden, modeled after Munich's Hofbrauhaus.

Dinner tonight is on the farm, ❺ **Liberty Hill Farm** in Rochester, to be precise, 30 miles northwest of the brewery on gorgeous Rte 100. Thanks to its owners' efforts to conserve the surrounding land, Liberty Hill features one of Vermont's best barn-and-mountain vistas. Overnight farm stays here include dinner and breakfast, served family style and making ample use of produce from the owners' garden. Other highlights include lounging on the front porch, getting to know the farm animals and sampling the ultrafresh dairy products you might expect from a herd of over 100 cattle.

Next morning, head west on Rte 73 to cross Brandon Gap. Near the summit, a pristine wetland popular with moose, beavers and waterfowl sits at the foot of lovely Mt Horrid. From the gap itself, a 1-mile hike north on the Long Trail leads to an overlook with spectacular views in all directions.

DETOUR West of Brandon Gap, a 3-mile detour north on forest service roads leads to **Green Mountain National Forest Blueberry Management Area**, a vast hillside patch of wild blueberries ripe (and free) for the picking. Berries reach their peak in late July/early August and the view over the surrounding mountains is fantastic. From Rte 73 initially follow signs toward Blueberry Hill Inn; once on the unpaved forest service road, look for signs for the Blueberry Management Area itself.

Descend to the pretty town of Brandon, which has spruced itself up in recent years and earned a reputation for colorful street art festivals featuring rocking chairs, pigs and an annually changing array of other items handpainted by local residents. Another welcome addition to the town's landscape is ❻ **Café Provence**, whose French cuisine lives up to its name. Founded by graduates of the New England Culinary Institute in Montpelier, this fabulous eatery cranks out croissants that could hold their own in any Parisian patisserie, and serves a seasonally changing menu sourced heavily from local farms.

A scenic meander west along Rte 73 follows the lazy curves of Otter Creek for a couple of miles before breaking into wide open farm country cascading toward Lake Champlain. Just shy of the lakeshore, double back eastward on Rte 74 to ❼ **Champlain Orchards**, where you can pick two dozen varieties of apples (including many New England heirlooms) or watch the pressing and bottling of ultrafresh cider. The orchard is famous for its free "while-you-pick" acoustic concerts and an annual harvest celebration in October with BBQ pork, apple sauce, cider and fresh-baked pies.

Speaking of pie, the orchard recently partnered with the Vermont Mystic Pie Company to create the world's tastiest and most butter-laden frozen apple pie, available in stores such as the ❽ **Middlebury Natural Foods Co-op**. Continue 17 miles northeast back toward the Green Mountains along Rte 74 and Rte 30 and you'll find Vermont Mystic pie sharing the freezer with its soul mate, Strafford Creamery's scrumptious cinnamon ice cream.

A must-see for microbrew fans in Middlebury is **9** **Otter Creek Brewery**, on Exchange St north of town. Tours three times daily (except Sunday) give you a chance to clamber amid vats of barley and hops, then taste samples to your heart's content. In addition to its many fine namesake brews, Otter Creek brews Wolaver's, one of America's oldest certified organic ales.

ASK A LOCAL

"The Small Farms Food Fest at **Shelburne Orchards** (www.shelburneorchards.com) is more than just an 'apple festival'; it captures everything I love about Vermont: fresh local foods, good music, community and natural beauty. Some of the components – pony rides, a corn maze, face painting – can be found at other county fairs, but the amazing energy and creativity at this event and the breathtaking location overlooking Lake Champlain cannot be beat. This event rocks even in the pouring rain!"

Katherine Quinn, Middlebury, VT

Continue your descent into decadence 10 miles north along Hwy 7 in the picturesque little city of Vergennes, home to the **10** **Daily Chocolate**. This sinfully seductive basement hole-in-the-wall, just opposite Vergennes' town square, specializes in weird but exquisitely tasty concoctions such as green-chili pistachio chocolate bark. Ride your chocolate buzz 5 miles further north along Hwy 7 through Ferrisburg. Just north of town, look for the round barn and camel – yes, a real live camel peacefully coexisting with alpacas and sheep – at Round Barn Merinos. Sighting the camel means you're nearing **11** **Starry Night Café**, a romantic little restaurant with intimate indoor seating plus a pond and patio out back for firefly-watching.

Head for the lakeshore just south of Burlington, where the century-old estate of the Vanderbilt-Webb family, Shelburne Farms, has been converted into a magnificent nonprofit working farm and environmental education center. The **12** **Inn at Shelburne Farms**, a lakeshore mansion serving high tea and some of Vermont's very best fresh-from-the-farm dinners, is reason enough to visit. But it's worth staying overnight for the chance to attend a dusk concert or roam the 1400-acre grounds next morning, watching the making of the farm's excellent cheddar cheese and visiting the architecturally magnificent 19th-century outbuildings, including the twin-turreted, castlelike Farm Barn.

A couple of miles north in South Burlington, **13** **Magic Hat Brewery** exudes an infectious creative energy. Tours and tastes at the "Artifactory" are free and plentiful, with over 20 beer varieties flowing from four-dozen taps at the brand new bar billed as Vermont's largest. Must-trys are the trademark No 9 (pale ale with a hint of apricot), the Orlio organic brews and Odd Notion, a whimsically changing seasonal creation.

Here, in the midst of Vermont's most urban corridor, you'd scarcely expect to discover pristine farmland. Surprise! Five miles north on Hwy 7, tucked between the hubs of Burlington and Winooski, the Intervale Center is a bucolic complex of community gardens and farms hugging the fringes of the Winooski River. Descending from Hwy 7, Intervale Rd turns to dirt and passes through a lush tunnel of trees to ⑭ **Adam's Berry Farm**, where pick-your-own strawberry, blueberry and raspberry operations run from late May till the first frost.

Even fermented berries have a place in Vermont's food culture. When harvest season is over, some of them go into the dessert wines at ⑮ **Boyden Valley Winery**, 20 miles north in the stunningly beautiful Lamoille River valley at the foot of Mt Mansfield. Savor the views and check out the award-winning Gold Leaf, a Vermont-inspired concoction that uses maple syrup straight from the farm combined with local apples.

You won't need any mind-altering substances to appreciate the serpentine curves of Smugglers Notch, the prettiest and narrowest paved mountain pass in the state. On the far side of the notch, as you drop down into Stowe, Sunday visitors should make sure to look for the ⑯ **Stowe Farmers Market** on the left side of Rte 108 shortly before its junction with Rte 100. Continue down Rte 100 and stop in for the night at ⑰ **May Farm Inn**, which incorporates its own home-grown asparagus, berries, herbs and tomatoes into guest menus.

For dinner, the ⑱ **Waterbury** area offers an embarrassment of riches. On Hwy 2 just west of town, ⑲ **Cider House BBQ & Pub** crosses the Mason-Dixon Line with panache, incorporating food from local producers into its Southern-influenced menu of barbecue, hush puppies and fried green tomatoes. Alternatively, kick back by the fire with a mint julep, or taste the wide range of hard and not-so-hard Vermont apple ciders.

Closer to downtown, a beautiful setting in a 19th-century grist mill at ⑳ **Hen of the Wood** complements a menu of ultrafresh, ever-changing seasonal cuisine featuring local meat and produce, wild mushrooms and over a dozen artisanal cheeses. For a nightcap, or a lighter meal, ㉑ **Alchemist Pub & Brewery** is an ultra-laid-back alternative with a friendly bartender who gladly offers free tastes of the in-house craft brews.

Wake up next morning and zip over to ㉒ **Red Hen Bakery**, east on Hwy 2 in Middlesex. Famous for its bread, Red Hen also makes amazingly buttery pastries – from traditional sticky buns to quirkier offerings such as strawberry

VERMONT FRESH NETWORK

Fresh local food is never far away in the Green Mountain State, thanks to the **Vermont Fresh Network**, a partnership between the state's restaurants and farmers. Restaurants commit to supporting local producers by buying direct from the farm, while "farmers' dinners" throughout the year allow diners to meet the people who put the food on their table. For a full list of participating restaurants and upcoming events, see www.vermontfresh.net/vfnfarmerdinner.

Danish with pistachios. The dining area is dotted with homey touches – a couch, a carpet and a wood stove – plus a viewing window into the bakery and photos of local growers such as Ben Gleason, whose organic wheat figures prominently in Red Hen's crusty loaves.

With 9000 residents, Montpelier (8 miles east on Hwy 2) is not only America's smallest capital city, it's also the only one without a McDonald's. Home to the prestigious New England Culinary Institute, it has an amazing crop of good eateries. A particularly congenial spot is ㉓ **Kismet**, which balances a commitment to locavore, vegetarian and vegan-friendly dining with a fun-loving spirit reflected in menu offerings such as green eggs and maple hot chocolate.

DETOUR If you've ever wanted to learn how hard cider and fruit brandies are produced, consider the stiff uphill detour near Vershire to **Flag Hill Farm** (www.flaghillfarm.com). Here cider master Sebastian Lousada patiently watches over the fermentation of 80 varieties of apples growing on the nearby hillside. Advance planning is essential as Flag Hill doesn't receive visitors on an everyday basis. Contact the farm directly via the website and make sure to ask for directions!

A different model for uniting farmers and community is ㉔ **LACE (Local Agricultural Community Exchange)**, 6 miles east in Barre. Here Ariel Zevon has launched a market-café-deli that stocks locally grown products and sells hearty soups and sandwiches at great prices. Zevon's efforts to "lace people back into the land that feeds them" also include participation in the Barre City Street Market, a Wednesday afternoon event featuring local produce, crafts and entertainment.

Next, head southeast along Rte 110 and Rte 113 to the Connecticut River, where you'll find ㉕ **Cedar Circle Farm**. Like a roadside farmstand on organic steroids, it offers endless opportunities to appreciate Vermont's summer bounty: pick-your-own berries, flowers and pumpkins; a great café where you can dose up your java with Strafford Creamery's rich organic half-and-half; and lounging in an Adirondack chair by the river. Cedar Circle's busy schedule of events includes dinners in the field, workshops on canning and freezing and popular strawberry and pumpkin festivals (in June and October, respectively).

As the sun sets, meander downstream to the ㉖ **Norwich Inn**, a grand old establishment with rockers perched on its front porch overlooking Norwich's architecturally distinguished Main St. The best part about staying here is the built-in brewery right downstairs, with a patio offering views of the home-grown hops in the backyard. Jasper Murdock's Ale House brews its beers in such small batches that they're only available at the source. And the food's good too! By the time you finish breakfast the next morning, you should be ready to (literally) roll down the interstate back home.

Gregor Clark

TRIP INFORMATION

GETTING THERE
From Boston, take I-93 to I-89 northbound. At the first Vermont exit (Quechee-Woodstock), take Hwy 4 westbound to Quechee.

DO

Adam's Berry Farm
A mile north of downtown Burlington, descend into the lush Winooski Valley for pick-your-own organic blueberries, strawberries and raspberries. ☎ 802-578-9093; Intervale Rd, Burlington; ☷ late May-first frost; ⚤

Cedar Circle Farm
Cedar Circle offers everything from dinners in the field to annual strawberry and pumpkin festivals. ☎ 802-785-4737; www.cedarcircle farm.org; Pavillion Rd, East Thetford; ☷ 10am-6pm Mon-Sat, 10am-5pm Sun; ⚤

Champlain Orchards
This lovely orchard near Lake Champlain specializes in pick-your-own apples, fresh-milled cider, and organic cherries, raspberries, peaches, plums and pumpkins. ☎ 802-897-2777; www.champlainorchards.com; 2955 Rte 74 W, Shoreham; ☷ 8am-6pm Jul-Oct; ⚤

EAT

Café Provence
Dine at the restaurant, or pop round the corner for French pastries at its Gourmet Provence bakery. ☎ 802-247-9993; www .cafeprovencevt.com; 11 Center St, Brandon; mains $8-26; ☷ 11:30am-9pm Tue-Fri, 9am-9pm Sat & Sun

Cider House BBQ & Pub
Hard and sweet cider mix intriguingly with barbecue and Southern fare. ☎ 802-244-8400; www.ciderhousevt.com; 1675 Hwy 2, Waterbury; mains $10-24; ☷ 11:30am-9pm Fri & Sat, 4-9pm Tue-Thu & Sun

Daily Chocolate
Using Vermont cream, butter and maple syrup, these creative chocolatiers make amazing stuff; watch them work while you order. ☎ 802-877-0087; www.dailychoco late.net; 7 Green St, Vergennes; chocolate per lb $28; ☷ 10:30am-5:30pm Tue-Fri, 11am-4pm Sat

Farmer's Diner
The "buy local" concept here is as old-fashioned as the diner itself. ☎ 802-295-4600; www.farmersdiner.com; 5573 Wood-stock Rd (Hwy 4), Quechee; mains $5-18; ☷ 6:30am-3pm Mon & Tue, 6:30am-8pm Wed-Sun

Hen of the Wood
The menu changes with the seasons; the old mill setting remains beautiful year-round. ☎ 802-244-7300; www.henofthewood.com; 92 Stowe St, Waterbury; mains $16-31; ☷ 5-9pm Mon-Sat

Kismet
Serious about locavore dining, Kismet provides links on its website for suppliers of everything it serves. ☎ 802-223-8646; www.kismetkitchen.com; 207 Barre St, Montpelier; mains $6.50-10; ☷ 8am-3pm Wed-Sun

LACE (Local Agricultural Community Exchange)
This community-minded market sources virtually everything from surrounding farms. ☎ 802-476-4276; www.lacevt.org; 159 N Main St, Barre; soups & sandwiches $4-5; ☷ cafe 9am-3pm, market 9am-7pm

Middlebury Natural Foods Co-op
A true community enterprise, the co-op displays pictures of the many Addison County farmers whose food fills the shelves. ☎ 802-388-7276; www.middleburycoop.com; 9 Washington St, Middlebury; ☷ 8am-7pm

Red Hen Bakery
From ciabatta to olive bread to morning pastries, Red Hen's baked goods are exceptional.

☎ 802-223-5200; www.redhenbaking.com; 961B Hwy 2, Middlesex; ⏱ 7am-5pm Mon-Sat, 8am-5pm Sun

Simon Pearce
Reserve ahead for a table overlooking the river in this renowned restaurant near Quechee's covered bridge. ☎ 802-295-1470; www.simonpearce.com; 1760 Main St, Quechee; mains $12-30; ⏱ 11:30am-2:45pm & 6-9pm

Starry Night Café
From local strawberry salad to asparagus-cheddar soup, Starry Night's menu is as enticing as its intimate atmosphere. ☎ 802-877-6316; www.starrynightcafe.com; 5371 Hwy 7, Ferrisburg; mains $17-26; ⏱ 5:30-9pm Wed-Sun

DRINK

Alchemist Pub & Brewery
The ever-popular Alchemist emphasizes the organic in its ales, pub food and vegetarian fare. ☎ 802-244-4120; www.alchemistbeer.com; 23 S Main St, Waterbury; ⏱ 4pm-midnight Mon-Thu, 3pm-1am Fri-Sun

Boyden Valley Winery
Boasting one of Vermont's prettiest settings,. Boyden Valley specializes in fruity creations, including cassis made with local black currants. ☎ 802-644-8151; www.boydenvalley.com; cnr Rte 15 & Rte 104, Cambridge; ⏱ 10am-5pm

Long Trail Brewing Company
Few beer garden settings can rival Long Trail's deck overlooking the Ottauquechee River. ☎ 802-672-5011; www.longtrail.com; cnr Hwy 4 & Rte 100A, Bridgewater Corners; ⏱ visitor center 10am-6pm, pub 11am-5pm

Magic Hat Brewery
With 48 taps and a penchant for creative experimentation, Magic Hat is just plain fun.

☎ 802-658-2739; www.magichat.net; 5 Bartlett Bay Rd, South Burlington; ⏱ 10am-6pm Mon-Sat, noon-5pm Sun

Otter Creek Brewery
Otter Creek offers free samples all day, plus brewery tours three times each afternoon. ☎ 802-388-0727; www.ottercreekbrewing.com; 793 Exchange St, Middlebury; ⏱ 10am-6pm Mon-Sat, 11am-4pm Sun

SLEEP

Inn at Shelburne Farms
No place in Vermont can match the elegance of Shelburne's lakefront setting or its afternoon teas. ☎ 802-985-8686; www.shelburnefarms.org; 1611 Harbor Rd, Shelburne; r$145-425

Liberty Hill Farm
With its magnificent red barn and White River Valley panoramas, this working farm is a Vermont classic. ☎ 802-767-3926; www.libertyhillfarm.com; 511 Liberty Hill Rd, Rochester; r incl dinner & breakfast per adult/child/teen $110/55/70; ♿

May Farm Inn
May Farm's many welcoming touches include an outdoor hot tub, homemade scones and fresh berries for breakfast. ☎ 802-244-7306; www.mayfarm.com; 4706 Waterbury-Stowe Rd, Waterbury; r $85-205

Norwich Inn
This inn in Norwich's village center has old-fashioned parlors, rocking chairs on the porch and a fine brewpub out back. ☎ 802-649-1143; www.norwichinn.com; 325 Main St, Norwich; r $99-209

USEFUL WEBSITES
www.vermontbrewers.com
www.vermontfresh.net

LINK YOUR TRIP

www.lonelyplanet.com/trip-planner

The Other Side of Winter Sports

WHY GO Vermont's big downhill ski resorts get all the press, but a parallel universe of alternative winter sports brings you closer to the land and far from the crowds. We discussed the various options with Lissy Heminway, a sled dog musher and longtime member of the Vermont Outdoor Guide Association (VOGA).

Suppose you want to get out and explore New England's winter wonderland, but mingling with snow bunnies in designer skiwear has never been your thing. Did you know Vermont still has low-key resorts where you can downhill ski for under $40? Add to that opportunities for dogsledding, sleigh rides, cross-country skiing, horseback riding and maple sugaring and there's more than enough variety to fill a long weekend.

Twenty minutes east of Middlebury lies the high, wild heart of Green Mountain National Forest. This is Lissy Heminway's backyard, where she's been mushing sled dogs for years. It's also home to the ❶ **Middlebury College Snow Bowl**, one of Vermont's most affordable, least crowded downhill ski areas. "There's a trail for everyone from beginner to advanced," says Heminway. "It has a friendly family atmosphere and a warm lodge with windows facing the mountain." You can ski all day here for pennies on the dollar and lift lines are rarely a problem.

A few miles southwest is another of Heminway's personal favorites, the ❷ **Blueberry Hill Cross-Country Ski Center**. "Blueberry Hill is a real gem, because it's way off the beaten path. It's on a forest service road that's kind of secretive, like a retreat. There are over 100 miles of trails, connecting into the forest service system. The Catamount Trail (running from Quebec to Massachusetts) skirts one edge of the property and keeps going. You can literally go anywhere. The groomed trails are

TIME
2 – 3 days

DISTANCE
90 miles

BEST TIME TO GO
Dec – Mar

START
Middlebury

END
Waterbury

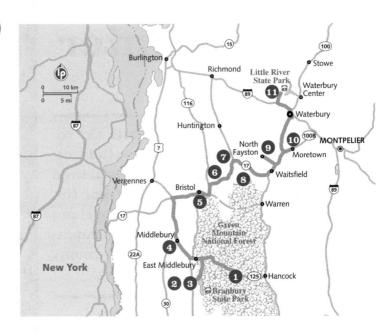

amazing and perfect for all levels. A big lunch is part of the package, with a pot of hearty soup and the center's famous Blueberry Hill cookies. You come into the lodge and there's a wood stove, very warm and cozy."

Across the road sits the ❸ **Blueberry Hill Inn**, an old blue farmhouse whose creaking and sloping wood floors bespeak centuries of use. "The bedrooms are simple but really elegant and the meals are exquisite, usually four or five courses. The dining room has a huge hearth and all these beautiful flowers. You sit as a family – all at one table, so you get to meet people. It also has a wood-fired sauna – don't forget to roll in the snow afterwards!"

For an après-ski experience with local flavor, try ❹ **American Flatbread** in Middlebury. Set below Otter Creek Falls in a cavernous marble building with 30ft ceilings, Flatbread still manages to retain an amazingly cozy feeling, thanks to cheery holiday lights, colorful wall hangings and a roaring wood-fired pizza oven. The menu couldn't be simpler – thin-crusted pizza, salads and a drinks list heavy on Vermont microbrews – but everything's ultrafresh, with many ingredients organic and locally sourced.

Thirteen miles northeast in Bristol, the old-fashioned bar at the brick-walled, tin-ceilinged ❺ **Bobcat Café & Brewery** makes an atmospheric place to taste home brews such as App-Gap IPA. Diners on a tight budget can grab a beer and a bite, but the Bobcat's also elegant enough for a romantic sit-down dinner.

North of Bristol where Rte 17 and Rte 116 meet, the **6** **Inn at Baldwin Creek** has its own fabulous restaurant and provides comfy overnight lodging.

Next morning, climb 10 miles northeast along Rte 17 and Gore Rd to family-run **7** **Hillsboro Sugarworks**, one of Vermont's largest organic maple sugar operations. Throughout the late March/early April sugaring season, you can taste syrup straight from the evaporator or don snowshoes to explore the sugarbush (that's maple groves, for you flatlanders out there!).

Just over Appalachian Gap along Rte 17 lies **8** **Mad River Glen**, an iconoclastic downhill ski area whose long single-chair lift (a relic unique in the US), cooperative ownership scheme and bargain lift tickets make it a darling of Vermonters. The runs are just plain fun and the views down to the Mad River Valley and north to Camel's Hump are dizzying.

The wintry smorgasbord continues in tiny North Fayston, just off Rte 100. **9** **Vermont Icelandic Horse Farm** offers rides on shaggy Nordic beasts with named Thor and Freia – an invigorating and unconventional way to experience the local mountain scenery.

10 **Atii Expeditions** in Morestown offers personalized two-hour lessons in skijoring. Ski-what? It's basically a way to share the wintry outdoors with your dog. Rover wears a harness with bungee towlines attached and you ski along behind! For more dog-based backcountry fun, Rob Farley of **11** **October Siberians** runs dogsled adventures in Little River State Park northwest of Waterbury. "His beautiful team of purebred Siberian Huskies combined with his 15 years of experience and passion for dogsledding make it a truly authentic and wonderful experience," says Heminway.

A SKIING GRADUATION

If you think mortarboards and moguls don't mix, you obviously haven't seen Middlebury College's winter graduation ceremony. In early February each year, dozens of midterm graduates can be seen slaloming down the slopes in full valedictory regalia, their dark robes fluttering amid the snowflakes. Come out and see it for yourself at the Middlebury College Snow Bowl, or at least check out the videos on YouTube!

XMAS TREES, & A SLEIGH RIDE TOO!

Next December, enjoy some "two-for-one" winter fun at **Dave Russell's Christmas Tree Farm** (www.russellchristmastrees.com) on Rte 116 north of Bristol. Dave himself will take you by horse-drawn sleigh or carriage up the hill above his third-generation dairy farm to cut your own Balsam fir (saws and blankets provided). The sleigh ride is included in the price of the tree ($50 for the first, $30 each additional tree) and you can bring along as many helpers as you like!

For a scenic trip home, make this a gorgeous loop trip by backtracking 35 miles south to Hancock on Rte 100, then returning to Middlebury on Rte 125.
Gregor Clark

TRIP INFORMATION

GETTING THERE
From Boston, take I-93 northbound to I-89. At Exit 3 (Bethel), follow Rte 107, Rte 100 and Rte 125 northwest to Middlebury Gap.

DO

Atii Expeditions
Try your hand at skijoring, an alternative to dogsledding that doesn't leave your dog behind. ☎ 802-496-3795; www.atiisleddogs.com; PO Box 550, Morestown; 2hr skijoring lesson $100; 🐾

Blueberry Hill Cross-Country Ski Center
Trails and rentals for all abilities in the heart of Green Mountain National Forest. ☎ 802-247-6735; www.blueberryhillinn.com/ski.htm; 1307 Goshen-Ripton Rd, Goshen; trail passes adult/child $16/free, ski rentals adult/child $16/12; ♿

Hillsboro Sugarworks
Taste maple syrup straight from the source, then snowshoe through the sugarbush. Call ahead and get detailed directions from the website. ☎ 802-453-5462; www.hillsborosugarworks.com; Mountainside Lane, Starksboro; 🕐 by arrangement; ♿

Mad River Glen
Short lines, long runs, great views and the incomparable single chair make this one of Vermont's best skiing areas. ☎ 802-496-3551; www.madriverglen.com; Rte 17, Waitsfield; lift tickets midweek/weekend $39/60; ♿

Middlebury College Snow Bowl
Ultra-low-key college ski area offering the cheapest lift tickets in central Vermont. ☎ 802-388-4356; www.middlebury.edu/campuslife/facilities/snowbowl; Rte 125, Hancock; lift tickets midweek/weekend $25/39; ♿

October Siberians
One of Vermont's best-established mushers leads trips through the wilds of Little River State Park. ☎ 802-482-3460; www.octobersiberians.com; 1088 Texas Hill Rd, Hinesburg; 2hr dogsled trips adult/child $150/100; 🐾

Vermont Icelandic Horse Farm
Ride horses through snowy fields high above the lovely Mad River Valley. ☎ 802-496-7141; www.icelandichorses.com; 3061 N Fayston Rd, Fayston; 1/2/3hr ride $50/80/100

EAT

American Flatbread
On a wintry night, few places have such a happy buzz as this firelit, marble-walled pizzeria. ☎ 802-388-3300; www.americanflatbread.com; 137 Maple St, Middlebury; flatbread $10-18; 🕐 5-9pm Fri & Sat

Bobcat Café & Brewery
From French onion soup to curry, the Bobcat knows how to warm a frozen skier's heart. ☎ 802-453-3311; www.bobcatcafe.com; 5 Main St, Bristol; mains $6-19; 🕐 5-9pm

SLEEP

Blueberry Hill Inn
This lovely old inn is the perfect mountaintop home for cross-country skiers. ☎ 802-247-6735; www.blueberryhillinn.com; 1307 Goshen Ripton Rd, Brandon; r per person incl dinner & breakfast $140-220

Inn at Baldwin Creek
Conveniently located at the foot of Appalachian Gap, its fine restaurant is also a pillar of Vermont's locavore movement. ☎ 802-424-2432; www.innatbaldwincreek.com; 1868 Rte 116, Bristol; r $95-170

USEFUL WEBSITES
www.voga.org

LINK YOUR TRIP

www.lonelyplanet.com/trip-planner

Down on the Farm: Vermont Dairies

FOOD & DRINK

WHY GO In southern Vermont, newly sprouted artisanal dairies share the landscape with venerable old-timers whose roots go back more than a century. Here you can meet cows, sheep and water buffaloes and watch cheesemaking in some of the state's most gorgeous historic villages.

TIME
1 – 2 days

DISTANCE
95 miles

BEST TIME TO GO
May – Oct

START
Putney

END
South Woodstock

ALSO GOOD FOR

HISTORY & CULTURE

Standing on the serenely pastoral 250-acre farm of ❶ **Vermont Shepherd**, it's hard to believe you're anywhere near the interstate. Yet a 6-mile jog north from Putney along Kimball Hill and Patch Rds is all it takes to reach this most revered of Vermont's "new" dairies. Vermont Shepherd started making its cave-aged sheep's milk cheese back in 1993 and almost instantly began bringing home blue ribbons. A small self-serve farmstand in the driveway reports the whereabouts of the rams and ewes, allowing you to wander in search of them among the barns and rolling pastures or, if you arrive at the right time, to watch the milking. Manufactured seasonally in small batches, the earthy-flavored rustic cheese typically sells out for a period each summer.

Continue north through Westminster West (the sign says 'thickly settled,' but blink and you'll miss it!), then turn west on Rte 121 in pretty Saxtons River. Six miles later, the ❷ **Scoop** – a popular local ice-cream stand on a working dairy farm – signals your arrival in Grafton.

❸ **Grafton** is *the* quintessential southern Vermont village. This clutch of 19th-century clapboard dwellings, with electrical lines moved underground to enhance the "bygone times" vibe, is a delightful place to stroll. Village streets and paths lead past galleries, museums and a lovely pond, through a covered bridge to ❹ **Grafton Village Cheese Company**, half a mile south of town. Revived in 1962 after half a century of dormancy, the factory makes some of Vermont's tastiest cheddar. You can watch

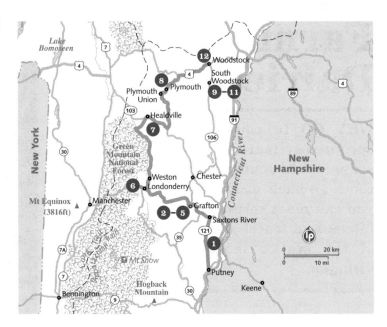

production six days a week and try free samples daily. Back in "downtown" Grafton, the historic **5** **Old Tavern at Grafton** sports pretty porches with rocking chairs and uses the home-town cheddar in its cheddar-ale soup.

Over the river and through the woods via an idyllic unpaved stretch of Rte 121, **6** **Taylor Farm** crowns a pretty hillside on Rte 11 west of Londonderry. Dogs hasten from the barn to welcome you, as does cheesemeister Jon Wright. "This is a terrible place to farm," says Wright. "In most states you can pasture your cows eight months and have them on feed grain for four, but here in Vermont it's more like four months of pasturing and eight of hay. It's crazy. But I'm here because I love it."

> *"This is a terrible place to farm… But I'm here because I love it."*

"What has made Vermont farming work is its proximity to several big cities and the excellent quality of Vermont milk. Most of our farms – even the big ones – are small by national standards. Smaller farms are better for animals. They're happier, healthier and they make better milk." Visitors can taste Taylor Farm's exceptional Vermont Gouda, meet the cows in the adjacent barn, or even stay overnight in the farm's small guesthouse.

Twenty miles northeast in Healdville, Vermont's oldest continuously operating cheese factory has been using the same recipe since the late 19th century. The long history of **7** **Crowley Cheese** is palpable in the photos on the factory wall. "See that guy?" asks Brad Hutchinson, pointing at an early-20th-century teenager riding a milk wagon. "He used to work here, still lives down the road; he's over 90 now." Turning to the subject of Crowley's creamy "Colby-like" cheese, Hutchinson explains, "It actually predates true Colby, but the federal government misclassified it and the name stuck." Whatever you call it, Crowley's cheese is smooth, delicious and still handmade.

Fifteen miles north, the bucolic hamlet of Plymouth – birthplace of President Calvin Coolidge – plays host to **8 Frog City Cheese Company**. Originally cofounded by Coolidge's father, Plymouth's cheese factory recently resumed production of a traditional farmhouse cheddar known as granular curd cheese. Its distinctively sharp tang and grainy texture are reminiscent of the wheel cheese traditionally found at general stores throughout Vermont. Panels downstairs tell the history of local cheese-making, while a museum upstairs displays cheese-making equipment from another era.

STROLLING OF THE HEIFERS

Brattleboro's fun-spirited multiday celebration of agriculture and community begins with flower-garlanded heifers mooing their way down Main St. Then come the bagpipes, nursery school floats, 4H-ers, Vermont politicians, bad cow jokes from the parade's commentators, excrement-scooping superheroes (complete with capes!), and everything from antique tractors to synchronized shopping cart performances by the local food co-op. Don't miss the crowning of Miss Ver-mooont, prettiest heifer of them all!

They don't make villages any prettier than Woodstock, 14 miles northeast along Hwy 4. Stop to appreciate the grand old town green, then follow Rte 106 to South Woodstock. At **9 Kedron Valley Inn** (worth a return trip for dinner), climb up Church Hill Rd to **10 Bufala di Vermont**, one of America's very few water-buffalo dairies. With lots of curly horned critters roaming the farm's pastures, buffalo-spotting is easy. Even better are the free samples of buffalo-milk yogurt available in the cheese-making area, where you can observe production of the dairy's trademark mozzarella.

For an overnight stay, return to the South Woodstock crossroads and take the other fork up Fletcher Hill Rd to **11 Top Acres Farm**, a maple syrup producer that also houses guests. Back in Woodstock, the innovative and intimate Italian eatery **12 Pane e Salute** is highly recommended for dinner, putting all this good Vermont cheese to use alongside locally raised meat and bushels of fresh organic produce.

Gregor Clark

APPEARING AT YOUR FOOD CO-OP

Some dairies are too small for visitors, but too good to miss. While in Vermont, make sure to taste locally produced **Butterworks Farm** yogurt (try the maple) and **Strafford Creamery**'s ice cream (the cinnamon and mint flavors deserve special mention here). Strafford also makes delectable eggnog in old-fashioned glass bottles throughout the holiday season. The products are available at food co-ops throughout Vermont. Get a moo-ve on and check 'em out!

TRIP INFORMATION

GETTING THERE
From Boston, follow MA-2 westbound to I-91. Take Vermont Exit 4 off I-91 and follow Hwy 5 north into downtown Putney.

DO
Bufala di Vermont
The United States' largest water-buffalo dairy makes ultrafresh mozzarella and ultracreamy blueberry, raspberry and maple yogurt. ☎ 802-457-4540; www.bufaladivermont .com; 2749-01 Church Hill Rd, South Woodstock; ⏱ 9am-5pm Mon-Fri

Crowley Cheese
Founded by Winfield Crowley in 1882, America's oldest continuously operating cheese factory makes a mild Colby-like cheese. ☎ 802-259-2340; www.crowley cheese-vermont.com; 14 Crowley Lane, Healdville; ⏱ 8am-4pm Mon-Fri

Frog City Cheese Company
Fabulous "old school" cheddar, interesting interpretive displays and a beautiful historical setting make Frog City unique. ☎ 802-672-3650; www.frogcitycheese.com; 106 Messer Hill Rd, Plymouth; ⏱ 9am-5pm

Grafton Village Cheese Company
Some of Vermont's tastiest cheddar, made in one of Vermont's prettiest villages. ☎ 800-472-3866; www.graftonvillagecheese.com; PO Box 87, Grafton; ⏱ 8am-5pm Mon-Fri, 10am-5pm Sat & Sun

Taylor Farm
One of the friendliest and most accessible of Vermont's working farms also makes fabulous cheese and rents a guesthouse. ☎ 802-824-5690; www.taylorfarmvermont.com; 825 Rte 11, Londonderry; ⏱ 10am-6pm; ♿

Vermont Shepherd
Billing itself as America's oldest producer of sheep's milk cheese, Vermont Shepherd is among the very best dairies in Vermont. ☎ 802-387-4473; www.vermontshepherd .com; 875 Patch Rd, Putney; ⏱ 9am-5pm; ♿

EAT
Kedron Valley Inn
Mixing tavern food with fancier fare, this inn features casual dining inside or out on its beautiful porch. ☎ 800-836-1193; www .kedronvalleyinn.com; Rte 106, South Woodstock; mains $9-28; ⏱ 5:30-9pm Wed-Sun

Pane e Salute
Intimate and outstanding, Pane e Salute uses fresh Vermont ingredients in ever-changing recipes sourced straight from Italia. Advance reservations essential. ☎ 802-457-4882; 61 Central St, Woodstock; mains $13-19; ⏱ 6pm-close Thu-Sun

Scoop
At the Rushton family's roadside scoop shop, tour the dairy, meet the cows and watch milking from 4pm to 6pm Friday to Sunday. ☎ 802-843-2719; Rte 121, Grafton; ⏱ 5-8pm Fri, 2-8pm Sat & Sun Jun-Aug; ♿

SLEEP
Old Tavern at Grafton
This inn's location – smack in the middle of one of New England's most picturesque historic villages – is unbeatable. ☎ 802-843-2231, 800-843-1801; www.oldtavern.com; 92 Main St, Grafton; r $160-420

Top Acres Farm
This maple syrup producer offers farm vacations at a hillside home on a gorgeous dirt road. ☎ 802-457-2135; www.vermont property.com/rentals/woodstock/fullwood .html; 3615 Fletcher Hill Rd, South Woodstock; r from $125

USEFUL WEBSITES
www.vtcheese.com

www.lonelyplanet.com/trip-planner

LINK YOUR TRIP
TRIP
13 Massachusetts: Farmstand Fresh p113
42 The Way We Lived p275

Tip to Tail by Bike & Rail

WHY GO Cyclist-friendly Vermont is a paradise for bike travel and Amtrak's *Vermonter* route is among the nation's most scenic train rides. This carbon-conscious loop does involve a few – ahem! – hills, but your reward is an up-close-and-personal look at one of the prettiest states in America, not to mention some of Vermont's finest bakeries.

Grab a pretrain bite at the **1** Brattleboro Food Co-op deli, then hit the rails for the exceptionally scenic four-hour train ride north to St Albans on Amtrak's *Vermonter*. One quick note: a boxed bike with wheels and pedals removed will fit behind the last seat in any *Vermonter* passenger car, but to avoid problems when boarding, it's crucial to mention your bike to the Amtrak phone agent who takes your reservation. The train follows the Connecticut River north, then turns northwest through the mountain-fringed valleys of the White and Winooski Rivers. Disembark at the end of the line in St Albans and turn in for the night at **2** Back Inn Time, a cyclist-friendly B&B just east of the station.

A mile north of St Albans on Hwy 7, a rusty bike suspended in midair marks the start of the **3** Missisquoi River Recreation Path. This 26-mile rail trail runs clear to the Canadian border, passing through wetlands filled with birds, crossing the Missisquoi on a grand old railway bridge, and affording sweeping views across cornfields to the northern Green Mountains.

Twenty miles out, turn south onto Rte 108 in Enosburg Falls, crossing into the gorgeous Lamoille River valley at the base of 4393ft Mt Mansfield. Recharge your batteries in Jeffersonville at the **4** Cupboard Deli & Bakery, whose sandwiches and pastries have fueled many a cyclist

TIME
4 – 7 days

DISTANCE
270 miles

BEST TIME TO GO
May – Oct

START
Brattleboro

END
Brattleboro

ALSO GOOD FOR

OUTDOORS

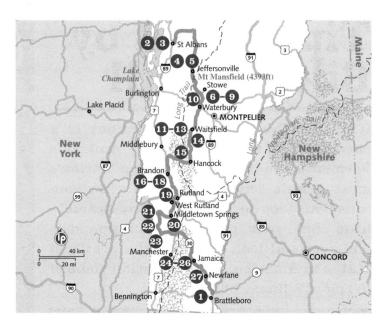

over 2162ft Smugglers Notch. For mechanical fine-tuning or moral support before your big climb, stop in at **5** **Foot of the Notch Bicycles** next door.

Vermont's most visually stunning mountain pass feels like something out of a fairy tale. As you crest the notch, the painted center line disappears in deference to encroaching cliffs and boulders that squeeze the roadway down to a scant lane and a half. The tight switchbacks on the far side more closely resemble those of a hiking trail than a numbered state highway. Just past the summit, **6** **Smugglers Notch State Park** makes a great overnight camping spot.

Cruise downhill 10 miles on Rte 108 to Stowe's **7** **Vermont Ski Museum**, where videos of hotshot skiers allow you to vicariously enjoy other people's exertion instead of sweating through your own. Then backtrack west 2 miles, paralleling Rte 108 on the beautiful **8** **Stowe Recreation Path**, which crosses the West Branch River repeatedly on graceful arched bridges. Turn south on Luce Hill Rd toward **9** **Trapp Family Lodge Bakery**, where the stunning mountain views and apple strudel are equally compelling.

After 10 more miles cycling down Trapp Hill Rd, Moscow Rd and Rte 100 south to Waterbury, you'll probably feel like you've already earned a milkshake. Or maybe a sundae. And why not throw in a factory tour? The folks at **10** **Ben & Jerry's** will be happy to oblige and you can feel virtuous as you chug up the hill past all the tour buses.

Next, wipe that ice-cream smile off your face and replace it with an ear-to-ear grin as you descend Rte 100 into the seriously scenic watershed of the Mad River. In downtown Waitsfield, ⑪ **Clearwater Sports** offers another opportunity to tune up your bike or, for serious masochists, a chance to rent a kayak and brave the local white-water.

For a hot shower and a night indoors, the ⑫ **Lareau Farm Inn** south of Waitsfield can't be beat. Why? Because you get priority seating at ⑬ **American Flatbread** next door, the cozy original location of Vermont's nationally distributed, organically minded pizza company. Grab a table by the fire and dream of tomorrow's downhills.

LAKE CHAMPLAIN BY BIKE & FERRY

Starting in downtown Burlington, the flat and easy **Island Line Trail** snakes northward to a "pedestrians and cyclists only" causeway jutting 3 miles into Lake Champlain. On August weekends, a bike ferry crosses every few minutes from the causeway to Grand Isle, the southernmost of the Champlain Islands, from where you can follow the Champlain Bikeway all the way to Canada. Info is available through Burlington-based **Local Motion** (www.localmotion.org).

Next morning, join other cyclists 5 miles south at the ⑭ **Warren Store**, popular for its sticky buns and sunny outdoor deck. From here the 10-mile cruise south through Granville Gulf is one of Rte 100's most scenic stretches. Look for moose in the ponds up top as you cross between the Mad River and White River watersheds. In Hancock, turn right on Rte 125 toward 2144ft Middlebury Gap. Halfway through the 8-mile ascent, check out the short side road to ⑮ **Texas Falls**, a raging torrent plunging through a pockmarked granite gorge. Rte 125 steepens considerably above the falls turnoff, but rest assured, your hard work will soon be rewarded. The amazingly pretty descent on the west side of Middlebury Gap sends you screaming down through Breadloaf Wilderness, then hugs the sinuous fringes of the Middlebury River.

Below Ripton, watch for Upper Plains Rd on the left, which provides a convenient shortcut south to ⑯ **Branbury State Park**. Nestled at the foot of the Green Mountains on pretty Lake Dunmore, the park's campsites adjoin a sandy beach, while across Rte 53 the ⑰ **Falls of Lana/Silver Lake Trail** climbs to an especially pretty section of Green Mountain National Forest.

With visions of fresh-baked croissants dancing in your head, cycle down Lake Dunmore's eastern shore to ⑱ **Gourmet Provence**, a French bakery 8 miles southwest along Rte 53 and Rte 73 in the town of Brandon. Follow Hwy 7 to Pittsford, then branch onto Rte 3 and cross the arched marble bridge into Proctor, where the ⑲ **Vermont Marble Museum** will help you appreciate the quarrying country you're about to pedal through.

Where Rte 3 dead-ends into Hwy 4, jog right 4 miles to West Rutland and pick up Rte 133 south. Restored 19th-century mansions pop up on all sides as you enter pretty Middletown Springs, once a thriving spa town popular with New Yorkers. The old spa hotel is long gone, but you can still fill your water bottles with springwater at shady riverside **20 Mineral Springs Park**.

Follow Rte 140 west to the **21 East Poultney General Store** for provisions before turning south on Rte 30 toward **22 Lake St Catherine State Park**, another dreamy place for a dip and a lakeside campout. The next 40 miles take you through an idyllic corner of Vermont. With the Taconics on your left and the lake on your right, head south on Rte 30 through Wells into the sweet little town of Pawlet. At **23 Mach's General Store**, built directly over a waterfall, you can watch the cascading water through a grate as you grab some snacks for the thinly settled stretch ahead.

CARBON CONSCIOUSNESS

Although this tour is written for cyclists, you could conceivably duplicate the same route by car. The difference? It's all in your carbon emissions. Consider this: a midsized car traveling 200 miles per month will emit 1.32 tons of CO_2 annually. By contrast, no matter how hard you huff and puff up those mountains, the extra CO_2 you emit annually through sheer exertion probably won't exceed 100lb. Something to contemplate as you're cursing that next climb...

Cycle 10 miles east to Danby on little-trafficked Danby-Pawlet Rd. Dodge the cars for two seconds as you cross Hwy 7 onto tranquil, unpaved Mt Tabor Rd, one of the wildest Green Mountain crossings in Vermont. After a stiff climb, the road flattens out before descending into the high mountain valley of North Landgrove, where horses graze and pavement resumes.

At Londonderry, join Rte 100 and begin racing downstream alongside the West River. End the day with a long downhill cruise into Jamaica, a community of artists tucked into the pine woods. Across the river, **24 Jamaica State Park** is the best place in the whole state for riverside camping. A semiannual kayaking event here draws participants from all over New England. There's good swimming right in the heart of the campground, but intrepid explorers can also head 3 miles upstream along a 19th-century railway bed to Hamilton Falls, a 50ft ribbon of water cascading into a natural swimming hole.

For breakfast, hit the colorful **25 Townshend Dam Diner**, 6 miles east of Jamaica on Rte 30. Pencil-on-index-card caricatures of past diners adorn the napkin holders, while a "Table Talk" wall has countless puns about the "dam" good food (including bogus quotes from Thomas Jefferson and Derek Jeter).

Two miles downriver on your right, look for the 166ft **26 Scott Covered Bridge**, Vermont's longest single-span covered bridge. Take a final break 5 miles further on in picture-perfect **27 Newfane**, decked out in green-shuttered, white clapboard buildings. Congratulations – you're on the home stretch! From here it's an easy 12-mile pedal down Rte 30 back "home" to Brattleboro.

Gregor Clark

TRIP INFORMATION

GETTING THERE
From Boston, take MA-2 westbound to I-91 northbound. At the first Vermont exit off I-91, take Hwy 5 eastbound to the Amtrak station.

DO
Ben & Jerry's
Come for the ice cream; stay for the ice cream. Oh yeah, and the tour too. ☎ 802-882-1240; www.benjerry.com; 1281 Waterbury-Stowe Rd, Waterbury; ✲ 9am-9pm Jul & Aug, 10am-6pm Sep-Jun; ♿

Clearwater Sports
Bike supplies and kayak rentals coexist happily at this venerable adventure outfitter. ☎ 802-496-2708; www.clearwatersports.com; 4147 Main St, Waitsfield; single/double kayak rentals $59/69; ✲ 10am-6pm Mon-Fri, 9am-6pm Sat, 10am-5pm Sun

Foot of the Notch Bicycles
Perfectly positioned to supply whatever you need for the climb to Smugglers Notch. ☎ 802-644-8182; 134 Church St, Jeffersonville; ✲ 10am-6pm Tue-Fri, 10am-5pm Sat, noon-4pm Sun

Vermont Marble Museum
Don't miss the psychedelic roomful of foot-square marble samples from around the world. ☎ 800-427-1396; www.vermont-marble.com; 52 Main St, Proctor; admission adult/child $7/free; ✲ 9am-5:30pm mid-May–late Oct

Vermont Ski Museum
See how far ski equipment has come since the 1930s and enjoy some truly crazy videos. ☎ 802-253-9911; www.vermontskimuseum.org; 1 S Main St, Stowe; admission $3; ✲ noon-5pm Wed-Mon

EAT
American Flatbread
Enjoy the mesmerizing glow of the wood fire as you watch Vermont's best pizza made before your eyes. ☎ 802-496-8856; www.americanflatbread.com; 46 Lareau Rd, Waitsfield; flatbreads $10-18

Brattleboro Food Co-op
Southern Vermont's best co-op has a natural-foods deli that just won't quit; try Chai Wallah's incredible chai. ☎ 802-257-0236; www.brattleborofoodcoop.com; 2 Main St, Brattleboro; ✲ 8am-9pm Mon-Sat, 9am-9pm Sun

Cupboard Deli & Bakery
Jeffersonville's finest deli is a good place to carbo-load before climbing up Smugglers Notch. ☎ 802-644-2069; 4837 Rte 15, Jeffersonville; ✲ 6am-10pm

East Poultney General Store
Across from one of Vermont's prettiest town greens, this store has everything you need for a lakeside barbecue. ☎ 802-287-4042; 11 On The Green, East Poultney; ✲ 7am-7pm Mon-Sat, 9am-2pm Sun

Gourmet Provence
Brandon's formidable French bakery wouldn't feel out of place on the streets of Paris. ☎ 802-247-3002; www.cafeprovencevt.com; 37 Center St, Brandon; pastries from $2; ✲ 7am-6pm Mon-Sat, 8am-3pm Sun

Mach's General Store
Two centuries old and still going strong, this venerable community store is the anchor of Pawlet's main street. ☎ 802-325-3405; 18 School St, Pawlet; ✲ 6am-8pm Mon-Sat, 7am-8pm Sun

Townshend Dam Diner
Names such as "The Best Dam Chili" say it all: these people have fun with words and know how to cook. ☎ 802-874-4107; 5929 Rte 30, West Townshend; breakfast $2-5; ✲ 5am-8pm Wed-Mon

Trapp Family Lodge Bakery
Enjoy quasi-alpine views along with your Bavarian chocolate cake at this Austrian-style bakery near Stowe. ☎ 802-253-8511; www.trappfamily.com; 700 Trapp Hill Rd, Stowe; ✲ 7am-1:30pm

Warren Store

Like manna from heaven for the hungry cyclist, the Warren Store's deli makes great sweet rolls and breakfasts. ☎ 802-496-3864; www .warrenstore.com; Main St, Warren; breakfast & sandwiches $3.50-8; ◷ 8am-7pm

SLEEP

Back Inn Time

The owners of this cyclist-friendly B&B can point you straight to the bike path after breakfast. ☎ 802-527-5116; www.backinn time.net; 68 Fairfield St, St Albans; r $99-139

Branbury State Park

Mountain-fringed Lake Dunmore forms the backdrop for this scenic park between Brandon and Middlebury. ☎ 802-247-5925; www.vtstateparks.com/htm/branbury.cfm; 3570 Lake Dunmore Rd, Salisbury; campsite /lean-to $18/25; ◷ Memorial Day–Columbus Day; ♿

Jamaica State Park

Vermont's best park for riverside camping draws outdoors enthusiasts of every persuasion. ☎ 802-874-4600; www.vtstateparks .com/htm/jamaica.cfm; 285 Salmon Hole

Lane, Jamaica; campsite/lean-to $18/25; ◷ early May–Columbus Day; ♿

Lake St Catherine State Park

Wide vistas and grassy lakefront lawns make this one of Vermont's most attractive parks. ☎ 802-287-9158; www.vtstateparks.com /htm/catherine.cfm; 3034 Rte 30, Poultney; campsite/lean-to $18/25; ◷ Memorial Day–Labor Day; ♿

Lareau Farm Inn

Set in a pleasant old farmhouse, this simple inn offers preferential seating at American Flatbread next door. ☎ 802-496-4949; www.lareaufarminn.com; 48 Lareau Rd, Waitsfield; r $85-135

Smugglers Notch State Park

This popular campground is pleasantly situated just downhill from "the notch," toward Stowe. ☎ 802-253-4014; www.vtstateparks .com/htm/smugglers.cfm; 6443 Mountain Rd, Stowe; campsite/lean-to $18/25; ◷ mid-May–mid-Oct

USEFUL WEBSITES

www.localmotion.org
www.mvrailtrail.com

LINK YOUR TRIP
www.lonelyplanet.com/trip-planner

Burlington's Backyard Playground

WHY GO Vermont's highest peak and largest lake – right in Burlington's backyard – provide some of the state's finest backdrops for outdoor fun. This compact state park loop includes opportunities for swimming, birding, apple picking, kayaking around traffic-free Burton Island and surveying the 60-mile views from the windswept tundra atop Mt Mansfield.

Cast off for the Champlain Islands, cruising 10 miles north of Burlington on I-89 to Exit 17, then west on Hwy 2. Within 5 miles, picnickers, sunbathers and windsurfers signal your arrival at the lakeshore. ❶ **Sand Bar State Park** is worth a stop just for the views, but its sandy beach and calm waters also make it one of the state's most popular swimming areas.

When you've had your fill of sand and sun, cross the causeway to Grand Isle, the largest of the Champlain Islands. Just outside the town of South Hero, grab a Creemee (that's Vermont-speak for soft-serve ice cream) at ❷ **Allenholm Orchards**, or pick a few apples for the road ahead.

After rejoining Hwy 2, cross the bridge onto North Hero Island, where day-use only ❸ **Knight Point State Park** offers more good swimming, plus hiking trails and kayak rentals.

Hungry boaters for miles around cast anchor at ❹ **Hero's Welcome**, a popular general store 3 miles north. The store's amusing wall display of "World Time Zones" – four clocks showing identical hours for Lake Champlain's North Hero, South Hero, Grand Isle and Isle LaMotte – reflects the prevailing island-centric attitude. Grab a sandwich and catch some rays on the outdoor terrace overlooking the boat landing.

TIME
2 – 4 days

DISTANCE
145 miles

BEST TIME TO GO
Jun – Aug

START
Burlington

END
Burlington

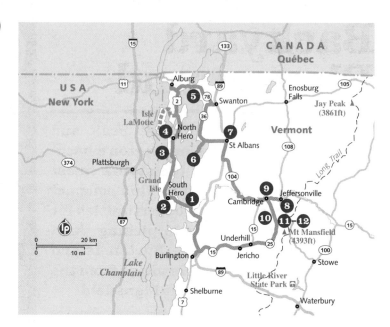

Near Alburg, turn off Hwy 2 onto eastbound Rte 78. Moments after rejoining the mainland, you'll enter the ⑤ **Missisquoi National Wildlife Refuge**. This pristine 6642-acre tract at the delta of the Missisquoi River provides an important resting place for migratory waterfowl along the Atlantic Flyway. Silver maples and eastern cottonwoods shimmer along the smooth-flowing waters of the wide Missisquoi, while songbirds trill and dart across open meadows. Visitors have seasonal access to six hiking trails through the wetlands, and the refuge offers free biweekly pontoon rides to view the blue heron rookery (arranged through the visitors center south of Rte 78).

Humans seeking a nest for the night should set sail for ⑥ **Burton Island State Park**, 20 miles south toward St Albans via Rte 78 and Rte 36. The park is accessible only by the Island Runner ferry, which departs Kill Kare State Park on the mainland several times daily between Memorial Day and Labor Day. After parking in Kill Kare's lot and unpacking your gear, enjoy the breeze and the pretty views as the ferry traverses the narrow channel to Burton Island. The island's limited but well-run infrastructure includes a nature center with daily programs for kids, and a store selling breakfast, lunch and very basic groceries. The sign outside epitomizes the island's laid-back beach-party atmosphere: "No shoes, no shirt, no problem!".

On this automobile-free island, visitors trundle their gear by handcart to the campsites and lean-tos along the shoreline (slackers can pay the park service to do the job!). The best sites are right on the lake, including Juniper, which sits in glorious isolation at the far end of the north shore. Hiking trails circle the island, and kayaks and canoes are available for rent, allowing exploration of the Lake Champlain Paddlers' Trail. Pay showers are a welcome hint of civilized life.

After a couple of nights on Burton Island, celebrate your return to the mainland at ❼ **Jeff's Maine Seafood**. On the north edge of St Albans' vast town green, it serves some of Vermont's finest chowder and crabcakes.

Continue southeast along Rte 104 into the gorgeous Lamoille River valley. If you're tempted to linger, consider a paddling trip offered by ❽ **Green River Canoe & Kayak** in Jeffersonville. Alternatively, stop in Cambridge to enjoy the views and buy barbecue provisions at ❾ **Boyden Farm**. At the junction of Rte 104 and Rte 15, the farm raises its own grass-fed beef and sells local cheese and wine. To round out the menu, head south along Pleasant Valley Rd to ❿ **Valley Dream Farmstand**, whose certified organic veggies, herbs and eggs are as beautiful as the idyllic setting under the hulking form of Mt Mansfield.

Speaking of Mt Mansfield, you'll be climbing it soon. A few miles further down Pleasant Valley Rd, a 2.6-mile dirt turnoff leads uphill to ⓫ **Underhill State Park**. Here, a peaceful series of clearings shelters a few campsites and lean-tos adjacent to the trailhead for the exceptionally scenic loop trip along ⓬ **Sunset Ridge and Laura Cowles Trails** to the 4393ft summit. Significant portions of Sunset Ridge Trail are above the tree line (a rarity in Vermont), affording breathtaking views of Lake Champlain, the Green Mountains and the St Lawrence River Valley all the way up to Montréal. Allow several hours for the 6-mile round-trip.

> **DETOUR**
>
> From Hwy 2, detour west 4 miles on Rte 129 to historic **Isle LaMotte**. Signs along the western shore signal its traditional importance as a crossroads for Native Americans and mark French explorer Samuel de Champlain's 1609 landing site. Nearby, the world's most ancient **fossil reef** – half a billion years old – once provided limestone for Radio City Music Hall and Washington's National Gallery. To visit the reef, inquire at **Fisk Farm** (www.fiskfarm.com), whose historic buildings and grounds also host summertime high teas and outdoor concerts.

THE SIXTH GREAT LAKE

Oh, those Vermont senators! Vermont's Patrick Leahy got Congress in 1998 to pass legislation that recognized Lake Champlain as the sixth Great Lake. The lake's new status lasted for all of 18 days, as senators from the *real* Great Lakes states quickly objected, with Ohio's Steven LaTourette insisting that Champlain should be renamed "Lake Plain Sham." For the record, Champlain measures a measly 435 sq miles, compared with Lake Superior's 31,700.

Return to civilization (and Burlington's great restaurants and breweries!) via Pleasant Valley Rd, River Rd and Rte 15 through Underhill and Jericho.
Gregor Clark

TRIP INFORMATION

GETTING THERE
From Boston, take I-93 northbound to I-89. At Vermont Exit 14, follow Hwy 2 westbound, which becomes Burlington's Main St.

DO

Allenholm Orchards
This perennially popular orchard sponsors VT's largest apple festival (South Hero Applefest) every October. ☎ 802-372-5566; www.allenholm.com; 150 South St, South Hero; ☀ 9am-5pm late May-Christmas Eve; ♿

Green River Canoe & Kayak
Self-guided kayak rentals, with a shuttle running upriver daily at 8am and 3pm. ☎ 802-644-8336; www.sterlingridgeresort.com/canoe.htm; Rte 15, Jeffersonville; kayak rentals & shuttles $40

Knight Point State Park
This pretty state park, open for day use only, hosts occasional summer concerts. ☎ 802-372-8389; www.vtstateparks.com/htm/knightpoint.cfm; 44 Knight Point Rd, North Hero; ☀ Memorial Day-Labor Day

Missisquoi National Wildlife Refuge
Vermont's largest tract of silver maple floodplain habitat and a refuge for birds. ☎ 802-868-4781; www.fws.gov; 29 Tabor Rd, Swanton; ☀ visitors center 8am-4:30pm

Sand Bar State Park
This gateway to the Champlain Islands takes its name from a natural sandbar between South Hero Island and the mainland. ☎ 802-893-2825; www.vtstateparks.com/htm/sandbar.cfm; 1215 Hwy 2, Milton; ☀ Memorial Day-Labor Day

EAT & DRINK

Boyden Farm
Featuring grass-fed beef, Vermont cheddar, ice cream and wine from the neighboring farm, this is the perfect one-stop picnic shop. ☎ 802-644-6363; www.boydenfarm.com; 44 Rte 104, Cambridge; ☀ 10am-8pm Tue-Sun; ♿

Hero's Welcome
Catch some rays while snacking on the waterfront deck, or indulge in shameless souvenir shopping upstairs. ☎ 802-372-4161; www.heroswelcome.com; 3537 Hwy 2, North Hero; sandwiches $6; ☀ 6:30am-6:30pm Mon-Sat, 7am-6pm Sun

Jeff's Maine Seafood
One of Vermont's finest seafood eateries sits right across from St Albans' historic town green. ☎ 802-524-6135; 65 N Main St, St Albans; mains $6.50-15; ☀ 11am-3pm Mon, 11am-3pm & 4:30-9pm Tue-Sat

Valley Dream Farmstand
Dreamy views of Mt Mansfield enhance your appreciation of the produce at this certified organic farmstand. ☎ 802-644-6598; 5901 Pleasant Valley Rd, Cambridge; ☀ 10am-6pm Jun-Nov

SLEEP

Burton Island State Park
With its short season and good infrastructure, Burton fills up quickly – reserve well in advance. ☎ 802-524-6353; www.vtstateparks.com/htm/burton.cfm; PO Box 123, St Albans Bay; campsite/lean-to $18/25; ☀ Memorial Day-Labor Day; ♿

Underhill State Park
Not just under a hill, this pretty park sits at the foot of Vermont's tallest peak. ☎ 802-899-3022; www.vtstateparks.com/htm/underhill.cfm; PO Box 249, Underhill Center; campsite/lean-to $14/21; ☀ Memorial Day–mid-Oct

USEFUL WEBSITES
www.vtstateparks.com

www.lonelyplanet.com/trip-planner

LINK YOUR TRIP
TRIP

Dog Parties & Bug Art: Offbeat Vermont

WHY GO If the Department of Tourism has convinced you that Vermont is all about fudge, fall leaves and teddy bears, think again. The Green Mountain State hides a host of quirkier attractions, each reflecting Vermont's longstanding tradition as a refuge for iconoclasts, artists and creative thinkers.

TIME
1 – 2 days

DISTANCE
125 miles

BEST TIME TO GO
Jun – Oct

START
Waterbury

END
Beebe Plain

ALSO GOOD FOR

It all begins with ice cream for breakfast. Yes, Ben & Jerry's Waterbury factory opens at 10am sharp (9am in summer) and yes, the staff will be happy to serve you whatever flavor you like. Just don't go asking for Bovinity Divinity, Dastardly Mash, Makin' Whoopie Pie or any of the other ex-flavors put out to pasture over the past two decades. To see these, you'll have to head up the hill to ❶ **Ben & Jerry's Flavor Graveyard**.

Quaintly perched on a knoll overlooking the parking lot, neat rows of headstones pay silent tribute to 27 flavors that flopped. Each memorial is lovingly inscribed with the flavor's brief lifespan on the grocery shelves of this earth and a poem in tribute. Rest in Peace Holy Cannoli, 1997–98! Adieu Miss Jelena's Sweet Potato Pie, 1992–93!

Twenty miles east in Barre, ❷ **Hope Cemetery** is a resting place of another sort. Names such as Bilodeau, Corti and Chiaravalli reflect Barre's heyday as the immigrant capital of Vermont. The headstones of Barre granite, some carved into whimsical forms such as a racing car, a soccer ball or a cube standing on end, celebrate the rock-carving tradition that's continued unabated here since the 1800s.

For an awe-inspiring look at the modern quarrying process, follow Rte 14 and Middle Rd 5 miles southeast of Barre to Graniteville, where massive granite blocks are liberated from the mountainside daily at ❸ **Rock of Ages Quarry**. Estimated to be 10 miles deep, the

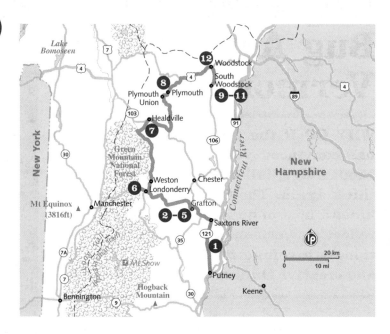

Barre granite field – one of the world's largest – yields a high-quality gray granite that supplies most of the nation's memorials. Quarriers have been working the same seam for over 100 years, literally digging themselves into a 620ft-deep pit. Guided bus tours whisk you to an observation platform high above, where on weekdays you can gaze down on the ant-sized workers cutting 1400-ton slabs of rock and hoisting them to the surface with gigantic derricks. Back down the hill, self-guided tours provide a glimpse of the factory floor where the cut stone is polished and carved.

For a more hands-on experience, test your industrial sandblasting skills at the newly opened Cut-in-Stone Center, or visit the adjacent outdoor bowling alley. Constructed from pure granite, this prototype never quite got off the ground commercially, but you can still roll a few frames if you don't mind setting up the pins yourself!

The landscape grows wilder as you follow Hwy 2 east into the Northeast Kingdom, an untamed domain of moose and dark pines. If the sight of so many trees makes you feel like climbing one – or even sleeping in one – the folks at ❹ **Twin Pines** can help. On their scenic 35-acre hillside horse farm just east of Danville, they offer three-hour classes in recreational tree climbing, plus a state-of-the-art tree house set in a forest full of chirping birds. Adventurous souls who don't mind heights or rustic living will appreciate the elegant hand-hewn stairway and deck, burl furniture, picture windows,

Vermont Castings wood stove and a fire pole for dramatic exits. Advance reservations are essential. Note that there's no electricity or indoor plumbing, although guests have access to a bathroom with lights and hot showers five minutes uphill. Those seeking a more traditional motel experience can continue 7 miles east to St Johnsbury.

Smack in the heart of "Saint J" (as it's known to the locals) stands the impressively Romanesque **5** **Fairbanks Museum & Planetarium**. First opened in 1891, the museum is packed to the rafters with an eclectic mix of history and nature exhibits, many from founder Franklin Fairbanks' original "cabinet of curiosities." Seekers of the truly unusual should make a beeline for the bug art display upstairs. Bug art? Yes, eccentric Victorian John Hampson meticulously assembled his "mixed-media pieces" from thousands of dead bugs. Seen from a distance these weird masterpieces artfully depict familiar themes such as the American flag and George Washington. Step a little closer and you can see – eeww! – nothing but dead beetles and moths!

Two miles east of town, clearly sign-posted on Spaulding Rd just off Hwy 2, internationally acclaimed artist Stephen Huneck has built another

> **DETOUR** Late summer travelers with a weakness for weird should check out the **Great Vermont Corn Maze** (www.vermontcornmaze.com), a seasonal operation 9 miles north of Hwy 2, reached from the town of Danville west of St Johnsbury. Attractions include a meticulously planned and seriously challenging corn maze, a barnyard golf game involving neither golf balls nor clubs and the ever-popular "Dead North: Farmland of Terror", a pre-Halloween event in a haunted cornfield. For directions and photos of past years' mazes, see www.vermontcornmaze.com.

unique tribute to the animal kingdom. Huneck's captivating **6** **Dog Chapel** perches on a grassy hillside, its sign proclaiming: "Welcome All Breeds, All Creeds; No Dogmas Allowed." Having survived a near death experience in 1994, Huneck awoke from his coma with a vision of a chapel that would celebrate the enduring spiritual bond between humans and animals. From the doggie weather vane crowning the steeple to the carved dog angel in the entryway, to the lovingly rendered stained-glass representations of dogs swimming after a ball or licking an ice-cream cone, Huneck's personal affection for the animal kingdom is readily felt. What makes this place doubly memorable is Huneck's invitation to visitors to commemorate their own pets through writings and photos. Thousands of heartfelt mementos from animal lovers are plastered on the walls throughout the chapel. Next door you'll find Huneck's gallery, where several happy hounds roam freely among the paintings and other artwork.

Ten minutes north of St Johnsbury (just off the I-91 Exit 24 in Lyndonville), take a gander at the parking lot of **7** **Bob's Welding**, where propane tanks have been transformed into sculptures of moose, dinosaurs, a totem pole and other expressions of inspired lunacy. A stone's throw further north is ⑧ **Miss Lyndonville Diner**, a great place to recharge your batteries and continue the dessert-for-breakfast tradition. The fresh strawberry pie (in season) is a local favorite.

Fifteen miles further north along Rte 122, near the town of Glover, the ⑨ **Bread & Puppet Theater** is a tour de force of avant-garde art. For nearly 50 years, the internationally renowned Bread & Puppet Theatre has been staging theatrical spectacles with a political twist. While the company can be seen both nationally and internationally, Vermont performances take place on weekends throughout the summer, starring gigantic puppets (some up to 20ft tall) borne through the fields on the company's hilltop farm. Even when no show is going on, you can visit the treasure trove of papier-mâché angels, devils, horses and other fantastic creatures from past performances, hauntingly displayed in a cavernous old barn.

BYOD (BRING YOUR OWN DOG)

When's the last time you went to a party and found yourself surrounded by dogs? At Stephen Huneck's semiannual **Dog Fest**, that's the whole point. In early August and October, Huneck invites the general public and their pets to his hillside farm for a day of free dog biscuits, Frisbee throwing and good-natured canine competitions. Humans will appreciate the apple pie and the superb views over the mountains of Vermont's Northeast Kingdom. For dates, see www.dogmt.com/events.php.

If you've worked up an appetite, this may or may not be a good time to visit ⑩ **Currier's Quality Market** in Glover, 2 miles north of Bread & Puppet on Rte 16. This community general store has a post office, a deli and shelves full of food and drink, but what's likelier to catch your attention are the dozens of animal trophies scattered throughout the store. Taxidermists gone wild have stuffed everything from moose to bear to a lynx tangling with a deer. As store patron Nancy Cressman puts it, "You reach for a box of Ritz crackers and suddenly you're petting a dead raccoon." Note that photos are encouraged but touching the stuffed animals is not.

"You reach for a box of Ritz crackers and suddenly you're petting a dead raccoon."

More animal-themed eating awaits 15 miles north off I-91, Exit 28. Near the corner of Routes 5 and 5A in Derby Center, an enormous archway of elk and deer antlers ushers you into the ⑪ **Cow Palace**, a steakhouse serving fresh elk venison from the adjoining ranch. Several not-yet-burgerized elk can be seen grazing in the adjacent field, while a stuffed polar bear presides over the tables inside.

To reach the trip's last two attractions, head north on Hwy 5. Here in the towns of Derby Line and Beebe Plain lie a pair of unusual points where you can stand with one foot in New England and one in Canada. In 1901 the cornerstone for Derby Line's ornate Queen Anne Revivalist library was laid squarely on the Vermont–Québec border, at a time when international boundaries were more porous than today. Seven years later, the US Congress passed legislation prohibiting new construction on the border, but the library was allowed to stand. Today a painted diagonal line indicates which country is which. The children's room is in Québec, the front entrance in Vermont. Bilingual staff from both countries work the reception desk. It's worth a stroll through just to see the gorgeous cherry, golden birch and bird's-eye maple details. However, the star attraction is the **12 Haskell Opera House** on the 2nd floor. In earlier times, this miniature theater regularly hosted traveling performers working the Boston–New York–Montréal circuit but fell into disuse when WWI spelled vaudeville's doom. Benign neglect, coupled with a strictly preservationist board of trustees, has left the original theater almost perfectly preserved, with its original painted curtain, dome, chandelier, ornamental plasterwork and stage backdrops still intact. The opera house hosts weekend performances throughout the summer, some in French and some in English.

If you enjoy this kind of borderline schizophrenia, continue west 3 miles along Elm St and Beebe Rd to the town of Beebe Plain, where you can stroll along the aptly named **13 Canusa Street**. Houses on the north side of the street are in Canada, while those on the south side are in the USA. A quick check of license plates in the local driveways will let you know where you stand. The sidewalk is on the Canadian side, so US citizens need to visit customs on both sides of the border before exploring this international oddity.

For a scenic return trip to Ben & Jerry's, with no backtracking, follow Hwy 5 to Newport, then Vermont Rtes 105 and 100 southwest to Waterbury.
Gregor Clark

TRIP INFORMATION

GETTING THERE
From Boston, take I-93 northbound to I-89. At Exit 10 (Waterbury), follow Rte 100 north 1 mile to Ben & Jerry's.

DO

Ben & Jerry's Flavor Graveyard
With 27 tombstones, this faux graveyard crowns a hilltop above the ice-cream factory. ☎ 802-882-1240; www.benjerry.com; 1281 Waterbury-Stowe Rd, Waterbury; ⏰ 9am-9pm Jul & Aug, 10am-6pm Sep-Jun; ♿

Bread & Puppet Theater
A funky old barn, stuffed to the rafters with giant puppets, showcases the artistic genius of Peter Schumann and his troupe. ☎ 802-525-3031; www.breadandpuppet.org; 753 Heights Rd, Glover; ⏰ 10am-6pm Jun-Oct

Dog Chapel
The Dog Chapel is Stephen Huneck's most personal and striking work of art. ☎ 800-449-2580, 802-748-2700; www.dogmt.com; 143 Parks Rd, St Johnsbury; ⏰ 10am-5pm Mon-Sat, 11am-4pm Sun; ♿ 🐾

Fairbanks Museum & Planetarium
This striking pink sandstone building houses Franklin Fairbanks' wide-ranging collection. ☎ 802-748-2372; www.fairbanksmuseum .org; 1302 Main St, St Johnsbury; adult/child under 5 $6/free; ⏰ 9am-5pm Tue-Sat, 1-5pm Sun; ♿

Haskell Opera House
A gift from lumber baron Martha Stewart Haskell, this early-20th-century gem straddles the US–Canada border. ☎ 802-873-3022; www.haskellopera.org; 93 Caswell Ave, Derby Line; tours adult/child $3/free; ⏰ 11am-4pm May-Oct

Hope Cemetery
The final resting place of many a quarrier. Displays the carving skills of generations of immigrants. ☎ 802-476-6245; 262 E Montpelier Rd, Barre; ⏰ dawn-dusk

Rock of Ages Quarry
The world's largest deep-hole granite quarry has operated continuously for over a century. ☎ 802-476-3119; www.rockofages.com; 558 Graniteville Rd, Graniteville; guided tours adult/child $4.50/2; ⏰ 9:15am-3:30pm Mon-Sat, 10:15am-3:30pm Sun Memorial Day–mid-Oct

EAT

Cow Palace
Eschew the golden arches in favor of Cow Palace's arch of antlers, the gateway to Vermont's freshest local elk venison. ☎ 802-766-4724; www.derbycowpalace.com; Main St, Derby; mains $7-24; ⏰ 4-8:30pm Mon, 11am-8:30pm Tue-Thu & Sun, 11am-9:30pm Fri & Sat

Currier's Quality Market
Grab a deli sandwich or run the gauntlet of stuffed animals in the grocery department. ☎ 802-525-8822; 2984 Glover St, Glover; ⏰ 6am-9pm Mon-Sat, 9am-6pm Sun

Miss Lyndonville Diner
This friendly local hangout specializes in hearty breakfasts and other American classics. ☎ 802-626-9890; 686 Broad St, Lyndonville; mains from $5; ⏰ 6am-3pm Mon & Tue, 6am-8pm Wed & Thu, 6am-9pm Fri & Sat, 7am-8pm Sun

SLEEP

Twin Pines
Sleep among the birds in a rustic tree house. Advance reservations are essential. Acrophobes need not apply! ☎ 802-684-9795; www.newenglandtreeclimbing.com/vermont .html; Maple Lane, Danville; tree house $75

USEFUL WEBSITES
www.travelthekingdom.com

www.lonelyplanet.com/trip-planner

LINK YOUR TRIP

The Way We Lived

WHY GO This wide-ranging history tour provides glimpses of early Vermont life and insights into the state's perennially free-thinking spirit. Visit the state historical society museum, a president's home village frozen in time, a working 19th-century farm, a museum tracing Vermont's role in the industrial revolution and a Smithsonian-caliber collection of early Americana.

TIME
2 – 3 days

DISTANCE
150 miles

BEST TIME TO GO
May – Oct

START
Plymouth Notch

END
Shelburne

Gazing across the high pastures of Plymouth Notch, you feel a bit like Rip Van Winkle – only it's the past you've woken up to. President Calvin Coolidge's boyhood home, preserved as the ❶ **President Calvin Coolidge State Historic Site**, looks much as it did a century ago, with homes, barns, a church, a one-room schoolhouse, a cheese factory and a general store gracefully arrayed among old maples on a bucolic hillside. At Plymouth's heart is the Coolidge homestead, where the vacationing vice president took the Presidential Oath of Office by kerosene lamp with his father after being awakened at 2am to news of Harding's death. (Asked later how he knew he could administer the oath, Coolidge's father, a notary public, quipped, "Didn't know I couldn't.")

The village's streets seem sleepy today, but museum exhibits tell a tale of elbow grease and perseverance. Tools for blacksmithing, woodworking, butter-making and hand-laundering are indicative of the hard work and grit it took to wrest a living from Vermont's stony pastures. As a boy, Calvin hayed with his grandfather and kept the woodbox filled. This vision of an earlier America is compelling for adults, but Plymouth is also fun for kids, hosting horse-drawn wagon rides, old-time crafts demonstrations, concerts and a pull-out-all-the-stops birthday party for the one president born on July 4.

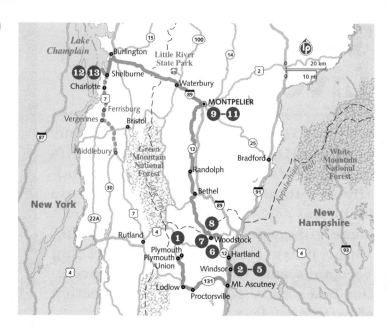

While we tend to think of Vermont's past in terms of its pastures, running a hill farm also took industry and Yankee ingenuity. Vermonters have a proud inventing history, from receiving USA's first patent in 1790 to developing the modern snowboard. Vermonters are credited with inventing the first electric motor, the steel square, the cast steel plowshare and the steamboat. Many were blacksmiths or gunsmiths, and it was guns that spawned an invention that changed not just Vermont but the world: interchangeable parts. The ❷ **American Precision Museum** in Windsor, housed in the 1846 armory and machine shop where this revolutionary innovation was first perfected, celebrates Vermont's role in the industrial revolution and the all-around ingenuity of Vermonters.

North of Windsor, two other points of historic interest appear along Hwy 5: the ❸ **Cornish-Windsor Covered Bridge** over the Connecticut River is the longest such span in the world, and half a mile north the ❹ **Old Constitution House** witnessed the signing of Vermont's groundbreaking 1777 constitution.

Two great food and drink stops lie just north of Windsor along Hwy 5 and Rte 12: the ❺ **Harpoon Brewery**, where tasty sandwiches accompany some of Vermont's finest craft brews, and the charming ❻ **Skunk Hollow Tavern** in Hartland Four Corners, dating to the 1790s. From here, follow Rte 12 north to the impeccably preserved village of Woodstock and the ❼ **Woodstocker Inn**, which has won awards for hospitality, guest satisfaction and environmental excellence.

Just outside Woodstock on Rte 12, Vermont's farming history comes to life at the **8** **Billings Farm & Museum**. Established in 1871, Billings is still a working farm and its prize-winning Jersey herd is the country's oldest. Visitor activities vary with the seasons, from horse and sleigh rides to the afternoon milking of the cows, to demonstrations of strawberry shortcake being made in the cast-iron stove at the Victorian farm manager's house.

Next it's the bright lights of America's smallest capital, Montpelier, following

THE VERMONT REPUBLIC 1777–91

Vermont was an independent Republic for 14 years (eat your heart out Texas!) before joining the union. In July 1777 Vermonters drafted the first constitution to outlaw slavery, authorize a public school system and give every man the right to vote. In recent years, the Second Vermont Republic movement has begun clamoring for secession. Vermont's independent spirit lives on!

Rte 12 through historic Bethel, Randolph and Northfield. Adjacent to the gold-domed state capitol, the award-winning "Freedom and Unity" exhibit at the **9** **Vermont Historical Society Museum** literally walks you through 400 years of Vermont history. From your first few steps into an Abenaki wigwam, you're asked to consider the true meaning of this state motto. Current controversies aren't brushed under the rug: a short film presents the early-20th-century debate over women's suffrage alongside footage from the 1999 statehouse hearings where citizens voiced their opinion on civil unions. In a very Vermontish way, you can ponder the issues on your own rather than assent to someone else's party line. Absolutely thought provoking, the panoply of voices and imaginative presentation keep this exhibit fun and lively. For lunch or dinner try try **10** **Restaurant Phoebe**, directly across from the museum. Nearby you can sleep at the **11** **Inn at Montpelier**.

An hour west via I-89 and Hwy 7, feast your eyes on the array of 17th- to 20th-century American artifacts – folk art, textiles, toys, tools, carriages, furniture – spread over the 45-acre grounds at **12** **Shelburne Museum**, which is set up as a mock village. The

DETOUR Several sites of interest line Hwy 7 south of Shelburne: Ferrisburg's **Rokeby Museum** (www.rokeby.org) is a Quaker farmstead that once served as a stop on the Underground Railroad; Vergennes' **Lake Champlain Maritime Museum** (www.lcmm .org) explores shipwrecks, Revolutionary War battles and other local maritime history; and Middlebury's **Vermont Folklife Center** (www .vermontfolklifecenter.org) exhibits photos and oral histories documenting Vermonters' lives.

39 buildings include a jail, lighthouse, schoolhouse, railway station and blacksmith's forge. The collection's sheer size lets you tailor your visit. Families can take in the carousel, Owl Cottage children's center or *Ticonderoga* steamship, while duck decoy and quilt aficionados can spend hours investigating their passion. The museum's collection is so vast that tickets give you two days to explore – a perfect excuse to spend the night at the luxurious **13** **Inn at Shelburne Farms**, 3 miles away and a historic attraction in its own right.

Gregor Clark

HISTORY & CULTURE

TRIP INFORMATION

GETTING THERE
From Boston, take I-93 to I-89 N. At Vermont Exit 1, take Hwy 4 W, then Rte 100A S to Plymouth Notch.

DO

American Precision Museum
Rotating exhibits in a historic mill examine the impact of early Yankee ingenuity. ☎ 802-674-5781; www.americanprecision.org; 196 Main St, Windsor; adult/student/family $6/4/18; ☽ 10am-5pm Memorial Day-Nov 1

Billings Farm & Museum
A 19th-century farmhouse and barns outside Woodstock tell of early Vermont farm life. ☎ 802-457-2355; www.billingsfarm .org; Rte 12, Woodstock; adult/child/senior $11/6/10; ☽ 10am-5pm May-Oct, 10am-4pm some winter weekends; ♿

President Calvin Coolidge State Historic Site
Coolidge's hilltop hometown, Plymouth, ex-udes the air of another century. ☎ 802-672-3773; www.historicvermont.org/coolidge; 3780 Rte 100A, Plymouth; adult/child/family $7.50/2/20; ☽ 9:30am-5pm late May–mid-Oct; ♿

Shelburne Museum
Acres of preserved historic buildings house the nation's premier collection of early New England Americana. ☎ 802-985-3346; www.shelburne museum.org; 5555 Shelburne Rd, Shelburne; admission adult/child/student $18/9/13; ☽ 10am-5pm mid-May–late Oct; ♿

Vermont Historical Society Museum
Multimedia exhibits trace Vermont's his-tory from Abenaki times to the present. ☎ 802-828-2291; www.vermonthistory.org; 109 State St, Montpelier; adult/child $5/3; ☽ 10am-4pm Tue-Sat year-round, noon-4pm Sun May-Oct

EAT

Restaurant Phoebe
Casually elegant Phoebe's serves a seasonally changing menu featuring Vermont produce. ☎ 802-262-3500; www.restaurantphoebe. com; 52 State St, Montpelier; mains $8-27; ☽ 11:30am-2pm & 5-9pm Mon-Fri, 5-9:30pm Sat

Skunk Hollow Tavern
At a sleepy rural crossroads, this rustic 18th-century tavern makes an atmospheric dinner spot. ☎ 802-436-2139; www.skunkhollow tavern.com; 12 Brownsville Rd, Hartland Four Corners; mains $9-27; ☽ from 5pm Wed-Sun

DRINK

Harpoon Brewery
Tour the brewery, or enjoy one of New Eng-land's best brews at tables outside. ☎ 802-674-5491; www.harpoonbrewery.com; 336 Ruth Carney Dr, Windsor; sandwiches $4.50-7, 5-beer sampler $5.80; ☽ 10am-6pm

SLEEP

Inn at Montpelier
Enjoy cookies and a wraparound porch at these two renovated homes from the early 1800s. ☎ 802-223-2727; www.innamontpe lier.com; 147 Main St, Montpelier; r $125-210

Inn at Shelburne Farms
This elegant lakeside mansion on a 1400-acre working farm is an absolute gem. ☎ 802-985-8686; www.shelburnefarms.org; 1611 Harbor Rd, Shelburne; r $145-425

Woodstocker Inn
An award-winning cute yellow inn at historic Woodstock's western edge. No children. ☎ 802-457-3896; www.woodstockervt.com; 61 River St, Woodstock; r $110-340

USEFUL WEBSITES
www.historicvermont.org
www.vermonthistory.org

www.lonelyplanet.com/trip-planner

LINK YOUR TRIP

A Community Arts Renaissance

WHY GO Community-based arts organizations are revitalizing downtowns throughout Vermont, preserving historic buildings, strengthening communities and exposing the public to art that's gritty, dynamic and unpredictable. For a first-hand view of their impact in four southern Vermont towns, we teamed up with Matthew Perry, artistic director of the Vermont Arts Exchange.

TIME
2 days

DISTANCE
120 miles

BEST TIME TO GO
Year-round

START
North Bennington

END
West Rutland

Before you even cross the threshold of the ❶ **Vermont Arts Exchange** in North Bennington, you feel its dynamism and sense of humor. A school bus parked outside has its sign altered to read "COOL BUS," while the homemade bumper decal asks, "How's your drawing? Call 802-442-5549."

"The arts are very empowering for communities," says Perry, sitting in the converted mill that he and Vermont Arts Exchange cofounder Patricia Pedreira helped rescue in the early 1990s in their quest to build a community arts organization in southern Vermont. "In other countries, the arts are woven in, whether you're in Bali, Spain, Mexico, kids are learning these things in their lives at home. Here in America it's definitely on the back burner, but when we put it forward, people see how we can transform community through art."

"Each place I'm going to recommend has its own story and each blends in a passion for historical buildings. We've all taken places that were falling down and instead of building a mall, preserved them by getting the whole community involved. This building had pigeons and raccoons living in it, and now...I like to say, now we're making art here in this factory."

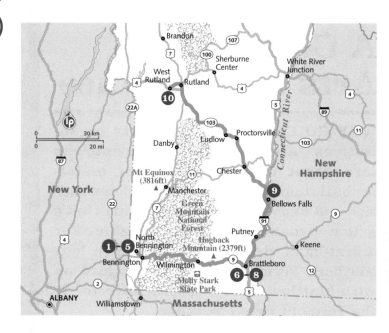

Inside the 19th-century mill building, creativity spills out in a thousand different forms: cutting-edge exhibits covering the walls in the gallery spaces, studios filled with works in multiple media, and signs advertising the Arts Exchange's many other projects, from kids' summer arts camps to a basement music series that brings in Cuban pianists, Portuguese fado singers and local artists who blow a jazz trombone as handily as they wield a paintbrush.

In North Bennington, creativity also extends into the kitchen. Just off the village square, Perry points to three eateries spanning the culinary spectrum: ❷ **Marigold Kitchen**, a hole-in-the-wall pizzeria using ultrafresh local ingredients ("if the motorcycle's out front, we're open," says chef-owner Chris Donza); ❸ **Powers Market**, a venerable 175-year-old general store and community gathering place; and ❹ **Pangaea**, serving gourmet dinners in its main dining room, with lighter fare in the bar and on the riverside deck below. For overnight visitors, ❺ **Eddington House Inn** is just up the street.

Transformative art of the kind Perry describes is happening all over Vermont. Ten years ago Brattleboro, east of Bennington on Rte 9, started looking like a ghost town as businesses short on walk-in customers moved their operations to the internet. Brattleboro today presents an entirely different picture. Local artists and – as Perry describes it – the ponytail-wearing select board teamed up to revitalize Main St, resulting in a visibly arts-oriented downtown. The first Friday of every month, an enthusiastically attended gallery walk takes in dozens of galleries and studios, plus Main St businesses such as **6** **Amy's Bakery Arts Café**, where local art hangs on the walls and patrons congregate in the back room overlooking the Connecticut River. Just down Main St, the **7** **Artist's Loft B&B** is a 3rd-floor artist's studio converted into a one-of-a-kind overnight lodging. Nearby, Brattleboro's historic train station houses the **8** **Brattleboro Museum & Art Center**, which holds regular juried shows focusing on artists living within a 100-mile radius.

Twenty-five miles upriver, the historic architecture of Bellows Falls reflects its early prosperity as home to America's first chartered canal in 1802. By the

THE OPEN STUDIO WEEKEND

Want to see sparks flying in a forge or mud turning on a wheel? Attend the Vermont Crafts Council's Memorial Day **Open Studio Weekend**, where you can visit painters, sculptors, photographers, blacksmiths, jewelers, potters, glassblowers and woodworkers in studios and galleries statewide. Maps listing artists, hours and directions are available at information kiosks around the state and at www.vermontcrafts.com.

1990s Bellows Falls had fallen on hard times, but today, the city's historic core is undergoing a small renaissance, thanks in large part to the efforts of Robert McBride, founding director of **9** **RAMP (Rockingham Arts & Museum Project)**. "In Bellows Falls," says Perry, "Robert has taken historic buildings and turned them into studios, galleries and affordable housing for artists." Visitors to RAMP's downstairs gallery in the historic Exner Block building can view the work of artists living in the studios above, and with prior planning can sometimes meet the artists themselves.

Another favorite of Perry's is the **10** **Carving Studio & Sculpture Center** in West Rutland, 50 miles northwest of Bellows Falls. Here an abandoned marble quarry has been converted into studios, classrooms and gallery space. "What's exciting is they've taken this quarry and they've turned it around. Outside they're working with some of the same stone that's been lying around since the Vermont Marble Company left in 1978. They're also preserving the grounds by using them for their annual juried SculptFest installations. In the studios you see marble chips, huge hydraulic machines, drills, sanders, grinders and polishers, and artists wandering around covered with stuff they've just been working for days. You see work in progress and finished work. For me it's kind of like going into Santa's Workshop. You've heard about this place and you know there's magic in making art, but now you're seeing the process. We've been so concerned with the product, but actually learning how an artist works – we just don't see that anymore. There's this excitement here, even if you don't know anything about art. You get this feeling like back in the olden days when artists would get together in the Adirondacks, the creativity and the talk and the wine flowing…".

Clearly, Perry could continue in this vein for hours, but he's got a class to teach and more people to meet. In southern Vermont, the arts must go on…
Gregor Clark

HISTORY & CULTURE

TRIP INFORMATION

GETTING THERE
From Boston, take Rte 2 or I-90 west to Hwy 7. Follow Hwy 7 north through Bennington, then Rte 67A northwest into North Bennington.

DO

Brattleboro Museum & Art Center
In Brattleboro's old train station, BMAC displays rotating exhibitions of local and contemporary art. ☎ 802-257-0124; www.brattleboromuseum.org; 10 Vernon St, Brattleboro; admission $4; ☻ 11am-5pm Wed-Mon

Carving Studio & Sculpture Center
This place is like an industrial sculpture garden, displaying contemporary works amid rusting machinery, marble heaps and revitalized quarry buildings. ☎ 802-438-2097; www.carvingstudio.org; 636 Marble St, West Rutland; ☻ 9am-5pm

RAMP (Rockingham Arts & Museum Project)
The historic Exner Block building houses arts-oriented businesses, gallery space and affordable live-work studios for artists. ☎ 802-463-3252; www.ramp-vt.org; 7 Canal St, Bellows Falls; ☻ by arrangement

Vermont Arts Exchange
This dynamic community arts center blends gallery, studio, classroom and concert space. ☎ 802-442-5549; www.vtartxchange.org; 29 Sage St Mill, North Bennington; ☻ 9am-5pm Mon-Fri, by appointment Sat & Sun

EAT

Amy's Bakery Arts Café
Always buzzing, Amy's serves sandwiches and salads against a backdrop of local artwork. ☎ 802-251-1071; 113 Main St, Brattleboro; sandwiches & salads $4-9; ☻ 8am-6pm Mon-Sat, 9am-5pm Sun

Marigold Kitchen
Marigold bakes delicious pizza with fresh Vermont mozzarella and local organic ingredients. ☎ 802-445-4545; www.marigoldkitchen.net; 25 Main St, North Bennington; pizzas from $9; ☻ 4:30-8pm Tue-Thu, 4:30-9:30pm Fri & Sat

Pangaea
With its cozy bar, dining room and riverside deck, Pangaea offers everything from pints to multicourse dinners. ☎ 802-442-4466; www.vermontfinedining.com; 3 Prospect St, North Bennington; mains $10-17; ☻ 5-10pm

Powers Market
In business for over 175 years, this elegant columned market is the architectural and social centerpiece of North Bennington. ☎ 802-442-6821; www.powersmarket.com; 9 Main St, North Bennington; sandwiches from $4; ☻ 7am-6pm

SLEEP

Artist's Loft B&B
This one-room B&B's spacious suite overlooks the Connecticut River and the seasonally changing canvas of Wantastiquet Mountain. ☎ 802-257-5181; www.theartistsloft.com; 103 Main St, Brattleboro; r $138-158

Eddington House Inn
The beautifully restored and conveniently located 1857 lodging in North Bennington is on the National Register of Historic Places. ☎ 802-442-1511; www.eddingtonhouseinn.com; 21 Main St, North Bennington; r $99-159

USEFUL WEBSITES
www.vermontartscouncil.org
www.vermontcrafts.com

LINK YOUR TRIP

www.lonelyplanet.com/trip-planner

NEW HAMPSHIRE TRIPS

Whether you've got a hunger for hiking to the top of a punishing peak or a lust for fine antiques buried within dusty barns, New Hampshire will thrill, enchant and mesmerize. Few parts of the country can equal New Hampshire for the variety of things to do and their proximity to each other. The wide roads and relative lack of traffic make this state ideal for road tripping – you can wake up to the sunrise over the Atlantic in the morning, hike up a mountain a few hours later, dine in soft candlelight by evening…all within a few hours' drive.

The ever-changing seasons play a huge part, too. A trip taken in spring will be a totally different experience in fall, when the splendor of the leaves turning color transforms the region. A town that seems all but deserted in summer may be packed with people when the ski season rolls around.

Don't be afraid to get off the beaten path, to stop and smell the roses (or the cows), to follow that river to where it curves around the bend, and to make these trips into your own journeys. The hard part isn't figuring out what to do, it's figuring out how to do it all.

PLAYLIST ♫

Ponder the scenic valleys and forest-lined lakes with this New Hampshire soundtrack, which includes the theme to the movie *On Golden Pond* (1981), filmed in the state. In the Durham area, you can tune into the University of New Hampshire college radio station WUNH (91.3FM).

- "New Hampshire Hornpipe," Dave Grusin
- "New Hampshire," Matt Pond PA
- "Leaving New Hampshire," Andy Leftwich
- "New Hampshire," Sonic Youth
- "Snow Outside the Mill," Bill Morrissey
- "New Hampshire Girl," Hutch
- "Farewell to Whiskey," Rodney Miller's New England Dance Band
- "Old New Hampshire Home," Smokey Greene

NEW HAMPSHIRE BEST TRIPS

NEW HAMPSHIRE TRIPS

White Mountains Loop

WHY GO Wend your way up majestic Mt Washington, come face to face with deer, moose and black bears, and let the week's worries slip away at a campfire or cozy inn's hearth. Trading posts, train rides, white steeples, sleepy ski towns and great restaurants all add to the fun.

Start in quiet ❶ Conway, the eastern end of the beautiful ❷ Kancamagus Scenic Byway. No matter what the season is, you'll be awed by the beauty of this spectacular road. Running alongside the Pemigewasset and Swift Rivers, the Kank is often a driving destination all by itself, especially in autumn when the maples and oaks paint the hills crimson and gold. It's not uncommon to startle a deer as you pick your way along the riverbanks. Stop for a picnic at ❸ Sabbaday Falls, a ten-minute hike to a spot where ribbons of water cascade through a series of granite channels and small pools. Shortly after Sabbaday, the road starts rising, the leafy maples are replaced by dark, somber conifers and the air begins to smell like real pine. At ❹ Kancamagus Pass, elevation 2890ft, only Mt Washington itself can beat the serene view. Seven miles east of Lincoln, the well-labeled ❺ Discovery Trail offers an easy meander through the forest with informative plaques along the way.

Turn onto Rte 3 and head north, where you'll either love or hate **Clark's Trading Post** in Lincoln, so unrepentantly tacky that it has become a New Hampshire institution. The Clark family has kept black bear for over 80 years, and the souvenir store has a surprisingly wide selection of good area literature as well as the usual trinkets, gifts and postcards.

If you need a bite to eat, check out the ❼ **Common Man**, nearby. The variety of good old home-style dishes fit with the homey, by-the-fireplace feel. Lines can be long, especially on weekends or holidays, and people have been known to drive hours out of their way to eat here.

TIME
2 days

DISTANCE
151 miles

BEST TIME TO GO
May – Oct

START
Conway

END
Conway

ALSO GOOD FOR

OUTDOORS

BEST TRIP

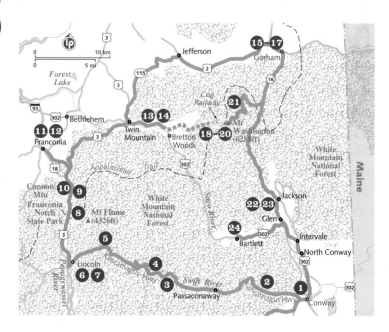

The **8** **Flume Gorge**, part of Franconia Notch State Park, is a natural granite sluice with 90ft walls. A sturdy walkway makes this accessible for everyone (sometimes too accessible – expect crowds) but the verdant, moss-covered cliffsides and the rushing stream are worth it. Nearby, check out the **9** **Cannon Mountain Aerial Tramway**, where a cable car whisks you up over the rolling hills to a lookout point so high and lofty you'll feel like you've sprouted wings. On a sunny, haze-free day you'll have a bird's eye view that can't be beat.

No New Hampshire landmark can match the fame of the **10** **Old Man of the Mountain**, a rock formation that remains the state symbol despite its collapse in May, 2003. In the ice-cream shop at the Aerial Tramway parking area, there are forensically accurate diagrams of "the Profile's" collapse and tributes to this beloved symbol who is no more.

"It's not uncommon to startle a deer as you pick your way along the riverbanks."

The **11** **Franconia Notch Motel** offers modest two-room cabins with white paint and green shutters; some have porches. It's a friendly place that is perfect for families, though pets are not allowed. For something more snazzy, try the **12** **Franconia Inn**, a giant 29-room white-clapboard inn where you'll have elegantly appointed rooms, a central location and lots of history and lore. Alternatively, for a closer-to-nature experience, head off Rte 3 along Rte 302 to **13** **Zealand**

Campground, in the Pemigewasset Ranger District, offers beautiful sites nestled along the Zealand Valley riverside, near Twin Mountain. The eleven campsites are spread out and private, and the pit toilets are well maintained. Take a walk down the nearby ⑭ **Trestle Trail** and you'll meander along the Ammonoosuc riverside, a nice, easy-to-moderate hike that offers a taste of New Hampshire's mountains without your needing to break a sweat.

From Franconia, follow the Daniel Webster Trail (still Rte 3), passing miles of undeveloped forest and rolling pasture lands. Keep on the lookout for moose and bear, especially in the evening when the animals come out to feed. Turn right onto Rte 115, then right again at Jefferson Highlands, following Rte 2 all the way into ⑮ **Gorham**, where you'll pick up Rte 16.

Gorham has one of the route's finest restaurants. ⑯ **Libby's Bistro**, housed in an old bank building that has a relaxed, speakeasy feel, has hand-prepared meals, often made using local produce, in-season vegetables, or New England seafood. For

MOAT MOUNTAIN SMOKEHOUSE

If Ben Franklin were alive today, there's a good chance he'd be a regular at **Moat Mountain Smokehouse** (www.moatmountain.com) on Rte 302 in North Conway, the modern-day equivalent of the travelers' inns of frontier days. There's no faux flair or hokey gimmicks, just good beer, great eats, and friendly smiles, and it makes a perfect bookend to begin or end your White Mountains Loop. Be sure to snag a growler of your favorite grog before you leave.

those on a budget, a very reasonable set menu option gives you a four-course meal for a very reasonable $30. Sink your teeth into the sublime duck sausage with peppered duck confit and you will never want to leave. Desserts, such as the prickley-pear sorbet with lavender or the hazelnut chocolate cake, are sublime. Don't leave without peeking at the original wall safes that speak of the building's banking past.

Only minutes away, the ⑰ **Top Notch Inn**, right on Rte 16 in the center of town, has both motel-style rooms and a more B&B-style building (the Pinkham House) for those wanting a more homey, New England vibe. Pets are welcome in the regular motel rooms, though there is a unique caveat: no moose are allowed at any time. You'll have to leave Bullwinkle at home.

From Gorham head southeast to ⑱ **Mt Washington**, New England's highest peak and the site of the world's highest recorded wind gust. The heavy chains wrapped around the ⑲ **Auto Road Stage Office** at the summit attest that winter on Washington is no laughing matter. It was here that the record-setting 231mph wind gust was recorded. The ⑳ **Sherman Adams Summit Building**, which includes an observatory, has souvenirs, refreshments and a lookout tower where you can gawk at the majestic landscape beneath you. If you time it right, the winding ㉑ **Washington Auto Road** will be open, but there will still be snow and ice at the summit, giving you a taste of what the winter holds. The world record ascent – set in 1998 in an Audi Quattro – is an absolutely mind-boggling six minutes 41.99 seconds, but most people take just under an hour.

Only a stone's throw off the highway in Jackson, stop at **22** **Glen Ellis Falls** for a few final snapshots. This easy walk brings you 0.3 miles to a 60ft waterfall, one of the prettiest in the White Mountains region, and most can make the hike without breaking a sweat. The **23** **Dana Place Inn** is where Peter Pan would surely stay if he wanted a vacation from Neverland. With its own Treehouse (named for the tree that used to grow through the private deck) and kid-friendly touches such as special kids' box lunches, activities lists and more, it's a great stop for anyone with rugrats in tow.

Return to Conway along Rte 16, making sure to turn right onto Rte 302 into the town of Bartlett. The **24** **White Mountain Cider Company** is in a rustic barn with unfinished wood beams and beautiful farm-style furnishings. Dine by lamplight, with local live music such as mellow jazz or crooning folk guitar in the background. The natural wood bar makes a perfect spot for slowly sipping a glass of red, and roasted duck breast with fresh bay rub, rhubarb compote and wild leek mashed potatoes, or succulent calamari with rhubarb and basil are a few of the possible dinner options. During the day they have freshly made doughnuts that are well worth a detour. Hot out of the fryer, they're as soft and succulent as a doughnut can be. A healthy dose of cinnamon in the batter is one of their secrets, along with cider – which they press themselves in the autumn. What could be better than hot doughnuts and fresh pressed cider as you're watching the maple leaves turn from green to gold?

Ray Bartlett

> **DETOUR**
>
> If you're looking for an alternate way to reach the Mt Washington Summit but aren't quite ready for the hike, try the **Mt Washington Cog Railway** (www.thecog.com), a 10-mile detour from Rte 3 on Rte 302, past Bretton Woods. This steam-powered cog train was originally built in 1869 and at the time was popular for its state-of-the-art engineering. Now it hearkens back to the days of yesteryear, but remains just as fun and just as scenic.

TRIP INFORMATION

GETTING THERE

To get to Conway, follow Rte 16 from Portsmouth, NH or Rte 302 from Portland, ME. Either trip takes just over 1½ hours.

DO

Auto Road Stage Office

Site of the record-setting 23mph wind gust, this building is replete with chains to keep it from blowing away. ☎ 603-466-3988; Mt Washington Summit; ☽ 10am-4pm May-Oct, hours are weather dependent

Cannon Mountain Aerial Tramway

Bird's-eye beauty from this fun-for-kids cable car that whisks you to the top of nearby Cannon Mtn. ☎ 603-823-8800; www.cannonmt .com; Exit 34B, Rte 93, Franconia; round-trip adult/child $12/9; ☽ 9am-5pm, May-Oct

Clark's Trading Post

A steam locomotive and a screaming, scooter-riding Wolfman are all popular attractions at this over-the-top tourist trap. Not everyone's cup of tea, black bears also perform here. ☎ 603-745-8913; www .clarkstradingpost.com; 110 US-3, Lincoln; admission $15; ☽ 10am-5pm, later in summer; ♿

Flume Gorge

A beautiful river and 90ft cliff walls plus a sturdy walkway make this a must-see, but arrive early to beat the bus tours. ☎ 603-745-8391; www.visitnh.gov/flume/; Rte 3, Franconia; adult/child $12/8; ☽ 9am-5pm, May-Oct

Mt Washington Auto Road

Built in the 1860s with blood, sweat and lots of black powder, the auto road remains one of the most popular ways to reach the peak. ☎ 603-466-3988; www.mountwashington autoroad.com; Rte 16, Pinkham Notch, Gorham; car & driver/child 5-12/extra adult $20/5/7; ☽ 8am-5pm May-Oct, hours vary seasonally

Old Man of the Mountain

Lost but not forgotten, this much-beloved state symbol site offers a fitting tribute and hope for the future. ☎ 603-271-3556; Profile Ice Cream Shop, Rte 93, Exit 34B, Franconia; admission free; ☽ 9am-5.30pm

Sabbaday Falls Trail

Beautiful hike to a scenic waterfall that offers a great introduction to the wonders of New Hampshire mountain trails in a 10-minute walk. Park admission $3; ☽ dawn-dusk

Sherman Adams Summit Building

The majestic views from the observatory here, site of the strongest-ever recorded wind gust, can't be beat. ☎ 603-356-2137; www.mountwashington.org; Mt Washington Summit; ☽ 8am-6pm, May-Oct, hours are weather dependent

EAT

Common Man

Uncommonly good food in a relaxed atmosphere, pulling in crowds from miles away. ☎ 603-745-3463; www.thecman.com; 10 Pollard Rd, Lincoln; mains $15-20; ☽ 3pm-11pm

Libby's Bistro

Old bank building with drop-your-fork goodness, served with style and smiles. ☎ 603-466-5330; www.libbysbistro.net; 115 Main St, Gorham; mains $15-25; ☽ high season 5.30pm-close Wed-Sat, low season 5.30pm-close Fri & Sat

White Mountain Cider Company

Great fresh doughnuts, gourmet locavarian dining, and yes, of course, cider in season. ☎ 603.383.9061; www.whitemountain cider.com; Rte 302, Bartlett; mains $18-25; ☽ 5pm-9pm, Thu-Sat

SLEEP

Dana Place Inn

Centrally located and happy to please, the Dana Place Inn also offers lots for children, including special lunches and activities lists. ☎ 800-537-9276; www.danaplace.com; 1143 Rte 16, Jackson; r $159-225; ♿

Franconia Inn

Elegant B&B with pool and great views of the surrounding hills, and a big porch for setting on as you watch the world go by. ☎ 800-473-5299, 603-823-5542; www.franconiainn.com; Easton Rd, Franconia; r with/without breakfast $135/115

Franconia Notch Motel

Cozy cabins and convenience at a great price make this place a perfect spot to stay, especially for couples with kids or pairs of travelers who each want a separate room. ☎ 800-323-7829, ☎ 603-745-2229; www.franconianotch.com; 572 Rte 3, Lincoln; r motel/cottage $65/80; 🚻

Top Notch Inn

No moose allowed at this pet-friendly, spic-and-span motel and B&B. ☎ 800-228-5496, ☎ 603-466-5496; www.topnotchinn.com; 265 Main St, Gorham; r $79-149; 🚻 🐾

Zealand Campground

First-come, first-served at these spacious, secluded, rustic riverside sites near the Trestle Trail. ☎ 603-536-1310; Rte 302, Zealand Rd, Twin Mountain; sites $16, extra car $5; 🗓 May-Oct; 🚻 🐾

USEFUL WEBSITES

www.visitnh.gov
www.visitwhitemountains.com

LINK YOUR TRIP

www.lonelyplanet.com/trip-planner

Antique Alley

WHY GO If you swoon when you enter a musty attic or show up at yard sales hours before the real birds have even begun to get the worms, then you'll love Antique Alley, where a lifetime's worth of everything "vintage" awaits – all of it wonderously well worn.

You could do this trip in a day, or even an afternoon, but why hurry? Pick up a copy of the very useful directory of New Hampshire Antiques Dealers and your favorite well-thumbed appraisal book and start bargain hunting. The stores themselves vary so widely from one to the next that there's really no "perfect" store – it all depends on what you're looking for, what you like and how much cash you're willing to part with to take something home.

Despite the constant visitors, the paucity of lodgings means slim pickings, but one of the nicest is the historic **❶ Three Chimneys Inn**, a two-building inn and tavern that has retained many of the antique touches, though certain amenities such as Jacuzzis and TVs are decidedly modern. The inn sits atop a knoll overlooking the Oyster River, with large white pines and even a cemetery on the grounds. A stay here may even include a visit from "Hannah," the inn's resident wandering spirit. The **❷ ffrost Sawyer Tavern** has hearty fare for those souls still wandering on this side of the River Styx.

Friendly, family-owned **❸ RS Butler's Trading Company** is as good a place to start off as any, and you'll be able to find one of the four owners right there behind the cash register if you've got questions. Located in an attractive pink barn right off Rte 4, this smorgasbord of antiques has something for everyone. Items are arranged roughly by style so, for example, there's a 1950s-era room with chrome stools and toys, and a china room with enough cups, plates, and saucers to

TIME
1 – 2 days

DISTANCE
25 miles

BEST TIME TO GO
Year-round

START
Northwood

END
Chichester

ALSO GOOD FOR

ROUTE

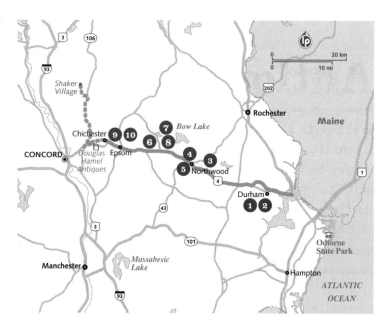

make a museum envious. There's even a route through the barn you can take if you want to be sure to see every nook and cranny.

Only a few moments away on the right (heading toward Concord) is ❹ **Evans & Wright at the Eagle**, also family owned. This "country store" setup (no, not original, it just looks that way) offers you the chance to see many of the antiques and decorations as they may have once been used. Civil War buffs will want to swing by for a gander, though there's more here than just 1860s memorabilia.

For delicious organic and vegetarian delights, stop at ❺ **Susty's**, a simple, no-frills café at the intersection of Rte 4 and Rte 43. Smoothies (though small for the price) are a sublime way to beat the heat. They also have a variety of tasty treats behind glass, many of which can be snagged for the road, and in-season fruit or produce.

"...chairs seem to be standing at attention like tired troops listening to a sarge."

Open "by chance or by appointment," the ❻ **Betty House** is off the beaten track, down a pretty country side road with fallow fields, forests, and (if you're lucky) bright blue sky overhead. An almost awe-inspiring collection of furniture and tools lines the walls, floor to ceiling...and then some. The barn seems more like a storehouse than a store – be sure to go through to the back then look toward the door, where hundreds of chairs seem to be standing at attention like tired troops listening to a sarge.

7 **Meadow Farm B&B** is a bright, quaint, cozy 1700s-era colonial with chickens scratching in the shade of giant maple trees. Flowers of all sorts, and roses in particular, spill out from the various gardens, and the hewn beams and original paneling make this a treat for anyone with a taste for what's old. And where else are horses welcome? Bring your own and have a dressage lesson out in the pasture.

If you're traveling with kids, a stay at **8** **Lake Shore Farm** may be just what the doctor ordered. As the name says, this rambling old farmhouse is right on the lake and specializes in family-style getaways. The rates include not one, not two, but three full meals. Rooms vary in size but have simple furniture and carpeted floors.

ASK A LOCAL

Heading off on a road trip and need a cash injection to fund it? Get that knick-knack you've had forever valued...you could just find yourself holding a small fortune disguised as a rather ugly pot pourri holder. Carla Penfield of RS Butler's Antiques explains how valuing works: "There are several values to an antique piece: retail value, wholesale value, and insurance value. Most antique dealers are interested in buying at a wholesale price so they can add their profit. You're best off getting an appraiser who charges by the hour."

9 **Landmark Furnishings**, after the Epsom traffic circle, is where you should go to find fine-quality replicas so your teething puppy won't leave its signature in that priceless Windsor chair. DR Dimes antique reproductions look so much like real antiques that many amateurs will have a hard time noticing the difference. Not for everyone, but for those with puppies who like wood...this could be an heirloom-saver.

Right next door you'll find friendly **10** **Keepers Antiques**, a clean, well-lit place with a collection of mainly colonial era items. Decoys watch demurely from their perches, brass telescopes sit atop antique dressers in a

DETOUR

Only 14 miles away from Chichester is the **Shaker Village**, where you'll find hand-crafted items ranging from chairs and furniture to curios and children's toys. The Shakers are still crafting these interesting items, but **Douglas Hamel Antiques** (www.shakerantiques.com) specializes in Shaker antiques. His hours vary, so set something up via his website prior to stopping by.

way that suggests a stately living room. The four owners are very active in the dealing circuits and are happy to offer advice for shoppers, be they newbies or old-timers.

Ray Bartlett

TRIP INFORMATION

GETTING THERE

Follow Rte 4 out of Portsmouth for 23 miles and you'll be in Northwood, the start of "Antique Alley" proper.

DO

Betty House

A beautiful old barn filled with chairs, hand tools, furniture and garden items. And did we mention chairs? ☎ 603-736-9087; 105 North Road, Epsom; ☽ by chance or appointment

Evans & Wright at the Eagle

The old-time country-store setup here will make you feel like you've stepped into yesteryear. ☎ 603-942-5020; 194 Rte 4, Northwood; ☽ 10am-5pm

Keepers Antiques

A clean store with lots of Colonial-era items to choose from, arranged a bit like a tastefully furnished living room. ☎ 603-798-3399; www.keepersantiques.biz; 114 Rte 4, Chichester; ☽ 9am-4pm Wed-Sat, 12-4pm Sun

Landmark Furnishings

Primarily offers a variety of antique replicas, many of which are on display. Custom orders can be made to suit your needs. ☎ 114 Rte 4, Chichester; ☽ 10am-4pm Mon-Sat, noon-4pm Sun

RS Butler's Trading Company

Great selection in a multiroom, multiperiod family-owned shop. ☎ 603-942-8210; 102 Rte 4, Northwood; ☽ 10am-5pm Wed-Mon Apr-Nov, hours vary seasonally

EAT

ffrost Sawyer Tavern

Varnished wood and ample room make this pub a good spot for washing down good grub with a pint or two. ☎ 603-868-7800; www.threechimneysinn.com; 17 Newmarket Rd, Durham; mains $25-30; ☽ 11:30am-2:30pm Tue-Sat, 5pm-9pm daily

Susty's

Slightly pricey but oh-so-good, with organic and sustainably produced items in a very casual café. ☎ 603-942-5862; 159 Rte 4, Northwood; mains from $6; ☽ 11am-3pm Mon-Wed, 11am-9pm Thu-Sat, 9am-3pm Sun

SLEEP

Lake Shore Farm

Fun for the whole family in a relaxing, summer-camp–style setting, right on the lake. The tariff includes three meals per day. ☎ 603-942-5921; www.lakeshorefarm.com; 275 Jenness Pond Rd, Durham; r from $112; ⛲

Meadow Farm B&B

Flowers, chickens, and – if you bring your own horse – dressage lessons at this cozy, country-style B&B. ☎ 603-942-8619; www.bbonline.com/nh/meadowfarm/; 454 Jenness Pond Rd, Northwood; r $80-110; ❀

Three Chimneys Inn

Beautiful 1700s-era inn with luxurious modern touches, a big tavern, and even its own ghost. ☎ 603-868-7800; www.threechimneysinn.com; 17 Newmarket Rd, Durham; r $159-239

USEFUL WEBSITES

www.nhantiquealley.com

LINK YOUR TRIP

www.lonelyplanet.com/trip-planner

TRIP

The Lakes Region

WHY GO Nothing symbolizes New Hampshire like Lake Winnipesaukee, whether it be the tackiness of Weirs Beach or a candlelit meal at a lake-view restaurant. Lakes Region local Stephanie Elsener, who tied the knot on a boat here in July 2008, shares some favorite spots in this loop of the Lakes.

TIME
2 days

DISTANCE
99 miles

BEST TIME TO GO
May – Oct

START
Weirs Beach

END
Wolfeboro

Start in wacky ❶ **Weirs Beach** by checking into the ❷ **Lake Winnipesaukee Motel**, a no-frills spot with room decor ranging from red-headed mermaids to whimsical fruits of the sea. The owners are laid-back and friendly, and you can always sneak cookies or candy from the reception desk. Gratis coffee greets you when you wake up. The motel is within walking distance of the various sights and activities below. You'll be able to dive in (literally) to Lake Winnipesauke (watch for rocks!) or wander the Weirs Beach sea of tourist traps, retro diners and ubiquitous souvenir stands. The ❸ **Weirs Beach Water Slides** are fun for everyone; you pay only for the slides and it's good for the whole family, whether sliding or not. There's also minigolf, go-carts and other things to do nearby.

❹ **Kellerhaus**, a Swiss-chalet–style place, is just down the road. Belly up to the weekend Belgian waffle bar (where you can pile the plate high with your choice of fruit, cream, or chocolate toppings) and then at least do some window shopping before you leave – the place is as stuffed with souvenirs as your stomach will be after you leave the buffet.

Always crowded, you'd expect ❺ **Donna Jean's Diner** to be just another service-with-a-snarl diner, but it rises above the rest and is a great place for good eats, with stick-to-your-ribs American breakfasts. Parking can be a bit crazy, especially during the Laconia Bike Week when there's more beards, chrome and black leather to make even ZZ Top feel wanting, but you can't beat the atmosphere.

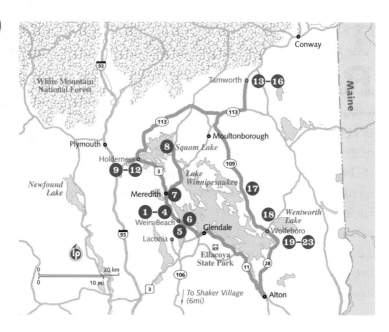

There are boat rides, lakeside attractions and fireworks to watch from the pier, and what could be better than catching a good ole drive-in movie at the **6 Weirs Drive-In**. Opened in 1949 and continually operating since then, the WDI has become a revered institution. For locals and tourists alike, summers in the Lakes just aren't complete without a flick, some nacho cheese goo and thou. One can only wonder how many of us might never have been conceived were it not for venerable drive-in theatres like the WDI.

For dinner away from the tacky Weirs Beach environment, you can't do better than **7 Abondante** in Meredith, where you'll find cheerful staff, copper-clad tables, candlelight, and dishes so good you'll wish you lived here. Abondante features local produce, be it fresh scallops or greens from a nearby farmers market, and has wonderful Italian wines. Artichokes in lemon egg-batter speak perfectly of "summer," as does the warm mussel salad, perfectly cooked, topped with slices of ripe orange. Yum!

Follow Rte 25 to **8 Squam Lake**, the most remote and wild of the Lakes Region water bodies. The road gets wild, the forests denser, and birders will want to keep the binoculars at the ready, as sightings of warblers, finches and a variety of waterfowl are common.

For a close-up of local fauna try the **9 Squam Lakes Natural Science Center** – they offer tours of the lake, demonstrations and activities, and there's a big zoo in the back where you can see exhibits of local wildlife. All of the cages are big and done in keeping with the animals' natural habitat.

In ❿ **Holderness**, you'll find a bit of civilization again, but it's the complete antithesis of the Weirs Beach attitude. The site of the movie *On Golden Pond*, Squam Lake and Holderness remain placid and peaceful, perfect for a pair of waders and fly-fishing, or for plopping your butt in a beach chair and soaking up the sun. If you hike in the shady forests you'll frequently surprise deer, moose, or even a black bear or two.

Bringing home the bacon takes on a whole new meaning at the **Fox Country Smoke House** (http://oldehousesmokehouse.com), where you can snag hand-cured bacon, smoked trout, salmon, and cheese at this family-built, almost creepy stone smoker. Be sure to ask for a quick tour, which will show both the original hand-built section and the more modern part. You can even bring your own pig! Head down Rte 106 to the Shaker Village and follow the hand-lettered signs.

The elegant ⓫ **Manor on Golden Pond**, an estate-turned-hotel in Holderness, has a stunning lobby that seems done with New Hampshire autumn in mind – greens and golds and maroons. The rooms have stately decks and gorgeous views, and most have fireplaces that help turn a chilly evening into a cozy one.

For provisions, head to the ⓬ **Holderness General Store** where, tucked behind things like rope, tire chains, beach chairs, kerosene and bug repellent, you'll find an awesome deli with fresh baked, multigrain breads, Boursin spreads and a list of sandwich options as long as your arm.

From there, teeny ⓭ **Tamworth**, 30 minutes northeast of Moultonborough on Rtes 25 and 113, is so quaint you expect to see hitching posts instead of parking spaces. Forget about stoplights – the main intersection here doesn't even have a stop sign, and there's a relaxed, this-is-how-it-should-have-been vibe that will make you want to sit down in the nearest rocking chair, grab a pitcher of lemonade and watch the world go by. Locals don't quite greet you with a drawling "Howdy, paaardner," but it's pretty close. The church here seems plucked straight out of a frontier movie set, as do some of the locals. There's a general store with everything you might need, from tools to toiletries, and, right next to it, the ⓮ **Other Store**, where the ⓯ **Daley Cafe** offers a selection of sweets, as well as freshly made coffee, soups and sandwiches. It's the kind of place where if you notice the coffee's getting low you can just pull out the grounds and make a new pot yourself. And where else can you find bulk Gummy Bears that cost only 25 cents per scoopful?

"Where else can you find bulk Gummy Bears that cost only 25 cents per scoopful?"

Right next door is the ⑯ **Remick Country Doctor Museum & Farm**, where you can step back into yesteryear and see what life as a rural doctor was like. House calls and influenza epidemics were all part of the territory. In addition to exhibits, the museum hosts a wide variety of seasonal events, such as maple sugaring in spring or apple cidering in fall.

Following Rte 109 south, you'll come to ⑰ **Abenaki Tower**: an 80ft, osprey's-eye view of the lake and mountains that's well worth the short hill climb and the many flights of stairs. There's something almost holy about looking out over the vast blue of Winnipesauke, and chances are you'll have the tower all to yourself. Bring a picnic lunch or a few blank postcards, don't forget the camera and, in season (which is just about year-round), the mosquito repellent.

Further down the road the ⑱ **New Hampshire Boat Museum** celebrates vessels in style. The building has a hokey but fun mural on the bow-shaped front door, and inside you'll find lots of exhibits about boats and their history, and in summer there are even boat-building classes where kids can try their hand at making a watercraft.

BIKE WEEK IN LACONIA

If black leather jackets, skimpily covered cleavage and more "hawgs" (read: Harley-Davidson motorcycles) than you can count get your engine running, don't miss Laconia during Bike Week in late June. Where else can you see gals old enough to be your grandmother decked out in black leather bras, hugging the trunk of a boyfriend who weighs as much as his Harley does? Revelry ranges from mild to wild – fist fights and (unsanctioned) nudity are all part of the spectacle.

Finishing up the trip on the other side of the lake from Weirs Beach, you'll come to the self-proclaimed "Oldest Resort in America," ⑲ **Wolfeboro**, It's worth stopping and taking a few hours to wander here: the waterfront is picturesque and there are lots of free concerts and music/art events so there's a good chance something will be on when you stop by. ⑳ **Mise En Place**, with its minimalist decoration and its nice three-table patio outside, is a wonderful spot for lunch or dinner, but reservations are almost always required. Right in the center is ㉑ **Bailey's Bubble**, which has giant ice-cream cones and shakes. Get a cone and then walk along the lakeshore until it's gone. ㉒ **Hampshire Pewter** has all kinds of gleaming metal goodies, from traditional tankards to crèche scenes, and tours show you how these items are made. ㉓ **Tuc' Me Inn** is in a beautiful 1850s-era building run by a friendly couple. Rooms are cosy with Colonial-style quilts and lots of cushions, and some have four-post beds. The inn serves full breakfasts and has a big common area and it's just a short walk from the center of Wolfeboro.

Ray Bartlett

TRIP INFORMATION

GETTING THERE
Follow I-93 north from Boston to Rte 104 then head east. The trip takes about two hours.

DO

Hampshire Pewter
Fine crafted pewterware and tours at this Wolfeboro factory, which makes everything from baby spoons to ale tankards. ☎ 603-366-4723; www.hampshirepewter.com; 43 Mill Street, Wolfeboro; tour free; ☽ store 9am-5pm Mon-Sat, tours hourly 10am-3pm Mon-Fri

Kellerhaus
Souvenirs galore at this tasty waffle buffet and ice-cream chalet, a feast for both the eyes and the belly. ☎ 603-366-4466, 1-888-557-4287; www.kellerhaus.com; 259 Rte 3, Weirs Beach; ☽ 10am-10pm daily Jun-Sep, 10am-6pm Wed-Mon Sep-Jun; ♿

New Hampshire Boat Museum
Fun exhibits and lots of nautically related activities at this small but sincere museum; especially good for kids. ☎ 603-569-4554; www.nhbm.org; 397 Center St, Wolfeboro Falls; adult/child $5/free; ☽ 10am-4pm Mon-Sat, 12noon-4pm Sun, Memorial Day-Columbus Day; ♿

Remick Country Doctor Museum & Farm
Real country life required real country doctors, and you can get great glimpses of what that entailed, as well as learn about the personal lives of the Remick doctors. ☎ 603-323-7591, 1-800-686-6117; www.remick museum.org; 58 Cleveland Hill Rd, Tamworth; admission $3; ☽ 10am-4pm Mon-Sat, hours vary seasonally; ♿

Squam Lakes Natural Science Center
Great activities and lots of animal exhibits at this modern, well-kept nature center. Don't miss the zoo out the back where bears, raccoons, eagles and more are on display.

☎ 603-968-7194; www.nhnature.org; 23 Science Center Rd, Holderness; adult/child $13/9; ☽ 9:30am-4:30pm daily May 1-Nov 1

Weirs Beach Water Slides
Slip-sliding fun for the whole family, especially since there's no general entry fee — you only pay for the rides themselves. ☎ 603-366-5161; www.weirsbeach.net/waterslide .html; Rte 3, Weirs Beach; 2 hr/one day $21/25; ♿

Weirs Drive-In
Four screens show double features at this rain-or-shine, much-loved Weirs Beach tradition, which first opened up almost a century ago. ☎ 603-366-4723; www.weirsbeach.net/drivein.html; 76 Rte 3, Weirs Beach; adult/child $8.50/free, 2 adults minimum; ☽ from 7pm; ♿

EAT

Abondante
Excellent ambience matches the great food and sweet staff at this candlelit, copper-clad Italian place. ☎ 603-279-7177; www .abondantenh.com; 30 Main St, Meredith; mains from $15; ☽ 5-9pm Wed-Sun

Bailey's Bubble
Big cones and small prices make this ice-cream shop a must stop for cone lovers and you can go from there to the waterfront. ☎ 603-569-3612; www.baileysbubble.com; Railroad Ave, Wolfeboro; cones from $3; ☽ 11am-10pm daily; ♿

Daley Cafe
Inside the Other Store, this one-person café is both casual and tasty, and it's a good spot to chew the fat with locals. ☎ 603-323-8872; 77 Main St, Tamworth; mains from $5; ☽ 8am-8pm Tue-Sat

Donna Jean's Diner
Service with a smile at this bustling biker favorite. Expect crowds and chrome during Bike Week and cycles any time of year. ☎ 603-366-5996; 1208 Weirs Blvd, Weirs Beach; mains from $7; ☽ 6am-close Mon-Sat, 6am-1pm Sun; ♿

Holderness General Store
Old times don't seem so far away when you step inside this everything-you-could-possibly-want country store. ☎ 603-968-3446; 863 Rte 3, Holderness; sandwiches from $6; ⏰ 7am-9pm

Mise En Place
Prepare to part with your pennies at this fine, tasteful and tasty Wolfeboro dining option. Patio seating is perfect on sunny afternoons. ☎ 603-569-5788; 96 Lehner St, Wolfeboro; mains from $20; ⏰ 11:30am-2pm Mon-Fri, 5-8pm Mon-Sat

SLEEP

Lake Winnipesaukee Motel
Simple motel in Weirs Beach, right on Lake Winnipesaukee, with cute, individually decorated rooms and free coffee in the morning. ☎ 603-366-5502; www.lakewinnipesau keemotel.com; 350 Rte 3, Weirs Beach; r $49-98; ⚷

Manor on Golden Pond
Private beach access and cozy fireplaces are just two of the amenities that this opulent option has for those with bling to fling. ☎ 800-545-2141; www.manorongolden pond.com; 31 Manor Dr, Holderness; r $200-500

Tuc' Me Inn
As charming as the name, this family-owned inn is close to Wolfeboro center and a nice spot for those who don't want a motel. ☎ 603-569-5702; www.tucmeinn.com; 118 Main St, Wolfeboro; r $135-175

USEFUL WEBSITES
www.visitnh.gov
www.thelakesregion.org

LINK YOUR TRIP
www.lonelyplanet.com/trip-planner

TRIP

Conway Scenic Railroad

WHY GO Head for the hills in style with these old engines of yesteryear. Four trains with restored vintage railcars so lustrous that they'd make even Pullman himself beam with pride chuff and whistle through verdant forests, over rushing rivers and past waving locals.

For anyone whose heart skips a beat when they hear that distinctive whistle, the **1** Conway Scenic Railroad will be a treat you'll remember for a lifetime, but you'll want to do it right and part of that means not missing the train. You're best off staying the night in the North Conway area. **2** Wildflowers Inn B&B has stunning views of the valley and (in season) gorgeous wildflower fields, with cozy rooms and a wide, flower-festooned porch for settin' on, and the hot tub makes it all the harder to leave. For motel-style overnights even closer to the depot and right in the center of North Conway, head to the **3** Colonial Motel. The pool is perfect for watching the sunset, and free coffee in the morning helps make sure you catch the train on time.

If you've time before boarding for a brewski you can't do better than the **4** Moat Mountain Smokehouse & Brewery. Try a sampler if you're not sure what you'll like best, or sip a seasonal brew like blueberry ale. If you like what you're tasting, they sell it in growlers or 5-gallon jugs to take home. They even have a few rooms available upstairs, making for an easy commute between your brews and your bed.

If it's too early to punish your liver, the **5** Stairway Cafe, directly opposite the depot, offers freshly brewed cups of joe along with hearty breakfasts and lunches. Look for it on the second floor, and if you're lucky, snag a balcony seat so you can watch the world go by as you munch your meal.

TIME
2 days

DISTANCE
27 miles

BEST TIME TO GO
Jun – Oct

START
North Conway

END
North Conway

ALSO GOOD FOR

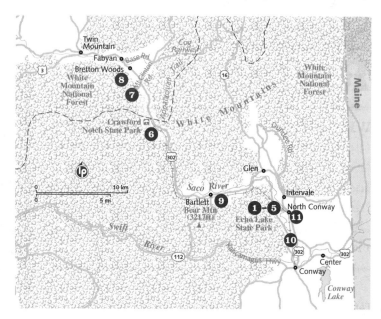

If you can, take the **6 Notch Train**, the railroad's longest and most scenic trip. You'll start by pulling out of the depot to the clack of the wheels and the whoooo-whooooooo of the whistle, and in minutes you'll be crisscrossing the Saco, East Branch and Ellis Rivers. The views include forests, train trestles and the occasional backyard. Past Bartlett, you'll be able to peer down at the rushing river or gasp in awe as the train makes its vertiginous way over the trestles. Those with a fear of heights may want to reach for the rosary, but it's worth it: as the train climbs higher, the cliffs get steeper and the white, silk-like ribbons of water over the rocks will take your breath away.

> *"The train climbs higher, the cliffs get steeper and the white ribbons of water take your breath away."*

If you're a shutterbug, try to travel in good weather, because on sunny days they attach the Open Coach car, a restored Pullman with bench seats and no windows, meaning you can lean out (be careful!) and snap much better shots than you could if you were stuck inside the train. Other seating options include indoor coach and first class, where you can choose either the futuristic Dome car, where you view the entire panorama through a plastic bubble, or the CP Reed car. Both were used in the 1950s for passenger transport through the United States and Canada and have been "reborn" here in North Conway.

At the **7 Crawford Notch summit**, you'll have 50 minutes to take photos, stretch your legs, or meander over to the **8 Highland Lodge**, where you can peruse the gift shop or have yourself a meal or malted beverage in the café. It's not fancy, but the outdoor patio is a great place to chat with other passengers, or to watch the various hikers coming off the Appalachian Trail.

The Notch and ❾ **Bartlett Train** excursions are identical until the latter stops in Bartlett. Check with the conductor to see if time permits a walk along the river bank – beautiful at any time of year, but especially so when the leaves are turning color.

If time is of the essence and you can't take the Notch Train but can't bear not to ride it somehow, there's the far less scenic ❿ **Conway Train**, a 55-minute round-trip from North Conway to Conway. You'll see mainly fields and backyards – none of the grandeur of the Notch trip, but it's a fun taste of train travel and you don't have to spend all day.

Last but not least, those who really want to do it in style can book their passage in the ⓫ **Dining Car "Chocorua."** Tuck your starched white nap-

ELEPHANT ROCK

At **Crawford Notch**, look down the valley from the depot and you'll see **Elephant Rock** on the left side – an elephantine hunk of granite visible right near the highway. The very sprightly can hit the ground running and hike up to the top and back in under 50 minutes, a great glimpse of what longer hikes hold. Just don't be late – it's a long hike back to North Conway if you're still in the woods when the "All Aboard" whistle blows.

kin under your chin and belly up to the table for travel in style. You'll have all the luxuries of a full liquor license and a full meal, and in a nice touch that hearkens back to train travel days of old, tables of two may be seated together – forcing you to meet some strangers and possibly make new friends. You may not find yourself across from Cary Grant or Eva Marie Saint, but it will still be fun.

Ray Bartlett

ROUTE

TRIP INFORMATION

GETTING THERE
From Boston, take I-95 N to Portsmouth, then follow Rte 16. It's about 140 miles or 3 hours to North Conway.

DO

Bartlett Train
This 1¾-hour trip goes from North Conway to Bartlett before turning around. ☎ 603-356-5251, 1-800-232-5251; www.conwayscenic.com; 38 Norcross Circle, North Conway; adult/child $21/14; ☽ daily, departures times vary; 🚼 🐾

Conway Scenic Railroad
Hop aboard these vintage trains for an engineer's view of New Hampshire's best scenery. ☎ 603-356-5251 or 1-800-232-5251; www.conwayscenic.com; 38 Norcross Circle, North Conway; ☽ 8:30-5pm daily; 🚼 🐾

Conway Train
The shortest and least scenic of the trips, this 55-minute zip connects North Conway to neighboring Conway. ☎ 603-356-5251, 1-800-232-5251; www.conwayscenic.com; 38 Norcross Circle, North Conway; adult/child $13/10; ☽ daily, departures times vary; 🚼 🐾

Dining Car "Chocorua"
Lunch and dinners by sunset are possible in this restored dining car, which gives you a taste (pun intended) of train travel of yesteryear. ☎ 603-356-5251 or 1-800-232-5251; www.conwayscenic.com; 38 Norcross Circle, North Conway; adult/child lunch $39/29 dinner $56/42; ☽ 11:30 & 6pm daily; 🚼

Notch Train
Chuff and chug through gorges, over rivers, through forests and past backyards up to Crawford Notch. ☎ 603-356-5251, 1-800-232-5251; www.conwayscenic.com; 38 Norcross Circle, North Conway; adult/child $44/28 ☽ daily, departures times vary; 🚼 🐾

EAT

Moat Mountain Smokehouse & Brewery
Popular spot to quench your thirst or grab a bite, with a few rooms as well for those who want it all in one package. ☎ 603-356-6381; www.moatmountain.com; 3378 White Mountain Hwy, North Conway; beers from $4; ☽ 11:30am-close Tue-Sun

Stairway Cafe
Snug little coffee and brunching spot directly across from the train depot. ☎ 603-356-5200; 2649 White Mountain Hwy, North Conway; mains from $9; ☽ 7am-3pm daily

SLEEP

Wildflowers Inn B&B
Gorgeous vistas, Jacuzzi and friendly owners make this a top stop for an overnight. ☎ 603-356-7567; www.wildflowersinn.com; 3486 White Mountain Hwy, North Conway; r $75-210

Colonial Motel
Clean and cheap with a nice pool, this motel is a great central stop for those on a budget. ☎ 603-356-5178; www.thecolonialmotel.com; 2431 White Mountain Hwy, North Conway; r $45-275

USEFUL WEBSITES
www.conwayscenic.com

LINK YOUR TRIP

www.lonelyplanet.com/trip-planner

Eating Portsmouth & the Seacoast

WHY GO With diners that draw presidents and restaurants with five-star views of a working seaport, Portsmouth has some of New England's finest fare. Whether you choose a simple plate of succulent fried clams or a juicy filet mignon, you'll wish you had room for more.

Step onto a Portsmouth street and you'll feel a hip, happening, youthful vibe that for a few moments is almost unnerving – streets are clean, people smile at you and even the skate punks make sure they shred where they won't scare anyone. Stay for longer and you start wondering why the rest of the world isn't this way. What other city could get away with having a funky red ant as its central icon in the middle of town? Best of all, from French haute cuisine to blue-collar specials, breakfast to midnight snacks, Portsmouth has everything a hungry stomach could ask for.

Begin your trip where everyone does, at ❶ **Colby's Breakfast & Lunch**, a bustling joint right in the center of town. It's the kind of place where most – if not all – of the waitstaff sport tattoos and piercings in addition to a smile. A multitude of Benedicts await egg lovers, but lighter fare is just as good. Scones, coffee, smoothies or juice round out the selections, but be prepared to wait…out the door, sometimes down the street if it's really busy.

If Colby's is too packed, and it often is, try ❷ **Popovers on the Square**, a few streets away. Like the name suggests, you'll find popovers of all kinds here, including an excellent salmon and herb spread one that will have you reaching for the Portsmouth real estate magazines and planning to set down roots here. Popovers is wide and open, the tables and chairs accented with brushed steel and light wood; one gets the

---

TIME
2 days

BEST TIME TO GO
Year-round

START
Town Center

END
Waterfront

ALSO GOOD FOR

CITY

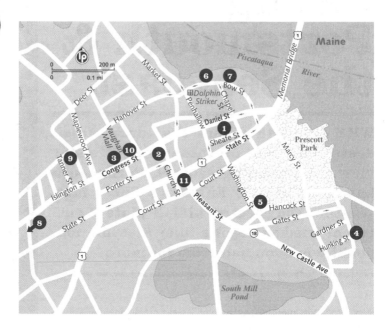

feeling that if Hemingway had happened upon the spot he might have come back with his typewriter to get some writing done here.

It's doubtful you'll have hunger pains yet, but when you do, lunchtime brings a host of great choices, all of them delicious. If you breakfasted at Colby's and then arrive at quirky favorite **3 Friendly Toast** for lunch, it would be easy to assume there's a Portsmouth bylaw stating all waitstaff in the town must have a tattoo. There's a bizarre collection of funky ceramic animals and mannequins crammed into every nook and cranny here. Some of the lampshades are so wild that they may make you wonder if that wacky tabbacy you smoked in the '60s is coming back to haunt you...and then you'll look at the menu and be sure it is: Green Eggs and Ham? (It's delicious.) Eat in or take out, this place has it all: the crunchiest of granolas to the most savory of burgers, and they offer a juicy, succulent portobello option for those who aren't fans of meat. If there's still a line at Colby's you can find solace here – breakfast is served, with pride, all day.

"...that wacky tabbacy you smoked in the '60s is coming back to haunt you..."

Be watched over by photos of George Bush, Mitt Romney and other Republicans at **4 Geno's Chowder & Sandwich Shop.** It's hard to beat the location – so close to the water that they invite you to come in your boat. The chowder is hugely popular, especially with GOP members on the election circuit, but Democrats may not enjoy the beams and grins from the photographs on the walls. And who knows, if it's approaching the New Hampshire primary you may just bump elbows with the next Republican nominee.

From Geno's you're only a few minutes walk from one of Portsmouth's biggest attractions: ❺ **Strawbery Banke**, a living history museum where you can visit numerous houses, talk with Pilgrims and Puritans (just don't ask to borrow their cell phone!) and learn about the curious history of Portsmouth from the 1650s until the present day. This is not a sponsored organization – it grew out of a grassroots desire from Portsmouth citizens and history buffs to preserve and protect a valuable part of the city center. Right nearby, you'll find the Point of Graves burial ground, a fun spot for making wax rubbings or just headstone hunting. Plaques describe several of the more famous people buried here and other tidbits about the headstones.

It's dinner time: this is when the real decisions have to be made. If you're doing this right you've given yourself

RED HOOK BREWERY

Hop out of Portsmouth center and you'll be within stumbling distance of one of New Hampshire's best microbreweries. The tour takes about 20 minutes and is a mix of beer-making info and some really awful puns, but the jokes get better at the end, when pitcher after pitcher of classic and seasonal brews get passed around. This is one tour when you may want to take a taxi – or a designated driver – along. Cheers!

a weekend or longer and can do it all in the fullness of time. If you've only got one day to spend in this taste-o-licious town, your biggest choice will be whether to go with one of America's best views of a working seaport, or to go with some of the tastier but viewless alternates.

It's hard to imagine that a great date could be any better than at a table for two by a window in the ❻ **Wellington Room**. The rough brick walls are intimate and classy, the food is wonderful, but you'll forget about it completely every time you glance outside. Your meal might include a perfect spinach and blue cheese soup with leeks and sherry, or duck medallions lightly basted with a reduction glaze, but it's impossible not to pause as you eat to watch the soft, rolling currents of the ever-changing Piscataqua, the tugboats pushing barges, the sailboats slipping dockside as the sun goes down – it's gorgeous. You do pay for the view, but it's well worth the splurge. Add a bottle of wine, a loaf of bread and thou…one couldn't ask for a more perfect meal. If you've still got a bit of room for dessert, try the chai sorbet with Chantilly cream. Then roll yourself outside and take a walk along the waterfront until you've digested the meal.

Close to the Wellington Room, in a similar brick building that was once a brewery, you'll find the aptly named ❼ **Bow Street Inn**. This B&B offers rooms with a view (though not all face the seaport) that face each other down a long corridor. The round arches and brick design in the common room where you eat breakfast is evidence of the building's brewery past. Due to smallish windows the views are less than what they could be, but it remains a top spot for anyone with a yen for the waterfront.

DETOUR If you're not prone to seasickness (it would be a shame to waste that delicious breakfast you just ate) then a trip out to the **Isle of Shoals** may be just the thing for a morning or afternoon. Trips take you out through the Piscataqua River to the Isles, a beautiful boat ride and the only way to view the Shoals. Birders will want to bring binoculars and keep their eyes peeled for pelagic species.

For the full B&B experience slip the shackles of the town center and head out to Islington St, only a few minutes drive away. The lemon-yellow **8 Martin Hill Inn** offers beautiful rooms decorated in lace and linens, a stately garden shaded by majestic maple, beech and ash trees, and a multilingual host (test her Spanish or Japanese) who bakes cookies for you to munch on in the afternoon. She's also happy to share restaurant tips or suggest activities. Rooms in this home-away-from-home do not have televisions so as to ensure peace and tranquility for all, but there is wi-fi: for internet junkies the web is just a few clicks away.

Judged on food alone, perhaps the finest restaurant in all of Portsmouth is **9 Café Mirabelle**. Real flowers sit nicely on the starched tablecloth, soft piano music sets the mood and then out comes the menu: the French influence here is clear – succulent escargot, genuine frogs' legs and baked brie; gingered carrot soup with just the right balance of sweetness and spice; a salmon crepe with dill that melts on the tongue. If you're lucky you'll have room for dessert, but don't count on it. Unlike some of the other dining options, Café Mirabelle has no gimmicks, no view to speak of, but dining here will convince you that you've flown to France rather than up I-95.

THE DOLPHIN STRIKER

This restaurant (www.dolphinstriker.com) and tavern's building once housed a brothel at the turn of the century (the 19th century, not this past one!) and, with the heavy beams across the ceiling and the worn wood floors, it has retained a festive tavern feel. Live music livens up the night and those in the know will want to tipple from the extensive wine list as they tap their toes to the tune.

10 Pesce Blue is a hip, minimalist café that brings a whole new meaning to the phrase "dinner by candlelight." Row upon row of votives complement the light of the overheads. A stately floor-to-ceiling wine rack lends authority to the place, as does the polite, professional service from the waitstaff. Some of the items are a bit like tapas – you can pick and choose a few small items rather than a big main dish. But the main course options are hard to resist. The house-cured salmon or rabbit with crimini mushrooms are tempting choices, but the skate wing

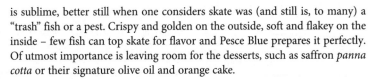

is sublime, better still when one considers skate was (and still is, to many) a "trash" fish or a pest. Crispy and golden on the outside, soft and flakey on the inside – few fish can top skate for flavor and Pesce Blue prepares it perfectly. Of utmost importance is leaving room for the desserts, such as saffron *panna cotta* or their signature olive oil and orange cake.

If you need a nightcap, head to the casual, almost campy ⑪ **Green Monkey**, where you can sip the signature Green Monkey Martini or opt for any of the smooth Spanish wines. The bar stretches most of the way across the restaurant, but there are dinner tables too – Asian pear salad is perfect for anyone looking for a lighter way to end the day. As with many Portsmouth establishments, the Green Monkey uses local produce when possible and sustainable day-boat seafood.

Ray Bartlett

TRIP INFORMATION

GETTING THERE
From Boston, follow I-93 N to I-95, then take I-95 N and follow the Portsmouth exit signs.

DO
Strawbery Banke
Fun living history museum with people dressed in the period costume of centuries ago. ☎ 603-433-1100; www.strawbery banke.org; 14 Hancock St, Portsmouth; adult/child $15/10; ☺ 10am-5pm daily May 1-Oct 31; ☒

EAT
Café Mirabelle
Perhaps the best food in Portsmouth, the understated Café Mirabelle really feels like France. ☎ 603-430-9301; www.cafemirabelle .com; 64 Bridge St, Portsmouth; mains from $18; ☺ 5:15pm-close Wed-Sun

Colby's Breakfast & Lunch
If you're lucky you'll wait in line only for a moment at this packed but worth-the-wait breakfast café. ☎ 603-436-3033; 105 Daniel St, Portsmouth; mains from $7; ☺ 7am-2pm daily

Friendly Toast
Wild, wacky and wonderful, with scrumptious meals with wild names to match the surroundings. ☎ 603-430-2154; 121 Congress St, Portsmouth; mains from $7; ☺ 7am-midnight Mon-Thu, 24hr Fri & Sat, 7am-9pm Sun

Geno's Chowder & Sandwich Shop
Republicans grin from every corner in this down-home chowder stop, a mainstay of the election trail. ☎ 603-427-2070; 177 Mechanic St, Portsmouth; mains from $4; ☺ 8:30am-4pm Mon-Sat

Green Monkey
This funky monkey has a long bar and is popular for dinner or for après-dinner drink. ☎ 603-427-1010; www.thegreenmonkey .net; 86 Pleasant St, Portsmouth; mains from $20; ☺ 5pm-close daily

Pesce Blue
Candlelit to the max, with sublime mains and even better desserts. ☎ 603-430-7766; www.pesceblue.com; 103 Congress St, Portsmouth; mains from $20; ☺ noon-2pm Mon-Fri, 5pm-close daily, 10am-2pm Sun

Popovers on the Square
Great popovers are the star attraction at this well-lit café. ☎ 603-431-1119; www .popoversonthesquare.com; 8 Congress St, Portsmouth; breakfast from $6; ☺ 8am-10pm daily; ☒

Wellington Room
Sublime waterfront views and intimate setting make this a perfect spot to celebrate something special. ☎ 603-431-2989; www .thewellingtonroom.com; 67 Bow St, Portsmouth; mains from $25; ☺ 5pm-close Tue-Sat

SLEEP
Bow Street Inn
Some rooms have great water views and it's in a fantastic central location. ☎ 603-431-7760; www.bowstreetinn.com; 121 Bow St, Portsmouth; r $120-185

Martin Hill Inn
Plush, comfortable and homey with a friendly host…and chocolate chip cookies to snack on. ☎ 603-436-2287; www.martinhillinn.com; 404 Islington St, Portsmouth; r $115-210

USEFUL WEBSITES
www.portsmouthchamber.org

LINK YOUR TRIP

www.lonelyplanet.com/trip-planner

MAINE TRIPS

Known mostly for its stone-strewn shoreline and plethora of frisky moose, Maine is a state of surprising superlatives. Not only is Maine the biggest state in New England, it is also about as large as all the other states combined.

Of course, we've all heard about the mighty Maine lobster – over 90% of the lobsters caught in America are plucked from the state's rocky coast. But as you venture inland through the endless acres of dense forest, you'll uncover the largest crop of blueberries in the nation – Maine produces 99% of the country's little blue fruits. And that's not all: Maine's grand pines (it is known as the Pine Tree State, after all) are felled to make 90% of the United States' total toothpick supply.

 PLAYLIST Although Mainers aren't the biggest chart-toppers, there are some local gems for your ears to feast upon while your eyes take in the scenery out the car window:

- "Dear Mother Ocean," Bruce Thulin
- "Land's End," The String Cheese Incident
- "Collide," Howie Day
- "Hold You in My Arms," Ray Lamontagne
- "How About You?" Johnny Smith
- "Social Quarantine," A Global Threat
- "Salem's Lot," Stephen King (MP3 audio book)

Visitors don't often look past the state's glossy holiday veneer of Cape Cod–style cottages, antiquing and dinner tables toppling over with the daily catch. But the truth is that this sparsely populated state has had a hard-knock life. A step off the tourist track reveals Maine's predominantly blue-collar history of hearty fisherman and lonely lighthouse keepers.

 MAINE'S BEST TRIPS

MAINE TRIPS

Art Appreciation in Portland

WHY GO Art aficionado Daniel Kany has worked in hipster hubs across the US. Now he's back in his home state, and with good reason: Portland is stepping up to bat with plans to hit an artful homerun. So we've created an all-star lineup of activities based on Daniel's insider tips.

In the last decade Portland, Oregon, has risen out of obscurity to become one of the hottest destinations in America. Journalists across the nation have lauded it as the ultimate liberal/green/artsy/boho destination, and trendsetters are lining up like lemmings to visit this hipster promised land. Wait…this is supposed to be about Portland, Maine? Oh. Well, even better! While the west coast Portland has been pushing all the right buttons on the marketing machine, east coast Portland is happily flying under the radar, attracting only the savviest of art oglers.

So, congratulations are in order. If you are reading this then you can officially take your place beside Mondrian, Duchamp, Picasso or any other player in the art world who was well ahead of his time. The spoils of arty Portland are yours for the taking.

A visit to the ❶ **Portland Museum of Art**, near Congress Sq, is a must before one begins a gallery gallivant. This first-rate museum, designed by illustrious architect IM Pei, is the crown jewel of Portland's thriving art scene. The modern gallery spaces feature a slew of notable American artists like Edward Hopper, Rockwell Kent, Andrew Wyeth and Winslow Homer (a Mainer). Be sure to check out the temporary exhibition hall, which usually houses the thematic works of heavy hitters like Georgia O'Keefe.

After exiting the museum, head to ❷ **Susan Maasch Fine Art**. Here visitors will find an impressive assortment of big names like Picasso,

TIME
2 days

DISTANCE
2 miles

BEST TIME TO GO
Jun – Aug

START
Portland

END
Portland

ALSO GOOD FOR

HISTORY & CULTURE

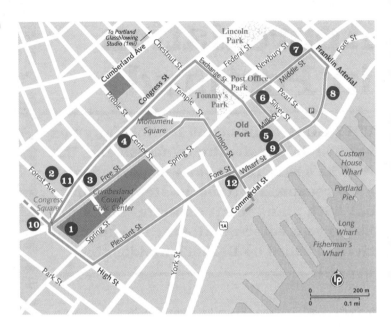

Robert Mapplethorpe and Ansel Adams. Have a chat with the owner and curator, Susan Maasch, who often gives the impression she's had a few espressos before bouncing in to work.

The two ❸ **June Fitzpatrick** galleries are also great spots. The space on High St features only works on paper, and the other space, squished among the storm of competing galleries on Congress St, partially serves the Maine College of Art (MECA). A Londoner by birth, June maintains her British accent with regular trips back to the motherland to run a drawing studio. June brings an old-meets-new vibe to her spaces – don't be surprised to find a clay pot next to a digital process installation piece.

Gallery gurus will relish bopping through downtown Portland, but if you're keen on seeing an artist in his element, then head a mile out of town to the **Portland Glassblowing Studio** (www.portlandglassblowing.com). Here local artist Ben Coombs mesmerizes onlookers as he swirls hot shards of glass into intricate Italianate goblets. It's best to call beforehand and make an appointment.

Stepping off Congress St into ❹ **Whitney Art Works** feels like entering a transporter and being zapped to Soho or Chelsea. This happening space focuses on cutting-edge sculpture, 2D and installation works. But don't be fooled; these bizarre pieces, including sculptures made from books and 'surveillance sandwiches' (you'll see), are the brainchild of local artists.

Continue on Congress St toward the Old Port then head along Exchange St until you reach **5** **Walter's**. Pause for lunch in the narrow storefront-cum-dining-room and taste-test the bouillabaisse or the succulent fish tacos.

One last gallery stop before becoming "art-ed out": **6** **Greenhut Galleries**, Portland's first private gallery and the anchor of the city's progressive art scene. The kind staff at Greenhut curates work in an intimate and friendly place and focuses their efforts on showcasing masterpieces by some of Maine's most accomplished artists, including John Whalley, a favorite among local gallerinas.

DETOUR After appreciating Art with a capital 'A' in its various forms – painting, sculpture and even cuisine – experience the fine art of massage? Day spas have been cropping up all over Portland to sate the recent yuppie influx. Give **Nine Stones** (www.ninestonesspa.com) on 250 Commercial St a whirl, and while you're indulging in a hot-stone massage, check out the interesting array of art adorning the treatment center.

Turn your arty adventure into a complete sensorial experience at **7** **Bresca**, Portland's hottest dining option. The duck breast with nectarines is a local fave, and the chorizo- and gorgonzola-stuffed dates will bring a tear to your eye. Like any other see-and-be-seen joint, this charming, jewel-box-sized restaurant is almost always full (because there are only five tables), so reservations are highly recommended. If you can't score a spot at Bresca, try **8** **Fore St**, which is arguably just as good. Owner and chef Sam Hayward has made apple-wood grilling and roasting his forte. The menu changes nightly, and features the best seasonal fruits of the land and sea, not to mention the most comprehensive wine list in town.

A late-night stroll is an absolute must after gorging on scrumptious fare served in intriguing positive-negative schemes. Casually work off those calories while moseying down **9** **Wharf St** and let the eclectic mix of live music and lounge chatter wash over you. Weekends in the heart of the Old Port bounce with a colorful clash of locals and weekenders, while weekdays tend to be a bit more slow-paced, fostering the ultimate mellow vibe. Sample some chilled-out bluegrass beats at **10** **Local 188** up on Congress St, or loosen your belt (in the name of art, of course) and make room for a heavenly desert at **11** **Five Fifty-Five**.

As the evening comes to a close it's time to retreat back to your wooden four-post bed at **12** **Portland Harbor Hotel** for comfy sleep amid soft linens and fluffy pillows. But don't rest too easy, intrepid traveler; even though your avant-garde adventure is indeed ahead of the curve, you've just started to scratch the surface of the city's hidden boho culture. Hopefully you've planned to stay a second day here in the better of the two Portlands…

Brandon Presser

TRIP INFORMATION

GETTING THERE

Heading north from Boston along I-95, drive two hours until you reach the exit for Portland, around 50 miles after entering Maine.

DO

Greenhut Galleries
The grandpapa of Portland galleries, this space showcases artists from all over Maine. ☎ 207-772-2693; www.greenhutgalleries.com; 146 Middle St; ⏰ 10am-5:30pm Mon-Fri, 10am-5pm Sat

June Fitzpatrick
A hip, white-washed space catering to contemporary painting, sculpture and works on paper. ☎ 207-772-1961; www.junefitzpatrickgallery.com; 112 High St; ⏰ noon-5pm Tue-Sat

Portland Museum of Art
A stunning, first-rate museum designed by the legendary IM Pei. ☎ 207-775-6148; www.portlandmuseum.org; 7 Congress Sq; adult/child $10/4; ⏰ 10am-5pm Tue-Thu & Sun, 10am-9pm Fri

Susan Maasch Fine Art
Features major works of art from Picasso to Ansel Adams. ☎ 207-699-2966; www.susanmaaschfineart.com; 29 Forest Ave; ⏰ 11am-6pm Tue-Fri, 11am-4pm Sat

Whitney Art Works
This smart Chelsea-style space oozes urban sophistication while featuring artists of all media. ☎ 207-774-7011; www.whitneyartworks.com; 492 Congress St; ⏰ noon-6pm Wed-Sat

EAT

Bresca
At this savvy little eatery in the city center, five tables nestle within the candlelit atmosphere. ☎ 207-772-1004; 111 Middle St; meals $18-26; ⏰ dinner Tue-Sat

Five Fifty-Five
One of Portland's best new chefs holds court at this handsome restaurant north of the West End. ☎ 207-761-0555; 555 Congress St; ⏰ dinner daily, brunch Sun

Fore St
This award-winning spot has a dining room of airy, exposed brick and pine paneling that faces an open kitchen. ☎ 207-775-2717; www.forestreet.biz; 288 Fore St; meals $20-31; ⏰ 5:30-10pm Sun-Thu, 5:30-10:30pm Fri & Sat, 5:30-9:30pm Sun Oct-May

Local 188
Fun and funky Local 188 features belle époque lanterns, loads of fluffy pillows and plenty of light. ☎ 207-761-7909; www.local188.com; 685 Congress St; ⏰ 11am-2pm & 5:30-10pm Sun-Thu, 5:30-10:30pm Fri & Sat

Walter's
Portland's best-loved bistro is a narrow storefront dining room with a high ceiling and even higher culinary aspirations. ☎ 207-871-9258; 15 Exchange St; meals $11-23; ⏰ lunch & dinner

SLEEP

Portland Harbor Hotel
A top-notch hotel with a classically coiffed lobby and bright rooms to match. ☎ 207-775-9090; www.portlandharborhotel.com; 468 Fore St; d $300

USEFUL WEBSITES

www.firstfridayartwalk.com
www.galleriesportlandmaine.com

LINK YOUR TRIP

www.lonelyplanet.com/trip-planner

Maine Lobster Tour

WHY GO Maine's amazingly fresh lobster is so ubiquitous that if you ask 10 Mainers where to find the best lobster, you'll probably get 20 different answers. Taste-test your way across the state enjoying the various lobster incarnations: lobster roll, lobster salad and the traditional steamed lobster.

When man ate his first lobster, it was surely an act of desperation. The crops must have failed and the fish stopped biting, so some poor soul was forced to trudge through thick strands of seaweed in search of anything remotely edible. He stuck his hand deep into a dark crevice and pulled out a wretched, googly-eyed creature with pincers wildly waving and furiously snapping shut. Eureka! This ghastly creature is delicious! Who'd have guessed this hideous arachnoid would wind up topping the price lists at fancy restaurants?

As you cross the state line into Maine, signs littered with superlatives crowd the streets attempting to lure those with lobster on the brain. Get some tail at ❶ **Mike's Clam Shack** in Wells. Mike's is definitely a tourist trap (the menus have detailed instructions about tipping in America), but its midsized lobster rolls, with a helping of unusually tasty fries, are delish. Those looking for a side order of sand and sun should try ❷ **Forbes Self Service Restaurant** along Wells Beach. The large, bright-blue-and-yellow hut offers a scrumptious lobster–mayo combo to go, so customers can chow down under the shade of their beach umbrella.

Before venturing deep into the heart of Maine's main lobster territory, make a pit stop in Portland, the state's largest city. The ❸ **Downeast Duck Tours**, aboard an amphibious bus–boat, is a unique way to learn about the region's vivid maritime history. The tour ambles around town then plunges into Casco Bay for a whole different perspective.

TIME
2 – 3 days

DISTANCE
200 miles

BEST TIME TO GO
Year-round

START
Wells

END
Bar Harbor

ALSO GOOD FOR

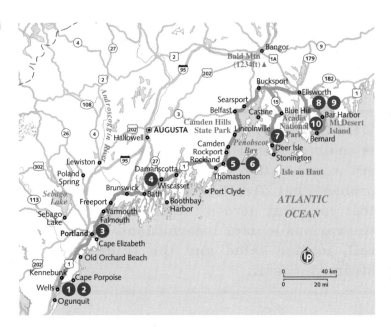

Hop back on Hwy 1 and continue your northward journey in search of an afternoon snack at ❹ **Red's**, in little Wiscasset. The throngs of lip-licking tourists make this wobbly lobster stand very hard to miss. The lobster-roll recipe is simple: take a toasted hot-dog bun and cram it with one lobster's worth of meat. There's a small plastic bowl of melted butter for dipping, and *voilà* – no gobs of mayo, just juicy red meat and a plastic fork shoved in the middle like a pioneer's flag.

A stop in Rockland, further north on Hwy 1, is a must for any true lobster junkie. This little port teems with crustacean-related events throughout the year including lobster-boat racing and the annual Maine Lobster Festival (www.mainelobsterfestival.com). A trip with ❺ **Captain Jack Lobster Boat Adventure** is a great way to get a behind-the-scenes look at lobster hunting in Maine. Spend an hour cruising the open seas on an authentic 30ft lobster boat while Captain Hale hauls his traps. Lunch and dinner cruises are also available for those who want some instant gratification. Sample some exquisitely prepared seafood at Rockland's favorite

YOU'VE GOT MAIL

The times they are a-changin'. Fresh Maine lobster used to be a luxury available only to those who made the pilgrimage. These days you can have the critters delivered to your doorstep with a click of your mouse and a quick call to FedEx. If you're too lazy to get off your keister and taste-test your way up the coast, then get in touch with **Browne Trading** (www.browne -trading.com) or **Maine Lobster Direct** (www .mainelobsterdirect.com).

restaurant, **6 Primo**, if you don't want your dishes rocking back and forth. Feast on modern twists of Italian faves like fresh vine-ripe antipastos and a heavenly espresso dessert float topped with vanilla and chocolate gelato.

To digest the lifetime's worth of lobster consumed earlier on in the day, settle for the night at the handsome **7 Pilgrim's Inn**, on the rugged, rock-strewn shores of Deer Isle. Built in 1793, the post-and-beam inn offers refined seaside charm in its 12 rooms and cottages.

Start the new day by continuing north to Bar Harbor, on Mount Desert Island (pronounced "dessert," for all you New England neophytes), where you can take a morning ride with the affable Captain John on **8 Lulu Lobster Boat**. Enjoy the postcard-worthy scenery around Acadia National Park while listening to colorful local legends and the faint claw clicking of recently caught creatures. After a tour with Lulu, swing by the **9 Thirsty Whale**, a favorite hangout for local lobstermen. Try an amber brew while eavesdropping on the conversations of gruff sailors as they swap exaggerate stories of whale sightings, rip tides and catching a lobster THIS BIG. For the best lobster on Mount Desert Island, locals turn to **10 Thurston's Lobster Pound** out in Bernard, overlooking Bass Harbor. Park yourself on the rickety plastic patio furniture, strap on a bib and savor some of the juiciest crustaceans around while watching fishing boats unload their daily catch.

Brandon Presser

YOU'VE GOT MALE

Show your skills at the dinner table and wow those surrounding you by identifying the gender of your steamed seafood. The secret lies in the swimmerets (the small, leafy limbs dangling on the underside of the tail). If the first pair of swimmerets are hard, then you've caught yourself a male – female lobsters' swimmerets feel more feather-like.

TRIP 50

TRIP INFORMATION

GETTING THERE
From Boston, take I-95 north, passing the New Hampshire and Maine state lines before arriving in Wells Beach.

DO

Captain Jack Lobster Boat Adventure
Experience life as a lobsterman aboard an authentic downeaster lobster vessel. ☎ 207-542-6852; www.captainjacklobstertours .com; 130 Thomaston St, Rockland; adult/child $25/15; ☽ mid-May–Oct; ♿

Downeast Duck Tours
This 65-minute amphibious bus putters through the Old Port, before plunging into the bay for a waterside tour. ☎ 207-774-3825; www.downeastducktours.com; 177 Commercial St, Portland; adult/child $22/17; ☽ mid-May–mid-Oct; ♿

Lulu Lobster Boat
A tour aboard a traditional lobster boat intermixed with local legends, great photo ops and traps full of lobster. ☎ 207-963-2341; www.lululobsterboat.com; Harborside Hotel and Marina, Bar Harbor; adult/child $27/15; ☽ 8am-8pm May-Oct; ♿

EAT

Forbes Self Service Restaurant
A bright-blue-and-yellow bastion of seafood serving beach bums some of the best lobster around. ☎ 207-646-7620; Wells Beach; lobster roll $15-18; ☽ breakfast, lunch & dinner late May-Aug

Mike's Clam Shack
An institution along the highway, Mike's is a bit touristy but serves up a great lobster roll with a tasty side of French fries. ☎ 207-646-5998; www.mikesclamshack.com; 1150 Post Rd, Wells; lobster roll $13-14; ☽ 11:30am-9:30pm; ♿

Primo
Set in a Victorian home and featuring expertly prepared seafood, Primo remains one of the top restaurants in the Northeast. ☎ 207-596-0700; 2 S Main St (ME 73), Rockland; meals $21-28; ☽ dinner Thu-Mon mid-May–Oct

Red's
A small stand overflowing with hungry tourists yearning for a lobster roll. ☎ 207-882-6128; cnr Main & Water Sts, Wiscasset; lobster roll $16-19; ☽ 11am-11pm Mon-Thu, 11am-2pm Fri & Sat, noon-6pm Sun

Thirsty Whale
Head here to mingle with locals and lobstermen over a pint of ale. ☎ 207-288-9335; 40 Cottage St, Bar Harbor; drinks from $3; ☽ noon-midnight

Thurston's Lobster Pound
Overlooking Bass Harbor in Bernard, this casual waterside spot with superb views serves amazingly fresh lobster. ☎ 207-244-7600; Steamboat Wharf, Bernard; meals $14-22; ☽ noon-8pm late May-Sep

SLEEP

Pilgrim's Inn
Sitting along the Northwest Harbor, this handsome post-and-beam inn was built in 1793 and offers refined seaside charm in its 12 rooms and cottages. ☎ 207-348-6615; www.pilgrimsinn.com; 20 Main St, Deer Isle Village; r with breakfast $99-209

USEFUL WEBSITES
www.meliving.com/lobster/index.shtml
www.visitmaine.com

LINK YOUR TRIP
www.lonelyplanet.com/trip-planner

60 Lighthouses in 60 Hours

WHY GO In the early freight and fishing days of Maine, lighthouses were vital to ship safety. Today, the 60 looming shafts of brick and steel from Kittery to Calais are charming and photogenic reminders of a bygone era.

After eons hidden under thick, frozen sheets of ice, the melting glaciers gave birth to Maine's rugged coastline. The stunning expanse would one day prove to be a big moneymaker for the tourism industry, but first this jagged realm of granite and sand would be a great hazard to the burgeoning community of sailors and fishermen. In order to protect the seamen and their ships from a watery grave, many lighthouses were erected along the coast casting their beams into the night sea. Today, over 60 lighthouses are peppered along the shoreline, and although many of them are no longer in use, they've become monuments to an earlier era and the perfect maritime Kodak moment.

Take a long weekend and wind your way up along the coast from Kittery to Calais clicking your camera at the dozen lights along the shore and the four-dozen lighthouses set adrift in the sea on wee islets. You will also learn about the difficult lives of keepers who sat in the towers all night long making sure the light burned brightly to warn passing ships. It was a lonely and tiresome life – the pay was poor and the extended periods of isolation often led to insanity. Eerie tales of shipwrecks, ghosts and murder will surely add some flavor to the journey.

Below you'll find the names of almost every light in the state, and a handful of other cool things to see along the way.

Start the trip in little Kittery, just over the border from New Hampshire. Here you'll find the first lighthouse on the trip, the ❶ **Whaleback Ledge**. Built in 1831, the light earned its name because it looks like it was constructed on the back of some mammoth sea

TIME
2 – 3 days

DISTANCE
375 miles

BEST TIME TO GO
Sep – Nov

START
Kittery

END
Calais

ALSO GOOD FOR

OUTDOORS

HISTORY & CULTURE

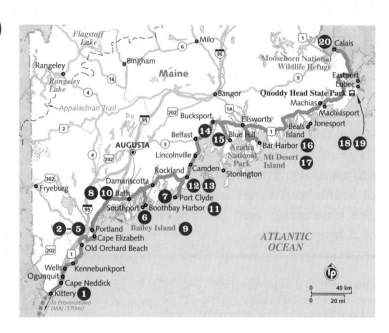

creature. Although it is not possible to visit the light, there are great views from Fort Foster.

As you wander up the coast you'll pass a half-dozen lighthouses before reaching Portland, including Boon Island Light, Cape Neddick (Nubble) Light, Goat Island Light, Wood Island Light, Cape Elizabeth Light and Spring Point Ledge Light. Portland, Maine's largest city and port, is graced with a handful of handsome lights including **2 Portland Breakwater (Bug) Light**, a veritable Greek temple with Corinthian columns, and just outside the city in Cape Elizabeth you will find **3 Portland Head Light**, Maine's oldest functioning lighthouse. During the American Revolution, the town of Cape Elizabeth posted soldiers at a rocky outcropping to warn locals of an eminent attack by the British.

"Today, over 60 lighthouses are peppered along the shoreline... monuments to an earlier era."

Afterwards, a lighthouse was built in the same location and was completed in the winter of 1791. Today, the keeper's house has been passed into service as the **4 Museum at Portland Head Light**, which traces the maritime and military history of the region. There is also a small on-site artist's studio featuring local paintings and photography of the surrounding area's topography.

For a unique vantage point of the bay, try a 90-minute kayak tour with **5 LL Bean**. The tours launch from the port and you can register at their kiosk next to the Portland Lobster Company.

For an eerie tale, make your way to the turtle-shaped Seguin Island to visit a lighthouse with the same name. The state's first offshore station, the ❻ **Seguin Island Lighthouse**, was built to guide sailors through one of the foggiest areas in the country. After months of complaining that there was nothing to do, the keeper's wife convinced her husband to buy her a player piano. Unfortunately, the piano played only one song, which soon drove the keeper crazy. He strangled his wife and took an axe to the baby grand. Locals claim that the creepy tune rides the fog on particularly dismal evenings.

Cross another dozen lighthouses off the list, including Ram Island Ledge Light, Halfway Rock Light, Pond Island Light, Fort Popham Light, Perkins Islands Light, Squirrel Point Light, Doubling Point Light, Kennebec River Range Lights, Cuckold Light (yes, actually named for a man whose wife left him for another lover), Burnt Island Light, Hendricks Head Light, Ram Island Light and Monhegan Island Light. Give yourself some extra time to explore ❼ **Pemaquid Point Light**, Maine's most famous lighthouse after being featured on the front of the special edition Maine quarter. The stone tower was constructed in 1835 and today the keeper's house has been transformed into a small museum and a one-bedroom apartment available for weekly vacation rentals. Don't miss the detailed map of the Maine coast in the museum. This nautical chart features every lighthouse in the state.

SEEN FROM SPACE?

Only a few man-made items on the planet can be seen from space, so would you believe us if we told you that one of Maine's lighthouses could be viewed by extraterrestrials? Well, it's true…sorta. When NASA compiled an image database of photographs from around the world to identify earth should the space shuttle make alien contact, they included a picture of **Nubble Lighthouse** in York.

Sneak back to the industrial town of Bath, home to the ❽ **Maine Maritime Museum & Shipyard**, which preserves the rich tradition of shipbuilding in the Kennebeck region. The museum features mostly paintings and models, but if you check out the Percy & Small Shipyard, you'll find scores of locals working to restore antique watercraft. In the summer, tourists can link up with a three-hour lighthouse tour offered by knowledgeable museum workers. As the evening shadows dance on the bobbing dinghies offshore, venture deep into the Harpswells for a sunset lobster dinner at ❾ **Cook's Lobster House** on Bailey Island. Stay in Bath for the night at ❿ **Popham Beach B&B**, which used to be a US Coast Guard station. Today, the four bright bedrooms sit directly on the sands of Popham Beach.

In the morning, stop in Boothbay Harbor for a leisurely cruise out to the lights on Monhegan Island and Burnt Island with ⓫ **Balmy Days Cruises**. Then, add tick marks to another 10 lights: Franklin Island Light, Marshall

Point Light, Matinicus Light, Tenants Harbor Light, Whitehead Light, Two Bush Island Light, Heron Neck Light, Browns Head Light, Goose Rocks Light and ⓬ **Owls Head Light**, where, according to local legend, the keeper's dog saved the day by continuously barking through a bad storm when the light couldn't penetrate the clouds and the foghorn was broken. Take a well-deserved break in Rockland to check out the ⓭ **Maine Lighthouse Museum**. Perched over Rockland harbor, the museum contains an array of nautical artifacts like lighthouse lights, foghorns and model ships. There's even a hands-on exhibit to keep young ones entertained.

Maine's biggest collection of mariner art and artifacts can be found in Searsport at the ⓮ **Penobscot Maritime Museum**. The center is spread throughout several historical buildings and is a stone's throw from the port to Sears Island, the largest uninhabited island on the East Coast.

"X"-off Rockland Harbor Southwest Light, Rockland Breakwater Light, Indian Island Light, Grindle Point Light, Fort Point Light, Dice Head Light, Eagle Island Light and Blue Hill Bay Light, and continue on to Blue Hill to have a look at the current maritime conditions documented at the ⓯ **Marine Environmental Research Institute**. Members of the institute study the relationship between pollution and marine life. Visitors can learn about MERI's activities in a series of changing exhibitions in the main gallery, often with hands-on exhibits for children. In the summer, a variety of tours taking tourists to small, scrubby islands just off the coast are on offer.

DETOUR ➤ In Provincetown, Massachusetts, you can have the chance to be a lightkeeper while staying at **Race Point Lighthouse** (www.racepointlighthouse .net). This 19th-century lighthouse sits amid unspoiled sand dunes in a remote corner of the National Seashore. Solar energy and gas run the lights and kitchen and your nearest neighbors are miles away…well, unless you count the seals and the dolphins just offshore.

For a look at life along the Maine coast before European colonization, have a peek at the ⓰ **Abbe Museum** in the town of Bar Harbor in Acadia National Park. The fascinating collection of over 50,000 artifacts from Maine's Native American heritage includes pottery, combs and fishing implements that span the last 2000 years. Contemporary pieces include finely wrought woodcarvings, birch-back containers and baskets. Campsites are available around the park on a first-come basis for those who decide to hang their hat for the evening. Lighthouses orbiting Acadia National Park include Burnt Coast Harbor Light, Great Duck Island Light, Baker Island Light and Bear Island Light.

A trip out to ⓱ **Mt Desert Rock Light**, Maine's most remote lighthouse, is not for the faint of heart; it's a challenge even to see this concrete conical shaft from a boat. Located on a scrubby little islet 20 miles from Mt Desert

Island, the lonely light gets battered and beaten throughout the year – even the smaller storms ravage the little island, leaving most of it submerged for the colder months of the year. Despite the harsh weather, the light has been burning strong since 1830.

After Acadia National Park, you've officially entered what Mainers call "Far Down East," a stretch of land far more rugged and unspoiled than any other rocky expanse you've seen thus far. Stop at ⓲ **Quoddy Head State Park**. The 531-acre park boasts a walking trail that passes along the edge of towering, jagged cliffs. The tides here are similarly dramatic, fluctuating 16ft in six hours. Follow the fantastic 4-mile loop trail and keep an eye on the sea for migrating whales (finback, minke, humpback and right whales), which migrate along the coast in the summer. The park also boasts intriguing sub-arctic bogland and the much-photographed red-and-white-banded ⓳ **West Quoddy Light**, built in 1858, which looks like a barber's pole.

After passing the last dozen lighthouses (Winter Harbor Light, Egg Rock Light, Crabtree Light, Prospect Harbor Light, Petit Maman Light, Narraguagus Island Light, Nash Island Light, Moose Park Light, Libby Island Light, Machias Seal Island Light, Little River Light, Lubec Channel Light), end the trip in Calais at ⓴ **Whitlocks Mill Light**, Maine's northernmost lighthouse. After checking off your 62nd lighthouse on the list, have a quick look around the grounds, which kiss the Canadian border.
Brandon Presser

TRIP INFORMATION

GETTING THERE
Follow I-95 north out of Boston and pass through New Hampshire until you reach the exit for Kittery in Maine.

DO

Abbe Museum
This fascinating museum contains a collection of cultural artifacts related to Maine's Native American heritage. ☎ 207-288-3519; www.abbemuseum.org; 26 Mt Desert St, Bar Harbor; adult/child $6/2; ☺ 10am-6pm

Balmy Days Cruises
This outfit takes day-tripping passengers to Monhegan Island and Burnt Island. ☎ 207-633-2284; www.balmydayscruises.com; Pier 8, Boothbay Harbor; adult/child $32/18; ☺ May-Oct

LL Bean
This well-known outfitter offers 90-minute kayak tours around the bay; tours launch from the port. ☎ 207-400-4814; www .llbean.com/ods; 180 Commercial Rd, Portland; adult/child $29/19; ☺ daily Jul & Aug, Sat & Sun Sep

Maine Lighthouse Museum
Collections here include lighthouse artifacts like enormous jewel-like prisms, foghorns, marine instruments and ship models, with hands-on exhibits for children. ☎ 207-594-3301; www.mainelighthousemuseum.com; One Park Dr, Rockland; adult/child $10/free; ☺ 9am-5pm Mon-Fri, 10am-4pm Sat & Sun

Maine Maritime Museum & Shipyard
This museum preserves the Kennec's long shipbuilding tradition. In summer, the museum offers a variety of tours leading out to nearby islands. ☎ 207-443-1316; www .mainemaritimemuseum.org; 243 Washington St, Bath; adult/child $10/7; ☺ 9:30am-5pm

LINK YOUR TRIP
TRIP

Marine Environmental Research Institute
An important center studying the relationship between pollution and marine life. ☎ 207-374-2135; www.meriresearch.org; 55 Main St, Blue Hill; ☺ 9am-5pm Mon-Fri

Museum at Portland Head Light
The keeper's house has been transformed into a museum, which traces the maritime and military history of the region. ☎ 207-799-2661; www.portlandheadlight.com; 1000 Shore Rd, Portland; adult/child $2/1; ☺ 10am-4pm Jun-Oct, 10am-4pm Sat & Sun Apr-May & Nov–mid-Dec

Penobscot Maritime Museum
This superb museum houses Maine's biggest collection of mariner art and artifacts, which are spread through a number of historic buildings. ☎ 207-548-2529; www.penob scotmarinemuseum.org; 5 Church St (US 1), Searsport; adult/child $8/3; ☺ 10am-5pm Mon-Sat, noon-5pm Sun late May-early Oct

Quoddy Head State Park
This 531-acre park boasts a walking trail that passes along the edge of towering, jagged cliffs. ☎ 207-733-0911; 973 S Lubec Rd, Lubec; adult/child $2/1

EAT

Cook's Lobster House
A great spot for some lobster at sunset. ☎ 207-833-2818; 68 Garrison Rd, Bailey Island; mains $12-20; ☺ 11:30am-8pm

SLEEP

Popham Beach B&B
Formerly a US Coast Guard station, this upscale 1880s B&B has four bright rooms directly on the sands of Popham Beach. ☎ 207-389-2409; www.pophambeach bandb.com; 4 Riverview Ave, Phippsburg; r with breakfast $150-215

www.lonelyplanet.com/trip-planner

Down East & Acadia National Park

WHY GO America's first national park on this side of the Mississippi is a rugged hinterland offering the best hikes along the Eastern Seaboard. We've put together the ultimate to-do list for those looking to uncover the region's natural treasures.

The **①** **Acadia Information Center** is the logical place to start your visit. Friendly rangers can provide you with all of the supplementary info needed to make your trip a success.

② **Pemetic Mountain Trail** is a great place to break in your walking stick. Take the bus out to Bubble Pond and start the 4-mile hike up and over Pemetic Mountain, a scenic bald peak offering breathtaking views of the haunting Cranberry Islands. The best part about the route is the noticeable lack of other hikers. Things get a bit more crowded at **③** **Jordan Pond House**, where you can swap your trailblazing tales with other nature-lovers over hot tea and popovers (a hollow roll made from egg batter). After filling your belly, it's time to hit the trails again. This time try the **④** **Penobscot Mountain Trail**, a more strenuous but rewarding trip. Start by taking the plank boardwalk on the west side of Jordan Pond to Deer Brook Trail. Then head to Sargent Pond and take a dip in this ancient lake, which formed over 13,000 years ago when the glaciers receded. Make your way to the Penobscot summit and down the trail along a steep slice of rock that requires a bit of down-climbing. A second round of popovers awaits, but if you are feeling particularly peckish, head to **⑤** **Burning Tree** for fresher-than-fresh seafood. Bookend your meal with the tantalizing squash blossom appetizers and two scoops of Earl Grey ice-cream.

When the stars are twinkling high in the cloudless evening sky, it's time to unfurl your sleeping bag for a cozy evening in the sticks. There are a few rustic campgrounds classified as Acadian National Park Camping, so choose your preferred sleeping spot (on a first come

TIME
3 – 4 days

DISTANCE
200 miles

BEST TIME TO GO
Year-round

START
Bar Harbor

END
Bar Harbor

ALSO GOOD FOR

HISTORY & CULTURE

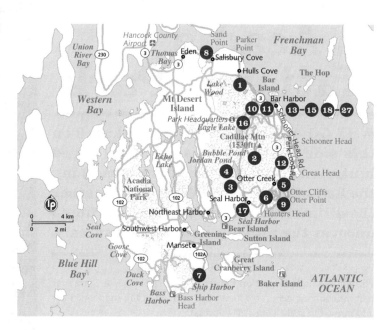

basis), be it ⑥ **Blackwoods Campground** near Seal Harbor or ⑦ **Seawall Campground** toward Bass Harbor.

For those looking to be one with nature *sans* the midnight mosquito bites, try a night at the ⑧ **Coach Stop Inn**, located 5 miles outside Bar Harbor and a mere 2 miles from the main entrance to the park. Built in 1804, this lonely carriage house is the oldest surviving hostelry in the region. A stroll around the 3 acres of garden reveals dappled apple trees and colorful petals.

Pack up your tent and greet the day with a 1-mile hike along ⑨ **Ocean Path** from the Gorham Mountain parking lot down to Otter Point. Due to the hike's popularity, it's best to tackle the route as early as possible to avoid the throng of tourists that flood the trail around 9am. Early-morning strollers will be wrapped in a thick blanket of fog as they glimpse local lobstermen checking their traps.

If you're feeling the urge to tackle some of the park's seemingly endless supply of granite, in Bar Harbor check out ⑩ **Acadia Mountain Guides** and ⑪ **Atlantic Climbing School**. Both offer a variety of programs tailored to all types of climbers. Newbies should sample a half-day introductory course.

Those who aren't so keen on monkeying around can still feel like a rock climber on a midmorning hike down the ⑫ **Beehive Trail**. Iron ladders and rungs, narrow wooden bridges and steep drop-offs make this an adventureous hike, not to mention a great outing for families. Park officials recommend a minimum age of six years old due to the height of the ladders and exposed cliff faces. And don't forget, dogs won't be able to climb the vertical steps!

Re-energize back in Bar Harbor town center with a late breakfast at ⑬ **Café This Way.** Go for the eggs benedict loaded with tomatoes, artichoke and spinach. If you miss breakfast at Café This Way, try ⑭ **2 Cats,** another uberpopular choice among tourists and locals. Don't miss the scrumptious biscuits and spicy home fries. Wash it all down with a freshly blended smoothie.

While you're in town, stop by the ⑮ **Bar Harbor Bicycle Shop** and rent some wheels. Explore the park's system of carriage roads (which are closed to motor vehicles) starting from the ⑯ **Eagle Lake Parking Lot** on Rte 233. Two stretches of carriage road extend in either direction from the car park and both are quite scenic – the southern routes winds around Eagle Lake.

JUST DESERTS

Tourists can be spotted a mile away fumbling over the local lingo. Blend in with the native Bar Harborites with a quick vocab lesson:

- Call the park "the island", or MDI (Mount Desert Island)
- If you do call the park "Mount Desert Island", pronounce the second word like "dessert" (as in "deserted").

The ⑰ **Flying Mountain Trail** and Valley Cove Rd make a short, sweet loop for one last jaunt through the pines before calling it a day. You can swim, picnic and sunbathe on the smooth boulders along the well-protected Valley Cove beach. Just watch out for the poison ivy at the edge of the sand.

For dinner, absorb the spirited nightlife along Bar Harbor's main street, the aptly named…Main St. Everyone can find something to suit at ⑱ **Poor Boy's,** a locally owned favorite, which features a lengthy menu of lobster, grilled fish, chicken, roast meats, pastas and salads. Nearby, ⑲ **Havana** is another Bar Harbor staple with lengthy menu of Latin-influenced dishes. Head to the comically named ⑳ **Carmen Verandah** down the street, for something a bit more upbeat. This second-story terrace bar serves up fruity cocktails and DJ-ed beats.

"Pull on the dangling flusher chain for 10 seconds and watch out for splinters in your bum!"

Tonight, instead of roughing it in the woods, treat yourself to a lovely stay at one of the B&Bs peppered around the fringes of the park, most of which boast a Victorian theme, with loads of antiques and period furniture. Decorations range from over-the-top displays of quotidian knickknacks to tasteful, more demure displays of turn-of-the-century country living. For those who shun floral print wallpaper and cotton doilies, the region around Acadia National Park has loads of cookie-cutter motel rooms as well. The affordable **㉑ Town Motel & Moseley Cottage Inn**, in central Bar Harbor, is great choice for all types of tastes. Catch your Zs in the Cadillac Room, which features an antique wooden toilet that used to draw its water from two cisterns in the attic. Be sure to pull on the dangling flusher chain for 10 seconds and watch out for splinters in your bum! Moseley also has eight motel units beside the main mansion for those who want turn down the volume on the antique-o-meter. The **㉒ Hearthside Inn** gives Moseley some healthy competition with nine inviting rooms, each set with wood and metal curios and period furnishings. The **㉓ Aysgarth Inn** is also located in town, and offers a handful of charming accommodations. Sprawl out on your four-post bed and take in the views of Cadillac Mountain.

> **ASK A LOCAL**
>
> "Yes, the park has rules, and yes, you need to be responsible, but it's a national park – it's your park! Don't be afraid to explore and get lost. Go hike, get hot, tired, dirty, hungry and thirsty. Then find a quiet place to sit down and pick blueberries while you figure out how you're going to get back to your car."
>
> *Charlotte Clews Lawler, Park Ranger, Acadia National Park*

After a restful slumber on goosedown pillows and hand-woven quilts, fulfill the second "B" in "B&B," then head back into the park. If you woke up early enough, try joining a morning bird walk (preregistration is required). Led by an affable park ranger, these quiet treks are an excellent way to learn about the diverse array of species hiding in the dense greenery. Too busy savoring your homemade pancakes to catch an early-morning guided tour? Sign up for 'Dive-In Theater' or 'Forests of Lilliput', two excellent ranger-led programs with plenty of time for Q&As.

ISLAND EXPLORER

The **Island Explorer Bus** (www.exploreacadia.com) is a godsend. It lets you trek along one-way hikes without having to retrace your steps, and you can use the service to transport your bike to the carriage roads (so you don't have to bike on the network of busy, narrow-shouldered streets). It's free if you have a park pass, and typically runs from mid-June through mid-October.

Spend the afternoon exploring the park from the sea by signing up at Bar Harbor for a half-day kayaking trip. Both **㉔ National Park Sea Kayak Tours** and **㉕ Coastal Kayaking Tours** offer four-hour expeditions along the jagged, boulder-strewn coast. If you aren't into manning your own vessel, consider booking a spot on a sailboat with **㉖ Downeast Windjammer Cruises**. You'll spend two windswept hours aboard the four-mast schooner *Margaret Todd*.

For those with the luxury of a fourth day to explore Down East Maine, end your holiday surveying your favorite trails and mountains from the sky. **㉗ Acadia Air Tours** offers 15-minute rides over the crags in a classic biplane.

Brandon Presser

TRIP INFORMATION

GETTING THERE

From Portland, take I-295 north for 46 miles and merge onto I-95. After another 80 miles merge onto I-395, hop onto US-1A and finally ME-3 until you arrive at the park gates.

DO

Acadia Air Tours

Takes tourists on scenic glider and biplane trips over the island. ☎ 207-667-7627; www.acadiaairtours.com; Hancock County Airport, ME-3, Bar Harbor; 20min trip $225; ⏰ May-Oct; ♿

Acadia Information Center (Hulls Cove)

A good first stop before entering the park, with loads of information and friendly staff. ☎ 207-667-8550; www.acadiainfo.com; ME-3, Bar Harbor; ⏰ early May–mid-Oct

Acadia Mountain Guides

Sets up courses for climbers of all levels along the granite surfaces around the park. ☎ 207-288-8186; www.acadiamountainguides.com; 198 Main St, Bar Harbor; half-day trips $100; ⏰ May-Oct; ♿

Atlantic Climbing School

Offers guided trips and instructional climbs all over the park. ☎ 207-288-2521; www.acadiaclimbing.com; 2nd fl, 67 Main St, Bar Harbor; half-day trips $100; ⏰ May-Nov; ♿

Bar Harbor Bicycle Shop

Rents out a wide variety of mountain bikes, perfect for the elaborate network of carriage roads in the park. ☎ 207-288-3886; www.barharborbike.com; 141 Cottage St, Bar Harbor; per day $21-35; ♿

Coastal Kayaking Tours

Offers paddlers the opportunity to go on guided trips, or you can simply rent equipment. ☎ 800-526-8615; www.acadiafun.com; 48 Cottage St, Bar Harbor; half-day tour $46; ⏰ May-Oct; ♿

Downeast Windjammer Cruises

Offers two-hour cruises on the majestic 151ft four-masted schooner *Margaret Todd*. ☎ 207-288-4585; www.downeastwindjammer.com; Bar Harbor Inn Pier, Bar Harbor; adult/child $32/22 ⏰ May-Oct; ♿

National Park Sea Kayak Tours

A popular option to explore the park in a unique way. Rentals and guided tours are available to all ages. ☎ 800-347-0940; www.acadiakayak.com; 39 Cottage St, Bar Harbor; half-day tour $46; ⏰ May-Oct; ♿

EAT

2 Cats

A splendid café with a heart of gold, 2 Cats serves delicious breakfasts and heartier fare for lunch. ☎ 207-288-2808; 130 Cottage St, Bar Harbor; meals $8-17; ⏰ breakfast & lunch

Burning Tree

One of the best restaurants on the island, Burning Tree prepares a rich and eclectic assortment of dishes, with local seafood being the pièce de résistance. It's 4 miles south of town, along ME-3. ☎ 207-288-9331; 69 Otter Creek Drive, Bar Harbor; meals $20-29; ⏰ dinner

Café This Way

This relaxed, quirky eatery is *the* place for breakfast, with plump Maine blueberry pancakes and eggs benedict with smoked salmon. ☎ 207-288-4483; 14 Mt Desert St, Bar Harbor; ⏰ breakfast, dinner

Carmen Verandah

The quirkily named venue has a festive atmosphere and a dance floor that sometimes sees DJ action. ☎ 207-288-2886; 119 Main St, Bar Harbor; drinks from $4.30; ⏰ 11am-1am

Havana

This dashing restaurant serves nicely seasoned meat and seafood dishes with a touch of Latin flair (Cuban this isn't). ☎ 207-288-2822; 318 Main St, Bar Harbor; meals $18-34; ⏰ dinner

Jordan Pond House

Beautifully set amid the park's lush greenery (it's the only restaurant actually in the park), this elegant teahouse is for afternoon tea and popovers. ☎ 207-276-3316; www.jordan pond.com; Park Loop Rd, Seal Harbor; meals $13-25; ☯ lunch, tea & dinner

Poor Boy's

This locally owned favorite spreads an enormous menu of surf and turf. ☎ 207-288-4148; 300 Main St, Bar Harbor; meals $14-25; ☯ dinner

SLEEP

Acadia National Park Camping

Sleep among the sticks at one of the campsites nestled within the pines of Acadia National Park. Backcountry camping is not allowed. ☎ 207-288-3338; www.npa.gov /acad; Acadia National Park; campsites per night from $15

Aysgarth Inn

This charming six-room B&B is well located in town and provides comfortable rooms with homey touches (some with views of Cadillac Mountain). ☎ 207-288-9655; www .aysgarth.com; 50 Roberts Ave, Bar Harbor; r incl breakfast $70-135

Coach Stop Inn

Five miles outside Bar Harbor and just 2 miles from the main entrance to Acadia National Park, this is the oldest surviving hostelry in the area. ☎ 207-288-9886; www.coachstop inn.com; 715 Acadia Hwy, Salisbury Cove; r $125-155

Hearthside Inn

Hearthside is an elegant Victorian inn with nine inviting rooms, each with antique and period furnishings. ☎ 207-288-4533; www .hearthsideinn.com; 7 High St, Bar Harbor; r incl breakfast $75-160

Town Motel & Moseley Cottage Inn

A stately white manor with elegant Victorian rooms that are so clean it's almost pathological. Delicious homemade breakfasts include eggs benedict and crispy bacon. ☎ 207-288-5548; www.moseleycottage.com; 12 Atlantic Ave, Bar Harbor; r incl breakfast from $105

USEFUL WEBSITES

www.acadia.nation-park.com
www.nps.gov/acad

LINK YOUR TRIP

www.lonelyplanet.com/trip-planner

Spooky Maine

WHY GO Maine's quiet coast and even quieter blue-collar towns are often chosen as the setting for eerie Hollywood plots. But it's a bit of a the-chicken-or-the-egg phenomenon: did Hollywood develop the state's chilling reputation, or did they simply discover it? Take this trip and come up with your own theory.

TIME
2 days

DISTANCE
170 miles

BEST TIME TO GO
Sep – Dec

START
Bangor

END
Kennebunk-port

ALSO GOOD FOR

HISTORY & CULTURE

Start your adventure in Bangor at ❶ **Betts Bookstore**, the ultimate bookstore dedicated to Mainer and master of the macabre, Stephen King. This narrow space features copies of virtually everything written by King, including the books he wrote using the alias Richard Bachman. Don't miss the creepy, larger-than-life cartoon bust of King at the back of the store while picking out your souvenir T-shirt. The owner of Betts has created several shirts that feature a drawing of Maine filled in with spooky King-related landmarks. Fanatics can even use the T-shirt to carve their own spooky Maine trail. In the summer, Betts offers Stephen King tours around Bangor, pointing out various locations featured in his novels and subsequent films. A print-out of the Bangor tour route is available at the cash register if you are stopping by off-season. The 14-stop tour visits ❷ **Mt Hope Cemetery**, a sprawling 264-acre tract known as America's second 'garden cemetery.' King's 1989 horror hit *Pet Sematary* was filmed on the property. The last stop on the tour is the ❸ **Bangor International Airport**. If you're already too creeped out, this is your chance to grab a ticket and get out of town. King's airplane thriller *The Langoliers* was shot here.

From Bangor, it's only a short drive down to the coast to the small seaside town of Bucksport. Head to Main St to visit the cursed tomb of Colonel Buck at ❹ **Buck Cemetery**. Buck was the founder of little Bucksport in the mid-1700s, and he also acted as the town's Justice of the Peace. According to legend, he convicted a townswoman of

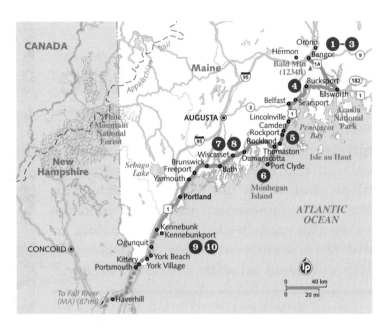

witchcraft, and before her execution she vowed to haunt him until the end of time. Seventy years after his death, a bizarre imprint of a witch's boot appeared on the tomb and despite the efforts of the crypt-keeper the mysterious bootprint could not be removed.

Follow US-1 along the ocean to Thomaston, the former site of Maine's state penitentiary and the compound that inspired Stephen King's compelling *Shawshank Redemption*. Although the jail has been completely demolished, visitors can still stop by the ⑤ **Thomaston Historical Society** to learn about the prison's two centuries of history.

Like many of King's thrillers, *Dolores Claiborne* is set on an isolated island spying on the Maine coast through the fog. Although Dolores' Little Tall Island was a figment of the author's imagination, there are many small, isolated islets along the state's jagged coast with the creepy, windswept vibes depicted in King's book. Spend the evening on Monhegan Island at the aptly named ⑥ **Hitchcock House** and wake up amid eerie early-morning mists.

As if the saccharine creaking of music boxes wasn't creepy enough, Wiscasset's music-box museum, ⑦ **Musical Wonder House**, is also haunted by an unidentified spirit in his mid-twenties who is often seen lurking in the front parlor and upstairs hallway. Before leaving Wiscasset, have one more ghoulish encounter at ❽ **Eastwind Restaurant**, which is haunted by 'Mother Dana,' who enjoys flipping cups and cutlery and unlatching sealed doors.

All you '80s TV addicts out there (and rerun junkies too) will fondly recall a prim-and-proper Angela Lansbury daintily clicking away on her typewriter during the opening credits of *Murder She Wrote*. Every gosh-darn episode, this mystery-writer-by-day–amateur-homicide-detective-by-night would somehow find herself entwined in a gruesome murder plot and would always save the day by identifying the true killer while police officers bungled the case. Although she often gallivanted around the world, *conveniently* winding up in a murderous situation each week, the crux of the action took place in Maine's idyllic coastal town of Cabot Cove. But where exactly was this seaside village with the highest murder rate in America? Scenery shots were filmed in Mendocino, California, because sadly Cabot Cove doesn't actually exist. The best you can do is spend the night at ❾ **Cabot Cove Cottages** in Kennebunkport. Although the cutesy cottage-strewn property is far from spooky, it's a nice place for a rest after a weekend of hauntings. If you're still in the spooky spirit, there's a spirit to spook you during your stay at the nearby ❿ **Captain Lord Mansion**. The wife of a crusty sea captain is known to haunt the Wisteria Bedroom and the spiral staircase leading up to the cupola on the roof.

Brandon Presser

> **DETOUR**
>
> Maine isn't the only creepy state – head to the town of Fall River, in Massachusetts, to learn about America's most famous murderess, Lizzie Borden. One quiet evening in 1892, Lizzie hacked her father and stepmother to bits with a hatchet, but somehow the judge didn't find her guilty. Today, the old Greek Revival home has been turned into the **Lizzie Borden Bed & Breakfast** (www.lizzie-borden.com) with all the original trappings left intact. Tours are also available for those without enough time (or guts) to spend the night ($10).

TRIP INFORMATION

GETTING THERE
Follow I-95 north of Boston until you reach the exit for Bangor, Maine.

DO

Bangor International Airport
Bangor's airport and the filming site of Stephen King's thriller *The Langoliers*. ☎ 207-992-4600; www.flybangor.com; 287 Godfrey Blvd, Bangor; ⊙ 9am-4:30pm Mon-Fri (customer service)

Betts Bookstore
The headquarters for all things Stephen King. ☎ 207-947-7052; www.bettsbooks.com; 584 Hammond St, Bangor; ⊙ 9am-4pm Mon-Fri, 9am-3pm Sat

Buck Cemetery
The infamous cemetery where the town's founder, Colonel Buck, is buried. His tomb has an indelible boot-shaped mark on its front. Main St, Bucksport; ⊙ dawn-dusk

Mt Hope Cemetery
Located just outside the center of Bangor, Mt Hope cemetery is known as the second-oldest garden cemetery in America and was the shooting location for the film *Pet Sematary*. ☎ 207-945-6589; www.mthopebgr .com; 1048 State St, Bangor; ⊙ dawn-dusk

Musical Wonder House
A museum dedicated to electrical music boxes of all shapes and sizes. The ghost of a young man haunts the building that houses the museum. ☎ 207-882-7163; www.musical wonderhouse.com; 16-18 High St, Wiscasset; ⊙ 10am-5pm Mon-Sat, noon-5pm Sun Jun-Aug

Thomaston Historical Society
This active historical society preserves the history of Thomaston and offers visitors a small information space during the weekday summers. ☎ 207-354-2314; Thomaston; ⊙ Tue-Thu 2-4pm Jun-Aug

EAT

Eastwind Restaurant
A restaurant in an old Victorian home regularly visited by a specter dubbed 'Mother Dana.' ☎ 207-882-5238; RR1, Wiscasset; ⊙ 7:30am-8:30pm May-Nov, to 9:30pm Jul & Aug

SLEEP

Cabot Cove Cottages
In an idyllic setting overlooking the Kennebunk River, these 16 cottages are a splendid alternative to a hotel or B&B. ☎ 207-967-5424; www.cabotcovecottages.com; 7 S Maine St, Kennebunkport; r with breakfast $175-325; ♿

Captain Lord Mansion
If money is no object, this former sea captain's home demands your attention. The meticulously restored rooms are more lavish than when lived in by their original occupants. ☎ 207-967-3141; www.captainlord .com; 6 Pleasant St, Kennebunkport; r with breakfast $250-475

Hitchcock House
On Horn's Hill, the secluded Hitchcock House has four old-fashioned rooms and two efficiency units that provide basic comforts (no more) after a day exploring. ☎ 207-594-8137; www.midcoast.com/~hhouse; Horn's Hill, Monhegan Island; r $90-150

USEFUL WEBSITES
www.stephenking.com
www.visitmaine.com

LINK YOUR TRIP

www.lonelyplanet.com/trip-planner

Behind the Scenes

THIS BOOK

This guidebook was commissioned in Lonely Planet's Oakland office, and produced by the following:
Product Development Manager Heather Dickson
Commissioning Editor Jennye Garibaldi
Coordinating Editor Averil Robertson
Coordinating Cartographer Andrew Smith
Coordinating Layout Designer Jim Hsu
Managing Editor Geoff Howard
Managing Cartographer Alison Lyall
Managing Layout Designer Celia Wood
Assisting Editors Michelle Bennett, Cathryn Game, Simon Williamson
Assisting Cartographers Hunor Csutoros, Pablo Gastar, Paul Iacono, Margie Jung, Carlos Solarte
Series Designer James Hardy
Cover Designers Gerilyn Attebery, Jennifer Mullins
Project Manager Glenn van der Knijff

Thanks to David Burnett, Jay Cooke, Catherine Craddock, Owen Eszeki, Suki Gear, Mark Germanchis, Chris Girdler, Michelle Glynn, Brice Gosnell, Liz Heynes, Lauren Hunt, Laura Jane, John Mazzocchi, Clara Monitto, Darren O'Connell, Paul Piaia, Wibowo Rusli, Julie Sheridan

THANKS

Ray Bartlett Jennye, thanks for putting me on this trip and for your help and handholding along the way – you were great, a pleasure to work for. Thanks to Brandon, Dan, and Gregor for being a pleasure to work with. Thanks to the great people I met along the way, especially Stephanie E, Melissa J, and David W, for your insight and expertise and for sharing it with me. But the lion's share of the thanks goes to my wife, who helped out in so many ways – from planning itineraries to dogsitting to sleuthing out neat spots to stop along the way and so much more. Thank you, thank you, thank you!

Gregor Clark Gregor Clark wishes to thank all the generous fellow Vermonters who helped with this project, especially Matthew Perry, Lissy Hemenway, Margo Whitcomb, Katherine Quinn, Sarah Pope, Jon Wright, David Alles, Saba Rizvi, Arshad Hasan, Sarah Shepherd, Lauri, Zara and Maya. Special hugs and kisses go to my dear Gaen, Meigan and Chloe – without whom this project wouldn't have been half as fun.

Dan Eldridge My deepest thanks go out to the three people who made this project possible: Jennye, for offering me the job in the first place; Justine, for the Dan Joy Compound accommodations and the absolutely priceless tips and connections on Cape Cod; and of course Carrie Ann, my traveling companion who once again saved me from an impending mental implosion. Thanks also to Silas Finch in New Haven, Taylor Brown in Cape Cod, and Susan Prout Webb for the insider Kennedy clan info.

Brandon Presser A huge thank you to: Nicolas L'Hermitte, Yagmur Nurhat, Carolyn Daly, Tatiana Giovanelli, James Doyle and Pablo Suarez. Thanks also to my lovely 'experts': Kimmie Keefe, Daniel Kany, and Charlotte and Jerome Lawther. Props to the kick-ass LP staff, especially Coordinating Author/ Commissioning Editor/superstar Jennye Garibaldi and my savvy co-authors.

ACKNOWLEDGMENTS

Many thanks to the following for the use of their content:

Internal photographs: p20 by James P. Blair/Corbis; p15 (bottom) by Catherine Karnow/Corbis; p8 by Phil Schermeister/Corbis; p14 by Paul Thompson Images/Alamy. All other photographs by Lonely Planet Images, and by Richard Cummins p6, p9, p18, p22 (top); Jon Davison p17; Lee Foster p12; Kim Grant p11 (bottom), p13 (bottom), p19 (top), p24 (bottom); Corinne Humphrey p6; Lou Jones p22 (bottom); Paul Kennedy p24 (top); Mark Newman p5, p19 (bottom); Angus Oborn p15 (top); Stephen Saks p21 (bottom); Neil Setchfield p21 (top); Philip & Karen Smith p8, p10; Glenn van der Knijff p11 (top), p13 (top), p16 (top), p23; Jim Wark p7; Frank Wing p16 (bottom).

All images are the copyright of the photographers unless otherwise indicated. Many of the images in this guide are available for licensing from Lonely Planet Images: www.lonelyplanetimages.com.

Index

000 map pages
000 photograph pages

000 map pages
000 photograph pages

n

000 map pages
000 photograph pages

000 **map pages**
000 **photograph pages**